THE NEW YORK CONSPIRACY

THE NEW YORK CONSPIRACY

by *DANIEL HORSMANDEN*

edited
with an Introduction by
THOMAS J. DAVIS

BEACON PRESS   BOSTON

CONTENTS

INTRODUCTION

THOMAS J. DAVIS

This usually unread rare book, published originally in 1744 and reprinted in its entirety twice since then,[1] is the fullest primary source of information on a neglected episode in the history of New York: the detection and prosecution of more than one hundred fifty slaves and twenty white persons for what the attorney general described at the time as "the most horrible and destructive plot that ever was yet known in these northern parts of America."[2] Mostly a day-by-day trial record, containing depositions, examinations and confessions, gathered from notes taken by the judges and lawyers during the various legal actions, its aim is to set forth the substance of "the proceedings . . . in the order of time they were produced," so that

> the reader will thereby be furnished with the most natural view of the whole, and be better enabled to conceive the design and dangerous depth of this *hellish project*, as well as the justice of the several proceedings.[3]

The book is more than a journal, however; as its aim partially indicates, it is a defense of those proceedings which between 11 May and 29 August 1741 resulted in thirteen blacks burning at the stake, sixteen hanging along with four whites, and more than seventy blacks and seven whites being banished from British North America.[4]

The events that led to those proceedings began about noon following St. Patrick's Day. The first and worst in a rash of ten fires (eight in six days), preceded and accompanied by robberies, broke out in the city, consuming within an hour and a quarter much of Fort George—a symbol of safety and the principal governmental structure in the province, containing the residence and seat of the royal governor. Whipped by violent winds that blew sparks onto the shingles of houses outside the fort, the fire temporarily threatened the whole town and excited anxious thoughts and uneasy feelings in the city, most of whose buildings were wooden and relatively close together.[5] A rain shower cooled the blaze, however, and although it smoldered until the next day, it did no further damage to the town. A week later fire slightly damaged another section of town. Then, two weeks after the fort burned, fire destroyed Winant Van Zant's storehouse. Three days after this, two fires broke out and the next morning (Sunday, 5 April) Joseph Murray's stable partially burned. The same morning a white woman overheard a slave say "Fire, Fire, Scorch, Scorch, a little, damn it, by-and-by." [6] The following day four fires burned parts of the city.

Many of the more than 9,000 white persons on the tip of Manhattan Island suspected that these outbreaks had not happened by chance.[7] To their minds the fires threatening their lives and property were too frequent to be accidents, and the robberies suggested that someone expected the fires as likely occasions to commit other crimes. This suspicion focused on the most distrusted element in the population—the more than 2,000 blacks and the few Indians enslaved in the city. And it increased so that when Cuffee, a slave of Adolph Philipse, was seen fleeing from the scene of a fire on Monday, 6 April, a shout went up *"that the negroes were rising."* [8]

Two days after this, John Hughson, an alehouse keeper, and his wife Sarah, were arrested for receiving goods stolen from Robert Hogg's shop. Earlier, Caesar—a slave of John Vaarck—was arrested after being seen and found with goods also stolen from Hogg's, and Prince, a slave of John Auboyneau, also was taken up in connection with that robbery. The investigation of the connection between these two blacks and Hughson produced evidence that confirmed in some minds the suspicion that the fires and robberies were part of some concerted criminal activity.

Hughson, several persons reported, illegally entertained frequently from twenty to thirty slaves at his alehouse. Not only were these gatherings patent violations of several laws such as those regulating the assembly of slaves, their movement in the city, their hours of curfew, their association with free persons, particularly with white women, and their consumption of liquor, but some persons reported that during these meetings "a design was conceived to destroy this city by fire and massacre its inhabitants." [9] The official investigation that followed up these reports interrupted the normal routine in New York for more than six months and resulted in the proceedings described in the book.

Obviously something that would attract attention and curiosity, the proceedings also attracted controversy. Even though the juries who heard the various cases were well enough convinced by the evidence and argument presented by the prosecution that they rendered verdicts of guilty which led to the punishments mentioned above, many persons doubted the accuracy of the prosecution's case, and during and after the proceedings they called into question almost everything connected with the trials, including their very basis and justice. Some persons declared that no plot at all had existed in fact. Others conceded the existence of some plot but denied that it was as deep and dangerous as the prosecution contended. Also some persons maintained that the manner and methods used in the proceedings prevented the alleged plotters from getting justice. In addition, some persons, who agreed that the trials were essentially just and fair, thought the sentences, especially the form and number of executions, were not merited by the crimes. These persistent and proliferating questions surrounded the entire proceedings with doubt.[10]

Much of that doubt resulted from the circumstances of the proceedings, including the character of the prosecution's argument and evidence as reflected in indictment of the alleged plotters for conspiracy. In law, conviction for conspiracy often requires no more than a flimsy case. The crux of the crime is an intention or agreement to act illegally and no proof of any illegal or other overt act is required. As the word "conspiracy" suggests, those charged with it stand accused of something concealed from public knowledge and most of the weight of proof hangs on implication from indirect evidence, usually an inference of guilt by association. So, although proven in court, cases of conspiracy frequently lack adequate substance to be convincing (outside of a strictly legal sense) and make it easy to draw conclusions contrary to the findings of a court. Thus, as happened in 1741, such proceedings often leave more than a few reasonable doubts.[11]

Furthermore, the condition and mood of the public during the proceedings increased doubt. Entangled as they were with the fires and robberies that provoked anxiety in the public mind, the proceedings were caught in questions as to whether they were a public search for scapegoats or products of delusion created among the populace by emotional excitement and excessive anxiousness. Indeed, an anonymous letter received in July 1741 by Cadwallader Colden (a prominent New Yorker, after 1761 lieutenant governor of the province) characterized the proceedings as a "Bloody Tragedy" similar to the infamous hysteria of the Salem witchcraft trials of 1692 during which nineteen persons hanged and one was pressed to death.[12] Almost unanimously, the few historians who have treated the episode take up this theme, portraying the affair as hardly more than demonstration of an agitated popular mood. Charles and Mary Beard, in their widely known survey, *The Rise of American Civilization*, call the plot "imaginary" and refer to the incident as a "massacre" exemplifying "plagues of popular frenzy." [13] Ulrich B. Phillips, in his monumental and controversial *American Negro Slavery*, briefly refers to the whole thing as "a panic among the white people." [14] Even Herbert Aptheker, trying somewhat ambiguously to use the incident for several purposes in his *American Negro Slave Revolts*, while suggesting it was not a complete hoax, an unaccountable mob delusion, nor an extensive conspiracy, nonetheless characterized it as "the hysteria of 1741." [15]

Clearly, the state of mind and conditions prevalent in the city affected the proceedings. And things were in an uproar. Several adversities already disturbed New York when the plot came to light. In fact, on 10 April, before any of the proceedings began, the lieutenant governor proclaimed a day of public fast and humiliation on account of, as one contemporary put it, "the calamities with which we had of late been visited." [16] These "calamities" included weather, war, and more. The coldest and most severe winter in the memory of New York's inhabitants had left ruinous results, particularly extensive losses of livestock and shortages of food, in the basically self-supplying agricultural province.[17] In addition, economic pressures lingered from the bad times of 1737, and both money and work (this due partly to the competition of slave labor) were scarce.[18] Moreover, the empire was at war with Spain. Unpopular because it drained men and money, the war interrupted commerce[19] and excited fears usual in a vulnerable coastal town in a frontier province—fears of betrayal from within and invasion from without.

More than that, though, the war helped to suggest why a conspiracy supposedly took place when it did and, thus, provided background that gave the notion of a plot coherence. War established opportunity and motive. On one hand it weakened the garrison in the city, by calling for armed expeditions,[20] and on another it brought in catalysts that stirred up action. One of these catalysts was a group of black Spaniards recently enslaved in the city. Among the crew of a captured Spanish ship condemned by the Admiralty Court, these blacks had been declared lawful prize and sold as slaves, although they protested that they were free and the more light-skinned members of the crew remained in jail as prisoners of war.[21] From the beginning these "Spanish negroes" were outspoken and recalcitrant; in time they convinced the "York negroes" that they could fight and suggested that other Spaniards might soon attack New York and would certainly come if the blacks rose up. Also, General James Oglethorpe, governor of Georgia, warned in a letter to lieutenant governor Clarke that during a recent expedition against the Spanish in Florida, he had discovered, through a captive, that spies in the guise of school teachers and dancing masters had been sent throughout British North America to burn the principal magazines and forts.[22] With the burning of Fort George and reports that a school teacher named John Ury—suspected as a "popish priest," thus in league with Spain—had frequented Hughson's and was concerned in the alleged plot, things seemed to fall into place.[23]

Further, New York remembered the slave uprising of 1712.[24] At almost the same time of year as the fires and robberies of

1741, insurgent blacks had killed ten whites during 1712. Armed with guns, knives, and swords, the blacks set the fires at about two o'clock in the morning on 7 April and ambushed the whites as they hurried sleepily to put out the blazes. Informed of the violence, Governor Robert Hunter dispatched a party of soldiers and fired a cannon from the fort to alarm the town. Confronted by heavy armed opposition, most of the blacks fled out of town, doing damage as they went. Several escaped or committed suicide, and of those captured nineteen were executed. As one white put it in 1741, "what they have done, they may at one time or other act over again." [25] This impressed New Yorkers more when they got some news in early May from about eight miles away. In a scheme similar to that suspected in New York, eight barns burned one morning at Hackensack, New Jersey, and two blacks —one caught at the scene with a gun, the other found loading one—confessed to the crimes and were burned at the stake.[26] Together, these events made it seem not unreasonable that blacks in New York had planned something.

Yet more than popular malaise, or the generally circulated suspicions of a mere possibility of a plot, drew concerned attention to the behavior of blacks from the city's white inhabitants. Many details and developments of that behavior showed clearly that blacks seriously were violating a wide range of restrictions against them. Caesar certainly was involved in the robbery at Hogg's; along with his fellow slave Prince, the Hughsons, and a woman commonly called Peggy who lodged with them and reportedly slept with several blacks, he was caught with the goods. Undeniably Hughson illegally entertained and served liquor to large groups of blacks—on a couple of occasions constables broke up such activities there. And such illegal parties took place elsewhere too: besides Hughson, ten alehouse keepers throughout the city were convicted of "keeping," as the judges called it, "a disorderly house," and were fined from six pence with immediate discharge to eight pounds and imprisonment until the fine was paid.[27] In addition to sneaking drinks and entertainment, blacks broke several other laws: they were out unidentified at night; they traveled throughout the city without permission; and they assembled, often undetected, in groups of more than twenty when the law forbade meetings by more than three.[28] Moreover, many engaged widely in theft and on occasion in arson, and also talked of doing serious harm to whites.

Not simply pilfering, blacks had organized a theft ring known as "the Geneva Club." As the story of its name indicates, it existed long before 1741. "It happened about five or six years ago," went the story in 1741, "that

> a cellar of one Baker, a tavern keeper in this city, had one night been broken open, and robbed of some Geneva [gin]; many of the parties concerned were detected, viz.—several negroes, of which Caesar and Prince were two principals; and all that were discovered were chastised at the public whipping-post. From thence . . . they became distinguished among each other by the name of the *Geneva Club*.[29]

Through experience, then, the members had contacts to dispose of stolen goods they could not use. Hughson fitted in there: he was a fence and was hanged in part for a conviction "of having feloniously etc. received . . . divers stolen goods, knowing them to be stolen." [30]

Several other whites also acted as fences, among them John Romme, a shoemaker and alehouse keeper; John Coffin, a peddler; and William Kane, a soldier. Romme apparently handled much business. Although he fled, was captured and deeply implicated during the proceedings, he got off lightly with discharge in security for transportation from the province, probably because "he had a great many friends in town," as he said, "and the best in the place [including, no doubt, a relative, alderman William Romme] would stand by him." [31]

Romme's connections with the blacks partially show the extent of their thievery. "[A]t several times," according to one report, he got from them "goods of several kinds." [32] On one occasion he got "fifty or sixty firkins of butter," after "making a bargain with Caesar to get him as much butter as he could, and he was to give him fifteen shillings a firkin for it; but Caesar insisted on twenty." [33] At another time it was said that the cloth coat Romme has now upon his back, with a cape to it was stolen by Caesar from a countryman's boat near Hughson's . . . ; [and] Romme gave Caesar ten shillings for it.[34]

An occasional fire or threat was added to these robberies. "[A]t the pump in the neighbourhood," Sawney—a seventeen-year-old slave of Thomas Niblet—said "G——d d——n all the white people; that if he had it in his power, he would set them all on fire." [35] Apparently he tried: three times he set fire to his master's house and once threw "fire over alderman Bancker's fence into his yard," but each time his master discovered it and finally sent him to Albany.[36] Another black, Diana, "put fire in the shingles of Mr. Machado's house" and frustrated with her condition, "in a passion, because her mistress was angry with her, *took her own young child from her breast, and laid it in the cold so that it froze to death.*" [37]

Other frustrated blacks also had ideas of getting even with whites. The lieutenant governor refused to allow Quack to visit his wife, a cook at the fort. Trying and failing, Quack got together with some others "on a Sunday afternoon, a month before the firing of the fort, over a bowl of punch . . . at Hughson's," and, he confessed, they "voted him . . . as having a wife in the fort to be the person who should fire the fort, Sandy, and Jack (Codweis's); Caesar, and Guy (Horsfield's); were to assist him in it." [38] Apparently this was serious: "Two days before the fort was burnt," shortly after being clubbed over the head by a sentry and thrown out into the street when he again tried in vain to see his wife, Quack told Fortune, "that in a few days there would be great alterations in the fort, . . . that [is,] the fort would be burnt," and he was going to do it.[39] Five of the "Spanish negroes" also had something to say; "about fourteen days before the fort was burnt," they declared

that if the Captain [John Lush, who captured them] would not send them back to their own country, they would ruin all the city; and the first house they would burn should be the Captain's, for they did not care what they did. . . .

[D]——n that son of a b——h, they would make a devil of him.[40]

Caesar made no declaration but he did "pay Hughson twelve pounds in eight shilling Spanish pieces . . . in order to buy guns"; and he got the goods: "Hughson . . . went abroad with his boat, and was absent three days, or thereabouts, and brought back with him seven or eight guns, three pistols and four swords." [41] Other blacks "whetted their knives . . . and some said their knives were sharp enough to cut off a white man's head." [42] By several reports, the common talk was to "set the houses on fire, and kill the white people," as Ben said, "in order to be free." [43]

But that did not happen: no white throats were cut and, while there was a rash of suspicious fires, the town was not burned down. Thus, when the prosecution pointed to this behavior as the foundation of its charges, it had little more than hearsay and an argument as to intention. Both left uncertainties that fed controversy: intentions are difficult to prove beyond doubt. Yet the authorities had a sound legal basis to justify the proceedings and executions.

In fact, the prosecution's case was more than adequate in court, and the indictments, trials, and sentences were well within the bounds of law. Under New York's "act for the most effectual preventing and punishing the conspiracy and insurrection of negroes and other slaves," the authorities had power to mete out summary justice in such cases; however, all accused during 1741 received jury trials.[44] Also, the act prescribed the punishment "of death, in such manner and with such circumstances as the aggravation or enormity of the crime, in the judgment of the justices . . . shall merit and require." [45] And the crime consisted in nothing more than agreement between two or more persons to do something illegal in manner, purpose, or consequence, regardless whether the thing agreed to was attempted, achieved, abandoned, or even renounced.[46] Furthermore, any statement by one conspirator was evidence against all. So, when Quack, Sawney, the Spanish Negroes, and others talked of burning the fort or houses, that was conspiracy. The Geneva Club was a conspiracy. Caesar's purchase of guns from Hughson involved conspiracy. Thus, the basic premise of the prosecution was incontestable: in law a conspiracy existed among "some White People, in conjunction with Negro and other slaves." [47]

Yet the prosecution's contention as to the details, dangers, and depths of that conspiracy still lacked credibility among some contemporaries; and that lack of credibility, along with uncertainties from other sources, affected the evaluation of its case later in time. Not only did the *Journal of the Proceedings* written in its defense share in those uncertainties, it produced more. Besides the questions surrounding the proceedings, the credibility of the *Journal* involved questions as to its partiality and the identity of its compiler.[48]

Questions of partiality issued almost naturally from the fact that the sources of the *Journal* were notes taken by judges and lawyers associated with the prosecution and the official version of the plot. Until the late nineteenth century, though, most American courts had no stenographers, so the notes of the justices, supplemented by those of the attorneys in the cases, usually were the most complete, if not the only, record of courtroom action. Undoubtedly, these minutes narrowed the perspective in which the proceedings were presented; however, they were as impartial as any set of non-verbatim, first-hand trial records.[49]

Also there were questions as to the identity and bias of the compiler.[50] The title page of the original edition indicated the compiler's identity only with the phrase "By the Recorder." The 1810 edition, however, carried the name Daniel Horsmanden, Esq. (1691–1778).[51] Son of an English clergyman and nephew of William Byrd of Westover (the founder of the aristocratic Virginia clan), Horsmanden emigrated to America and read law in New York where he took a place in provincial politics, befriending the powerful DeLanceys. From that connection he received several public appointments including that of Recorder, Admiralty Judge, and third justice of the Supreme Court of Judicature.[52] In the last position he presided over the conspiracy trials in 1741 and so had a real stake in the controversy over their judicial propriety. As compiler, then, he might be suspected of presenting the court in the best possible light. There is a dispute, however, as to whether he was recorder at the time of the trials and publication of the *Journal*. In the *Manual of the Corporation of the City of New York for 1858*—an earlier version of the present annual *Official Directory*—Daniel T. Valentine listed Daniel Horsmanden on page 492 as recorder from 1735 to 1737; from 1737 to 1769 he listed Simeon Johnson as Recorder. Earlier in the same book, however, in "A List of the Members of the City Government from 1653 up to the Present," Valentine·identified Horsmanden as recorder from 1735 to 1746. Johnson, an alderman from 1734 to 1747, is described there as recorder after 1747. In the *Manual* for 1870, Horsmanden again is listed as recorder from 1735 to 1746, and Johnson as recorder between 1747 and 1766. Yet, twenty-five pages earlier, the *Manual* showed Horsmanden as recorder during 1735 to 1737, and Johnson in the office from 1737 to 1769. Several histories of the city, such as Martha Lamb's multivolume study and I. N. P. Stokes' *Iconography of Manhattan Island 1498 to 1909*, refer to Horsmanden as recorder from 1736 to 1747.[53] Both the New York Public Library and the New-York Historical Society, on the catalog cards describing their holdings of the *Journal*, declare that "although Simeon Johnson was recorder of the city of New York, 1737–1769, the authorship of this volume is universally attributed to Daniel Horsmanden, recorder during the years 1735–1737." The internal evidence from the *Journal* is somewhat clearer, though, strongly suggesting that in fact Horsmanden was the compiler. In the preface, the compiler refers to himself as a person who continuously examined the alleged conspirators, as one who

> had borne a sufficient fatigue, under an ill state of health, in the share he had in the proceedings themselves for a course of six months daily attendance.[54]

Furthermore, as a person who "had the advantage of being all along privy to the proceedings, and all the motions concerning them," [55] only a judge had these "advantages." In addition, a further reference to "the duties of his offices and profession" convincingly suggests that the compiler was Horsmanden.[56] Besides, he was certainly Recorder at the time of the trials and publication of the *Journal*; one only need look in the *Minutes of the Common Council of the City of New York* (1740–1754) to see Horsmanden listed at meetings from 1740 through 1744 as Recorder.

Yet although its compiler is undoubtedly biased, its purpose admittedly polemical and although its preface, introduction, and conclusion consciously present one side of the story, the bulk of the book, being a journal gathered and put together from materials composed by others with little revision of substance or wording, admits the compiler's partiality in any large degree only in his comments and notations. In addition, even though the compiler selected and arranged the materials, the content and organization of a journal of the entire proceedings, along with his assumption that the justice of those proceedings was obvious, held him to a strictly chronological development that included the substance of each of the trials, although several—such as those of Caesar, Prince, Cuffee, the Hughsons, and John Ury, on which heavily rested the disputes as to the existence and nature of the plot—are given in more detail. But the detail of that reportage results mostly from the particular public and private attention focused on them during the proceedings. Also, the flavor produced by the proceedings was so pervasive that the compiler could not have altered it significantly without suffering immediate rejection.

Besides an account of the proceedings, the compiler unconsciously provided much other valuable information. There are lingering looks at the colonial judicial system in practice, glimpses into the minds of colonial justices and lawyers, glances at the social relationships in the city, views of the circumstances of slaves, occasional suggestions as to the level of political consciousness among them, and evidence of the prevalent attitudes of whites toward blacks and their justification of slavery. With attitudes typical for the times as shown in Winthrop Jordan's masterly *White Over Black: American Attitudes toward the Negro 1550–1812*,[57] many white New Yorkers considered blacks mischievous, unintelligible, without conception of truth, beastly, ungrateful, silly, but simultaneously with "a great deal of craft." These attitudes come together in justifications of slavery very similar to those in *Slavery Defended: The Views of the Antebellum South,* edited by Eric McKitrick.[58] John Smith, one of the lawyers in New York in 1741, showed this in his comments on the plot. To him, the plot indicated "the monstrous ingratitude of this black tribe." In an argument heard often a century later, Smith asserted that

> slavery among us is generally softened with great indulgence; they live without care, and are commonly better fed and clothed, and put to less labour, than the poor of most Christian countries.[59]

Moreover, he described slavery as an agency of civilization, uplifting blacks from the natural backwardness of the "Dark Continent." [60] "They are indeed slaves," he conceded, "but under the protection of law, none can hurt them with impunity."[61] Further, somewhat contradictorily, considering the circumstances, Smith declared that "they are really more happy in this place, than in the midst of the continual plunder, cruelty, and rapine of their native countries." [62] Although Smith could not understand the plot in light of "all the kindness and tenderness" of whites, the comments offered from the blacks suggest ample explanation. Some admitted they "lived well":[63] the names of the owners of the principal slaves involved in the plot read like "Who's Who" in colonial New York. The Roosevelts, the DeLanceys, the Courtlandts, the Jays, the Livingstons, and the Philipses "indulged" their slaves; yet they were in the vanguard of conspiracy "to be free." [64]

Many white New Yorkers could not understand such behavior because it contradicted so much of their notion of the nature of blacks and their enslavement. Supposedly blacks were happy under slavery and wanted no more than what they had. Moreover, supposedly they were incapable of thinking up such a nihilistic scheme as a conspiracy to destroy the city and murder the inhabitants. As the attorney general said in 1741, "it cannot be imagined that these silly unthinking creatures could of themselves have contrived so deep, so direful and destructive a scheme, as that we have seen with our eyes." [65] To explain the apparent contradiction between the conventional characterization of the slaves as ignorant and docile and the evidence of their involvement in the conspiracy, in an era when many men believed that supernatural forces of good and evil intervene directly in human life, the attorney general maintained that

> these stupid wretches [were] seduced by the instigation of the devil, and Hughson his agent, to undertake so senseless as well as wicked enterprise; which must inevitably end in their own destruction.[66]

Although few persons now would use such an explanation as that of the attorney general, the assumptions on which that explanation was based and the stereotype it presented are still prevalent: enslaved blacks remain in many minds as Sambos—content, naturally ignorant of "liberty and the pursuit of happiness," and unrebellious.[67] Any evidence to the contrary is given little recognition; hence this too has tended to depreciate the credibility of a conspiracy by blacks.[68]

So, something broader in scope than controversy over courtroom procedures, or the partiality of sources and compiler of the *Journal* buried this book and the episode it recounts. Both were relegated to the unremembered past because they contain contradictions to the much flaunted consensus conception of America as a land of freedom, justice, and harmony. Moreover the book is an important and much revealing document of the times, full of information about many aspects of life in colonial New York, suggestions as to the nature of society then, and details of the attitudes and relations between rich and poor, black and white. Those attitudes and relations continue to exist in America and on several levels the proceedings against the conspiracy in New York during 1741 are similar to the "Chicago 8" trial and that of the "Panther 21." Thus, for those who need present reminders that problems in the past have not succumbed to repression or drifted away if neglected—benignly or otherwise—here is a book to be ruminated over. It is a piece for thought in all the uneasy times when men of different means or complexions suspiciously look at one another.

NOTES TO INTRODUCTION

1. The title of the original edition was *A Journal of the Proceedings in The Detection of the Conspiracy formed by Some White People, in Conjunction with Negro and other Slaves, for burning the city of New-York in America, and Murdering the Inhabitants*. In 1741 at London, under the same title, it was reprinted and sold by John Clarke. A second edition appeared at New York in 1810, printed and published by Southwick & Pelsue. In 1851 William B. Wedgwood produced an edited incomplete version of the text in four parts, under the title *The Negro Conspiracy in the city of New York, in 1741* (New York, G. W. Schott). In addition, a fifty-eight-page abridgment entitled *The Trial of John Ury* appeared at Philadelphia in 1899 from the press of M. I. J. Griffin.

2. Infra, p. 155. For background and discussion of slave uprisings and plots in colonial America, see Herbert Aptheker, *American Negro Slave Revolts* (New York, 1943).

3. Infra, p. 5–6.

4. See "A List of White Persons, Taken into Custody on account of the Conspiracy, in 1741," and "A List of Negroes Committed on Account of the Conspiracy," at the end of the book (infra, pp. 466–472).

5. See discussion of the threat of fire and the flammability of the town in *New York as an Eighteenth Century Municipality* (New York, 1917), pt. 2, by George W. Edwards, pp. 168–181.

6. Infra, p. 27, 64.

7. See E. B. O'Callaghan, *Documentary History of the State of New York* (4 vols.; Albany, 1850–1851), I, 471–474; for a discussion of the growth, composition, and distribution of the slave and white population in New York from 1698 to 1790, see Thomas J. Davis, "Population and Slavery in New York" (unpublished master's essay, Department of History, Columbia University). For suspicions, infra, p. 29 ff.

8. Infra, p. 29.

9. Infra, p. 37.

10. For the contemporary controversy, see *The Letters and Papers of Cadwallader Colden, 1711–1767*, published as volumes 50–56 and 67–68 of The New-York Historical Society, *Collections* (New York, 1918–23, 1934–35), vol. 67, pp. 265–66, 270–272, 288–289; especially look at the anonymous letter from the province of Massachusetts to Colden, vol. 67, 270–272, the Boston *Weekly News-Letter* for 7–14 May, 4–11 and 18–25 June, the issues for July, 6–13 August, and 3–10 September 1741. Also see E. B. O'Callaghan, ed., *Documents Relative to the Colonial History of the State of New York* (15 vols., Albany, 1855–57), VI, 186–87, 196–202, 213; VII, 528.

11. On the nature of conspiracy in law, see P. W. Winfield, *The History of Conspiracy and Abuse of Legal Procedure* (New York, 1921); Milton Handler, *Contract, Combination or Conspiracy* (New York, 1953); and Herbert L. Packer, "The Conspiracy Weapon," *New York Review of Books*, 13 (6 November 1969), 24–30.

12. See *The Letters and Papers of Cadwallader Colden*, vol. 67, 270–272.

13. (New edition; New York, 1936), 81.

14. (2nd pb. ed.; Baton Rouge, 1969), 470–471.

15. (New York, 1943), 192–193. For other interpretations, see T. Wood Clarke, "The Negro Plot of 1741," *New York History*, 25 (1944), 167–181; Annette K. Dorf, "The Slave Conspiracy of 1741" (unpublished master's essay, Department of History, Columbia University, 1958); Henry H. Ingersoll, "The New York Plot of 1741," *The Green Bag*, 20 (1908); Edgar J. McManus, *A History of Negro Slavery in New York* (Syracuse, 1966); Walter F. Prince, "New York 'Negro Plot' of 1741," [New Haven, Conn.] *Saturday Chronicle*, 28 June and 23 August 1902, a typescript of which is at The New York Public Library; and Ferenc M. Szasz, "The New York Slave Revolt of 1741: A Re-Examination," *New York History*, 48 (1967), 215–230.

16. Infra, p. 69. See remarks of lieutenant governor George Clarke to provincial Assembly in Charles Z. Lincoln, ed., *Messages from the Governors, Comprising Executive Communication to the Legislature and Other Papers* (11 vols.; Albany, 1909), I, 260; and Richard B. Morris, *Government and Labor in Early America* (New York, 1946), 183 ff.

17. *Ibid.*

18. *Ibid.*

19. On frontier predicament, see Douglas E. Leach, *The Northern Colonial Frontier 1607–1763* (New York, 1966); Robert Leckie, *The Wars of America* (2 vols.; New York, 1968), I, 29–30. The unpopularity shows in part in the initial refusal of the general assembly to allocate monies to supply the war effort. Later it did allocate £200. See James G. Wilson, ed.,

The Memorial History of the city of New York (4 vols.; New York, 1892), II, 256; [New York], *Journal of the Votes and Proceedings of the General Assembly of the Colony of New-York, 1691–1743* (2 vols.; New York, 1764), I, 802–803. For expression of some of the fears, see E. B. O'Callaghan, ed., *Documents Relative to the Colonial History of the State of New York* (15 vols.; Albany, 1854), VI, 187.

20. By 22 April 1741 New York had raised five companies for an expedition against the Spanish West Indies—see O'Callaghan, *Documents Relative to the Colonial History*, VI, 185.

21. On color as the measure of bondage in colonial America, see Richard B. Morris, "The Measure of Bondage in the Slave States," *Mississippi Valley Historical Review*, 41 (September 1954); Oscar and Mary Handlin, "Origin of the Southern Labor System," *William and Mary Quarterly*, 7 (1950); and Carl N. Degler, "Slavery and the Origin of American Race Prejudice," *Comparative Studies in Society and History*, 2 (October 1959).

22. Infra, pp. 350–351.

23. Infra, pp. 338 ff.

24. Infra, p. 59n; also see Aptheker, *American Negro Slave Revolts*, 172–173.

25. Infra, p. 11.

26. For an account of the plot at Hackensack, see Henry S. Cooley, *A Study of Slavery in New Jersey* (Baltimore, 1896), 42–43; also, infra, p. 50.

27. Infra, p. 330.

28. For summary and comment on slave code in New York, see Ansel Judd Northrup, "Slavery in New York," *State Library Bulletin, History*, No. 4 (May 1900); and Edwin Olson, "The Slave Code in Colonial New York," *Journal of Negro History*, 29 (1944), 147–165.

29. Infra, p. 67n.

30. Infra, p. 31.

31. Infra, p. 60.

32. Infra, p. 74.

33. Infra, p. 77.

34. Infra, p. 78.

35. Infra, p. 88.

36. Infra, p. 85.

37. Infra, p. 87.

38. Infra, pp. 110–111.

39. Infra, p. 84.

40. Infra, p. 117.

41. Infra, p. 72.

42. Infra, p. 121.

43. Infra, p. 202.

44. Infra, pp. 8, 89n; also see William Livingston and William Smith, eds., *Laws of New York, from the Year 1691 to 1751 Inclusive* (New York, 1752).

45. *Ibid.*

46. Cf. note 11.

47. Infra, p. 415; see original title page.

48. Cf. notes 10 and 15.

49. See David McAdam, et al., eds., *History of Bench and Bar of New York* (2 vols.; New York, 1897); George A. Billias, ed., *Law and Authority in Colonial America* (Barre, Mass., 1965); and Hans Glatte, *Shorthand Systems of the World* (New York, 1959).

50. Cf. notes 10 and 15.

51. For details on Horsmanden see Charles W. Spencer's entry on him in the *Dictionary of American Biography*, IX, 236–237; and Mary P. McManus, "Daniel Horsmanden, Eighteenth Century New Yorker" (unpublished doctoral dissertation, Department of History, Fordham University, 1960).

52. *Ibid.*

53. Lamb, *History of the City of New York* (3 vols.; New York, 1877–1896), II, 577–578; Stokes (6 vols.; New York, 1915–1928), IV, 566.

54. Infra, p. 10.

55. *Ibid.*

56. *Ibid.*

57. (Chapel Hill, 1968).

58. (Englewood Cliffs, 1963).

59. Infra, p. 105.

60. *Ibid.*; see Jordan, *White Over Black*, 28 ff. and 252 ff., and McKitrick, *Slavery Defended*, 57–68 and 69–85.

61. Infra, p. 105.

62. Infra, pp. 105–106.

63. Infra, p. 202.

64. *Ibid.*

65. Infra, p. 168.

66. *Ibid.*

67. For discussion and recent support of Sambo see Stanley Elkins, *Slavery: A Problem in American Institutional and Intellectual Life* (2nd ed.; Chicago, 1968).

68. Cf. notes 13, 14, and 15.

A NOTE ON THIS EDITION

This text is a full and complete representation of the original edition, with the same wording (although not always spelling), structure, notes, commentary, paraphrases, translations, appendixes, and tables that appeared in the original, and with addition of the "Preface to the Second Edition." The text is based on the edition of 1810, which is a veritable reproduction of the original edition of 1744, except for changes from early eighteenth-century spelling, re-setting of the pages in single rather than double columns, the removal of printer's errors, and the insertion of the page and a half of errata of the original in the proper places throughout the text. In preparing this text for publication (except for removal of printer's errors), the present editor made no revisions of any kind in the form and content of the 1810 edition, which was checked carefully against the original so as to ensure its correspondence. The editor wished to leave each reader with the full flavor of the original, undistracted by the seasoning of additional annotations, which to be most helpful would have been most extensive. As a document of the time, the book stands on its internal structure and ought to be judged thereon. A full history of the plot is something else and another volume.

T.J.D.

THE NEW YORK CONSPIRACY

A
JOURNAL
OF THE
PROCEEDINGS
IN
The Detection of the Conspiracy
FORMED BY
Some *White* People, in Conjunction with *Negro* and other *Slaves*,

FOR
Burning the City of *NEW-YORK* in America,
And Murdering the Inhabitants.

Which Conspiracy was partly put in Execution, by Burning His Majesty's House in Fort George, within the said City, on Wednesday the Eighteenth of *March*, 1741. and setting Fire to several Dwelling and other Houses there, within a few Days succeeding. And by another Attempt made in Prosecution of the same infernal Scheme, by putting Fire between two other Dwelling-Houses within the said City, on the Fifteenth Day of *February*, 1742; which was accidentally and timely discovered and extinguished.

CONTAINING,

I. A Narrative of the Trials, Condemnations, Executions, and Behaviour of the several Criminals, at the Gallows and Stake, with their *Speeches* and *Confessions*; with Notes, Observations and Reflections occasionally interspersed throughout the Whole.

II. An Appendix, wherein is set forth some additional Evidence concerning the said Conspiracy and Conspirators, which has come to Light since their Trials and Executions.

III. Lists of the several Persons (Whites and Blacks) committed on Account of the Conspiracy; and of the several Criminals executed; and of those transported, with the Places whereto.

By the Recorder of the City of New-York.

Quid faciant Domini, audent cum talia Fures? Virg. Ecl.

NEW-YORK:
Printed by *James Parker*, at the New Printing-Office, 1744.

THE

NEW-YORK CONSPIRACY,

OR A

HISTORY OF THE NEGRO PLOT,

WITH THE

JOURNAL OF THE PROCEEDINGS

AGAINST THE

CONSPIRATORS AT NEW-YORK IN THE YEARS

1741-2.

TOGETHER WITH

SEVERAL INTERESTING TABLES,

Containing the Names of the White and Black Persons arrested on
account of the Conspiracy—the times of their Trials—their
Sentences—their Executions by Burning and
Hanging--Names of those Transported, and those Discharged.

With a variety of other useful and highly interesting matter

BY DANIEL HORSMANDEN, ESQ.

NEW-YORK:

PRINTED AND PUBLISHED BY SOUTHWICK & PELSUE,
No. 3, NEW-STREET.

1810.

PREFACE TO THE SECOND EDITION

The History of the Great Negro Plot in 1741, has always been a subject of curiosity, and highly interesting to the citizens of New-York. Never having been republished, the work had become so extremely scarce, that it was with the utmost difficulty a perfect copy could be obtained for the present edition.

After a lapse of nearly three quarters of a century, we look back with astonishment on the panic occasioned by the negro plot, and the rancorous hatred that prevailed against the Roman catholics. To judge from tradition, and the "Journal of the Proceedings against the Conspirators," no doubt can be had of the actual existence of a plot; but its extent could never have been so great as the terror of those times depicted. The very mode adopted to discover abettors, by mutual criminations and confessions, tended, in the progress of the trials, to inculpate every negro slave in the city. We accordingly find that the number of conspirators daily increased. As it was impossible to prove all equally guilty, the ringleaders only were executed, and those who, to save their lives, plead guilty and threw themselves on the mercy of the court, were transported.

The city of New-York, at this period, contained a population of about 12,000 souls, of which one-sixth were, in all probability, negro slaves. Insurrections and conspiracies were, at this juncture, frequent in the West India islands, and great apprehensions were entertained of an invasion by the French and Spanish. These circumstances aggravated the horrors of a domestic plot to such a degree, that the white inhabitants, regarding every negro slave as an incendiary and an assassin, carried their apprehensions and resentments beyond all bounds.

A holy hatred of the Roman catholics was inculcated by

[1]

church and state. Our Dutch forefathers, glowing with all the zeal of the early reformers, emigrated to this country, shortly after the emancipation of the United Netherlands from the Spanish yoke, and fostered all the rancour of their race against papists and Spaniards. It was the policy of the English government, after the conquest, to cherish this animosity, and those of our readers, who were born and educated before the American revolution, will recollect how religiously they were taught to abhor the Pope, Devil and Pretender. The act of our provincial assembly against Jesuits and popish priests, passed II William and Mary, and which continued in full force until our independence, was owing, not only to these prejudices, but to the exposed situation of the colony, the northern frontier of which was bounded by Canada, at that time in possession of France, the natural and ever-during enemy of England. The predominating influence of the French over the aborigines of this country, was principally ascribed to their priests. The pomp and pageantry of the Romish church powerfully appealed to the senses of the rude savage, who could not so easily comprehend the abstract truths of the protestant religion. To counteract this influence, and prevent the Indians from being seduced from their obedience to the English crown, this law was enacted against

every Jesuit, seminary, priest, missionary, or other spiritual or ecclesiastical person, made or ordained by any authority, power, or jurisdiction, derived, challenged or pretended, from the pope or see of Rome, or that shall profess himself, or otherwise appear to be such, by practising or teaching of others, to say any popish prayer, by celebrating of masses, granting of absolutions, or using any other of the Romish ceremonies, or rites of worship, by what name, title or degree soever such person shall be called or known, who shall continue, abide or come into this province, or any part thereof, after the first day of November aforesaid; shall be deemed and accounted an incendiary, and disturber of the public peace and safety, and a disturber of the true christian religion, and shall be adjudged to suffer perpetual imprisonment. And if any person, being so sentenced and actually imprisoned, shall break prison, and make his escape, and be afterwards retaken; he shall suffer such pains of death, penalties and forfeitures, as in cases of felony.

The intolerant spirit of this act shows the horror and detestation in which the Roman catholics were held, and will account, why so few of this profession existed in this city and colony before the revolution.

In estimating this singular event in our colonial history, the circumstances of the times should be duly considered, before we too hastily condemn the bigotry and cruelty of our predecessors. The advantages of a liberal, indeed of the plainest education, was the happy lot of very few. Intercourse between the colonies and the mother country, and between province and province, was very rare. Ignorance and illiberal prejudices universally prevailed. Their more favoured and enlightened posterity will, therefore, draw the veil of filial affection over the involuntary errors of their forefathers, and emulating their simple virtues, endeavour to transmit a brighter example to their successors.

New-York, April 5th, 1810

ORIGINAL PREFACE

The reader must not expect in the following sheets, a particular and minute relation of every formality, question and answer, that passed upon the trials; it may suffice, if he be assured he has the substance; for indeed more cannot be expected, when it is considered, that we have no one here, as in our mother country, who make it a business to take notes upon such occasions, or any others, that we know of, who are so dexterous at short-hand, as to be sufficiently qualified for such a purpose; but he will be sure to have all that could be collected from the notes that were taken by the court, and gentlemen at the bar; with all which the compiler has been furnished.

Upon a review of the proceedings, in order for this undertaking, the bulk of them, which was the product of about *six months inquiry*, seemed somewhat discouraging: No doubt they might have been contracted, if this work had been proceeded upon in the method of an historical relation only, wherein the compiler would have been more at liberty to abstract the several originals; but it was concluded, a *journal* would give more satisfaction, inasmuch as in such a kind of process, the depositions and examinations themselves, which were the ground-work of the proceedings, would appear at large; which most probably would afford conviction, to such as have a disposition to be convinced, and have *in reality* doubted whether any particular convicts had justice done them or not, notwithstanding they had the opportunity of *seeing* and *hearing* a great deal concerning them; and others, who had no such opportunities, who were prejudiced at a distance in their disfavour, by frivolous reports, might the readier be undeceived: for as the proceedings are set forth in the order of time they were produced, the reader will thereby be furnished with the most natural view of the whole, and be better enabled to conceive the design and dangerous depth of this *hellish project,* as well as the justice of the several prosecutions.

Thus far, however, the compiler thinks proper to premise, that as he found it convenient to divide the originals into numbered sections, for the more ready reference to the several parts of them, as occasion should offer, he took the liberty also of lopping off from them, what, in print, he thought would be a superfluous formality, such as, *the deponent further saith,* and such like, which he thought would have been a needless incumbrance to the book.

The parties accused of the conspiracy were numerous, and business by degrees multiplied so fast upon the grand jury, *which bore the burthen of this inquiry,* that there would have been an immediate necessity for others to have lent a helping hand in taking examinations *from the beginning,* if the judges had not found it expedient to examine the persons accused, upon their first taking into custody, whereby it seemed most likely the truth would bolt out, before they had time to cool, or opportunity of discoursing in the jail with their confederates, who were before committed.

The examinations thus taken by the judges, were soon after laid before the grand jury, who interrogated the parties therefrom in such manner, as generally produced from them the substance of the same matter, and often something more, by which means there accrued no small advantage; for though where the last examination brought to light new discovery, yet it will be seldom found, there is any thing in such further examinations contradictory to the former, but generally a confirmation of them; and in such case, the setting forth the same at large, may not be thought a useless tautology; not that this will happen often, and where it does, it will be chiefly found in the examinations and confessions of negroes, who, in ordinary cases, are seldom found to hold twice in the same story; which, for its rarity therefore, if it carried not with it the additional weight of the greater appearance of truth, may make this particular the more

[6]

excusable; and further, this is a *diary* of the proceedings, that is to be exhibited, therefore, in conformity to that plan, nothing should be omitted, which may be of any use.

All proper precautions were taken by the judges, that the criminals should be kept separate; and they were so, as much as the scanty room in the jail would admit it of; and new apartments were fitted up for their reception: but more particular care was taken, that such negroes as had made confession and discovery, and were to be made use of as witnesses, should be kept apart from the rest, and as much from each other, as the accommodations would allow of, in order to prevent their caballing from each other first, as well upon the trials, as otherwise, and then generally confronted with the persons they accused, who were usually sent for and taken into custody upon such examinations, if they were to be met with; which was the means of bringing many others to a confession, as well as were newly taken up, as those who had long before been committed, perhaps upon slighter grounds, and had insisted upon their innocence; for they had generally the cunning not to own their guilt, till they knew their accusers. But notwithstanding this was the ordinary method taken, both by the judges and grand jury, to send for the parties as soon as impeached, (which however might sometimes through hurry be omitted) yet several who happened then to be out of the way, were afterwards forgot, and slipped through our fingers, from the multiplicity of business in hand, as will hereafter appear; which *therefore* is particularly recommended to the notice of their owners.

The trouble of examining criminals in general, may be easily guessed at; but the fatigue in that of negroes, is not to be conceived, but by those that have undergone the drudgery. The difficulty of bringing and holding them to the truth, if by chance it starts through them, is not to be surmounted, but by the closest attention; many of them have a great deal of craft; their unintelligible jargon stands them in great stead, to conceal their meaning; so that an examiner must expect to encounter with much perplexity, grope through a maze of obscurity, be obliged to lay hold of broken hints, lay them carefully together, and thoroughly weigh and compare them with each other, before he can be able to see the light, or fix those creatures to any certain determinate meaning.

Though for the reasons before mentioned, all the trials could not be set forth at large; yet on the principal trials, such as, *the Hughsons, Ury the Priest, Quack*, and *Cuffee*, (the two first negroes executed for the conspiracy) and that of *the five Spanish slaves*, the court and gentlemen at the bar took notes more largely; but as to the rest, though there were here and there some minutes taken, (which are also set forth in their proper places) yet they did not think them equally worth the pains; therefore upon other trials, the paragraphs or sections of the depositions of whites, and the examinations and confessions of slaves, taken by the judges, grand jury, or others, upon the credit whereof such slaves were indicted, are referred to upon their respective trials: which method, if any should object to, as subject to uncertainty, and say, the witnesses might not declare exactly the same things, and in the same words, or the substance of them, before the court, as are contained in those depositions, examinations and confessions referred to, the answer is,

1st. It is most likely they did not, (nor could it be expected they should) deliver themselves precisely in the same words: but abstracts were taken of those evidences, and briefs prepared for the counsel concerned in each trial, pointing out the several articles affecting each criminal, whereby the counsel were readily led to ask a witness such questions as would naturally draw out the substance of the same matter in answer, as if it were the truth; and it was observed by those more immediately concerned in these affairs, and whose province it was to give close attention to them, that the witnesses both whites and blacks, generally kept close to the text, and delivered in court the substance of the evidence they had before given in their depositions, examinations and confessions.

2dly. That what the witnesses did actually declare in court upon the trials, was sufficient to convince *twelve* honest men upon their oaths, that the accused were guilty; and there is no other way to furnish the reader with the grounds which gave such conviction to the juries.

[8]

For the further *enlightening* the masters and owners of slaves accused, convicted upon their own confessions, and transported, and of others who were discharged from confinement, *(for want of sufficient evidence, as it was said, before the second grand jury, who were charged to continue the inquiry concerning this infernal scheme)* the evidence affecting each, is referred to under every such negro's confession, excepting as to such of them as were made use of as witnesses, which was thought needless; for their testimony having gained sufficient credit, it can scarce be supposed there will be any doubt of their own guilt: but if there should be any who hesitate concerning it, all that can be said is, it will behove such to give the closer attention to the several depositions, examinations and confessions, which impeach them.

The evidence likewise affecting each white person apprehended upon the account of this conspiracy, that was afterwards discharged for want of prosecution, is referred to under their respective names, that it may appear what reason there was for their commitment and accusation, though they were discharged for want of indictment.

It has been thought proper to add, at the end of this journal, lists of all the whites and blacks accused of this conspiracy, those who were executed, and those who were pardoned upon condition of transportation, or otherwise discharged from jail, shewing the respective times of their commitment, arraignment, conviction, execution or discharge; whereby the reader will be enabled to turn to almost any part of the journal to satisfy his curiosity, as to what most materially concerns each respective conspirator; and with a view also to shew to what places such of them as were transported (according to information received) were shipped; which is premised, as a modest hint to our brethren in the *West Indies,* and the more neighbouring English colonies, that they may see how tender we have been of *their* peace and security, by using all the precaution in our power, *that none of our rogues should be imposed upon them;* for it was made an express condition in the several pardons, and likewise the recognizances entered into by the securities for slaves transported, "that the persons pardoned should be transported to the dominion of some foreign prince or state, or the island of *Newfoundland,* (by a time therein limited) and if any of the negroes or slaves (pardoned by the letters patent) should at any time after (the day therein limited) *be found* in *any of his majesty's dominions,* except *Newfoundland,* the letters patent as to all and every the person and persons so found, would be null, void, and of no force or effect"; which terms have been strictly pursued and complied with, some few instances only excepted.

Many, it seems, have wondered that this journal has not made its appearance long ago; for, say they, the thing dies away, and is almost forgotten (the more is the pity) and now people will hardly take the pains to give it perusal.

To which it is answered, that it was some time before the compiler could submit himself to undergo a drudgery of this kind, for several reasons; the task was not very inviting, and he had borne a sufficient fatigue, under an ill state of health in the share he had in the proceedings themselves, for a course of six months daily attendance, and it was some time before he could absolutely determine to undertake it, and did set about it in earnest; and since that, the duties of his offices and profession have occasioned many interruptions; and when the attention is withdrawn for a time from a subject, it may not always suit the humour to reassume it, especially a matter of this nature; nor perhaps can the thoughts concerning it be easily collected again; not that this business required much intention, but recollection and care were necessary to introduce every matter properly, and give it connexion in its due order of time, towards which the compiler had the advantage of being all along privy to the proceedings, and all the motions concerning them.

There were reasons indeed, for making these matters public, which could not be withstood.

There had been some wanton, wrong-headed persons amongst us, who took the liberty to arraign the justice of the proceedings, and set up their private opinions in superiority to the court and grand jury; though God knows (and all men of sense know) they could not be judges of such matters; but nevertheless, they declared with no small assurance (notwithstanding what we *saw* with our eyes, and *heard* with our ears, and every one might have judged of by his intellects, that had any) *that there was no plot at all!* The inference *such* would have drawn from thence, is too obvious to need mentioning; however this moved very little: It was not to *convince* (for that would have been a vain undertaking; *the Ethiopian might as soon change his skin*) much less was it to gratify *such*.

But there were two motives which weighed much; the *one*, that those who had not the opportunity of *seeing* and *hearing*, might judge of the justice of the proceedings, from the state of the case being laid before them; the *other*, that from thence, the people in general, might be persuaded of the necessity there is, for every one that has negroes, to keep a very watchful eye over them, and not to indulge them with too great liberties, which we find they make use of to the worst purposes, caballing and confederating together in mischief, in great numbers, when they may, from the accounts in the ensuing sheets, from what they *see* has happened, *feel* the consequence of giving them so great a latitude, as has been customary in this city and province, and thereby be warned to keep themselves upon a strict guard against *these enemies of their own household,* since we know what they are capable of; for it was notorious, that those among them, who had the kindest masters, who fared best, and had the most liberty, nay, that those in whom their masters placed the greatest confidence, insomuch, that they would even have put their own swords into their hands, in expectation of being defended by them against their own colour, did nevertheless turn out the greatest villains. It even appeared that these *head fellows* boasted of *their superiority* over the more harmless and inoffensive; that they held them in an inferiority and dependence, a kind of subjection, as if they had got such dominion over them, *that they durst not, at any time, or upon any occasion, but do as they would have them*; from whence it may be guessed, how likely the defection was to be general.

The principal inducement, therefore, to this undertaking was, *the public benefit*; that those who have property in slaves, might have a lasting memento concerning the nature of them; that they may be thence warned to keep a constant guard over them; since what they have done, they may one time or other act over again, especially if there should in future times, appear *such monsters in nature*, as the *Hughsons, Ury the priest, and such like*, who dare be so wicked as to attempt the seducing them to such execrable purposes: and if any should think it not worth their while to learn from the ensuing sheets (what by others perhaps may be esteemed) *a useful lesson*, the fault will be their own; and really it was thought *necessary*, for these and other reasons needless here to mention, that there should be a standing memorial of so unprecedented a scheme of villainy.

But though the compiler was willing to make an offering of his *own time*, to the public service, by laying these matters in order for the press, yet being under no other influence so to do, but his inclination and readiness to oblige the public, he was at liberty, however, to suit his own convenience; and therefore, considering the multiplicity of the proceedings, it may, *after all*, rather be thought *matter of wonder*, that it makes its appearance so soon.

Perhaps it may not come forth unseasonably at this *juncture*, if the distractions occasioned by this mystery *of iniquity*, may be thereby so revived in our memories, as to awaken us from that supine security, which again too generally prevails, and put us upon our guard, lest the enemy should be yet within our doors.

City of New-York, 12th April, 1744

INTRODUCTION

As a robbery committed at Mr. Hogg's, paved the way to the discovery of the conspiracy, it may not be improper to introduce the ensuing journal and narrative, with an account of that felony, as well as the many fires which alarmed this city, close upon the heels of each other, within less than three weeks, occasioned by this infernal scheme, till they both came under the inquiry and examination of the grand jury, at the Supreme Court: and indeed there is such a close connexion between this felony and the conspiracy, as will appear by the several steps and examinations taken by occasion of the former, that the narrative of the robbery could not well be omitted; for the inquiry concerning that, was the means of drawing out the first hint concerning the other; nay, this felony and such like, were actually ingredients of the conspiracy, as will appear by the sequel.

On Saturday night the 28th February, 1740-1, a robbery was committed at the house of Mr. Robert Hogg, in the city of New-York, merchant, from whence were taken divers pieces of linen and other goods, and several silver coins, chiefly Spanish, and medals, and wrought silver, etc. to the value in the whole, of sixty pounds and upwards.

The occasion of this robbery, as was discovered, and will appear more fully hereafter, was one Wilson, a lad of about seventeen or eighteen years of age, belonging to the Flamborough man of war, on this station, who having acquaintance with two white servants belonging to gentlemen who lodged at Mr. Hogg's house, Wilson used frequently to come thither on that pretence, which gained him easy admittance: but Wilson, it seems, had a more familiar acquaintance with some negroes of very suspicious characters, particularly Caesar, belonging to John Vaarck, baker; Prince, to Mr. John Auboyneau, merchant; and Cuffee, to Adolph Philipse, Esq.

[13]

The Thursday before this robbery was committed, Wilson came to Mr. Hogg's shop, with one of the man of war's people, to buy some check linen, and having bargained for some, part of the money offered in payment, was of Spanish coin, and Mrs. Hogg opening her bureau to change the money, pulled out a drawer in the view of Wilson, wherein were a considerable quantity of milled Spanish pieces of eight; she soon reflected that she had done wrong in exposing her money to an idle boy in that manner, who came so frequently to her house, and immediately shut up the bureau again, and made a pretence of sending the money out to a neighbour's to be weighed.

Mrs. Hogg's apprehensions happened to be right; for this having a sight of the money, was charmed with it, and, as it seems, wanted to be fingering of it. He told his comrades of the black guard, the beforenamed Caesar, Prince and Cuffee, where they might have a fine booty, if they could manage cleverly to come at it; he said it was at Hogg's house in the Broad street; his wife kept a shop of goods, and sold candles, rum, molasses, etc.

The negroes catched at the proposal, and the scheme was communicated by them to John Hughson, who kept a public house by the North River, in this city, a place where numbers of negroes used to resort, and be entertained privately (in defiance of the laws) at all hours, as appeared afterwards, and will be shewn at large in the ensuing sheets. Thither they used to bring such goods as they stole from their masters or others, and Hughson, his wife and family, received them: there they held a consultation with Hughson and his family, how they should act, in order to compass the attainment of this booty.

The boy (Wilson) told them the situation of the house and shop; that the front was towards Broad-street, and there was a side door out of the shop into an alley, commonly called the Jews-Alley, and if they could make an errand thither to buy rum, they might get an opportunity to shove back the bolt of the door facing the alley, for there was no lock on it, and they could come in the night afterwards, and accomplish their designs. (a)

(a) At nights they usually let people in at the front door, in another street, and went through the parlour into the kitchen, which Wilson well knew.

At Hughson's lodged one Margaret Sorubiero, alias Saling-burgh, alias Kerry, commonly called Peggy, or the Newfoundland Irish beauty, a young woman about one or two and twenty; she pretended to be married, but no husband appeared; she was a person of infamous character, a notorious prostitute, and also of the worst sort, a prostitute to negroes; she was here lodged and supported by Caesar (Vaarck's) before mentioned, and took share (in common with Hughson's family) of the spoils and plunder, the effects of Caesar's thefts, which he brought to Hughson's; and she may be supposed to have been in most of their wicked secrets; for she had lodged there the summer before, and removed from thence to a house by the new battery, near one John Romme's, a shoemaker, and was well acquainted with him and his wife: thither also Caesar used frequently to resort, with many other negroes; thither he also conveyed stolen goods, and some part of Hogg's goods, of which John Romme had his choice, if what Caesar said, after his condemnation, be true; and by what will appear hereafter against Romme, and from his inti-macy with Hughson, his merits may be concluded to fall little short of his companions.

With this Peggy, as she will be hereafter commonly called, Caesar used frequently to sleep at Hughson's with the knowl-edge and permission of the family; and Caesar bargained with and paid Hughson for her board; she came there to lodge a second time in the fall, not long before Christmas, 1740, big with child by Caesar, as was supposed, and brought to bed there not many days before the robbery at Hogg's, of a babe largely partaking of a dark complexion.

Here is laid the foundation of the characters of Hughson and his family, Peggy and John Romme, which will afford frequent occasion of enlarging upon; and from such a hopeful earnest the reader may well expect a plentiful harvest.

Wilson coming to Mrs. Hogg's on Sunday morning, to see his acquaintance as usual, she complained to him, that she had been robbed the night before, that she had lost all the goods out of the shop, a great deal of silver Spanish coins, medals and other silver things, little suspecting that he had been the occasion of it, notwithstanding what she apprehended upon pulling out the drawer of money before him, as above; but as she knew he belonged to the man of war, and that several of those sailors frequented idle houses in the Jews-Alley, it happened that her suspicions inclined towards them; she imagined he might be able to give her some intelligence about it, and therefore described to him some things that she had missed, viz. snuff-boxes, silver medals, one a remarkable eight square piece, etc. Whereupon Wilson said, he had been the morning at Hughson's house, and there saw one John Gwin, who pulled out of his pocket a worsted cap full of pieces of coined silver; and that Mr. Philipse's Cuffee, who was there, seeing John Gwin have this money, he asked him to give him some, and John Gwin counted him out half a crown in pennies, and asked him if he would have any more; and then pulled out a handful of silver coin, amongst which, Wilson said, he saw the eight square piece described by Mrs. Hogg.

Sunday, March 1.

This morning search was made for John Gwin at Hughson's, supposing him to have been a soldier of that name, a fellow of suspicious character, as Mrs. Hogg conceived; and the officers making inquiry accordingly for a soldier, they were answered, there was no such soldier used that house; but it fell out, that Caesar, the real person wanted, was at the same time before their faces in the Chimney corner: the officer returned without suspecting him to be the person meant, but the mistake being discovered by the boy (Wilson) that the negro Caesar before mentioned went by that name, he was apprehended in the afternoon, and being brought before Wilson, he declared that he was the person he meant by John Gwin.

Caesar was committed to prison.

Monday, March 2.

Caesar (Vaarck's negro) was examined by the justices, and denied every thing laid to his charge concerning Hogg's robbery, but was remanded.

Prince (Mr. Auboyneau's negro) was this day also apprehended upon account of the same felony: upon examination he denied knowing any thing of it. He was also committed.

Upon information that Caesar had shewn a great deal of silver at Hughson's, it was much suspected that Hughson knew something of the matter, and therefore search was made several times at his house, yesterday and this day, but none of the goods or silver were discovered.

Hughson and his wife were sent for, and were present while the negroes were examined by the justices, and were also examined themselves, touching the things stolen, but discovered nothing; and they were dismissed.

Tuesday, March 3.

Hughson's house having been searched several times over by Mr. Mills, the under-sheriff, and several constables, in quest of Hogg's goods, without effect, it happened this evening, that Mary Burton (b) came to the house of James Kannady, one of the searching constables, to fetch a pound of candles for her master; Kannady's wife knew the girl by sight, and who she belonged to living in the neighbourhood near them, and having heard of the robbery, and the several searches at Hughson's, she took upon her to examine Mary, "whether she knew any thing of those goods, and admonished her to discover if she did, lest she herself should be brought into trouble, and gave her motherly good advice, and said if she knew any thing of it, and would tell she would get her freed from her master." Whereupon at parting, the girl said, "she could not tell her then, she would tell her tomorrow; but that her husband was not cute enough, for that he had trod upon them," and so went away. This alarmed Kannady and his wife, and the same evening Ann Kannady went to Mr. Mills, the under-sheriff, and told him what had passed between her and Mary Burton. "Whereupon Mills and his wife, Mr. Hogg and his wife, and several constables, went with Ann

(b) An indented servant to John Hughson, came to him about midsummer, 1740.

Kannady and her husband, down to Hughson's house; and Ann Kannady desired the under-sheriff to go in first, and bring Mary Burton out to her; but he staying a long time, Ann Kannady went into Hughson's house; and found the under-sheriff and his wife, and Mary Burton, in the parlour, and she then denied what she had before said to Ann Kannady, as above; then Ann Kannady charged her home with it; till at length, Mary Burton said she could not tell them any thing there, she was afraid of her life; that they would kill her. Whereupon they took the girl out of the house, and when they had got a little way from thence, she put her hand in her pocket, and pulled out a piece of silver money, which she said was part of Hogg's money, which the negro had given her. They all went to alderman Bancker's with her, and Ann Kannady informing the alderman, that she had promised Mary Burton to get her freed from her master; he directed that she should lodge that night with the under-sheriff at the City-Hall for safety; and she was left there accordingly." For Mary Burton declared also, before the alderman, her apprehensions and fears, that she should be murdered or poisoned by the Hughsons and the negroes, for what she should discover.

The alderman sent for John Hughson, and examined him closely, whether he knew any thing of the matter? but he denied that he did at first, until the alderman pressed him very home and admonished him (if it was in his power) to discover those who had committed this piece of villainy; little suspecting him to have been previously concerned; he was at last prevailed with to acknowledge he knew where some of the things were hid, and he went home, fetched and delivered them.

Wednesday, March 4.

This day the mayor having summoned the Justices to meet at the City-Hall, several aldermen met him accordingly, and sent for Mary Burton and John Hughson and his wife; and Mary Burton, after examination, made the following deposition before them.

"Mary Burton, of the city of New-York, Spinster, aged about sixteen years, being sworn, deposed,

1. "That about two o'clock on Sunday morning last, a negro man who goes by the name of John Gwin (or Quin) came to the house of John Hughson, the deponent's master, and went in at the window where one Peggy lodges, where he lay all night.

2. "That in the morning she saw some speckled linen in the said Peggy's room; that the said negro then gave the deponent two pieces of silver, and bid Peggy cut off an apron of the linen and give to the deponent, which she did accordingly.

3. "That at the same time the said negro bought a pair of white stockings from her master, for which he was to give six shillings; that the said negro had two mugs of punch, for which, and the stockings, he gave her master a lump of silver.

4. "That her master and mistress saw the linen the same morning.

5. "That soon after Mr. Mills came to inquire for one John Quin, a soldier, who he said, had robbed Mr. Hogg of some speckled linen, silver, and other things.

6. "That after Mr. Mills was gone, her mistress hid the linen in the garret; and soon after some officers came and searched the house; and when they were gone and found nothing, her mistress took the linen from the place she had before hid it in, and hid it under the stairs.

7. "That the night before last, her master and mistress gave the said linen to her mistress's mother, (c) who carried it away.

8. "That yesterday morning, one John Romme was at her master's house, and she heard him say to her master, if you will be true to me, I will be true to you; and her master answered, I will, and will never betray you. (d)

(c) Elizabeth Luckstead.
(d) Romme had received part of Hogg's goods from Caesar, John Gwin, or Quin, as before.

[19]

9. "That the said negro usually slept with the said Peggy, which her master and mistress knew of."

Upon this occasion, it seems, Hughson and his wife, finding that Mary Burton was inclinable to discover them in their villainy, touching this robbery, thought proper to say something to blacken her character, in order to take off from the credit of her testimony, and declared that she was a vile, good-for-nothing girl, or words to that purpose; that she had been got with child by her former master, etc. the truth whereof, however, was never made out. But at length Hughson finding that he was near going to jail, and as fearing the consequence of provoking her, changed his note, and said she was a very good girl, and had been a trusty servant to them: that in the hard weather last winter, she used to dress herself in man's clothes, put on boots, and went with him in his sleigh, in the deep snows into the commons, to help him fetch firewood for his family, etc.

The deputy town clerk, when Mary Burton was under examination, as he was taking her deposition, exhorted her to speak the truth, and all she knew of the matter; she answered him, that she hardly dared to speak, she was so much afraid she should be murdered by them; or words to that purpose. Whereupon the clerk moved the justices, that she might be taken care, not knowing that she had been removed from her master's the night before, by order of a magistrate.

After Mary Burton, John Hughson and his wife, and Peggy, were examined: Peggy denied every thing, and spoke in favour of Hughson and his wife: Peggy was committed, and John Hughson confessed as followeth:

Examination.—1. John Hughson said,

1. "That on Monday evening last, after Mr. Mills had been to search his house for goods which had been stolen from Mr. Hogg, one Peggy, who lodged at his house, told him that John Quin had left some checked linen and other things with her; that she delivered to the examinant the said checked linen, which he delivered to the mother-in-law Elizabeth Luckstead, with directions to hide them: that

soon after the said Peggy delivered him sundry silver things in a little bag; which he carried into the cellar, and put behind a barrel, and put a broad stone upon them, where they remained till last night about ten or eleven o'clock, when he delivered them to alderman Johnson and alderman Bancker.

2. "That while the said silver things lay concealed in his cellar, the constables came and searched his house for the said stolen goods, but did not find them.

3. "That this morning the said Peggy gave him a little bundle with several silver pieces in it; which he soon afterwards brought into court, and delivered it to the justices then present."

Hughson absolutely refused to sign the examination, after it was read over to him; and thereupon the deputy town clerk asked him if it was not true as he had penned it; he answered, yes, it was, but he thought there was no occasion for him to sign it. He was admitted to bail, and his wife Sarah likewise; and recognizances were entered into with two sureties each, for their appearance in the Supreme Court on the first day of the next term.

Caesar and Prince were likewise again examined, but would confess nothing concerning the robbery; Caesar was remanded, and Prince admitted to bail upon his master's entering into recognizance in ten pounds penalty, for his appearance at the next Supreme Court.

But Caesar acknowledged, that what Mary Burton had deposed concerning him and Peggy, as to his sleeping with her, was true.

Deposition.—John Vaarck, of the city of New-York, baker, being duly sworn and examined, saith,

1. "That about two o'clock this afternoon, his negro boy told him, there were some things hid under the floor of his kitchen: that thereupon he went to look, and found the linen and plates, now shewn him, which he took out, and carried to the mayor.

2. "That his said kitchen adjoins to the yard of John Romme, is a framed building, and the said linen and plates

[21]

could easily be put there from the said Romme's yard, but could not be put there from his house, without taking up a board of the floor."

These were supposed to be part of the goods stolen from Mr. Hogg, and carried to Romme's, by Caesar, alias John Gwin.

Upon Vaarck's deposition, orders were given for the apprehending John Romme, but he absconded.

Wednesday, March 18.

About one o'clock this day a fire broke out of the roof of his majesty's house at fort George, within this city, near the chapel; when the alarm of fire was first given, it was observed from the town, that the middle of the roof was in a great smoke, but not a spark of fire appeared on the outside for a considerable time; and when it first broke out it was on the east side, about twenty feet from the end next the chapel, and in a short time afterwards it made its way through the roof in several places, at a distance from the first and each other. Upon the chapel bell's ringing, great numbers of people, gentlemen and others, came to the assistance of the lieutenant governor and his family; and as the people of this city, to do them justice, are very active and diligent upon these occasions, most of the household goods, etc. were removed out and saved, and the fire engines were in a little time brought thither; but the wind blowing a violent gale at S.E. soon as the fire appeared in different places of the roof, it was judged impossible to save the house and chapel, so that endeavours were used to save the secretary's office over the fort gate, where the records of the colony were deposited; and also the barracks which stood on the side of the quadrangle opposite to the house; such diligence was used in removing the records, books and papers from the former, many of which for despatch were thrown out of the windows next the town, that most of them were preserved; and though from the violence of the wind the papers were blown about the streets, we do not hear that any very material writings were lost; but the fire had got hold of the roof of the office soon after they began to remove the records, and though the engines played some time upon it and afterwards upon the barracks, they were of little service, the wind blowing very hard and the flames of the house being so near them, all seemed to be at their mercy; and an alarm being given that there was gun powder in the fort, whether through fear and an apprehension that there was, or whether the hint was given by some of the conspirators themselves, with artful design to intimidate the people, and frighten them from giving further assistance, we cannot say; though the lieutenant governor declared to every body that there was none there, yet they had not the courage to depend upon his honour's assurance: but however, it happened most of them deserted it, until they found that many gentlemen remained upon the spot; though, had they all stayed, it was thought it would have been to little purpose; for such was the violence of the wind, and the flames spread so fast, that in about an hour and a quarter's time the house was burnt down to the ground, and the chapel and other buildings beyond human power of saving any material part of them: at length the fire got to the stables without the fort, and the wind blew, fired shingles upon the houses in the town next the North river, so that there was the utmost danger of its spreading further, which occasioned many families to remove their goods; but at last it was stopped at the governor's stables, with very little damage to the houses in the town.

While the records were removing from the secretary's office, there fell a moderate shower of rain, which was of some small service; and when the buildings were down to the ground floor, some hand-grenade shells, which had lain so long as to be forgotten, took fire, and went off, which few or none but the officers of the fort, could account for, or imagine what was the matter, nor would it have been worth while to have attempted their removal, if they had been thought of; for the buildings in the fort were at that time all given over for lost: but this served to confirm the generality of the people, in the notion that there was powder in the fort, and if they could have done any good, this would probably have prevented them.

But though the floors of the several buildings soon tumbled

in, there were many pieces of timber which were laid in the walls of the house, chapel steeple, and other buildings, which continued burning almost all the night after; so that we could not think the town quite out of danger of further mischief, till those timbers were entirely consumed; for it was apprehended, as the fort stood upon an eminence, that the wind, according as it should have happened to change, might have blown some of the fire upon the houses in the town, which, for the most part, have shingled roofs: therefore, care was taken to keep a watchful guard all the night, to prevent further damage.

Mr. Cornelius Van Horne, a captain of one of the companies of the militia, very providentially beat to arms in the evening, and drew out his men with all expedition; had seventy odd of them under arms all night, and parties of them continually going the rounds of the city until day light. This incident, from what will appear hereafter, may be thought to have been a very fortunate one, and deserving of a more particular remark, though at that time *some people were so infatuated, as to reproach that gentleman for it, as a madman.*

The only way of accounting for this misfortune at this time was, the lieutenant governor had ordered a plummer that morning to mend a leak in the gutter between the house and the chapel which joined upon one another, and the man carrying his fire-pot with coals to keep his soddering-iron hot, to perform his work; and the wind setting into the gutter, it was thought some sparks had been blown out upon the shingles of the house; but some people having observed, that upon the first alarm, as before, near half the roof, as they guessed, was covered with smoke, and that no spark of fire appeared without, nor could any be seen, but within; it was by them concluded, that the reason assigned was not likely to be the right one, especially when it was considered, that at length the fire broke out in several places of the roof, distant from each other, but no one imagined it was done on purpose.

Friday, March 20.

Prince, the negro of Mr. Auboyneau, who was bailed out of prison, as before mentioned, was recommitted by the mayor, and alderman Bancker.

Wednesday, March 25.

A week after the fire at the fort, another broke out between 11 and 12 o'clock at the house belonging to captain Warren, near the long bridge, at the S.W. end of the town; the roof was in flames, supposed at that time to have been occasioned by the accidental firing of a chimney; but when the matter came afterwards to be canvassed, it was not altogether clear of grounds of suspicion, that it was done designedly; but the fire engines were soon brought thither, and they played so successfully, though the fire had got to a considerable head on an old shingled roof, that by their aid, and the assistance and activity of the people, it was soon extinguished, without doing much damage to the house.

Wednesday, April 1.

Another week from the last, a fire broke out at the storehouse of Mr. Van Zant, towards the east end of the town. It was an old wooden building, stored with deal boards, and hay at one end of it; the fire was said to be occasioned by a man's smoking a pipe there, which set fire to the hay: but it is said, the fire was first discovered in the N.E. side of the roof, before it had taken the hay: this house was near the river, and by the side of a slip out of it, convenient for handing water to the engines; it was thought morally impossible to hinder its spreading further, there being many wooden buildings adjoining; but the people exerted their usual diligence, handed out the boards into the slip, all in flames, played the engines, and handed and threw the buckets of water, with such extraordinary activity, it stopped the progress of the fire so successfully, that it ended with little more damage than the entire consumption of the warehouse and most of the goods in it.

Saturday, April 4.

This evening there was an alarm of a fire at the house of one Quick, or Vergereau, (for they both lived under one roof) in the Fly: Upon inquiry, the fire was found to be in a cow-stable near the houses; the hay was on fire in the middle of it; but by timely assistance, it was suppressed.

As the people were returning from Quick's fire, that was succeeded with a second cry of fire, at the house of one Ben Thomas, next door to captain Sarly, on the west side; this was in the dusk of the evening. It began in the loft of the kitchen, was discovered by the smoke before the fire had got any head, and was soon extinguished. Upon examination, it was found that the fire had been put between a straw and another bed laid together, whereon a negro slept, but who did it, or how the fire happened at Quick's remained to be accounted for.

Sunday, April 5.

A discovery was made in the morning early, that some coals had been put under a haystack, standing near the coach-house and stables of Joseph Murray, Esq. in the Broadway, and near some dwelling-houses, which had it taken fire, would have been in great danger but the coals went out of themselves, as supposed, having only singed some part of the hay. It was said there were coals and ashes traced along from the fence to a neighbouring house next adjoining the stables, which caused a suspicion of the negro that lived there.

The *five* several fires, viz. at the fort, captain Warren's house, Van Zant's store-house, Quick's stable, and Ben Thomas's kitchen, having happened in so short a time succeeding each other; and the attempt made of a sixth on Mr. Murray's haystack; it was natural for people of any reflection, to conclude that the fire was set on purpose by a combination of villains, and therefore occasioned great uneasiness to every one that had thought; but upon this supposition nobody imagined there could be any further design; than for some wicked wretches to have the opportunity of making a prey of their neighbour's goods, under pretence of assistance in removing them for security from the danger of flames; for upon these late instances, many of the sufferers had complained of great losses of their goods, and furniture, which had been removed from their houses upon these occasions.

This Sunday as three negroes were walking up the Broadway towards the English church, about service time, Mrs. Earle looking out of her window, overheard one of them saying to his companions, with a vaporing sort of an air, *"Fire, Fire, Scorch, Scorch, A LITTLE, damn it, BY-AND-BY,"* and then threw up his hands and laughed; the woman conceived great jealousy at these words, and thought it very odd behaviour at that juncture, considering what had so lately happened; and she putting the natural construction upon them her apprehensions made her uneasy, and she immediately spoke of it to her next neighbour Mrs. George, but said she did not know any of the negroes.

About an hour after, when church was out, Mrs. Earle saw the same negroes coming down the Broadway again, and pointed out to Mrs. George the person who had spoke the words, and Mrs. George knew him, and said that it is Mr. Walter's Quaco.

These words, and the airs and graces given them by Quaco when he uttered them, were made known to a neighbouring alderman, who informed the rest of the justices thereof at their meeting the next day.

Monday, April 6.

About ten o'clock in the morning, there was an alarm of a fire at the house of serjeant Burns, opposite fort Garden. This, it was said, was only a chimney; which, upon inquiry, the man declared, had been swept the Friday before; but from the great smother in the house, and some other circumstances, there were grounds to suspect a villainous design in it.

Towards noon a fire broke out in the roof of Mrs. Hilton's house, at the corner of the buildings next the Fly-Market, adjoining on the East side of captain Sarly's house: it first broke out on that side next Sarly's, but being timely discovered, was soon prevented doing much mischief, more than burning part of the shingles of the roof. Upon view, it was plain that the fire must have been purposely laid on the wall-plate adjoining to the shingle roof; for a hole had been burnt deep in it, next that part of the roof where the fire had taken hold to the shingles; and it was suspected that the fire had been wrapped up in a bundle of tow, for some was found near the place; thus the fact was plain, but who did it, was a question remained to be determined; But there was a cry among the people, *the Spanish negroes; the Spanish negroes; take up the Spanish negroes.* The occasion of this was the two fires (Thomas's and Hilton's) happening so closely together, only one day intervening, on each side of captain Sarly's house; and it being known that Sarly had purchased a Spanish negro, some time before brought into this port, among several others, in a prize taken by captain Lush; all which negroes were condemned as slaves, in the court of Admiralty, and sold accordingly at vendue; and that they afterwards pretending to have been free men in their own country, began to grumble at their hard usage, of being sold as slaves. This probably gave rise to the suspicion, that this negro, out of revenge, had been the instrument of these two fires; and he behaving himself insolently upon some people's asking him questions concerning them, which signified their distrust; it was told to a magistrate who was near, and he ordered him to gaol, and also gave direction to constables to commit all the rest of that cargo, in order for their safe custody and examination.

In the afternoon the magistrates met at the City-Hall, with intent to examine them; and while the justices were proceeding to examination, about four o'clock there was another alarm of fire. Upon inquiry, and looking out of the hall windows, it was seen from thence, and found to be at col. Philipse's storehouse. Upon the view of it, there was a small streak of fire running up the shingles, like wildfire, from near the bottom to the top of the roof, on the side directly *against the wind as it then blew.* It not being far from the engines, they were instantly brought to the place; and the fire, to one's great surprise, almost as soon extinguished. This was the middlemost of three large storehouses next each other in a row, old timber buildings, and the shingles burnt like tinder. These storehouses were not inhabited, nor had they a chimney in them, but were at a great distance from any. The fire upon examination, must have begun within side; for between the side of those storehouses and the houses nearest them, opposite to the wind, there was a large space of garden ground; so that no spark from these chimneys could have occasioned this mischief, had the wind blown the contrary way; but to discover by whom the fire was put, was the difficulty.

While the people were extinguishing the fire at this storehouse, and had almost mastered it, there was another cry of fire, which diverted the people attending the storehouse, to the new alarm, very few remaining behind; but a man who had been on the top of the house, assisting in extinguishing the fire, saw a negro leap out at the end window of one of them, from thence making over several garden fences in great haste; which occasioned him to cry out, *a negro; a negro;* and that was soon improved into an alarm, *that the negroes were rising:* The negro made very good speed home to his master's; he was generally known, and the swiftness of his flight occasioned his being remarked, though scarce any knew the reason, but a few which remained at the storehouse, why the word was given, *a negro, a negro;* it was immediately changed into *Cuff Philipse, Cuff Philipse:* The people ran to Mr. Philipse's house in quest of him; he was got in at the back door; and being found, was dragged out of the house, and carried to jail, borne upon the people's shoulders. He was a fellow of general ill character; his master being a single man, and little at home, Cuff had a great deal of idle time, which, it seems, he employed to very ill purposes, and had acquired a general bad fame.

Many people had such terrible apprehensions upon this occasion, and indeed there was cause sufficient, that several negroes (and many had been assisting at the fire at the storehouse, and many perhaps that only seemed to be so) who were met in the streets, after the alarm of their rising, were hurried away to jail; and when they were there, they were continued some time in confinement, before the magistrates could spare time to examine into their several cases, how and for what they came there, many others first coming under consideration before them, against whom there seemed to be more direct cause of suspicion; but in a few days, those against whom nothing in particular was alleged, were discharged.

It was said, there was like to have been another fire this day, though it has by some been supposed to have been an accident. The cellar of a baker near Coenties market, was all of a smother, and the chips in a blaze, but was soon suppressed. This also occasioned some alarm.

Quack (Walter's) was sent for and committed; he remained in confinement some days without examination, from the hurry the magistrates were in; but at length, Mrs. Earle and Mrs. George being sent for by the justices, they declared concerning him to the effect before mentioned: (e) and Quack being brought before them, and examined, by his excuse admitted he had spoken the words he was charged with; but it being soon after we had the news of admiral Vernon's taking Porto Bello, he had contrived a cunning excuse, or some abler heads for him, to account for the occasion of them, and brought two of his own complexion to give their words for it also, that they were talking of admiral Vernon's taking Porto Bello; and that he thereupon signified to his companions, that he thought that was but a small feat to what this brave officer would do by-and-by, to annoy the Spaniards, or words tantamount; so that it happened Quack was enlarged from his confinement for some time.

Others considering that it was but eighteen days after the fort was laid in ashes, that these words were uttered; and that several other fires had intervened, as before related, and but the next day after Quick's stable and Ben Thomas's house were on fire; and the attempt upon Mr. Murray's haystack discovered that very morning; they were apt to put a different construction upon

(e) Sunday, 5th April.

[30]

Quack's words and behaviour; that he thereby meant, "that the fires which we had seen already, were nothing to what we should have by-and-by, for that then we should have all the city in flames, and he would rejoice at it;" for it was said he lifted up his hands, and spread them with a circular sweep over his head, after he had pronounced the words (by-and-by) and then concluded with a loud laugh. Whether these figures are thus more properly applied, the reader will hereafter be better able to judge; but the construction of them at that time confirmed many in the notion of a conspiracy; though they could not suspect one of so black a dye, as there were afterwards flagrant proofs of, and will appear by and by.

His honour the lieutenant governor was pleased to order a military watch to be kept this evening, and the same was continued all the summer after.

John Hughson and Sarah his wife were committed to jail by the mayor and three aldermen, being charged as accessories to divers felonies and misdemeanors.

Saturday, April 11.

At a common council, held this day at the city of New-York, present, John Cruger, esq. Mayor—the recorder—Gerardus Stuyvesant, William Romme, Simon Johnston, John Moore, Christopher Bancker, John Pintard, John Marshall, esquires, aldermen—Henry Bogert, Isaac Stoutenbergh, Philip Minthorne, George Brinkerhoff, Robert Benson, and Samuel Lawrence, assistants.—The recorder taking notice of the several fires which had lately happened in this city and the manner of them, the frequency of them, and the causes being yet undiscovered; must necessarily conclude, that they were occasioned and set on foot by some villainous confederacy of latent enemies amongst us; but with what intent or purpose, time must discover; that it could not be doubted, but the lieutenant governor and his majesty's council had taken the alarm at this time of danger, and were watchful, and anxious for the safety of the city; and though they were of opinion, that it was highly proper and necessary that a proclamation should be issued by the government, promising proper rewards to such person and persons as should make such discovery of the incendiaries, their confederates and accomplices, as that they should be convicted thereof; yet it was well known that the governor and council had not the liberty of drawing upon the colony treasury for any sum of money whatsoever, upon any emergency—and it could not be reasonably expected the governor should subject himself to pay such rewards out of his own pocket, for the use and necessities of the public; that as the safety of the city, so immediately concerned, seemed absolutely to require such a measure to be taken; so the public, who were also interested in the preservation of it, would reap the benefit in common with them, by the corporation's laudable resolution, should they determine to engage to pay proper rewards, and request the governor to issue a proclamation agreeable thereto; which, he was persuaded, the governor was well inclined to do and the gentlemen of the council to advise thereto: he therefore moved, "that the board should come to a resolution to pay such rewards as should by them be thought a proper and sufficient temptation to induce any party or parties concerned to make such discovery."

Upon consideration whereof, it was

ordered, That this board request his honour the lieutenant governor to issue a proclamation, offering a reward to any white person that should discover any person or persons lately concerned in setting fire to any dwelling-house or storehouse in this city (so that such person or persons be convicted thereof,) the sum of *one hundred pounds,* current money of this province; and that such person shall be pardoned, if concerned therein. Any slave that should make discovery, to be manumitted, or made free; and the master of such slave to receive *twenty-five pounds* therefor; and the slave to receive, besides his freedom, the sum of *twenty pounds,* and to be pardoned; and if a free negro, mulatto, or Indian, to receive *forty-five pounds,* and also to be pardoned, if concerned therein. And that this board will issue their warrant to the chamberlain, or treasurer of this corporation for the payment of such sum as any person, by virtue of such proclamation, shall be entitled unto. And that the mayor and recorder wait on his honour the lieutenant governor, and acquaint him with the resolution of this board.

The mayor and recorder waited on his honour accordingly, and a copy of the order was also delivered to him.

Many persons in the neighbourhood of the several fires before mentioned, thought it necessary to remove their household goods for safety; and in their consternation, as was natural, suffered any body who offered their assistance, to take them away; by which means, some villains had the cruelty to make prey of them; for there were great complaints of losses upon those occasions, which the magistrates took this day into their consideration: and it being much suspected that there were some strangers lurking about the city, who had upon the supposition only, that by those means, they might have opportunities of pilfering and plundering. A scheme was proposed, that there should be a general search of all houses throughout the town, whereby it was thought probable discoveries might be made, not only of stolen goods, but likewise of lodgers, that were strangers, and suspicious persons. The proposal was approved of, and each alderman and his common council-man, with constables attending them, undertook to search his respective ward on the south side of the fresh water pond; and the Monday following was the day fixed upon for making the experiment.

The scheme was communicated to the governor, and his honour thought fit to order the militia out that day in aid of the magistrates, who were to be dispersed through the city, and sentries of them posted at the ends of streets to guard all avenues, with orders to stop all suspected persons that should be observed carrying bags or bundles, or removing goods from house to house, in order for their examination; and all this was to be kept very secret till the project was put in execution.

Monday, April 13.

Pursuant to the scheme concerted on Saturday last, the *general search* was made; but there were not any goods discovered which were said to have been lost, nor was there any strange lodger or suspicious persons detected. But some things were found in the custody of Robin, Mr. Chamber's negro, and Cuba his wife, which the alderman thought improper for, and unbecoming the condition of slaves, which made him suspect they were not come honestly by; and therefore ordered the constable to take them in possession, to be reserved for further inquiry: and these two negroes were committed.

Friday, April 17.

The lieutenant governor, by and with the advice of his majesty's council, issued a proclamation, therein reciting the before mentioned order and resolution of the common council, promising the rewards agreeable thereto.

In the mean while, between the sixth and seventeenth instant, a great deal of time had been spent by the magistrates in the examination of the negroes in custody, upon account of these fires, but nothing could be got out of them.

Cuff (Philipse's) was closely interrogated, but he absolutely denied knowing any thing of the matter. He said he had been at home all that afternoon, from the time he returned from Hilton's fire, where he had been to assist and carry buckets. That he was at home when the bell rung for the fire at Col. Philipse's storehouse. It appeared, upon inquiry and examination of witnesses, that he, according to his master's orders, had been sawing wood that afternoon with a white boy; and that when his master came home from dinner, he took him off from that work, and set him to sew on a vane upon a board for his sloop; the white boy testified, "that he stood by him to see him sew it, and that he left him but a little before the bell rung for the fire." And when the alarm of the fire was, and that it was supposed to be at his master's storehouse, it was said, Cuff asked whether he would go

[34]

out with the buckets, and that he should answer, he had enough of being out, in the morning. Some of the neighbours also declared, that they had seen him looking over his master's door but a little before the bell rung; but an old man who had known Cuffee for several years, deposed, that he had seen him at the fire at the storehouse, and that he stood next him: there seemed to be some objection against the man's evidence; it was thought he might be mistaken, being very near sighted. Upon examination, it was found he could distinguish colours, and he described the clothes he had on, and moreover declared, he spoke to him, and asked him, why he did not hand the buckets; and that thereupon he answered him, and did hand water, and that he knew his voice.

There was very strong proof that he was the negro that leaped out of the window of one of the storehouses as the fire was extinguished, and most of the people drawn away upon the new alarm of a fire; that he was seen to leap over several garden fences, and to run home in great haste.

Upon the whole, it was thought proper Cuff should remain in confinement, to await further discovery.

JOURNAL OF THE PROCEEDINGS AGAINST THE CONSPIRATORS, AT NEW-YORK IN 1741

At a supreme court of judicature held for the province of New-York, at the city-hall of the city of New-York, on Tuesday, April 21, 1741—Present, Frederick Philipse, esq. second justice; Daniel Horsmanden, esq. third justice.

The grand jury were called. The following persons appeared, and were sworn—viz.:

Mr. Robert Watts, merchant, foreman; Messrs. Jeremiah Latouche, Joseph Read, Anthony Rutgers, John M'Evers, John Cruger, jun. John Merritt, Adoniah Schuyler, Isaac De Peyster, Abraham Keteltass, David Provoost, Rene Hett, Henry Beekman, jun. David Van Horne, George Spencer, Thomas Duncan, Winant Van Zant, merchants.

Mr. Justice Philipse gave the charge to the grand jury, as followeth:

Gentlemen of the grand jury,

It is not without some concern, that I am obliged at this time to be more particular in your charge, than for many preceding terms there hath been occasion. The many frights and terrors which the good people of this city have of late been put into, by repeated and unusual fires, and burning of houses, give us too much room to suspect, that some of them at least, did not proceed from mere chance, or common accidents; but on the contrary, from the premeditated malice and wicked pursuits of evil and designing persons; and therefore, it greatly behoves us to use our utmost diligence, by all lawful ways and means, to discover the contrivers and perpetrators of such daring and flagitious undertak-

[37]

ings: that, upon conviction, they may receive condign punishment; for although we have the happiness of living under a government which exceeds all others in the excellency of its constitution and laws, yet if those to whom the execution of them (which my lord Coke calls the life and soul of the law) is committed, do not exert themselves in a conscientious discharge of their respective duties, such laws which were intended for a terror to the evil-doer, and a protection to the good, will become a dead letter, and our most excellent constitution turned into anarchy and confusion; every one practising what he listeth, and doing what shall seem good in his own eyes: to prevent which, it is the duty of all grand juries to inquire into the conduct and behaviour of the people in their respective counties; and if, upon examination, they find any to have transgressed the laws of the land, to present them, that so they may by the court be put upon their trial, and then either to be discharged or punished according to their demerits.

I am told there are several prisoners now in jail, who have been committed by the city magistrates, upon suspicion of having been concerned in some of the late fires; and others, who under pretence of assisting the unhappy sufferers, by saving their goods from the flames, for stealing, or receiving them. This indeed, is adding affliction to the afflicted, and is a very great aggravation of such crime, and therefore deserves a narrow inquiry: that so the exemplary punishment of the guilty (if any such should be so found) may deter others from committing the like villainies; for this kind of stealing, I think, has not been often practised among us.

Gentlemen,

Arson, or the malicious and voluntary burning, not only a mansion house, but also any other house, and the out buildings, or barns, and stables adjoining thereto, by night or by day, is felony at common law; and if any part of the house be burned, the offender is guilty of felony, notwithstanding the fire afterwards be put out, or go out of itself.

This crime is of so shocking a nature, that if we have any

[38]

in this city, who, having been guilty thereof, should escape, who can say he is safe, or tell where it will end?

Gentlemen,

Another Thing which I cannot omit recommending to your serious and diligent inquiry, is to find out and present all such persons who sell rum, and other strong liquor to negroes. It must be obvious to every one, that there are too many of them in this city; who, under pretence of selling what they call a penny dram to a negro, will sell to him as many quarts or gallons of rum, as he can steal money or goods to pay for.

How this notion of its being lawful to sell a penny dram, or a pennyworth of rum to a slave, without the consent or direction of his master, has prevailed, I know not; but this I am sure of, that there is not only no such law, but that the doing of it is directly contrary to an act of the assembly now in force, *for the better regulating of slaves.* The many fatal consequences flowing from this prevailing and wicked practice, are so notorious, and so nearly concern us all, that one would be almost surprised, to think there should be a necessity for a court to recommend a suppressing of such pernicious houses: thus much in particular; now in general.

My charge, gentlemen, further is, to present all conspiracies, combinations, and other offences, from treasons down to trespasses; and in your inquiries, the oath you, and each of you have just now taken will, I am persuaded, be your guide, and I pray God to direct and assist you in the discharge of your duty.

Court adjourned until to-morrow morning ten o'clock.

SUPREME COURT
Wednesday, April 22.

Present, the second justice. The court opened, and adjourned until ten o'clock to-morrow morning.

[39]

The grand jury having been informed, that Mary Burton could give them some account concerning the goods stolen from Mr. Hogg's, sent for her this morning, and ordered she should be sworn; the constable returned and acquainted them, that *she said she would not be sworn, nor give evidence*; whereupon they ordered the constable to get a warrant from a magistrate, to bring her before them. The constable was some time gone, but at length returned, and brought her with him; and being asked why she would not be sworn, and give her evidence? she told the grand jury she would not be sworn; and seemed to be under some great uneasiness, or terrible apprehensions; which gave suspicion that she knew something concerning the fires that had lately happened: and being asked a question to that purpose, she gave no answer; which increased the jealousy that she was privy to them; and as it was thought a matter of the utmost concern, the grand jury was very importunate, and used many arguments with her, in public and private, to persuade her to speak the truth, and tell all she knew about it. To this end, the lieutenant governor's proclamation was read to her, promising indemnity, and the reward of one hundred pounds to any person, confederate or not, who should make discovery, etc. She seemed to despise it, nor could the grand jury by any means, either threats or promises, prevail upon her, though they assured her withal, that she should have the protection of the magistrates, and her person be safe and secure from harm; but hitherto all was in vain: therefore the grand jury desired alderman Bancker to commit her; and the constable was charged with her accordingly; but before he had got her to jail, she considered better of it, and resolved to be sworn, and give her evidence in the afternoon.

Accordingly, she being sworn, came before the grand jury; but as they were proceeding to her examination, and before they asked her any questions, she told them she would acquaint them with what she knew relating to the goods stolen from Mr. Hogg's, but would say nothing about the fires.

This expression thus, as it were providentially, slipping from the evidence, much alarmed the grand jury; for, as they naturally concluded, it did by construction amount to an affirmative, that she could give an account of the occasion of the several fires; and therefore, as it highly became those gentlemen in the discharge of their trust, they determined to use their utmost diligence to sift out the discovery, but still she remained inflexible, till at length, having recourse to religious topics, representing to her the heinousness of the crime which she would be guilty of, if she was privy to, and could discover so wicked a design, as the firing houses about our ears; whereby not only people's estates would be destroyed, but many persons might lose their lives in the flames: this she would have to answer for at the day of judgment, as much as any person immediately concerned, because she might have prevented this destruction, and would not; so that a most damnable sin would lie at her door; and what need she fear from her divulging it; she was sure of the protection of the magistrates? or the grand jury expressed themselves in words to the same purpose; which arguments at last prevailed, and she gave the following evidence, which however, notwithstanding what had been said, came from her, as if still under some terrible apprehensions or restraints.

Deposition, No. 1.—Mary Burton, being sworn, deposeth,

1. "That Prince (a) and Caesar (b) brought the things of which they had robbed Mr. Hogg, to her master, John Hughson's house, and that they were handed in through the window, Hughson, his wife, and Peggy receiving them, about two or three o'clock on a Sunday morning. (c)

2. "That Caesar, Prince, and Mr. Philipse's negro man (Cuffee) used to meet frequently at her master's house, and that she had heard them (the negroes) talk frequently of burning the fort; and that they would go down to the Fly (d) and burn the whole town; and that her master and mistress said, they would aid and assist them as much as they could.

3. "That in their common conversation they used to say,

(a) Mr. Auboyneau's negro.
(b) Vaarck's negro.
(c) 1st March, 1740 (1741, editor's note).
(d) The east end of the city.

that when all this was done, Caesar should be governor, and Hughson, her master, should be king.

4. "That Cuffee used to say, that a great many people had too much, and others too little; that his old master had a great deal of money, but that, in a short time, he should have less, and that he (Cuffee) should have more.

5. "That at the same time when the things of which Mr. Hogg was robbed, were brought to her master's house, they brought some indigo and bees wax, which was likewise received by her master and mistress.

6. "That at the meetings of the three aforesaid negroes, Caesar, Prince, and Cuffee, at her master's house, they used to say, in their conversations, that when they set fire to the town, they would do it in the night, and as the white people came to extinguish it, they would kill and destroy them.

7. "That she has known at times, seven or eight guns in her master's house, and some swords, and that she has seen twenty or thirty negroes at one time in her master's house; and that at such large meetings, the three aforesaid negroes, Cuffee, Prince, and Caesar, were generally present, and most active, and that they used to say, that the other negroes durst not refuse to do what they commanded them, and they were sure that they had a number sufficient to stand by them.

8. "That Hughson (her master) and her mistress used to threaten, that if she, the deponent, ever made mention of the goods stolen from Mr. Hogg, they would poison her; and the negroes swore, if ever she published, or discovered the design of burning the town, they would burn her whenever they met her.

9. "That she never saw any white person in company when they talked of burning the town, but her master, her mistress, and Peggy."

This evidence of a conspiracy, not only to burn the city, but also destroy and murder the people, was most astonishing to the grand jury, and that any white people should become so abandoned as to confederate with slaves in such an execrable and detestable purpose, could not but be very amazing to every one that heard it; what could scarce be credited; but that the several fires had been occasioned by some combination of villains, was, at the time of them, naturally to be collected from the manner and circumstances attending them.

The grand jury therefore, as it was a matter of the utmost consequence, thought it necessary to inform the judges concerning it, in order that the most effectual measures might be concerted, for discovering the confederates; and the judges were acquainted with it accordingly.

SUPREME COURT
Thursday, April 23.

Present, the second and third justices.

The grand jury came into court and were called over.

The foreman desiring that Margaret Sorubiero, alias Kerry, a prisoner might be brought before them, Ordered, that the sheriff do carry the said Margaret Sorubiero, alias Kerry, before the grand jury, and see her safe returned again.

The court adjourned until to-morrow, ten o'clock.

This morning the judges summoned all the gentlemen of the law in the town, to meet them in the afternoon, in order to consult with them, and determine upon such measures as on the result of their deliberations should be judged most proper to be taken upon this emergency; and Mr. Murray, Mr. Alexander, Mr. Smith, Mr. Chambers, Mr. Nicholls, Mr. Lodge, and Mr. Jamison, met them accordingly; the attorney general being indisposed, could not attend.

It was considered, that though there was an act of the province for trying negroes, as in other colonies, for all manner of offences by the justices, etc. in a summary way; yet as this was a scheme of villainy in which white people were confederated with them, and most probably were the first movers and seducers of the slaves; from the nature of such a conjunction, there was reason to apprehend there was a conspiracy of deeper design and more dangerous contrivance than the slaves themselves were capable of; it was thought a matter that required great secrecy, as well as the utmost diligence, in the conduct of the inquiry concerning it: and upon the whole, it was judged most advisable, as there was an absolute necessity that a matter of this nature and consequence should be fathomed as soon as possible, that it should be taken under the care of the supreme court; and for that purpose, that application should be made to his honour the lieutenant governor, for an ordinance to enlarge the term for the sitting of that court, which in the ordinary method would determinate on the Tuesday following.

The gentlemen of the law generously and unanimously offered to give their assistance on every trial in their turns, as this was conceived to be a matter that not only affected the city, but the whole province.

Margaret Kerry, commonly called Peggy, committed for Hogg's Robbery, being impeached by Mary Burton, as one of the conspirators, the judges examined her in prison in the evening; they exhorted her to make an ingenuous confession and discovery of what she knew of it, and gave her hopes of their recommendation to the governor for a pardon, if they could be of opinion that she deserved it, assuring her (as the case was) that they had his honour's permission to give hopes of mercy to such criminals as should confess their guilt, and they should think proper to recommend to him as fit and proper objects; but she withstood it, and positively denied that she knew any thing of the matter; and said, that if she should accuse any body of any such thing, she must accuse innocent persons, and wrong her own could. She had this day been examined by the grand jury, and positively denied knowing any thing about the fires.

SUPREME COURT
Friday, April 24.

Present, the second and third justices.

The king against Caesar and Prince, negroes.

The grand jury having found two bills of indictment for felonies, against the prisoners; Mr. Attorney General moved, that they might be brought to the bar, in order to be arraigned.

It was ordered, and they being brought, were arraigned accordingly, and severally pleaded, *not guilty*.

The king against John Hughson, Sarah, his wife, Margaret Sorubiero, alias Kerry.

The grand jury having found a bill of indictment for felony, against the defendants in custody, Mr. Attorney General moved, that they might be brought to the bar in order to be arraigned.

It was ordered, and the prisoners being brought, were arraigned accordingly, and severally pleaded, *not guilty*.

Ordered, that the trials of the two negroes, the Hughsons, and Kerry, do come on to-morrow morning.

Court adjourned till to-morrow morning, nine o'clock.

SUPREME COURT
Saturday, April 25.

Present, the second justice.

The king against Caesar and Prince, negroes.

The king against John Hughson, Sarah, his wife, Margaret Kerry.

Ordered, that the prisoners' trials be put off till Tuesday the 28th instant.

Court adjourned till Monday morning, nine o'clock.

SUPREME COURT
Monday, April 27.

Present, the second justice.

His majesty's ordinance published in court for enlarging the present term to the last Tuesday in May next.

Court adjourned till to-morrow morning, ten o'clock.

SUPREME COURT
Tuesday, April 28.

Present, the second and third justices.

The king against Caesar and Prince, negroes.

[45]

The king against John Hughson, Sarah, his wife, Margaret Kerry.

Upon motion of Mr. Attorney General, ordered, that the trials of the prisoners in both causes be put off till the first day of May.

Court adjourned till Friday, 1st May, ten o'clock in the morning.

The following letter, dated this day at New-York, was some time afterwards intercepted in New-Jersey, and sent up from a magistrate there to another here.

The original in female Dutch followeth, so much of it as is material to the present purpose.

Nieu York den 21 April 1741

Beminde Man Johannis Romme

 Dit is om U bekent te maken dat ik U brief ontfangen heb by de brenger van deze en daer nyt verstaen dat gey van sins ben om weer na huis te komen myn beminde ik versoek van U dat gy het best van U wegh maekt om varder te gaen en niet in Niu Yorck te komen en om U self niet bekent te maken waer gey ben voor John Husen die is van dese dagh zyn tryell te hebben enook zyn vrou en de mydt is king evidens tegen baye gar en zy het U naemook in kwetze gebrocht en ik ben bang det John Husen en zyn vrou gehangen sall worden by wat ik kan horen en de schout en bombeles soeken voor U over all want Fark neger die houdt zyn woort standen voor jou Brother Lucas is voor een jeure man gekosen en die hoort hoe het is So niet maer maer blyvende U eerwarde vrou Elezabet Romme tot ter doet toe.

Thus translated

"Beloved Husband John Romme,

 "This is to acquaint you that I have received your letter by the bearer hereof and understand out of it that you intend to return home again my dear I desire of you that you make the best of your way to go further and not to come to New-York and not to make yourself known where you are for John Hughson is this day to have his tryal as also his wife and the servant maid is king evidence against both and she has brought your name likewise in question and I am afraid that John Hughson and his wife will be hanged by what I can hear and the sheriff and bumbailiffs seek for you every where. Vaarck's negro (e) he keeps his word stedfast for you Brother Lucas is chosen one of the jurymen and he hears how it is So no more but remaining your respectful wife Elezabet Romme even till death.

Superscribed, *for Mr. John Romme,* Q D G

SUPREME COURT
Friday, May 1.

Present, the second and third justices.

The king against Caesar and Prince, negroes. On trial.

The jury called, and the prisoners making no challenge, the following persons were sworn, viz.:

Roger French, John Groesbeek, John Richard, Abraham Kipp, George Witts, John Thurman, Patrick Jackson, Benjamin Moore, William Hamersley, John Lashier, Joshua Sleydall, John Shurmur.

These two negroes were arraigned on two indictments, the twenty fourth of April last: the one for their entering the dwelling house of Robert Hogg, of this city, merchant, on the first day of March then last past, with intent then and there to commit some felony; and for feloniously stealing and carrying away then and there the goods and chattels of the said Robert Hogg, of the value of four pounds five shillings sterling, against the form of the statutes in such case made and provided, and against the peace of our sovereign lord the king, his crown and dignity.

The other for their entering the dwelling house of Abraham Meyers Cohen in this city, merchant, on the first day of March

(e) Caesar.

[47]

with intent then and there to commit some felony; and for feloniously stealing and carrying away then and there the goods and chattels of the said Abraham Meyers Cohen of the value of five pounds sterling, against the form of the statutes, etc. and against the king's peace, etc.

To each of which indictments they pleaded, *not guilty.*

The Attorney General having opened both the indictments, he with Joseph Murray, Esq. of council for the king, proceeded to examine the witnesses, viz.,

For the king, Mrs. Hogg, Mrs. Boswell, Christopher Wilson, Rachina Guerin, Mr. Robert Hogg, Mr. Robert Watts, Margaret Sorubiero, alias Kerry, Abraham Meyers Cohen, James Mills, Thomas Wenman, John Moore, Esq. Cornelius Brower, Anthony Ham, Mary Burton.

For the prisoners, Alderman Bancker, Alderman Johnson, John Auboyneau.

The prisoners upon their defence denied the charge against them. And,

The evidence being summed up, which was very strong and full, and the jury charged, they withdrew; and being returned, found them guilty of the indictments.

Ordered, that the trials of the Hughsons and Margaret Kerry, be put off until Wednesday of the 6th inst.

Court adjourned until Monday morning, 4th May, at ten o'clock.

Sunday, May 3.

Arthur Price, servant to captain Vincent Pearse, having been committed, upon a charge of stealing out of his master's house several goods belonging to the lieutenant governor, which had been removed thither for safe custody from the fire at the fort; he informed the under-sheriff, that he had some discourse in the jail with Peggy, which he would communicate to a magistrate: the under-sheriff acquainted one of the judges therewith, and he examined Price in the evening, and the following deposition was taken.

[48]

Deposition, No. 1.—Arthur Price being duly sworn, saith,

1. "That about the beginning of last week, Peggy Carey, or Kerry, now in jail, came to the hole in the prison door, in which he is confined, and told him, she was very much afraid of those fellows (meaning the negroes, as he understood) telling or discovering something of her; but, said she, if they do, by God, I will hang them every one; but that she would not *forswear* (e) herself, unless they brought her in. Upon which the deponent asked her, Peggy, how *forswear* yourself? To which she answered, there is fourteen sworn. Upon which he further asked her, what, is it about Mr. Hogg's goods? And she replied, no, by G——d, about the fire. Upon which the deponent asked here, was John and his wife in it? (meaning John Hughson and his wife.) And she answered, yes, by G——d, they were both sworn as well as the rest. Then the deponent asked her, if she was not afraid that the negroes would discover her? And she said no; for Prince, Cuff and Caesar, and Forck's (Vaarck's) negro, were all true-hearted fellows. Then he asked her, if Caesar was not Forck's negro? And she answered, no, by G——d, it was the other; (f) but what other she meant he did not know.

2. "That yesterday in the afternoon the said Peggy came to him again, and told him, she had no stomach to eat her victuals; for that bitch (meaning Hughson's maid (g) as he understood) has fetched me in, and made me as black as the rest, about the indigo, and Mr. Hogg's goods: but if they did hang the two poor fellows below (meaning Caesar and Prince, as understood) they (meaning the rest of the negroes) would be revenged on them yet; but if they sent them away, it was another case. Upon which this deponent said to Peggy, I don't doubt but they will endeavour to poison this girl that has sworn, (meaning Hughson's maid.)

(e) What she meant by forswearing herself, will be better guessed at hereafter.
(f) Bastian, alias Tom Peal, also belonging to Vaarck.
(g) Mary Burton.

[49]

And Peggy replied, no, by G——d, I don't believe that; but they will be revenged on them some other ways: And she further said to the deponent, for your life and soul of you, you son of a b——h, don't speak a word of what I have told you."

About this time, i.e. the beginning of this month, at Hackensack, in New-Jersey, eight miles from this city, the inhabitants of that place were alarmed about an hour before day, and presented with a most melancholy and affrighting scene! No less than seven barns in that neighbourhood were all in flames; and the fire had got such head, that all assistance was in vain; for in a short time they were burnt down to the ground. Two negroes, the one belonging to Derick Van Hoorn, the other to Albert Van Voerheise, were suspected to have been guilty of this fact; the former having been seen coming out of one of the barns with a gun laden, who pretended on his being discovered, that he saw the person who had fired the barns, upon which his master ordered him to fire at him, and the negro thereupon immediately discharged his piece; but no blood was drawn from any mortal that could be discovered. The latter was found at his master's house loading a gun with two bullets which he had in his hand ready to put in. Upon these and other presumptive circumstances and proofs, both negroes were apprehended, and in a few days tried, convicted, and burnt at a stake: the former confessed he had set fire to three of the barns; the latter would confess nothing; nor would either of them discover that any others were concerned with them in this villainy.

SUPREME COURT
Monday, May 4.

Present the second and third justices.

The court opened and adjourned till to-morrow afternoon 8 o'clock.

SUPREME COURT
Tuesday, May 5.

Present, as before.

The court opened and adjourned till to-morrow morning 9 o'clock.

SUPREME COURT
Wednesday, May 6.

Present, the second and third justices.

The king against John Hughson, Sarah his wife, Margaret Sorubiero, alias Kerry, on trial.

The jury were called and the following jurors sworn, viz.— Henry Lawrence, William Hammersley, Sidney Breese, John Smith, Samuel Weaver, Patrick Jackson, John Shurmer, John Hastier, John Robins, Henry Vandewater, Aaron King, Alexander Ward.

Benjamin Peck and Joseph North, jurors challenged by the prisoners.

They were indicted for feloniously, etc. receiving on the third day of March then last past, divers stolen goods, knowing the same to have been stolen, (i) against the form of the statute, etc. and the king's peace, etc.

To which indictment they all pleaded, *not guilty*, upon their arraignment as before.

Council for the King, the Attorney General, and Joseph Murray, esq.

The Attorney General opened the indictment, and then he and Mr. Murray examined the witnesses against the criminals, viz.—Witnesses for the King—Robert Hogg, Mrs. Hogg, Rachina Guerin, Anthony Ham, constable, alderman Romme, Robert Watts, esq. Richard Nicholls, esq. James Mills, Mary Burton, alderman Moore, Thomas Wenman, constable, John Cruger, esq. mayor, alderman Johnson, William Jamison, esq.

(i) They received the goods of Caesar and Prince, principal convicts.

The conviction of Caesar and Prince read.

The examination of Hughson before the justices read.

Witnesses for the prisoners—John Nichols, capt. Lee, Peter Anderson, and his wife.

And the charge against them being fully proved; the evidence summed upon; the arguments closed, and the jury charged, they withdrew; and being returned, found them *all guilty*.

Sarah Hughson, single woman, daughter of John Hughson and Sarah his wife, was this morning committed as one of the confederates in the conspiracy, being apprehended while the court was sitting.

Court adjourned till to-morrow morning ten o'clock.

Jack (Sleydall's negro) was this day committed on suspicion of putting fire to Mr. Murray's haystack.

SUPREME COURT
Thursday, May 7, A.M.

Present the second and third justices. Court opened, and adjourned until 4 o'clock in the afternoon, P.M.

Present, as before. Court opened and adjourned until tomorrow morning, ten o'clock.

Deposition taken before the judges—No. 2. Arthur Price being duly sworn, saith,

1. "That yesterday morning having discourse with Sarah, the daughter of John Hughson, about the fires which have lately happened in the town; she told him, that she had been with a fortune teller, who told her that in less than five weeks time, she would come to trouble, if she did not take good care of herself; but after that she would come to good fortune; then he inquired of her father's fortune; and she said, her father would be tried and condemned, but not hanged; but was to go over the water.

2. "That then, after some other discourse, the deponent told her, that some of the negroes who were concerned in the plot about the fires, had discovered; upon which she

said, she did not know of any plot; and thereupon he told her, that they that were sworn in the plot, had discovered, and brought them every one in: upon which she coloured, and put her bonnet back, and changed colour several times, and asked him if he knew who it was and when he had heard it? and he told her, he had heard it by the by, and it was kept private: upon which she made a long stop; and then said, it must be either Holt's negro, or Todd's; for, said she, we were always afraid of them, and mistrusted them, though they were as bad as the rest, and were to have set their own master's houses on fire; and then she said, I wish that Todd had sent his black dog away, or sold him, when he was going to do it. (j)

3. "That then the deponent told her, sure you had better tell every thing that you know; for that may be of some service to your father; upon which she said no, for that they were doing all that they could to take his life away; and that she would sooner suffer death, and be hanged with her daddy (if he was to be hanged) than she would give them that satisfaction of telling or discovering any thing to them; or words to that effect: that she was to have gone up into the country (like a fool that she was that she did not go) but staid to see what would become of her mammy and daddy; but that now she would go up in the country, and that she would be hanged if ever they should get her in York again; but if they (meaning the people of this city, as he understood) had not better care of themselves, they would have a great deal more damage and danger in York, than they were aware of; and if they did hang her daddy, they had better do something else; and as to the fire at the fort, they did not set the saddle on the right horse.

4. "That on Monday last Peggy came to him, and bid him not discover any thing for his life, that she had told him; for if he did, by G——d she would cut his throat.

5. "The deponent further saith, that as to the expression

(j) Dundee. Todd, it seems, did threaten, and was going to send this negro beyond sea last fall; so that her intelligence was right.

made use of by Sarah Hughson, viz., As to the fire at the fort, they did not set the saddle on the right horse; the occasion of these words was, the deponents telling her, that they had been picking out of him what they could concerning the fire at the fort, and thought that he knew something of it; but he said to her, that he took God to be his judge, that he did not know any thing of it. (k)

Upon the information by this deposition, Dundee (Todd's negro) was apprehended and committed; but, upon examination, denied knowing any thing of the conspiracy.

The other negro was at this time gone with his master (Holt) a dancing master, to Jamaica, in the West Indies, who thought it proper to remove from hence soon after the fire at the fort.

Voluntary confession.—Margaret Sarinbirr, alias Keary, declares,

"That she was several times at the house of John Romme, shoemaker, and tavern-keeper, and saw several meetings of the negroes from time to time; and in particular, in the month of December last past, she saw assembled there in or about ten or twelve in number, viz.—Cuff, belonging to Mr. Philipse; Brash, Mr. Jay's; Curacoa Dick, a negro man; Caesar, Pintard's; Patrick, English's; a negro belonging to Mr. Breasted, in Pearl-street, (Jack) Cato, Alderman Moore's.

"The rest of the names that were in the combination, I cannot remember, or their master's names. They proposed, to burn the fort first, and afterwards the city; and then steal, rob and carry away all the money and goods they could procure, and was to be carried to Romme's and were to be joined by the country negroes; and that they were to murder every one that had money.

(k) Upon the supposition, that Arthur knew nothing of the secrets of the conspiracy before he came to jail, the reader may be apt to judge, that he acted with more than ordinary acuteness for one of his station, in pumping so much out of Peggy and Sarah, (Hughson's daughter) and their confidence in him, if he were a stranger to them, was somewhat extraordinary on the occasion.

"The reason why I did not make this discovery before, Romme swore them all never to discover, and swore me too; and I thought, I would wrong my own soul, if I discovered it. And that all the rest of the negroes in city and country were to meet in one night.

"All the above I am ready to declare upon oath." (*)

Signed with her mark X

This declaration was sent from the jail, by the under-sheriff, to one of the judges late this night.

The conviction of the two negroes, Caesar and Prince, as principals in the two robberies; and of Hughson, his wife, and Peggy herself, as accessories in receiving the goods stolen; alarmed her so, that she seemed now to think it high time to do something to recommend herself to mercy; and this confession coming voluntarily from her, it gave hopes that she was in earnest, and would make some material discoveries.

SUPREME COURT
Friday, May 8.

Present, the second and third justices.

The king against Caesar and Prince, negroes.

The prisoners having been capitally convicted on two several indictments for felony, and being brought to the bar the court proceeded to give sentence; which was passed by the second justice as followeth:

You, Caesar and Prince, the grand jury having found two indictments against each of you, for feloniously stealing and taking away from Mr. Hogg, and Mr. Meyers Cohen, sundry goods of considerable value. To these indictments you severally pleaded *not guilty*; and for your trials put yourselves upon God and the country; which country having found you guilty, it now only remains for the court to pronounce

---

* This confession was penned by a jail secretary.

that judgment which the law requires, and the nature of your crimes deserve.

But before I proceed to sentence, I must tell you, that you have been proceeded against in the same manner as any white man, guilty of your crimes, would have been. You had not only the liberty of sending for your witnesses; asking them such questions as you thought proper; but likewise making the best defence you could; and as you have been convicted by twelve honest men upon their oaths, so the just judgment of God has at length overtaken you.

I have great reason to believe, that the crimes you now stand convicted of, are not the least of those you have been concerned in; for by your general characters you have been very wicked fellows, hardened sinners, and ripe, as well as ready, for the most enormous and daring enterprizes, especially you, Caesar: and as the time you have yet to live is to be but very short, I earnestly advise and exhort both of you to employ it in the most diligent and best manner you can, by confessing your sins, repenting sincerely of them, and praying God of his infinite goodness to have mercy on your souls: and as God knows the secrets of your hearts, and cannot be cheated or imposed upon, so you must shortly give an account to him, and answer for all your actions; and depend upon it, if you do not truly repent before you die, there is a hell to punish the wicked eternally.

And as it is not in your powers to make full restitution for the many injuries you have done the public; so I advise both of you to do all that in you is, to prevent further mischiefs, by discovering such persons as have been concerned with you, in designing or endeavouring to burn this city, and to destroy its inhabitants. This I am fully persuaded is in your power to do if you will; if so, and you do not make such discovery, be assured God Almighty will punish you for it, though we do not: therefore I advise you to consider this well, and I hope both of you will tell the truth.

And now, nothing further remains for me to say, but that you Caesar, and you Prince, are to be taken hence to the place from whence you came, and from thence to the place of execution, and there you, and each of you, are to be hanged by the neck until you be dead. And I pray the Lord to have mercy on your souls.

Ordered, that their execution be on Monday next, the eleventh day of this instant, between the hours of nine and one of the same day. And further ordered that after the execution of the said sentence, the body of Caesar be hung in chains.

Court adjourned till Monday morning next ten o'clock.

Peggy was examined by the judges touching the matter of her confession delivered in writing last night, which she declared for truth; and for the greater solemnity was sworn to it, after having been seriously admonished not to dare to say anything but the truth, or to accuse innocent persons: she was told, that we had dived so far into this mystery of iniquity already, that we could easily discern whether she prevaricated or not; and that if she did, she must not flatter herself with the hopes of being recommended to mercy; so that such disingenuous behaviour would but deceive herself, and make her case desperate, or words to that purpose: she put on the air of sincerity, as if disposed to make a discovery, but seemed to be under terrible apprehensions. What she said, corresponded with the scheme of the plot so far as we had got light into it, and in a great measure confirmed what Arthur Prince said in his deposition, No. 1. before, with this difference, that she shifted the scene from John Hughson's to John Romme's and protested that she did not know that the Hughsons were any wise privy to, or concerned in the conspiracy.

At this examination, she related a great many particulars, which for want of time, were not committed to writing; but her further examination deferred to the next day.

Romme at this time absconded; orders having been given for apprehending him long before, upon suspicion of his having received some of the goods stolen from Mr. Hogg's; and Peggy and her advisers might think as he was out of reach, she might have been brooding at both places, and with her knowledge; but one may be persuaded, from the course of the evidence, that Romme was apprized at least of the conspiracy carrying on at Hughson's. Upon this examination, Romme's wife was apprehended and committed.

Saturday, May 9.

Many hours were taken up in Peggy's examination yesterday and this day; which was committed to writing, as followeth.

Examination taken before the judges, No. 1. Margaret Salingburgh, (1) alias Kerry, saith,

1. "That some time last fall she took lodgings with one Frank, a free negro, fronting the new battery, within this city, about three or four doors from the house of John Romme, shoemaker, and continued there till the beginning of February last during which time she employed the said Romme in making shoes for her; and on that account became acquainted with him and his wife, and used often to go backwards and forwards to and from the said house; by which means she had the opportunity of seeing many negroes there at several different times, who used to resort thither to drink drams, punch and other strong liquors, the said Romme keeping a public house; and that often numbers of them have continued at the said Romme's house till two or three o'clock in the morning, to her knowledge, drinking, singing and playing at dice.

2. "That on or about the beginning of November last, on a Sunday evening, between the hours of 11 and 12, she (the examinant) being returning home to her said lodging, by the way of Whitehall, saw two negroes coming towards her with each of them a firkin upon their shoulders, and saw them turn into Romme's gate, sixteen of the said firkins: and the reason of the examinant's staying under the said

(1) How she came by the name Sorubiero, by which she stands indicted we know not; she saith she was married to one Salingburgh.

[58]

Hunt's shed to observe the motions of the said negroes was, because she suspected them to be stolen goods. (m)

3. "That one evening, some time about Christmas last, about eight or nine o'clock, she was at the house of the said John Romme, where she saw in company, together with the said Romme and his wife, ten or eleven negroes, all in one room, and the said John Romme was observing to the negroes, how well the rich people at this place lived, and said, if they (meaning the negroes, as she understood) would be advised by him, they (including himself and the negroes as she understood) should have the money. To which Cuff (Mr. Philipse's negro) replied, how wilt you manage that? Well enough, said Romme, set them all a light fire; burn the houses of them that have the most money, and kill them all, as the negroes would have done their masters and mistresses formerly. (n)

"That he (Romme) should be captain over them (meaning the negroes, as the examinant understood) till they could get all their money, and then he (Romme) would be governor. To which Cuff said, they could not do it. Yes, says Romme, we'll do well enough; we'll send into the coun-

(m) These firkins were said to have been stolen out of Jeneau's storehouse.

(n) There was a rising of the negroes in this city, in the year 1712. On the 7th of April, about one or two o'clock in the morning the house of Peter Van Tilburgh was set on fire by the negroes who being armed with guns, knives, etc. killed and wounded several white people as they were coming to assist in extinguishing the flames. Notice thereof being soon carried to the fort, his excellency governor (Robert) Hunter, ordered a cannon to be fired from the ramparts, to alarm the town, and detached a party of soldiers to the fire; at whose appearance those villains immediately fled, and made their way out of town as fast as they could, to hide themselves in the woods and swamps. In their flight they also killed and wounded several white people; but being closely pursued, some concealed themselves in barns, and others sheltered in the swamps or woods; which being surrounded and strictly guarded till the morning, many of them were then taken. Some finding no way for their escape, shot themselves. The end of it was, that after these foolish wretches had murdered eight or ten white people, and some of the confederates had been their own executioners, nineteen more of them were apprehended, brought upon their trials for a conspiracy to murder the people, etc. and were convicted and executed; and several more that turned evidences were transported.

try for the rest of the negroes to help, because he could write, and he knew several negroes in the country that could read. And he encouraged them, and said, he would stand by them, and that the sun would shine very bright by and by, and never fear, my láds: But that if it should happen that any thing should come out, he would make his escape, and go to North Carolina, Cape Fear, or somewhere thereabouts; or into the Mohawks country, where he had lived before; but besides, the D——L could not hurt him; for he had a great many friends in town, and the best place would stand by him; or the said Romme expressed himself in words to the effect before mentioned.

4. "That during all the discourse of the said Romme to the negroes as above mentioned, she did not observe any of the said number of ten or eleven, to make any answer to Romme's discourse aforesaid, excepting Cuffee (Philipse's), Curacoa Dick, Pintard's Caesar, Will (Weaver's, since dead), and Mr. Moore's Cato; but Cuffee spoke the most, and said, "The Devil take the failer;" though the other four seemed to be as forward for the plot as Cuff.

5. "That the other negroes that were present at the above discourse, whose persons or names she now remembers, were Patrick (English's), Jack (Breasted's), and Brash (Mr. Jay's.)

6. "That at the same meeting, there were several other negroes, which made up the number ten or eleven, whose names, or the names of their masters, she does not now remember; but believes she should remember their faces again if she should see them.

7. "That at the same meeting, the said John Romme proposed to the said negroes present, 'To burn the fort first, and afterwards the city; and then to steal and rob, and carry away all the money and goods they could procure;' and that they should be brought to Romme's house, and he would take care to hide them away.

8. "That Romme said further, that if the fire did not succeed, and they could not compass their ends that way; then he proposed to the negroes present, that they should steal

all that they could from their masters; then he would carry them to a strange country, and give them their liberty, and set them free. After this, Romme asked them, if it would do? That is whether the negroes then present liked his proposals, (as she understood.) To which Cuff answered, "There's great talking, and no cider;" and so they broke up: And the negroes remaining at that time all departed; some of them, to wit, Brash, Patrick, Jack, and the several other negroes (whose names the examinant cannot at all remember) having left the company about an hour before; but Cuff, Curacoa Dick, Weaver's Will, Cato, and Pintard's Caesar staid till the last.

9. "That she well remembers, that Cuff, Curacoa Dick, Weaver's Will, Pintard's Caesar, and Mr. Moore's Cato; and also Auboyneau's Prince, and Vaarck's Caesar, used much to frequent that house in the evenings, and to stay often late in the night, drinking and playing at dice; but she never heard any discourse amongst them concerning burning the fort, or setting fire to the town, but the time above mentioned.

10. "That immediately after the negroes broke up the meeting before mentioned, the said John Romme insisted upon this examinant's being sworn to secrecy, that she would not discover any thing that she knew had passed in his house, either relating to the butter, or the fire, or discourse at the said meeting, which she accordingly was and kissed a book; what book it was, knows not.

11. "That Romme's wife was by, all or most of the time, during the meeting and discourse aforesaid; and when Romme insisted that this examinant should be sworn as aforesaid, as well as his wife; for the said Romme declared, they were both sworn to secrecy, and all the negroes; but the examinant saith, that the said Romme's wife did not at all join in any of the discourse before mentioned."

Elizabeth Romme, wife of John Romme, was sent for and examined concerning what Peggy had declared to have passed at her house.

Examination.—1. She denied,

"That she knew any thing at all about the conspiracy for firing the fort and the town, and murdering the people.

2. "Denied there were ever such companies of negroes met at her house as Peggy declared.

3. "She confessed there had been some firkins of butter brought thither about the time mentioned by Peggy; but said that they were received by her husband, and she knew nothing of them.

4. "Denied she had ever heard or knew of any oath of secrecy imposed by her husband; or administered by him to her or Peggy, or any other person whatsoever, with regard to secrecy concerning the stolen butter, or any other goods, or concerning the conspiracy.

5. "Confessed, that a negro (the father of Mr. Philipse's Cuffee) kept game-fowls at their house, and used to come there to bring them victuals, but never used to stay long. Confessed that he was there about Christmas last. And

6. "That the last winter Cuffee's father brought them sticks of wood now and then, and she believed he had them out of his masters' yard.

7. "Confessed, that negroes used to come to their house to drink drams, but never used to stay; that Caesar (Vaarck's negro) used to come morning and evening often; Auboyneau's Prince sometimes; Mr. Moore's Cato once or twice, and not oftener, as she remembered; never saw Breasted, the hatter's negro, there at all; nor Mr. Jay's Brash; nor Patrick, (English's negro) but had seen Bastian (Vaarck's negro) there, and Mr. Pintard's Caesar; but never saw above three negroes at a time there, and that very seldom; and that when there were three, they were always Cuffee (Philipse's), Caesar (Vaarck's,), and Prince (Auboyneau's)."

This afternoon orders were given for apprehending the several negroes mentioned by Peggy, to have been present at Romme's, at the time she said Romme and the negroes were talking of the conspiracy; those of them whom she knew by name, and were not before committed, were soon found and brought to jail.

In the evening the judges came to the city-hall, and sent for Peggy, and had the several negroes brought one by one, and passed in review before her, viz., Patrick (English's), Cato (col. Moore's), Curacoa Dick, Caesar (alderman Pintard's), Brash (Mr. Jay's), and Jack (Breasted's), and she distinguished them every one, called them by their names, and declared, those were at the above mentioned meeting.

These negroes were each of them separately examined, and denied being at any such meeting, or that they knew any thing of the conspiracy.

At first, Cork (English's negro) was brought by mistake instead of Patrick, and Peggy declared, he was not English's negro which she meant; Cork was unfortunately of a countenance somewhat ill-favoured, naturally of a suspicious look, and reckoned withal to be unlucky too; his being sent for before the magistrates in such a perilous season, might be thought sufficient to alarm the most innocent of them, and occasion appearance of their being under some terrible apprehensions; but it was much otherwise with Cork; and notwithstanding the disadvantage of his natural aspect, upon his being interrogated concerning the conspiracy, he shewed such a cheerful, open, honest smile upon his countenance (none of your fictitious hypocritical grins) that every one that was by, and observed it (and there were several in the room) jumped in the same observation and opinion, that they never saw the fellow look so handsome: Such an efficacy have truth and innocence, that they even reflect beauty upon deformity!

On the contrary, Patrick's visage betrayed his guilt: those who are used to negroes may have experienced, that some of them, when charged with any piece of villainy they have been detected in, have an odd knack or (it is hard what to call or how to describe it) way of turning their eyes inwards, as it were, as if shocked at the consciousness of their own perfidy; their looks, at the same time, discovering all the symptoms of the most inveterate malice and resentment: this was Patrick's appearance, and such his behaviour upon examination, as served to induce one's

[63]

credit to what Peggy had declared; so far at least, that he was present at a meeting when the conspiracy was talked of, and was one of the persons consenting to act a part in that infernal scheme; so that he was committed to jail, and the rest of them, whom Peggy declared, as they were produced, to be the persons she meant.

These negroes, impeached by Peggy, and committed upon her information, and which had passed in review before her, were likewise shewn to Mary Burton, who declared, that she did not remember, that ever she saw any of them at Hughson's which seemed to add strength to what Peggy had declared in her examination, that this villainous scheme was carrying on at Romme's as well as Hughson's.

Deposition taken before one of the judges.—Abigail Earle, being sworn, deposeth,

"That just before the going in of the afternoon church, on the same Sunday that coals were found in Mr. Murray's haystack, (o) she saw three negro men coming up the Broadway; that she was then looking out of her window up one pair of stairs in the house where Mr. Williams now lives; and as they passed under the window, she heard one of them say, viz., *Fire, Fire, scorch, scorch,* A LITTLE, *damn it,* BY AND BY! and then threw up his hands and laughed. That after the said negroes were gone by she went into Mrs. George's house (p) and told her what she had heard: and about an hour after, when church was out, she saw the same negroes coming down the Broadway; and then shewed Mrs. George the negro that had spoke the aforesaid words: whereupon Mrs. George said, that is Mr. Walter's Quaco."

Lydia George being sworn, deposed, "that she heard the above written deposition of Abigail Earle read, and knows that all

(o) Sunday, April 5.
(p) Which was the next door.

therein mentioned, which any ways relates to her the deponent, is true."

Upon these depositions Quaco was recommitted this evening.

Sunday, May 10.

A young negro fellow of Mrs. Carpenter's had given some information, that Sarah (Niblet's negro wench) had told him that Sawney, alias Sandy (Niblet's negro boy of about 16 or 17 years of age) had been concerned in setting the fort on fire; that he had likewise set Muchado's house, next door to his master's, on fire; and had also thrown fire over alderman Bancker's fence into his yard. This negro fellow was sent for, and likewise Sarah (Niblet's) and he declared before one of the judges and others, to Sarah's face, to the same purpose. The wench seemed to be under great terror, and trembled much; but nothing could be got out of her more than a peremptory denial that she had ever said any such things to the above negro.

Sarah was committed.

Sandy had then lately been sent away by his master to Albany in order to be sold; but orders were immediately sent to bring him back.

Niblet the master was sent for, and examined as to the characters of these servants; but he said, *he knew no harm of them.*

SUPREME COURT
Monday, May 11.

Present, the second justice.

Ordered, that the gibbet on which the body of the negro Caesar is to be hanged in chains, be fixed on the island near the powder-house.

Court adjourned till Monday morning, ten o'clock.

Caesar and Prince were executed this day at the gallows, according to sentence. They died very stubbornly, without con-

[65]

fessing any thing about the conspiracy; and denied they knew any thing of it to the last. The body of Caesar was accordingly hung in chains.

These two negroes bore the characters of very wicked idle fellows; had before been detected in some robberies, for which they had been publickly chastised at the whipping-post, and were persons of most obstinate and untractable tempers; so that there was no expectation of drawing any thing from them which would make for the discovery of the conspiracy, though there seemed good reason to conclude, as well from their characters as what had been charged upon them by information from others, that they were two principal ringleaders in it amongst the blacks. It was thought proper to execute them for the robbery, and not wait for the bringing them to a trial for the conspiracy, though the proof against them was strong and clear concerning their guilt as to that also; and it was imagined, that as stealing and plundering was a principal part of the hellish scheme in agitation, amongst the inferior sort of these infernal confederates, this earnest of example and punishment might break the knot, and induce some of them to unfold this mystery of iniquity, in hopes thereby to recommend themselves to mercy, and it is probable, that with some it had this effect.

SUPREME COURT
Tuesday, May 12.

Present, the second and third justices.

The king against John Hughson, and Sarah, his wife.

The prisoners, John Hughson and Sarah his wife, having been indicted for conspiring, confederating and combining with divers negroes and others, to burn the city of New-York, and also to kill and destroy the inhabitants thereof, were set to the bar and arraigned on the said indictment; and thereupon pleaded, *not guilty.*

Margaret Kerry was also included in this indictment; but she being in a disposition, as it was thought at that time, for making a discovery, it was judged proper to postpone her arraignment.

Court adjourned to Friday the 15th instant, ten o'clock in the morning.

Arthur Price having been found by experience to be very adroit at pumping out the secrets of the conspirators, in the two instances of Peggy and Sarah Hughson the daughter, before set forth; the under-sheriff was ordered to put Cuffee (Mr. Philipse's negro) into the same cell with him, and to give them a tankard of punch now and then, in order to cheer up their spirits, and make them more sociable. These directions were accordingly observed, and produced the desired effects; and one of the judges being acquainted that Arthur had something to communicate he went up this morning in order to examine him.

Deposition taken before one of the judges, No. 3.—Arthur Price being duly sworn, saith,

1. "That having discourse on Saturday night last, with Cuffee, a negro slave belonging to Mr. Philipse, he the said Cuffee, amongst other discourse, said, that he was one of the Geneva club (q) that was sworn; but being overcome with sleep, he did not go to their meeting at that time: that Cuffee asked the deponent what could be the reason that

(q) There was a confederacy of negroes, of which Caesar (Vaarck's) and Prince (Auboyneau's) both hanged yesterday, and Cuffee (Mr. Philipse's) were the heads and ringleaders; who robbed, pilfered and stole whenever they had an opportunity: and it happened about five or six years ago, a cellar of one Baker, a tavern-keeper in this city, had one night been broken open, and robbed of some Geneva; many of the parties concerned were detected, viz., several negroes, of which Caesar and Prince were two principals; and all that were discovered were chastised at the public whipping-post. From thence it may be supposed they became distinguished among each other by the name of the *Geneva Club*; for they used frequently to be junketting together at nights with Cuff, upon the produce of the spoils of their pilfering. But it came out upon the examination of these negroes, that they had been that time the impudence to assume the style and title of *Free Masons*, in imitation of a society here: which was looked upon to be a gross affront to the provincial grand master and gentlemen of the fraternity at that time, and was very ill accepted: however, from this time the negroes may be supposed to have declined their pretensions to this title; for we heard nothing more of them afterwards under that stile. But it is probable that most of this Geneva Club that were sworn (as Cuffee said) were of the conspiracy; and it is likely that by the swearing, Cuff meant, sworn of the conspiracy.

[67]

Peggy was called down so often? (r) The deponent replied, he thought Peggy was discovering the plot about the fire; Cuffee replied, she could not do that unless she forswore herself, he knew; for that he that had done that was sworn after she (Peggy) was in prison; he (Cuffee) left his master's house in the evening, and went along the wharves to the Fly-Market, and waited there till one Quack came out of his master's house; they two then went to the house of John Hughson, where they met nobody but John Hughson, his wife, and daughter Sarah; that they (the two negroes) called for a tankard of punch; that Hughson swore Quack three times; that they only drank out their punch, and then went down to the Fly. That this deponent then said, I believe I know this Quack, and that he lived with a butcher; Cuffee replied, no; he doth not live with a butcher, but he lived with a painter, who lived within a few doors of a butcher; which painter's name he understood to be Roosevelt, according to the best of his remembrance.

2. "That Cuffee told him, that Quack was married to a negro wench who is cook to the fort, to the governor as he understood; that they were all to meet at Hughson's the Sunday after Quack was sworn; but some came and some did not. That the deponent, upon some further discourse, asked Cuffee how Quack could do it? (meaning the setting fire to the house in the fort) Cuffee answered, he could not tell how he did it; but that Quack was to do it, and did do it.

3. "That Cuffee said, they were to meet and have a club at John Hughson's in the Easter hollidays, but that the d——d constables hindered them.

4. "That he asked Cuffee, whether he did not think that the firing would be found out; he replied, no, by G——d, he did not think it ever would.

5. "That he further asked Cuffee, if he was not afraid, that the two negroes who were to be executed on Monday, would discover (the affair about the firing of the fort and

(r) She had been frequently sent for to be examined.

[68]

town meaning) Cuffee answered, he was not afraid of that; for that he was sure they would be burnt to ashes before they would discover it; he would lay his life on it.

6. "That yesterday the deponent having some further discourse with Cuffee, he said, he wondered why they only took up the Long Bridge boys, and did not take up those of the Smith's Fly; for he believed, if the truth was known, they (the Smith's Fly negroes meaning) were as much concerned as they (of the Long Bridge meaning.)"

Upon this deposition, Quack (Roosevelt's) was apprehended and committed; who was one of the *Smith's Fly Boys*, as Cuff called them.

Wednesday, May 13.

This being the day appointed by the lieutenant governor's proclamation, issued the tenth of April last, to be observed throughout the province, as a day of public fasting and humiliation, the same was reverently and decently observed, particularly in this city, by persons of all persuasions, the shops were all shut up, and persons of all ranks resorted to their respective places of divine worship, and seemed deeply affected with a sense of the calamities with which we had of late been visited: his most gracious majesty, for the vindicating the honour of his crown, having declared war against the king of Spain, the visitation which the province underwent with the severity of the cold weather the last winter, which reduced many families to extremity and want, by the loss of their cattle, etc. the many houses and dwellings that had been fired about our ears, without any discovery of the cause or occasion of them, which had put us into the utmost consternation: all these distresses succeeding upon the heels of each other, were surely most likely to awaken us to our duty, and a due sense of our demerits.

Deposition before the judges, No. 2.—Mary Burton being duly sworn, deposed,

1. "That a day or two after she was examined before the grand jury, she was coming by Vaarck's door in the Broadstreet of this city, and saw a negro of the said Vaarck's, who (now at the time of her examination being produced) called himself by the name of Bastian, but use to be called by the negroes, Tom Peal, who asked the deponent, whether she had discovered any thing about the fires? To which the deponent answered no. To which he replied, d——n you, it was not best for you, for fear you should be burnt in the next.

2. "That Quaco (s) the negro man now produced to her, she has often seen at Hughson's door along with Philipse's Cuff, Caesar (Vaarck's), and Prince (Auboyneau's), but never saw Quaco within Hughson's house, as she remembers.

3. "That she has seen Jack (Sleydall's, the tallow chandler) very often at Hughson's house, and believes he was very well acquainted with Hughson's eldest daughter Sarah; but does not remember she ever saw him there at the times of the meetings of the negroes, when they talked about fires; but from the kindness shewn to him by Hughson, his wife, and daughter aforesaid, she had great reason to think he was in their secrets.

4. "That she hath often times seen many negroes at Hughson's house, she believes thirty together, especially on a Sunday; many of them playing at dice, whose faces she could remember if she saw them; and she believes there were thirty of them concerned in the conspiracy about the fires; and some country negroes, particularly one Jamaica.

5. "That Hughson and his wife, and Peggy, and Sarah Hughson the daughter, used, at the meetings of the negroes, to be the forwardest of any of them in talking about fires, (that is to say) that they would burn the fort; then they would go to the Fly (t) and burn the whole town, and destroy all the people; to which all the negroes present were

(s) Roosevelt's
(t) Towards the east end of the town.

[70]

consenting; and by name Cuff, (u) Caesar and Prince, (v) Albany, Tom Peal, alias Bastian, amongst the rest.

6. "That she knows Hughson and his family, and John Romme were very intimately acquainted, and the latter used frequently to be at Hughson's house, where they used to retire to a private room, where Peggy afterwards lay in, and used to have a great deal of discourse together; but when the deponent over-heard them, they were talking Dutch; but Romme used to tell Hughson, he was afraid of the deponent. To which Hughson replied, he need not be afraid of her, for that she was bound to him, and she dared not tell; for if she did he would murder her; And afterwards Romme would be more free before the deponent.

7. "That she knows Jonneau (Vaarck's negro) and has seen him at Hughson's house a drinking with other negroes; but don't remember he was present at any time of the discourse about the fires, or killing the white people."

Jonneau, Albany and Bastian were immediately apprehended and committed.

Thursday, May 14.

This day Sandy alias Sawney (Niblet's negro boy) was brought down from Albany, and committed to jail.

Deposition before the judges—No. 3.—Mary Burton deposed,

1. "That at the time when she saw the meetings of the several negroes at Hughson's house, as mentioned in the deponent's deposition of yesterday, the said Hughson said, *they were all sworn*, meaning the negroes and all the white people present, (as she understood) that is, Hughson himself, his wife, and daughter Sarah, and Peggy, and she understood by Hughson, that the purport of the oath was, *that*

(u) Philipse's.
(v) Vaarck's and Auboyneau's.

[71]

*they were not to discover the secrets about firing the fort,
the houses at the Fly, and the whole town;* and about murdering the white people: and Hughson said to the negroes
present, which were Cuff, Caesar and Prince; *now you must
take care, for you are all sworn;* and the deponent at the
time saw a bible (as she took it to be) in Hughson's hand;
and when the deponent came into the room, he laid it upon
the table: and then Caesar spoke to the deponent, and cautioned her not to tell; and Hughson made answer, that she
dared not; and Cuff said, *d——n his bl——d, if he would
tell of any, if he was burnt;* and so said the other two negroes; and so said Hughson, his wife, their daughter Sarah,
and Peggy.

2. "That Hughson asked Caesar if he could get any others (meaning the negroes) to help them? Caesar answered,
he could get enough, who dared not but go if he spoke.

3. "That she saw Caesar pay Hughson twelve pounds in
eight shilling Spanish pieces, as Hughson said, after count-
ing them; which was paid him, in order to buy guns; and
that Hughson afterwards went abroad with his boat, and
was about three days, or thereabouts, and brought back
with him seven or eight guns, three pistols and four swords,
which were hid away under the boards in the garret floor in
Hughson's house.

Examination, before the judges, No. 2.—Margaret Salingburgh, alias Kerry, saith,

1. "That about a fortnight after she came to lodge at
Hughson's house (she believes it was about the beginning
of February) John Romme came there, when Hughson was
gone into the woods to cut fire-wood; but Hughson's wife
being at home Romme entered into conversation with her,
when the examinant was present; and she heard him say to
her (after calling for a mug of punch, and after observing
how hard the winter was) that he did not know how it was
with them; and though he had money enough himself; yet
he could not buy wood for it; but that he had a parcel of

good children (meaning the negroes, as she understood) who brought him wood almost every night, or words to that purpose; so that he had done well enough hitherto. And the examinant saith, that the reason why she understood the said Romme to mean the negroes by the words, *good children*, was, because she herself several times saw Cuff (Mr. Philipse's) and Caesar (Vaarck's) and sometimes Cuff's brother, and the white boy called Yorkshire (w) bring wood there a-nights: That Hughson's wife answered, that it was poor enough with them; that he (Romme) was a gentleman, and could live without work: to which Romme said, that if Hughson would join with him, and take a quantity of fifty or sixty firkins of butter in; meaning, as the deponent understood, into Hughson's house, to conceal them; for, Romme said, it was too hard for him to conceal such a quantity; but that Hughson, in his large house, might much easier make away with them, and conceal them. To which Hughson's wife, said, she did not know, but she believed her husband would not have any hand in it: oh! says Romme, I want to talk to him myself; for that he knew how circumstances were with them: by and by towards the evening he would come again and talk to him; for that he wanted a load of wood.

2. "That she was afterwards informed by Hughson himself, that Romme was returning to Hughson's house in the evening, and met Hughson with a sleigh load of wood in the street, which Hughson carried down to Romme's house.

3. "That at the time of Romme's discoursing with Hughson's wife about receiving butter as aforesaid, he further said, that as to butter, the weather was so hard, and the ground so frozen, that he did not know how to hide them away; and as no vessels could go out, he could not ship them off; and he believed gammon would do better; that his brother was going to Carolina, and that he could stow them in his cabin, when there could not be room to stow there fifty or sixty firkins of butter. And by the discourse, the de-

(w) Christopher Wilson.

ponent understood that Romme proposed to get the butter and gammons both from the weigh-house, or some of the storehouses thereabouts.

4. "That she had at several times seen goods of several kinds brought to Romme's house, that she suspected to have been stolen: and that after the oath of secrecy taken by the deponent, and mentioned in a former examination, the said Romme would talk freely to her about such stolen goods as she happened to see brought to his house; and Romme's wife used to help receive such stolen goods, and used to conceal them away."

From what had hitherto come to light concerning this mystery of iniquity, it was scarce to be doubted but Peggy had it in her power to unfold a great deal more of it, as she lodged at Hughson's; which, from the course of the other evidence, was the principal place the conspirators resorted to for holding their consultations: and though what Peggy had already disclosed seemed to merit something, yet it was not altogether satisfactory; and it was thought proper she should be arraigned upon the indictment for the conspiracy, upon the supposition that this step might probably be a means of bringing her to a resolution of making a full discovery of what she knew.

SUPREME COURT
Friday, May 15.

Present, the second and third justices.

The king against Margaret Kerry, and others.

The prisoner, Kerry, being brought to the bar and arraigned on an indictment for a conspiracy, etc. pleaded *not guilty*.

Ordered, that her trial, together with Hughson and his wife, be on Wednesday next.

Note. This was the same indictment upon which Hughson and his wife were arraigned the twelfth instant.

Court adjourned till Tuesday next, the 19th inst. at ten o'clock in the morning.

The examination of Sarah Hughson, the daughter, was deferred thus long, in expectation that Arthur Price might succeed further in drawing more secrets concerning the conspiracy from her, as he had before done from Peggy, and the negro Cuffee; but Price being often sent for, it was apprehended they began to suspect him, for after Quack (Roosevelt's) was brought to jail, none of the three before mentioned would hold any discourse with him: and this being understood to be the case, Sarah was sent for, and interrogated upon the matter of the conspiracy in general, and particularly as to what passed between her and Arthur Price, as set forth in his deposition of the 7th inst. but she positively denied that she knew any thing of the conspiracy, though part of the conversation she confessed, as followeth.

Examination, before one of the judges, No. 1.—Sarah Hughson, single woman, acknowledges

"she had some discourse with Arthur Price soon after she came into jail. That she talked to him about some conversation passed between her and a fortuneteller, who said to her, that her father would escape narrowly with his life, if he did escape at all; and that if he did escape, he would go over the water."

Owns "that Price said to her, that if she knew any thing about the fires, that she had better tell it: to which she answered, if she knew any thing she would tell the truth."

As soon as the examination was taken, Arthur Price was sent for to confront with her; and he told all that had passed between him and Sarah, agreeable almost word for word with his deposition of the 7th inst. and most of which she had denied very positively before he was brought into the room; and after all, when Price vouched the thing to her face, she did but faintly contradict what he said: and it being proposed to her to ask him any questions, she answered she had no questions to ask him, but at length denied in gross all that Price had charged upon her, which any ways related to the fires. The high-sheriff being present, he perused Price's deposition whilst he was telling his story before Sarah; and he declared Price had repeated the substance very exactly, and almost word for word.

Deposition, before one of the judges, No. 4.—Arthur Price being duly sworn, saith,

1. "That Cuffee (Philipse's negro) told him, that he knew he was to suffer death, and wondered why they did not bring him to his trial, for he was sure he was to go the same way the other two went. (x)

2. "That after Quack (mentioned in this deponent's examination of the 12th inst.) was committed, Cuffee never mentioned any thing concerning the former discourse, but read sometimes, and cried much."

Monday, May 18.

A few days ago John Romme was stopped and secured by a magistrate at Brunswick, in New-Jersey, which he very prudently did, and notified to a magistrate of this city; whereupon Romme was sent for, and this day committed to our jail.

Romme, upon examination, also confessed, as his wife had done before, that some firkins of butter had been brought by the negroes into his house; and he was even with his wife, saying, they were received by her, that he had no hand in it; and he also positively denied that he knew any thing of the plot, and that any such discourse had passed at his house, as before declared by Peggy in her examinations. He was remanded, and examined several times afterwards; but not a word would he own about the conspiracy.

Then Romme's wife was sent for down again to be farther examined: but nothing more could be got out of her. But in the course of her examination some hints having dropped, that her husband had acknowledged the negroes brought the butter to their house, but that he knew nothing of it, and said it was re-

(x) Meaning Caesar and Prince hanged, as may be supposed.

[76]

ceived by her; she being remanded to her prison, and going by her husband's apartment, and he putting his head out of the wicket, she civilly saluted him with a smart slap on the chops.

SUPREME COURT
Tuesday, May 19.

Present, the third justice.

The court opened and adjourned till Thursday morning 10 o'clock.

Wednesday, May 20.

Examination, before one of the judges—No. 3.—Margaret Salingburgh saith,

1. "That as to the butter brought by the negroes to Romme's house, as mentioned in one of her former examinations; that Caesar was one of the negroes that brought the butter, as Romme informed her himself; and that about a week before, she herself heard Romme making a bargain with Caesar to get him as much butter as he could, and he would give him fifteen shillings a firkin for it; but Caesar insisted on twenty.

2. "That the next day she was asking Romme who those negroes were that brought the butter in the night before? and he answered, Caesar, but the other he did not know; for that it was dark, and he did not care to light a candle for fear of being discovered.

3. "That Romme said, he lay abed, and that his wife was up and saw the butter put in the yard; and that after the negroes were gone, he himself got up and stowed it away under the wood in an old house in the yard.

4. "That Caesar told Romme, in her presence, that they had got the butter from a Frenchman's near the Long Bridge, and that he thought it belonged to a countryman,

who had left it in the said Frenchman's storehouse till it could be sold, or shipped off in the spring; or words to that effect.

5. "That the cloth coat Romme has now upon his back, with a cape to it, was stolen by Caesar from a countryman's boat near Hughson's, as she heard Caesar tell Romme; and heard both Romme and Caesar say, that Romme gave Caesar ten shillings for it.

6. "That Caesar and Prince had stolen twenty pieces of eight out of Ellis' boat, and a speckled new shirt and a pair of new stockings, which were brought by them directly to Romme's house, and the money they delivered into Romme's hands, and they told Romme, in her hearing, where they had got it, and two pieces of eight a-piece they gave to Romme, and the rest they were to leave in his hands to drink out."

For the greater solemnity of the matter, Peggy also swore to and signed her three several examinations.

The history of Peggy's, contained in her three examinations, corresponds so exactly as to the persons of, and charges against such negroes, mentioned by others, which she brings in question, and also with the matter and circumstances of the conspiracy, which the reader may hereafter perceive from the whole current of depositions and examinations of whites and blacks, that one may be very apt to conclude, she only shifted the scene, and laid it in a wrong place.

Peggy very well knew that Romme had fled the country upon the inquiry about the robbery at Hogg's; and probably that finding her own life in jeopardy concerning that felony, as well as the conspiracy, which she now was sensible had got air, and was like to be detected, and partly by her own frank talk and openness with her fellow-prisoner, Price; she might therefore think it high time to provide for her own safety, if she could do it so cheap as by amusing us with a narrative of the plot; which, though real and true in other respects, nevertheless she charged the confederacy and consultations about it to have been held solely at Romme's, as to the knowledge she had concerning it;

and so screened the other confederates, Hughson, his wife and family, at whose house principally these miscreants associated; though what she declared might be true as to both places, and there seems to be too much reason to mistrust it was so; yet she absolutely denied to the last, that she had ever heard any such discourse at Hughson's though frequently interrogated very strictly to that purpose, and admonished in the most solemn manner to declare the whole truth, if she intended to do herself any service, or induce the judges to recommend her as an object deserving of mercy.

However, though there was little reason to think that Peggy had told all she knew of the matter, yet that what she said was, in the main, true, there seemed no doubt; as said before, from the correspondence between her story and that of the other evidences, so far as they had discovered with relation to the conspiracy; the only question was, whether it was carried on at Romme's as well as Hughson's? From her lodging and intimacy with the Hughsons, she might be inclined to favour them, and lay the scene at Romme's only, who was then thought to be out of reach, and so make a merit of a fallacious sort of discovery. But we had great hopes, that if she should be convicted upon the in-dictment for the conspiracy, she would come to a resolution to make an ingenuous confession in order to save herself; and with this expectation, and considering what she had confessed al-ready, the judges were induced to recommend her to the lieuten-ant governor for a pardon, on this condition nevertheless, that it should not pass the seal till she should be thought amply to have merited it.

And a pardon was accordingly prepared for her, ready to pass the seal when it should be sent for by the judges.

SUPREME COURT
Thursday, May 21.

Present the second and third justices.

The court opened and adjourned till to-morrow morning, 10 o'clock.

Present, the second justice. Court opened, and adjourned until 4 o'clock in the afternoon, P.M.

Present, as before. Court opened and adjourned until to-morrow morning, ten o'clock.

The grand jury having been informed that Sawney, Niblet's negro boy, was brought to town and committed upon suspicion of being a confederate in the conspiracy, they requested the court that he might be brought before them; which being accordingly done; upon interrogation Sawney denied he knew any thing of the fires, or any conspiracy concerning them. The grand jury for a long time argued with him, to persuade him to speak the truth; being convinced from the evidence of Mrs. Carpenter's negro, (y) who already had been examined by them, that he could give some account of the fires. They told him if he would speak the truth, the governor would pardon him, though he had been concerned in them; and this was the time for him to save his life by making a free and ingenuous confession; or in words to this purpose. He answered, that the time before (z) after that the negroes told all they knew, then the white people hanged them. The grand jury assured him, that it was false; for that the negroes which confessed the truth and made a discovery, were certainly pardoned, and shipped off: (which was the truth)—and upon this assurance he began to open, and gave the following evidences.

Examination of Sawney (Niblet's negro) before the grand jury, No. 1.—He said,

1. "That about three weeks before the fire at the fort, Quack (Mr. Roosevelt's negro) asked him to assist him to set the fort on fire; and that he answered no, he would not run the risk of being hanged; but that he might go to hell and be d——d.

(y) A young negro man not accused of the conspiracy.
(z) Hinting at the conspiracy in 1712, before noted on Peggy's examination and confession, No. 1, 9th May.

2. "That he heard the said Quack and Mr. Philipse's Cuffee say, they would set fire to Mr. Philipse's storehouse.

3. "That Cuffee said, d——n him, that hang him or burn him, he would set fire to the town.

4. "That William (capt. Lush's Spanish negro) told him, that if they did not send him over to his own country, he would ruin the city.

5. "That Curacoa Dick said, he would set fire to Mr. Van Zant's storehouse; and that he was to be a captain.

6. "That Juan (capt. Sarly's negro) said, he would set fire or help to set fire to Hilton's house; and was to be captain of the Fly company.

7. "That Francis (capt. Bosch's negro) threw fire into Mr. Bancker's yard, and told him so.

8. "That Anthony (Mr. Peter Delancey's negro Spaniard) said, he would burn his master's house.

9. "That Augustine (McMullen's Spanish negro) said, he would burn his master's house; and was to have been an officer.

10. "That Jack and an old man (a) (Gerardus Comfort's) said, they would set fire to their master's house, and assist in their designs.

11. "That Cuffee (Gomez's) said, he would burn his master's house; and was to have been an officer in the Fly company; said so to a country fellow, and he heard him.

12. "That just by Coentics-market he heard Patrick (English's negro) and Cato (col. Moore's) say, they would set fire to their master's houses.

13. "That Fortune (Wilkins') was to set fire to his master's house.

14. "Sawney being asked what the negroes proposed by rising and doing all this mischief? He answered, "that their design was to kill all the gentlemen, and take their wives;" and that Quack (b) and Cuffee (Philipse's) were particular persons that talked so.

(a) Cook.
(b) Roosevelt's.

[81]

15. "That while he was in jail, Francis (capt. Bosch's) said, he would kill him if he told any thing; and that when Mr. Mills came for him, (c) several negroes winked as he came out.

16. "Being asked if Quack (Mr. Walter's negro) was knowing or concerned in the affair: he answered, no, though he was always cursing the white people.

17. "Being asked if he had much acquaintance with Danby, the governor's negro, and if he knew any thing? he answered, he had very little; and he believed not.

18. "That Caesar (Vaarck's) that was hanged, was concerned and was to have been captain of the Long Bridge company. (d)

19. "That about a fortnight before the fire at the fort, at Comfort's house, he overheard Jack and the old man (Cook) in company with four other negroes he did not know, talk about the rising of the negroes; and Jack said, that there was not enough of them, and he would stay longer, or to that purpose."

(c) To bring him down to be examined.

(d) It seems that the conspirators had divided the city, as it were, into two districts, and the confederates in each were distinguished by the denominations of the *Fly Boys*, and the *Long Bridge Boys*; being remarkable places, the one towards the east, and the other towards the west end of the town. This may be drawn from Cuffee's confession to Arthur Price, set forth in this deposition, 12th May, No. 3, section 6. And in these districts, it should seem, were several companies; for several of the officers were appointed captains, and others, as appears not only by this, but several other examinations, as well as depositions; and this seems to strengthen the evidence given by Peggy in her examinations, that the conspirators held their cabals at Romme's as well as Hughson's; the former being more convenient for the *Long Bridge Boys*, as Hughson's for the *Smith's Fly Boys*, for the mustering the companies, with regard to the respective distances from their homes. And if Peggy told the truth as to Romme, these were the two lodges in the two districts (as may be concluded from the course of the evidence) where the conspirators met; though the ringleaders, or heads of the negroes, such as Caesar (Vaarck's) Prince (Auboyneau's) and Cuffee (Philipse's) might resort to both places, for transacting those deeds of darkness and inhumanity, in combination with the most flagitious, degenerated, and abandoned, and scum and dregs of the white people, and others of the worse hearts, if possible, because of abler heads, who entitled themselves to be ten times more the children of *Belial*, than the negroes themselves.

[82]

Fortune (Wilkins's negro) was apprehended, examined and committed.

The Examination of Fortune, the negro of John Wilkins, before the grand jury, No. 1.—He said,

1. "That Quack, the negro of John Roosevelt, about a week or ten days before the fort was burnt, desired him the examinant, to take a walk with him (being Sunday afternoon) and that he went with him into the common; where Quack left him a little while, and went down into the swamp, near the powder-house, where he gathered something, and soon returned to him again.

2. "That when Quack came back, the examinant asked him what he had got? To which Quack replied, he would not tell him; but asked him the examinant to go with him to the fort, and he would give him some punch, and see his wife; that accordingly they went to the fort, though the examinant says, that he did not go very willingly.

3. "That when they came to the fort, Quack carried him into the kitchen, where he kept him till it began to grow dark, and then the examinant told Quack, that he must be going, for that the watch would take him up; to which Quack answered, that there was no danger of that.

4. "That Quack gave him no punch, but asked him to drink a dram, which the examinant refused; and so they both came from the fort, keeping company till they came by the house of captain Pearse, where they parted; the examinant returning through Beaver-street, and Quack (as the examinant believed) went back to the fort.

5. "That what is above recited was all that passed between them at their first meeting, on Sunday afternoon; but that two or three days after, Quack met him at the pump near the great slip, but nothing was said or passed between them remarkable.

6. "That about three days after that he met with Quack again, near the house of Mrs. Carpenter, at which place he (Quack) asked him why he was in such haste when he was

last at the fort? to which the examinant answered as before, that he was afraid of the watch; to which Quack replied again, that there was no fear of that, and invited him to come and see him again at the fort, but the examinant refused, saying that he had promised him punch before and gave him none.

7. "That about two days before the fort was burnt, he met with Quack again, near the house of Mrs. Rickets, where he told the examinant, that in a few days there would be great alterations in the fort; on which the examinant asked him what alterations? to which Quack answered, that the fort would be burnt: the examinant on that asked him who would do it? Quack replied, you may ask Niblet's negro, and he will tell you. That he did ask Niblet's negro who was to burn the fort? to which he answered, Quack, himself, and Cuffee (Gomez's) they would do it.

8. "That next day after the fire, the examinant met Sandy (Niblet's) who said to him, we have done the business; and the same day he met Quack, who likewise said to him, the business is done; that when Quack told him that the business was done, he asked him what business? to which Quack answered, the fort is burnt; do you not remember that I told you, there would be a great alteration in the fort? and that he told him at the same time, that he (Quack) Niblet's Sandy, and Gomez's Cuffee had done it.

9. "Being further interrogated whether he knew of any other negroes concerned in burning the fort, besides those above named? he answered, that he knew not of any but Sandy, Quack and Cuffee.

10. "Being further asked, if he knew any person concerned in setting fire to any of the houses in the town? he answered, No."

Jamaica (Ellis's negro, a fiddler) apprehended and committed.

SUPREME COURT
Saturday, May 23.

Present, the second justice.

The court opened and adjourned till Monday morning, 10 o'clock.

Examination, of Fortune (Wilkins's) before the grand jury— No. 2.

Memorandum.—The examination foregoing was read over distinctly to the negro Fortune who acknowledged it to be agreeable to the evidence which he gave yesterday.

1. The examination being continued, the examinant was asked (since he had time to recollect) whether he did not remember some others concerned in the late fires, besides Quack, Sandy, and Cuffee? (e) If he did, it was expected he should name them, without any regard to persons, be they white men or negroes; he answered in the negative; only that Sandy told him a day or two before his master sent him to prison, that his master was going to send him to Albany; on which the examinant asked him for what? to which Sandy replied, I set fire to the house three times, but my master discovered and extinguished it, and therefore is resolved to send me away.

2. "That on Sunday, the day before the storehouse of Mr. Philipse was set on fire in New-street, being sent towards the evening by his master, on an errand to their apprentice boy, who lived in the Broadway, he went by way of New-street, where he saw Cuffee (Mr. Philipse's negro man) and spoke with him, who said that he was going to one of his master's storehouses, on which they parted; and he went to the Broadway, and tarried there till it was duskish: that he returned the same way, and as he came by the house of captain Phoenix, at the corner of New-street, he saw Cuffee, and two negroes more at some small distance from him, but being dark, who they were knew not.

(e) Gomez's.

[85]

3. "That he spoke with Cuffee, and asked him what he did there so late? to which Cuffee made answer, that he waited there for his master, who wanted something out of the storehouse, and that he was to come and bring the key with him, on which they parted: but he believes one of the two negroes was a Spaniard, because when he left Cuffee, he heard one of them call to him, *venez a qui seignior.*

4. "The question being asked the examinant, whether he was acquainted with Hughson and his family? he answered, that he had been frequently asked by Caesar, Prince, and Cuffee (Philipse's) to go there, but never did go, but was told that they had a dance there every other night.

5. "Being asked if he ever went to Romme's house, or knew what negroes frequently resorted thither? he answered, that he never went there himself, nor was he acquainted with those that did."

Sunday, May 24.

This evening Will, or Gill (Lush's) and Cuffee (Gomez's) negroes were committed.

SUPREME COURT
Monday, May 25.

Present, the second and third justices.

Court opened and adjourned till to-morrow morning, ten o'clock.

Examination of Sawney, or Sandy, before the grand jury—No. 2.—He said,

1. "That going by Comfort's one Sunday evening, about a month before the fort was set on fire, Jack called him in, where were about twenty negroes, of which he only knew the said Jack and the old man (Comfort's negroes), Fortune (Vanderspiegle's), Caesar (Peck's), Cato (Cowley's),

Sarah (Burk's negro wench) and the only negro woman there.

2. "That upon his coming into the room, they gave him drink, and then asked him to burn houses; and he not giving a ready answer, Sarah swore at him, and the negroes did also; and with knives in their hands, that they frightened him, and he was afraid they would kill him; and upon it, he promised he would, and would burn the Slip-Market, and soon after he went home.

3. "That he saw in his master's yard, Mr. Machado's negro wench called Diana, put fire in the shingles of Mr. Machado's house; and on his telling of it, and saying that it might be laid on him, she gave him four shillings to hold his tongue.

4. "That Sarah and Fortune (Vanderspiegle's) were to have set fire to the meal market.

5. "That at their meeting at Comfort's house, they swore to be true to one another, on the oath, *that God Almighty would strike them dead with the first thunder.*

6. "That being asked, if he used Hughson's and Romme's houses with the other negroes, he said, "he never was at either of their houses." And who told him of what he had related? he answered, "that Jack did, and of the Spanish negroes who were concerned." Also, that if he did assist in setting the fort on fire? he answered, "no; only before it, Quack did ask him to help him, and he gave the answer before mentioned, and that then Quack said he would do it.

7. "That Diana (Mr. Machado's negro) in a passion, because her mistress was angry with her, *took her own young child from her breast, and laid it in the cold, that it froze to death.*"

Caesar (Peck's), Cato (Cowley's), Sarah (Burk's), Fortune (Vanderspiegle's) committed.

Examination of Sarah, (Mrs. Burk's negro wench) before the grand jury—No. 1.—After abundance of questions upon Sawney's evidence, she said, "she knew nothing of the matter; evaded about her being at Comfort's house;" but on confronting Sawney with her, and Peck's Caesar, she at last said, "that Sawney had, at the pump in the neighbourhood, said, supposing his master had been angry with him, G——d d——n all the white people; that if he had it in his power, he would set them all on fire."

SUPREME COURT
Tuesday, May 26.

Present, the second and third justices.

The king against (Roosevelt's) Quack, and (Philipse's) Cuffee.

These negroes were arraigned upon two indictments, for a conspiracy to burn the town, and murder the inhabitants; and for two actual burnings, the house in the fort, and Mr. Philipse's storehouse; whereto they pleaded *not guilty*.

Ordered, their trials be on to-morrow morning ten o'clock.

Court adjourned till to-morrow morning ten o'clock.

SUPREME COURT
Friday, May 29.

Present, the second and third justices.

The king against (Roosevelt's) Quack, and (Philipse's) Cuffee, negroes, on trial upon two indictments.

The prisoners brought to the bar. Jury called and sworn, viz., Samuel Weaver, John Shurmer, John Lashier, Charles Arding, George Witts, Thomas Bohenna, Daniel Bonett, John Robins. (f)

The negro Quack having been indicted for wickedly, voluntarily, feloniously and maliciously conspiring, combining and confederating with Cuffee and with divers other negroes, to kill and

(f) The panel being mislaid, no more of the jurors could be recollected.

[88]

murder the inhabitants of this city; and also for setting on fire, burning and consuming the house of our sovereign lord the king, then standing at the fort in this city; contrary to the form of an act of assembly (g) in such case made and provided, and against the king's peace.

The negro Cuffee had been also indicted for wickedly, etc. conspiring, etc. with Quack and divers other negroes, to kill and murder the inhabitants of this city; and also for setting on fire and burning an out-house belonging to Frederick Philipse, esq. then standing and being in this city; contrary to the form of the act of assembly, and against the king's peace.

To which indictments each of these criminals, upon their arraignment, pleaded *not guilty*.

The Attorney General having opened the indictments, spoke to the court and jury as followeth:

May it please your honours, and you, gentlemen of the jury,
This is a cause of very great expectation, it being, as I conceive, a matter of the utmost importance that ever yet came to be tried in this province; wherefore, before I call the witnesses to prove these two negroes guilty, I shall briefly mention to you something concerning this mystery

---

(g) By an act of assembly of this province, passed in the fourth year of his present majesty's reign, entitled, "An act for the more effectual preventing and punishing the conspiracy and insurrection of negroes and other slaves; for the better regulating them, and for repealing the acts therein mentioned relating thereto"—it is enacted, (*inter alia*) That all and every negro, Indian, or other slave, or slaves, who, after the publication of this act, shall murder or otherwise kill (unless by misadventure or in the execution of justice) or conspire or attempt the death of any of his majesty's liege people, NOT BEING SLAVES; or shall wilfully burn any dwelling house, barn, stable, out-house, stacks of corn or hay; and shall thereof be convicted before three or more of his majesty's justices of the peace for the county where such fact shall be committed, one whereof to be of the quorum, who are thereby authorized to hear and determine the same, in conjunction with five of the principal freeholders of the county, without a grand jury, seven of whom agreeing, shall put their judgment in execution according to this act; or before any court of oyer and terminer or general jail delivery; he, she or they, so offending, shall suffer the pains of death, in such manner and with such circumstances as the aggravation or enormity of their crimes, in the judgment of the justices of those courts aforesaid, or as in the judgment of seven of the said justices and freeholders shall merit and require.

of iniquity in general, how and where it was formed and carried on, and what share these two criminals had in it.

Gentlemen,

Not only these two negroes, but divers others, and several white people, as will appear to you in the course of our evidence, have been concerned with these wretched offenders, in this most wicked and devilish conspiracy.

Gentlemen,

You will hear from the mouths of our witnesses, that these two negroes, with divers others, frequently met at the house of one John Hughson, in this city. It was there they were harboured—there was the place of their general rendezvous—and there it was this hellish conspiracy was brooded, formed, consented, and agreed to. It was there that these two negroes and the rest of the conspirators came to a resolution of burning the king's house at the fort, and this whole town, and of murdering the inhabitants as they should come to extinguish the flames. Crimes, gentlemen, so astonishingly cruel and detestable, that one would think they never could have entered into the minds, much less the resolution of any but a conclave of devils to execute; and yet such monsters in iniquity are these two criminals and the rest of their confederates.

Gentlemen,

It will likewise appear to you, by Quack's own confession, (as we shall in the course of our evidence for the king upon this trial show you) that in prosecution of such their most abominable conspiracies, the king's house was by him (at the instigation of the rest of the conspirators) set on fire, burnt down, and consumed.

And then as to Cuffee, we shall show you that he is doubtless guilty of the charge against him.

Gentlemen,

The eyes of the inhabitants of this city and province are upon you, relying on and confiding in you, that by the justice of your verdict in this cause this day, the peace and safety of this city and province may for the future be secured to them; which at present (until some examples are made) seem very precarious.

Gentlemen,

It is in you, the people in general place their hopes and expectations of their future security and repose; that they may sit securely in their own houses, and rest quietly in their beds, no one daring to make them afraid.

I shall now proceed to examine the witnesses for the king, to support the charge against each of these criminals; and can make no doubt, gentlemen, but when you have heard the evidence against them, you will for your own sakes, your oaths sake, and for the peace, quiet and security of your country, find these two negroes.

Mr. Murray and Mr. Smith, of council also for the king.

Witnesses for the king, called and sworn, Mary Burton, Sarah Higgins, Jacobus Stoutenburgh, Arthur Price, John Peterson, Daniel Gautier, Isaac Gardner, Mr. Hilliard, James McDonald.

Negro evidence, Fortune (Wilkins's), Sandy (Niblet's.)

Evidence against Cuffee.—Mary Burton said,

"That Cuffee, with Caesar and Prince, the two negroes hanged, used frequently to meet at her master's (Hughson's) house, and that she heard them often talk of burning the fort, and that they would go down to the fly and burn the whole town; and that her master and mistress said they would aid and assist them as much as they could.

"That in their common conversation they used to say, that when all this was done, Caesar should be governor, and Hughson (her master) king.

"That Cuffee used to say, that a great many people had too much, and others too little; that his old master had a great deal of money, but that in a short time, his master would have less and himself have more.

"That at the meetings of the said three negroes, Cuffee, Caesar and Prince, at her master's house, they used to say in their conversations, that when they set fire to the town,

[91]

they would do it in the night; and as the white people came to extinguish it, they would kill and destroy them.

"That she has known at times, seven or eight guns in her master's house, and some swords; and has seen twenty or thirty negroes at one time there; and that at such large meetings the three aforesaid negroes Cuffee, Caesar and Prince, were generally present and most active; and used to say, that the other negroes durst not refuse to do what they commanded them; and that they were sure they had a number sufficient to stand by them: that the negroes swore, that if ever she published or discovered their design of burning the town, they would burn her whenever they met her."

Court. Did the prisoner Cuffee ever threaten you so?
M. Burton. Yes, he, Caesar and Prince, and the rest.

"That about three weeks after she came to Hughson's, which was about midsummer last, the negroes were there talking of the plot and some of them said perhaps she would tell; and Cuffee said no, she would not, he intended to have her for a wife; and then run up to her; and she had a dishclout in her hand, which she dabbed in his face, and he ran away.

"That at a meeting of the negroes at Hughson's house, Hughson said they were all sworn, negroes and white people present, as she understood; that is, Hughson, his wife, daughter Sarah, and Peggy, and that the purport of the oath was, that they were not to discover the secrets about firing the fort, the houses at the Fly, and the whole town, and about murdering the white people; and Hughson said to the negroes present, which were Cuffee, Caesar and Prince, now you must take care, for you are all sworn; and at the same time the witness saw a bible, as she took it to be, in Hughson's hand, and when the witness came into the room he laid it upon the table; and then Caesar spoke to the witness and cautioned her not to tell, and Hughson made answer that she dared not; and Cuffee said, d——n his bl——d, if he would tell of any, if he was burnt; and so said the other two negroes, and so said Hughson, his wife, daughter Sarah, and Peggy."

Arthur Price said,

"That soon after Cuffee, the prisoner at the bar, came to jail, he had some discourse with him over a bowl or tankard of punch, being confined in the same room together, and that, amongst other things, Cuffee said, that he was one of the Geneva Club (h) that was sworn, but being overcome with sleep, he did not go to their meeting at that time: that Cuffee asked the witness, what could be the reason that Peggy was called down so often? The witness answered, he knew; for that he that had done that was sworn after she was in prison; that he left his master's house in the evening, and went along the wharves to the Fly-Market, and waited there till one Quack came out of his master's house; they two went then to John Hughson's, where they met nobody but John Hughson, his wife, and daughter Sarah; that they called for a tankard of punch; that Hughson swore Quack three times; that they only drank out their punch, and then went down to the Fly. That the witness thereupon said to Cuffee, that he believed he knew that Quack, and that he lived with a butcher; Cuffee replied, no; he doth not live with a butcher, but he lives with a painter, who lives within a few doors of a butcher; which painter's name he understood to be Roosevelt, to the best of the witnesses remembrance.

"That Cuffee told him, that Quack was married to the negro wench who is cook to the fort (to the governor) as the witness understood him.

"That Cuffee said, they were all (the negroes as he understood him) to meet at Hughson's the Sunday after Quack was sworn, but some came and some did not.

"That the witness asked Cuffee how Quack did do it?

(h) See note upon Arthur Price's deposition, No. 3, after letter (q) Tuesday, May 12.

[93]

(meaning the setting fire to the fort) that Cuffee answered he could not tell how he did it, but that Quack was to do it, and did do it.

"That Cuff said they were to meet and have a Club at Hughson's in the Easter hollidays, but that the d——d constables hindered them.

"That the witness asked Cuffee, whether he was not afraid that the two negroes who were to be executed next Monday, would discover the fires about the fort and town? Cuffee answered, he was not afraid of that, for that he was sure they would be burnt to ashes before they would discover it, he would lay his life on it.

"That afterwards, upon further discourse with Cuffee, he said he wondered why they only took up the Long Bridge Boys, and not those of the Smith's Fly, for he said he believed, if the truth was known, the Smith's Fly negroes were as much concerned as the others.

"That Cuffee said to the witness, he knew he was to suffer death, and wondered why they did not bring him to his trial, for he was sure he was to go the way the other two went; meaning (as he understood him) the negroes Caesar and Prince, hanged.

"That after Quack, the other prisoner at the bar, was committed, Cuffee never mentioned any thing concerning the former discourse to the witness, but read sometimes, and cried very much."

Sarah Higgins said,

"That on Sunday afternoon, the day before col. Philipse's storehouse was set on fire, she saw four negroes lurking about the Garden behind that storehouse, but she knew but one of them, and him only by sight, which was Cuffee, the prisoner at the bar.

"That in the dusk of the evening, she saw four negroes in the same garden again, and they seemed to keep mostly about Kip's brewhouse, which was on the side of the garden opposite to the said storehouse, they shuffled about as though they would hide themselves; she distinguished Cuffee to be one (i) that he had on a blue coat; she imagined they were upon some ill design, and therefore got capt. Phoenix's sons to go along with her with small arms (swords she meant) and they went in with her, and searched Kip's brewhouse for the said negroes, but did not find them.

"The said Cuffee had come several times to the house where she used to live, but she did not know before then, who he belonged to."

John Peterson said,

"That when col. Philipse's storehouse was on fire, he went to assist there, and coming up to it he met Cuffee (Philipse's) coming out of the door of the storehouse, and he asked Cuff, what he did there: Cuff swore a great oath, and said the people were looking for negroes. That the witness had a bucket of water in his hand, and gave it to Cuff, and bid him hand it; and he took the bucket from the witness: that Cuff had a blue coat on lined or faced with red, and he knew his voice very well when he answered him. The witness said, he used to work for Cuff's master, and knew the negro very well.

"That after the fire at the storehouse was extinguished, and the people were drawn away from thence by a new cry of fire, Mr. Philipse (Cuff's master) and Mr. Chambers were standing together in the garden near the storehouse, and somebody came up and told Mr. Philipse that they had taken Cuff out of his house, and were carrying him to jail, and that it was he that had set the fire; Mr. Philipse made answer, how can that be, I left him at home at work, making a vane for the boat? that he the witness standing near by and hearing that, said I am sure I saw him here just now at the fire and spoke to him, and he answered me, and I handed him a bucket of water."

(i) See Fortune's examination, Number 2, section 2, 23d May.

[95]

Jacobus Stoudenburgh said,

"That he had known the prisoner (Cuffee) by sight a long time, but did not know who he belonged to.

"That he (the witness) went to assist at the fire at Mr. Philipse's storehouse; and when that fire was extinguished he was at the top of the roof, when there was another alarm of fire, which drew most of the people away from thence; when somebody cried out there were negroes in the storehouse; and there being a great many shingles pulled off the roof, he could see down into them, and he espied out Cuff in the storehouse next to that on fire, and he was letting himself down through the laths in order to catch him, but he was hindered by a nail catching hold of his breeches, or he believed he had taken him; that he saw him leap out of the window at the end of the storehouse, and so made haste away, leaping over several garden fences, and made his escape; that then the witness went back with the fire-engines towards the City-Hall, and he heard the people say they had got the negro; and then he said if it was the same negro he should know him again; and there was a great crowd of people bringing him to jail, and when the witness saw him he knew him to be the same (Cuffee) the prisoner at the bar."

Isaac Gardner said,

"He saw Cuffee the prisoner at the bar, at the fire at the fort, there were rows made of people in the garden, negroes as well as white men, from the water side through the sally port, in order to hand water along to the fire, and the witness observed that when the buckets came to Cuffee, instead of handing them along to the next man, he put them upon the ground and overset them, by which means the ground which was at first dry and hard, became so wet that the witness who stood next him, was almost up to the ankles in mud, and that the witness then observed Cuff when the flames of the house blazed up very high, he huzza'd, danced, whistled and sung, and that the witness said to

[96]

him, you black dog, is this a time for you to dance and make game upon such a sad accident; and he only laughed and whispered to Albany (Mrs. Carpenter's negro) who stood next him on the other side: whereupon the witness seeing col. Moore, he said to him he wished he would speak to those negroes, who only laughed and made game whenever he forbid them oversetting the water, and that col. Moore did speak to them, but after his back was turned, they went on again in the same manner, and so continued until they broke up from the fire."

Evidence affecting both prisoners.—Daniel Gautier, carpenter said,

"That he was one of the first who went up to the fort upon the alarm of the fire. When he came up towards it, he observed that a great part of the outside of the roof was covered with smoke, but none for a considerable distance from the end next the chapel; when he came upon the ramparts next the chapel, he was asking how it came, and was told it was occasioned by the Plumber's carrying his fire-pot into the gutter, which he was mending between the house and the chapel (as it was a leaden gutter which the plumber had been soddering to stop a leak) and some sparks of the fire had blown out of the pot and catched the shingles; whereupon the witness seing a ladder set up against the gutter, he went up, and looking in at the dormant window at the end of the house towards the chapel, he saw the inside of the garret roof in a blaze, but there was no fire within, he believes, twenty foot of the end he looked in at; wherefore he was then of opinion it could not have been occasioned by the plumber's working there; for when the fire broke out at the top of the roof, it was, as he thought, twenty foot from the end next the gutter, and he observed the fire broke out in several places further; and the witness said, that upon his first view of it, he gave the house over for lost."

Hilliard, the plumber, said,

"That he thought the fire could not have been occasioned by his working there, for that he was very careful of the fire he carried up, and he had a soldier to attend him; that his fire-pot was set on a board which laid over the gutter from the chapel to the house, but was much lower than the dormant window; that he did not think that any sparks of fire did fly out of the fire-pot; for it was an inclosed pot like a dark lanthron, with an opening only before to put his soddering iron in, and that he was careful to put the back of it towards the wind; that the fire was on the other side of the roof, not near where he was at work."

Mr. Murray observed, that by an act of assembly of this province, as in all other of his majesty's colonies where there are negroes, the negro evidence is good against each other; and he read the particular clauses in the act to this purpose, and further remarked upon the reasonableness and necessity of this law.

(The title of it is mentioned in the note upon the abstract of the first indictment in this trial.)

Negro evidence affecting Cuffee.—Fortune (Wilkins' negro) said,

"That on Sunday, the day before col. Philipse's storehouse in New-street was set on fire, being sent by his master, towards evening on an errand to their apprentice boy, who lived in the Broadway, he went by the way of New-street, where he saw Cuffee and spoke with him, and that he said he was going to one of his master's storehouses, on which they parted, and the witness went to the Broadway, and tarried there till it was darkish; that he returned the same way, and as he came by the house of Captain Phoenix, at the corner of New-street, he saw Cuffee again, and two negroes more at some small distance from him, but who they were knew not: that he spoke with Cuffee, and asked him what he did there so late? he answered, he waited there for his master, who wanted something out of the storehouse, and that he was to come and bring the key with him, on which they parted again, but the witness believed one of the other

[98]

two negroes was a Spaniard, because when he left Cuffee, he heard one of them call him, *venez a qui seignior.*

The witness said, "That he had been often asked by Caesar (Vaarck's) Prince (Auboyneau's) and Cuffee, the prisoner, to go with them to Hughson's, but that he never did, but was told they had a dance there every other night."

Negro evidence affecting Quack and Cuffee.—Sandy said,

"That he heard Quack and Cuffee say, they would set fire to Mr. Philipse's storehouse.

"That Cuffee said, d——n him, that hang him or burn him, he would set fire to the town."

Evidence affecting Quack only.—Mary Burton said,

"That she had often seen Quack at Hughson's door, along with Cuffee (Philipse's) Caesar (Vaarck's) and Prince (Auboyneau's) but never saw him within the house."

Negro evidence against Quack.—Fortune, (Wilkin's) said,

"that Quack, about a week or ten days before the fort was burnt, (being on a Sunday afternoon) desired the witness to take a walk with him, and that he went with him into the common, where Quack left him a little while, and went down into the swamp, near the powder-house, where he gathered something, and returned to him again.

"That when he came back, the witness asked him what he had got? He answered, he would not tell him; but then asked the witness to go down with him to the fort, and said he would give him some punch; that accordingly the witness went with him to the fort, though he did not go very willingly.

"That when they came to the fort, Quack carried him into the kitchen, where he kept him till it began to grow dark, and then the witness told him he must be going, for that the watch would take him up; Quack answered, there was no danger of that.

"That Quack gave him no punch at the fort, but asked him to drink a dram, which he refused; and so both came away from thence together, keeping company till they came to captain Pearse's house, where they parted; the witness returning home, and Quack, as the witness believed, went back to the fort.

"This was all that passed between the witness and Quack at their first meeting, on Sunday afternoon.

"That about three days after that, the witness met Quack again, near Mrs. Carpenter's, where Quack asked the witness, why he was in such haste when he was last at the fort? To which the witness answered, that he was afraid of the watch. Quack replied, there was no fear of that, and invited him to come and see him again at the fort, but the witness refused, saying that he had promised him punch before and gave him none.

"That about two days before the fort was burnt, he met Quack again, near Mrs. Rickets's, where he told the witness, that in a few days there would be great alterations in the fort. The witness asked him what alterations? to which Quack replied, that the fort would be burnt: the witness asked him, who would do it? Quack replied, you may ask Niblet's negro, and he will tell you. That the witness did ask Niblet's negro who was to burn the fort? To which he answered, Quack, himself (Sandy), and Gomez's Cuffee, they would do it.

"That the next day after the fire at the fort, the witness met Sandy (Niblet's negro) who said to him, we have done the business; and the same day the witness met Quack, who likewise said to him, the business is done; thereupon the witness asked him what business? to which Quack replied, the fort is burnt; don't you remember that I told you, there would be great alterations in the fort? and Quack told him at the same time, that he himself, Niblet's Sandy, and Gomez's Cuffee, had done it."

Sandy, alias Sawney (Niblet's negro) said, "that about three weeks before the fire at the fort, Quack asked him to set the fort on fire, and he the witness, answered no, he would not run the risk of being hanged; but that he might go to h——ll and be d——d. That then Quack said, he would do it himself."

Against Quack and Cuffee.—Sandy said,

"that they two particularly talked of killing the gentlemen, and taking their wives to themselves; that he heard Quack say, since he came to jail, that he burnt the fort."

Witnesses called at the request of the prisoners.—Jacob Bursen, Peter Jay, Lewis Parent, Gerardus Beekman, Mr. Niblet, captain Rowe, John Roosevelt and his son, Catherine Wells, Adolph Philipse, esq.

Adolph Philipse, esq. (Cuffee's master) said, that all he could declare about him was,

"that the afternoon his nephew's (col. Philipse's) storehouse was on fire, he had left him at home not long before the alarm of the fire at work, sewing a vane upon a board for his boat; that as to his character he could say nothing."

Quack's master (Mr. Roosevelt) and his son, both declared,

"that Quack was employed most part of that morning the fort was fired, from the time they got up, in cutting away the ice out of the yard; that he was hardly ever out of their sight all that morning, but a small time while they were at breakfast; and that they could not think he could that morning have been from their home so far as the fort."

James McDonald being called and sworn for the king, said,

"that the day the fort was fired, he stood sentry at the gate about eleven o'clock in the morning, a little before or after, and that Quack came up to the gate and offered to come in;

[101]

the witness said, he knew that the governor had some time before forbid him coming to the fort, and therefore he scrupled to let him in; Quack answered, that he was free now and had liberty to come, and so he let him pass.

"That not long before that, the witness was posted one night at the same gate, and Quack (the prisoner) came up in order to go to the governor's house, and the witness knew that the governor had before then lately forbid him coming there, and therefore opposed his entrance within the gate; but Quack was resolute, and pushed forward whether he would or no, and said he would go in. The witness then bid him take what followed, and clubbed his firelock, and knocked him down; that then Quack got up again and collared the witness, and cried out murder; and the witness was going to strike him again, and the officer of the guard hearing a bustle, called to the witness, and forbid him striking him any more; and Quack then run in a-doors into the governor's kitchen, and they went and fetched him, and turned him out of the fort."

Captain Rowe and Beekman said,

"Quack was employed last year to work at the new battery, and that he minded his business very well."

The other witnesses called at the request of the prisoners, said nothing more material.

The Prisoners being asked what they had to offer in their defence, they offered nothing but peremptory denials of what had been testified against them, and protestations of their innocency.

Mr. Smith then proceeded to sum up and remark upon the evidence, and spoke as followeth:

May it please your honours, and you, gentlemen of the jury,
  The part assigned to me on this trial, is to sum up the evidence which you have heard; and in general it may be ob-

served, that a most horrid conspiracy has been formed, to burn this city, and to destroy the white people.

That great numbers of persons have been concerned in the plot; some whites, and many blacks. That the place of their general rendezvous was the house of John Hughson. That there thirty negroes have met at a time. That their meetings were chiefly on Sundays. That Hughson, as the captain of this hellish band, swore himself and others into this dark confederacy. That some arms and ammunition were provided by Hughson for the purpose; and that the night season was agreed on for the putting it in execution.

Gentlemen, no scheme more monstrous could have been invented; nor can any thing be thought of more foolish, than the motives that induced these wretches to enter into it! What more ridiculous than that Hughson, in consequence of this scheme, should become a *King!* Caesar, now in gibbets, a *Governor!* That the white men should be all killed, and the women become a prey to the rapacious lust of these villains! That these slaves should thereby establish themselves in peace and freedom in the plundered wealth of their slaughtered masters! It is hard to say whether the wickedness or the folly of this design is the greater; and had it not been in part executed before it was discovered, we should with great difficulty have been persuaded to believe it possible, that such a wicked and foolish plot could be contrived by any creatures in human shape.

Yet, gentlemen, incredible as such a plot would have seemed to have been, the event has in part proved it to be real. Whence else could so many fires have been lighted up all around you in so short a time, with evident marks of wilful design? A design that could not be executed but by several hands.

Now gentlemen, the prisoners at the bar stand charged with being principal parties in this tragical design, and two of the prime incendiaries: Quack for burning his majesty's house in the fort, and Cuffee for burning col. Philipse's storehouse.

Afterwards Mr. Smith proceeded to observe on the several parts of the evidence against each of the prisoners, particularly to shew, that Cuffee was one of the first of the negroes that were sworn into the plot to burn and murder; that he appeared one of the most forward and active in promoting it; that Mr. Philipse's storehouse, by divers circumstances, appeared to have been wilfully set on fire; that the prisoner declared that he would burn that storehouse; that he was seen there before the fire broke out, in a suspicious appearance, and was present at the time of it; and at the cry of some persons that negroes were in the storehouse, the prisoner jumped out of a window, leaped over two fences, and ran away, etc. that he seemed exceedingly well pleased with the fire at the fort; overset the buckets that were filled with water, and did what he could to prevent the extinguishing of that fire, etc. and then inferred, from the facts proved, and circumstances attending them, that there appeared violent presumption of guilt, which the law esteems full proof.

As to Quack, he observed, that the witnesses proved that Quack was sworn into the conspiracy, and particularly that he had agreed to burn the fort; that he repeatedly said he would do it; that the fire where it broke out could not easily be accounted for from any accidental cause; that the prisoner had confessed the crime both before he was apprehended and since he had been in jail; all which amount to full proof.

The particular remarks on the testimony of the witnesses to the several points before mentioned, are here omitted for the sake of brevity, and because the substance of the evidence is before related. Then concluded,

Thus, gentlemen, I have distinguished the several points of the evidence against the prisoners, and have repeated the substance of what each witness has said to each point, and shall leave it to you to determine whether the prisoners are guilty or not. I have endeavoured to lay no more weight upon any part of the evidence, than it will well bear; and I hope I have not urged any consequence which the fact proved will not fairly warrant.

Gentlemen, the prisoners have been indulged with the

[104]

same kind of trial as is due to free men, though they might have been proceeded against in a more summary and less favourable way. The negro evidence, in the manner in which it has been produced is warranted by the act of assembly that has been read to you; the law requires no oath to be administered to them, and indeed it would seem to be a profanation of it, to administer it to a Heathen in the legal form. You have seen that the court has put them under the most solemn caution, that their small knowledge of religion can render them capable of. The being and perfections of an Almighty, all knowing, and just God, and the terrors of an eternal world, have been plainly laid before them, and strongly pressed upon them. Unless they were professed Christians, and had taken upon them the bonds and obligations of that religion, their word, with the cautions that have been used, I suppose will be thought by you, as satisfactory as any oath that could have been devised. But, gentlemen, the court has no power to administer an oath, but in the common form, and if Pagan negroes could not be received as witnesses against each other, without an oath in legal form, it is easy to perceive that the greatest villanies would often pass with impunity.

Before I conclude, I cannot help observing to you, gentlemen, that by divers parts of the evidence, it appears that this horrid scene of iniquity has been chiefly contrived and promoted at meetings of negroes in great numbers on Sundays. This instructive circumstance may teach us many lessons, both of reproof and caution, which I only hint at, and shall leave the deduction of the particulars to every one's reflection.

Gentlemen, the monstrous ingratitude of this black tribe, is what exceedingly aggravates their guilt. Their slavery among us is generally softened with great indulgence; they live without care, and are commonly better fed and clothed, and put to less labour, than the poor of most Christian countries. They are indeed slaves, but under the protection of the law, none can hurt them with impunity: they are really more happy in this place, than in the midst of the

[105]

continual plunder, cruelty, and rapine of their native countries; but notwithstanding all the kindness and tenderness with which they have been treated amongst us, yet this is the second attempt of the same kind, that this brutish and bloody species of mankind have made within one age. (k) That justice that was provoked by former fires, and the innocent blood that was spilt in your streets, should have been a perpetual terror to the negroes that survived the vengeance of that day, and should have been a warning to all that had come after them. But I fear, gentlemen, that we shall never be quite safe, till that wicked race are under more restraint, or their number greatly reduced within this city. But I shall not insist further, but refer you, gentlemen, to the direction of the court; and if the evidence against these prisoners proves sufficient in your judgment to convict them, I make no doubt but you will bring in a verdict accordingly, and do what in you lies to rid this country of some of the vilest creatures in it.

Then the jury were charged, and a constable was sworn to attend them as usual; and they withdrew; and being soon returned, found the prisoners guilty of both indictments.

The prisoners were asked, what they had to offer in arrest of judgment, why they should not receive sentence of death? and they offering nothing but repetitions of protestations of their innocence; the third justice proceeded to sentence, as followeth:

Quack and Cuffee, the criminals at the bar,
You both now stand convicted of one of the most horrid and detestable pieces of villainy, that ever satan instilled into the heart of human creatures to put in practice; ye, and the rest of your colour, though you are called slaves in this country; yet are you all far, from the condition of other slaves in other countries; nay, your lot is superior to that of thousands of white people. You are furnished with all the

(k) Alluding to the negro plot in 1712, before noted upon Peggy's examination, No. 1, May 9.

necessaries of life, meat, drink, and clothing, without care, in a much better manner than you could provide for yourselves, were you at liberty; as the miserable condition of many free people here of your complexion might abundantly convince you. What then could prompt you to undertake so vile, so wicked, so monstrous, so execrable and hellish a scheme, as to murder and destroy your own masters and benefactors? nay, to destroy root and branch, all the white people of this place, and to lay the whole town in ashes.

I know not which is the more astonishing, the extreme folly, or wickedness, of so base and shocking a conspiracy; for as to any view of liberty or government you could propose to yourselves, upon the success of burning the city, robbing, butchering, and destroying the inhabitants; what could it be expected to end in, in the account of any rational and considerate person among you, but your own destruction? And as the wickedness of it, you might well have reflected, you that have sense, that there is a God above, who has always a clear view of all your actions, who sees into the utmost recesses of the heart, and knoweth all your thoughts; shall he not, do ye think, for all this bring you into judgment, at that final and great day of account, the day of judgment, when the most secret treachery will be disclosed, and laid open to the view, and every one will be rewarded according to their deeds, and their use of that degree of reason which God-Almighty has entrusted them with.

Ye that were for destroying us without mercy, ye abject wretches, the outcasts of the nations of the earth, are treated here with tenderness and humanity; and, I wish I could not say, with too great indulgence also; for you have grown wanton with excess of liberty, and your idleness has proved your ruin, having given you the opportunities of forming this villainous and detestable conspiracy; a scheme compounded of the blackest and foulest vices, treachery, blood-thirstiness, and ingratitude. But be not deceived, God Almighty only can and will proportion punishments to men's offences; ye that have shewn no mercy here, and have been for destroying all about ye, and involving them in one general massacre and ruin, what hopes can ye have of mercy in the other world? For shall not the judge of all the earth do right? Let me in compassion advise ye then; there are but a few moments between ye and eternity; ye ought therefore seriously to lay to heart these things; earnestly and sorrowfully to bewail your monstrous and crying sins, in this your extremity; and if ye would reasonably entertain any hopes of mercy at the hands of God, ye must shew mercy here yourselves, and make what amends ye can before ye leave us, for the mischief you have already done, by preventing any more being done. Do not flatter yourselves, for the same measure which you give us here, will be measured to you again in the other world; ye must confess your whole guilt, as to the offences of which ye stand convicted, and for which ye will presently receive judgment; ye must discover the whole scene of iniquity which has been contrived in this monstrous confederacy, the chief authors and actors, and all and every the parties concerned, aiding and assisting therein, that by your means a full stop may be put to this horrible and devilish undertaking. And these are the only means left ye to shew mercy; and the only reasonable ground ye can go upon, to entertain any hopes of mercy at the hands of God, before whose judgment seat ye are so soon to appear.

Ye cannot be so stupid, surely, as to imagine, that when ye leave this world, when your souls put off these bodies of clay, ye shall become like the beasts that perish, that your spirits shall only vanish into the soft air and cease to be. No, your souls are immortal, they will live forever, either to be eternally happy, or eternally miserable in the other world, where you are now going.

If ye sincerely and in earnest repent you of your abominable sins, and implore the divine assistance at this critical juncture, in working out the great and momentous article of the salvation of your souls; upon your making all the amends, and giving all the satisfaction which is in each of your powers, by a full and complete discovery of the conspiracy, and of the several persons concerned in it, as I have observed to ye before, then and only upon these conditions can ye reasonably expect mercy at the hands of God Almighty for your poor, wretched and miserable souls.

Here ye must have justice, for the justice of human laws has at length overtaken ye, and we ought to be very thankful, and esteem it a most merciful and wondrous act of Province, that your treacheries and villanies have been discovered; that your plot and contrivances, your hidden works of darkness have been brought to light, and stopped in their career; that in the same net which you have hid so privly for others your own feet are taken: that the same mischief which you have contrived for others, and have in part executed, is at length fallen upon your own pates, whereby the sentence which I am now to pronounce will be justified against ye; which is,

That you and each of you be carried from hence to the place from whence you came, and from thence to the place of execution, where you and each of you shall be chained to a stake, and burnt to death; and the lord have mercy upon your poor, wretched souls.

Ordered, that the execution of the said Quack and Cuffee be on Saturday the 30th of this instant, between the hours of one and seven o'clock in the afternoon of the same day.

The court adjourned till Tuesday the 2d of June next, ten o'clock in the morning.

Saturday, May 30.

This day Quack and Cuffee were executed at the stake according to sentence.

The spectators at this execution were very numerous; about three o'clock the criminals were brought to the stake, surrounded with piles of wood ready for setting fire to, which the people were very impatient to have done, their resentment being raised to the utmost pitch against them, and no wonder. The criminals shewed great terror in their countenances, and looked as if they would gladly have discovered all they knew of this accursed scheme, could they have had any encouragement to hope for a reprieve. But as the case was, they might flatter themselves with hopes: they both seemed inclinable to make some confession; the only difficulty between them at last being, who should speak first. Mr. Moore, the deputy secretary, undertook singly to examine them both, endeavouring to persuade them to confess their guilt, and all they knew of the matter, without effect; till at length Mr. Roosevelt came up to him, and said he would undertake Quack, whilst Mr. Moore examined Cuffee; but before they could proceed to the purpose, each of them was obliged to flatter his respective criminal that his fellow sufferer had begun, which stratagem prevailed: Mr. Roosevelt stuck to Quack altogether, and Mr. Moore took Cuff's confession, and sometimes also minutes of what each said; and afterwards upon drawing up their confessions in form from their minutes, they therefore intermixed what came from each.

Quack's confession at the stake. He said,

1. "That Hughson was the first contriver of the whole plot, and promoter of it; which was to burn the houses of the town; Cuffee said, to kill the people.

2. "That Hughson brought in first Caesar (Vaarck's); then Prince (Auboyneau's); Cuffee (Philipse's); and others, amongst whom were old Kip's negro; Robin (Chambers's); Cuffee (Gomez's); Jack (Codweis's) and another short negro, that cooks for him.

3. "That he Quack did fire the fort, that it was by a lighted stick taken out of the servants hall, about eight o'clock at night, that he went up the back stairs with it and so through Barbara's room, and put it near the gutter, betwixt the shingles, and the roof of the house.

4. "That on a Sunday afternoon, a month before the firing of the fort, over a bowl of punch, the confederates at Hughson's (amongst whom were the confederates above named, Albany, and Tickle, alias Will, Jack and Cook

[110]

(Comfort's); old Butchell (l); Caesar, and Guy (Horsfield's); Tom (Van Rants's); Caesar (Peck's); Worcester, and others) votéd him Quack, as having a wife in the fort, to be the person who should fire the fort (m), Sandy, and Jack (Codweis's); Caesar, and Guy (Horsfield's); were to assist him in it.

5. "That Hughson desired the negroes to bring to his house, what they could get from the fire, and Hughson was to bring down country people in his boat to further the business, and would bring in other negroes.

6. "That forty or fifty to his knowledge were concerned, but their names he could not recollect (the mob pressing and interrupting).

7. "That Cuffee (Gomez's); and Caesar (Peck's), fired Van Zant's storehouse.

8. "That Mary Burton had spoke the truth, and could name many more.

9. "Fortune (Wilkins's), and Sandy, had done the same; and Sandy could name the Spaniards, and say much more, which Cuffee particularly confirmed.

10. "Being asked what view Hughson had in acting in this manner? He answered, to make himself rich.

11. "That after the fire was over, Quack was at Hughson's house, Jack (Comfort's), a leading man, Hughson, wife and daughter present, and said, the job was done, meaning the fire; that he went frequently to Hughson's house, and met there Tickle and Albany.

12. "Quack said his wife was no ways concerned, for he never would trust her with it: and that Denby (n) knew nothing about the matter.

13. "Jamaica (Ellis's) not concerned that he knew of, but was frequently at Hughson's with his fiddle.

(l) It was not discovered who this negro was.
(m) The reader may perceive hereafter, that the whole current of the testimony of the witnesses, white and black, do agree, that there was a great meeting of the negroes at Hughson's, on a Sunday evening, about a month before the fort was burnt.
(n) The governor's negro boy. Quack's wife was the governor's cook.

14. "Said he was not sworn by Hughson, but other were." (o)

McDonald (the witness against Quack upon the trial) at the stake desired Mr. Pinhorne to ask Quack, whether he had wronged him in what he had said of him at court? He answered no; it was true he did pass him at the fort gate, about eleven o'clock that morning.

The witness then went up to him himself, and asked him the same question; and he answered the same as to Mr. Pinhorne, that he had not wronged him, and further, "that he, Quack, thought the fort would have been on fire the night before; for that he had taken a firebrand out of the servants' hall, and carried it up into the garret, on the seventeenth at night, (St. Patrick's) and when he came up the next morning into the garret, he found the brand alight, and blew it, and then went away again." (p)

(o) If this be true, then he was sworn there by somebody else: but Cuff told Arthur Price, as he says, that he (Cuff) went down with Quack to Hughson's and that Hughson swore Quack three times. See Price's deposition, No. 3, section 1, 12th May. Perhaps Cuff said no more than that he saw Quack sworn there three times. From what had been discovered of this villainy at that time, and for some time afterwards, it was the general opinion, that Hughson was the contriver and chief schemist of the conspiracy, and these two negroes, it should seem, knew no better; and from Quack's being carried to Hughson's and sworn three times there. Price might naturally enough conclude he was sworn by Hughson himself and understand Cuffee so. It will scarce be expected a witness should depose precisely the same words which pass in a long discourse, but the substance of them only, according to his own apprehension and remembrance. It was thought that the false, ensnaring, damnable notion (which had, no doubt, with great art and industry, been instilled into these wretches) of the obligation of that infernal oath, which had been so often administered to them by Hughson and other principal conspirators, was the true reason of the backwardness and hesitancy of the others opening first. The hopes and promises of paradise for doing the devil's work, is no new invention of worldly, wicked and blood-thirsty politicians, for involving such as they are pleased to style heretics, in butchery and destruction.

Tantum religio potuit suadere malorum, falsa!

(p) This to some may seem incredible; but those who have experienced hickory or walnut firewood, which has the preference of all other firewood in this country (amongst other reasons for the durableness of the coal) have affirmed, that they have known when a fire has been laid up, and brands-ends

Cuffee's confession at the stake.—He said,

1. "That Hughson was the first contriver of all, and pressed him to it: that he Cuffee was one of the first concerned.

2. "The fire was intended to begin at Comfort's shingles, and so through the town.

3. "Old Kip's negro; Robin (Chambers's); Jack (Comfort's); and Cuffee (Gomez's); were of the conspirators: Albany and Tickle were concerned.

4. "That he was sworn, and Caesar and Prince (q) also by Hughson.

5. "That Cuffee (Gomez's); and Caesar (Peck's); burnt Van Zant's storehouse.

6. "That Sandy set fire to Mr. Machado's house; Niblet's negro wench can tell it, and Becker's Bess (r) knows it.

7. "That he set fire to the storehouse as sworn against him, that when his master went to the Coffee-House, he ran out of the other door, and went the back way into the storehouse, having lighted charcoal in his pocket between two oyster shells, he put the fire between the ropes and the boards, and leaving it on fire, went home.

---

or sticks put by in the chimney corner, that they have mouldered slowly away, and been often found alive twenty-four hours afterwards; which is much longer than this brand lay upon the beam in the garret at the fort; and this was in a place where little or no air came to quicken it, and where it lay, being upon a beam next the shingle roof, it was possible there might have been some leak which had made it damp or wet, which by the brand and the ashes mouldering from it, was at length dried by the time Quack came up there the next morning, about eleven o'clock, which was about eleven hours after the brand was laid there, by Quack's account; and the ashes which in that time had mouldered from the brand, might possibly guard the beam from the fire, till Quack had blown them away, and enlivened the brand, by which means it might afterwards take effect, though it was about an hour and a half after this, that the smoke and smother appeared on the outside of the roof. But however it was, these were declared by the witness McDonald, to be part of Quack's dying words, whatever objections they may be liable to. And Quack, it seems, was the occasion of this mischief.

(q) Vaarck's and Auboyneau's.
(r) This wench not apprehended.

8. "That Hughson's people were to raise a mob to favour the design.

9. "That the evidence that Peterson, did see him (was true); that Fortune did see him the night before. (s)

10. "That Fortune knew and was as deeply concerned as he; and Sandy was concerned, and knew the Spaniards. (t) —And (being asked) did confess there was a design to kill the people, but not told to all. (v) And said,

11. "There was about fifty concerned; (w) and that all were concerned that a constable who stood by (x) had seen (all) at Hughson's house."

After the confessions were minuted down (which were taken in the midst of great noise and confusion) Mr. Moore desired the sheriff to delay the execution until the governor be acquainted therewith, and his pleasure known touching their reprieve; which, could it have been effected, it was thought might have been means of producing great discoveries; but from the disposition observed in the spectators, it was much to be apprehended, there would have been great difficulty, if not danger in an attempt to take the criminals back. All this was represented to his honour; and before Mr. Moore could return from him to the place of execution, he met the sheriff upon the common, who declared his opinion, that the carrying the negroes back would be impracticable; and if that was his honour's order it could not be attempted without a strong guard, which could not be got time enough; and his honour's directions for the reprieve being conditional and discretionary, for these reasons the execution proceeded.

Cuffee, from the course of the evidence, was one of the principal negroes who was first initiated into this detestable en-

(s) See Fortune's evidence on the trial and his examination, No. 2. section 2. Saturday, 23d May. Also, Sarah Higgins's evidence on the trial.

(t) i.e. The Spanish negro conspirators.

(v) So that Cuff was more in the secret than others engaged.

(w) This seems to be a random guess under great confusion, for it is most probable he knew more.

(x) North, the whitsuntide before, he had interrupted a number of negroes feasting at Hughson's, and cudgelled them away.

[114]

terprize; one that Hughson, no doubt, found so thoroughly qualified for this purpose, that he might put more than ordinary confidence in him, and entrust him with a greater share of this infernal secret than others of his colour; but more especially as to the parties of blacks and whites engaged in it. It was notorious Cuff had a great deal of idle time upon his hands, perhaps more than any negro in town, consequently was much at large for making frequent daily or nightly visits at Hughson's, the head lodge, where those deeds of darkness and inhumanity were brooding; and therefore indeed must of course have become personally acquainted with a greater number of the conspirators, than others who had fewer of the like opportunities.

Quack had a master who kept him fully employed, adays at least, and it seems he was a much later convert; (for Cuff, in his discourse with Arthur Price, about the person that set fire to the fort, see Price's deposition again, No. 3, section 1. May 12; for the manner of this secret bolting from Cuff to a fellow-prisoner, as there related, is somewhat remarkable, and may be very apt to induce one's credit.) Price having told Cuff, "that he had heard Peggy had discovered about the fire at the fort, Cuff replied, she could not do that unless she forswore herself, he knew, for he that had done that was sworn" (perhaps he meant into the conspiracy also, but at least he must mean to do that fact) "after Peggy was in prison." And so Cuff goes on and tells the circumstances of his meeting Quack (it should seem according to appointment) and carrying him down to Hughson's, and Hughson's swearing him three times, to make sure of him. This could not have been long before the fort was burnt the 18th, but intended for the 17th at night; and by Cuff's saying, "she could not do that unless she forswore herself he knew," i.e. (Cuff must mean) she could not discover the person who set fire to the fort. Quack must therefore have been engaged in this wicked purpose but a little before he put it in execution, and though Hughson and his advisers might have known long before that Quack was a fit tool for him, and as such made very much of him, because he had pretensions to go to the fort and stay there a night with his wife, and though probably he might have been engaged and sworn into the general design of the conspiracy (which was the artifice, it seems, they constantly practised upon a negro's saying yes, i.e. consenting to their abominable proposals) yet they might not think it so safe to attempt the engaging him for this particular fact, long before the time calculated for the execution of it, for they might apprehend some danger in that; during a long interval there would have been more hazard of his talking of it, and perhaps to his wife, who, if she had any influence over him, and had happened to have a grain of honesty or gratitude towards her master and his family, she possibly might have persuaded him to make a merit of them both, of detecting this informal confederacy, and therefore it seems most probable the Devil and his agents deferred the attempting his resolution upon this grand article, till some short time before the execution of it; if they found Quack of a pliable disposition, they might think if they could, upon a surprize, fix him in the persuasion that such an oath was at all obligatory; by the reiterating of it, they might make the deeper impression upon him, and fix him the more firmly, and that there would be less hazard of his failure in the engagement, the shorter time he had to cool and deliberate upon it.

Both these criminals declare their opinions, that Hughson was the first contriver and promoter of the conspiracy, so far as they knew of the matter; that he was the first promoter as to them they were sure of; he drew Cuff into it several years before, as will appear hereafter. But if the foregoing reflections are right, surely they import a train of policy beyond what could be expected from an illiterate cobler, Hughson!

However, from these confessions, there was another satisfaction beyond these criminals' acknowledgment of their own guilt —that the testimony of Mary Burton, Sandy and Fortune, negroes, witnesses upon the trial (upon the credit whereof chiefly these criminals were convicted) was by them particularly and expressly confirmed in the midst of flames, which is the highest attestation; and by consequence from the whole, Arthur Price's also, who was the first that gave information that Quack was the person who set fire to the fort, and Cuffee told him so.

Upon the confessions of these two criminals, one of the judges issued a warrant for apprehending the negroes on Nassau island by them impeached, belonging to Mr. Codweise, and the Horsfields; and in consequence thereof, and the orders given to the constables in town, the following slaves were committed this evening, viz.

Harry (Kip's), Tickle alias Will, Caesar (Israel Horsfield's), Cambridge (Codweise's), Gusie alias Galick (Tim Horsfield's), Tom (Van Rants's), Worcester (Varian's).

The other negroes, mentioned in the confessions, were in custody before.

Monday, June 1.

Examination of Sandy (Niblet's negro) before one of the judges —No. 3.—He said,

1. "That he heard by captain Lush's house, about six of the Spaniards (about fourteen days before the fort was burnt) say, that if the captain would not send them to their own country, they would ruin all the city; and the first house they would burn should be the captain's, for they did not care what they did: He (Sandy) stood by Arden's door, and they did not (as he thought) see him; and that (pointing to Lush's house) they said, *d——n that son of a b——h, they would make a devil of him*: which was the first time he ever heard of the conspiracy.

2. "That the second time Quack (y) called to him by Coentics Market, and told him he wanted to speak to him; and said, will you help to burn the fort? and answered as he said at the trial, and in his examination before the grand jury; said that Quack told him the first time he met him, he would make an end of him.

3. "That the third time, at Comfort's house, one Sunday, when Comfort's Jack called to him to come to him, and he went in, Sarah (Burk's negro wench) d——d him, and bid him drink, having before refused.

(y) Roosevelt's negro.

[117]

4. "That there was a great number of negroes present, and about six Spanish negroes among them; but none of them were the same that he saw at Lush's. That he did drink.

5. "That Comfort's Jack brought out about eleven pen-knives, which were rusty; some complained their knives were dull and would not cut, which they went to sharpen on a stone; Jack (Comfort's) said his knife was so sharp, that if it came a-cross a white man's head, it would cut it off; on which he (Sandy) said, if you want to fight, go to the Spaniards, and not fight with your masters.

6. "That they asked him (and Comfort's Jack in particular) if he would help to burn some houses; he cried: on which Jack (Comfort's) said, d——n you, do you cry? I'll cut your head off in a hurry, and surrounded him; on which Burk's wench said he deserved it, if he would not say yes, on which he consented, and said yes; whereupon they did not threaten him, but bid him say nothing to black or white about it, and every one would do his part, and take a round, and fire the town.

7. "That Jack (Comfort's) said they had not men enough this year, but next year would do it, every one present was to set his master's house on fire first, and then do the rest at once, and set all the houses on fire in the town, which when they had done, they would kill all the white men, and have their wives for themselves.

8. "That Mr. Moore's Cato, Caesar (Pintard's negro), Mr. Jay's Brash, Jack (that is in jail) knows him if he sees; Todd's Dundee, Chambers's Robin, Patrick (English's), Peck's Caesar, a Caromantee, Cowley's Cato, Comfort's Maph alias Cook, Kip's Harry, and three country negroes, who called Comfort's Jack, uncle, and brother, and cousin. burnt) Ben Moore's Tom, Leffert's Pompey, Duane's Prince, Comfort's old Caromantee woman, Vaarck's Caesar (hanged) were there also; the room being quite full.

9. "That Augustine and Wilkins' Fortune were to burn their master's houses, which he heard them say, as they were

[118]

talking by Frazier's corner, about a week before the fort was burnt.

10. "That at the aforesaid meeting at Comfort's Jack, the old man, and the old woman, and three of the Spaniards were sworn to the effect, that the first thunder that came, might strike them dead, if they did not stand to their words.

11. "That they asked him to come again the next day to be sworn; the rest said they would come to be sworn the next day."

The negroes Tom (Ben Moore's), Prince (Duane's), and Pompey (Leffert's), apprehended and committed.

Examination of Fortune, (Wilkins's negro) before one of the judges—No. 3.—He said,

1. "That Quack (z) one Sabbath day afternoon, asked him to walk into the fields, and pressed him to it: third meeting, told him he should see a great alteration at the fort; and told him that they were going to burn the fort; threatened that some of his mates would poison him if he told.

2. "That Niblet's boy (a) told him that Gomez's negro was to assist in burning the fort.

3. "That he heard Quack talk to Gomez's negro Cuffee on the dock, that he must meet him to burn the house, and if white people came, to shoot them with pistols; which was before the meeting him by Mr. Rickets's.

4. "That when he asked Sandy (Niblet's negro) who was to burn the fort? He answered, Quack, himself, and Gomez's Cuffee; that he asked him (Sandy, Niblet's negro) to be concerned and that he said to Quack, he had no mind to be hanged, he might go to h——ll and be d——d.

5. "That he never talked to any negro but Quack and Niblet's about any conspiracy or design of firing.

6. "Never heard of a house where they met, nor knew Hughson. Cuffee however has asked him to go down to a

(z) Roosevelt's negro.
(a) Sandy.

house by the north river, and dance with him; but he never did."

Examination of Sarah, (Burk's negro wench) before one of the judges, Mr. Chambers, and others—No. 2.—She said,

1. "That one Sunday afternoon, about four or five of the clock, she was at Comfort's house, in the kitchen, about five weeks before the fort was fired; a great many negroes sitting round the table, betwixt twenty and thirty, amongst whom were Dr. Fisher's *Harry, Bagley's *Jemmy, widow Schuyler's tall slender *negro, Abeel's mulatto *Tom, Niblet's Sandy. She staid there about an hour, and rum was there; Mrs. Clopper's *Betty, Robin (Chamber's negro), Mr. Clarkson's *Tom, Old Frank, Philipse's Cuffee, Teller's *Sarah, Vaarck's Caesar, Auboyneau's Prince, Comfort's Jack, Comfort's Cook, Comfort's *Jenny, Jack a busy man, Patrick (English's boy), Hunt's Warwick (a negro that cut his throat), Todd's Dundee, Brinkerhoff's *Tom, Pintard's Caesar, Old Kip's Harry, Teneyck's Bill, Silvester's *Sambo, a tall negro living at John Dewit's (a stranger), Kierstead's Braveboy, John Hunt's *Jenny, the Long Bridge Boys. Patrick (English's boy) used to say, let us go to Romer's (b) — Alsteyn's *Cato, Shurmur's Cato, Leffert's Pompey: Comfort's Jack and others sharpened their knives, and said they would go and set fire along the docks; Comfort's Jack proposed the fort first; Cook said no, they would find them out if they did: every one was to set their master's house on fire; Clopper's Betty carried her there; they swore, and said they wished thunder might strike them to the hearts if they told. Three negroes, viz.—Comfort's two, and old Harry, swore; Cuffee was sworn, and Caesar, Auboyneau's Prince. All that made the right bargain swore, the rest were to come the next day; De Lancey's Anthony there, and Roosevelt's Quack: Comfort's Jack drew out his knife and threatened the negro of Niblet, on which Sandy consented.

(b) For Romme's.

[120]

2. "That they whetted their knives on a stone, some complaining that their knives were rusty and blunt, and some said that their knives were sharp enough to cut a white man's head, that they would kill the white men, and have the white women for their wives.

3. "That on a dispute between them, Quack was pitched upon to fire the fort; others having refused, Quack undertook it; Curacoa Dick there, and consented.

4. "Confessed she threatened Niblet's negro, and bid them cut his head off, if he did not drink.

5. "That she believed there were Spanish negroes there, and that Mr. Moore's Cato was there, and consented."

Notwithstanding this wench had brought so many negroes in question, at length when the examination came to be read over to her, she retracted, and excused many persons, saying, such a one, and such a one, went away before the bargain was made. (c). *Those she so excused are marked with an *asterisk* (in section 1 above). This was one of the oddest animals amongst the black confederates, and gave the most trouble in her examinations; a creature of an outrageous spirit. When she was first interrogated upon this examination about the conspiracy, she absolutely denied she knew any thing of the matter; threw herself into most violent agitations; foamed at the mouth, and uttered the bitterest imprecations; if ever she was at Comfort's in her life, or knew where his house was. But at length, being apprized that there was positive evidence against her, that she was at a meeting there amongst the confederates, when they were talking of the conspiracy, and that she was one consenting and advising thereto, and some items also given her of her behaviour and expressions with respect to Sandy; (d) and that she could entertain no hopes of escaping with life, or recommending herself to mercy, but by making an ingenuous confession and discovery of the whole truth of what she knew of the matter, and the persons concerned; she stood aghast and silent for some

(c) i.e. Before they took this execrable oath.
(d) See Sawney's examination, No. 2, sections 1, 2, 4. Monday, 25th May.

[121]

time, but at last declared she would tell the whole truth, and began to open, and so by degrees grew more calm, and seemed abundantly easier after disburthening part of the secret. But her conduct was such upon the whole, that what she said, if not confirmed by others, or concurring circumstances, could not deserve entire credit. She, no doubt, must have had extraordinary qualifications to recommend her to the confidence of the confederates; for she was the only wench against whom there was strong and flagrant evidence of having consented to and approved this execrable project.

About noon this day, the under-sheriff informed the recorder, that John Hughson wanted to speak to the judges, and (as he had said) to open his heart to them, and they should know more, and was very urgent that somebody should go to them to acquaint them therewith. Pursuant to Hughson's desire, the recorder did go up to the City-Hall in the afternoon, expecting he would make some material discovery, and having sent for him, he was asked, what it was that he wanted with the judges? Whereupon Hughson asked if there was a bible, and desired that he might be sworn. He was told that no oath would be administered to him; if he had any thing to say, he had free liberty to speak, but he wanted very much to be sworn. The recorder thereupon reproached him with his wicked life and practices, debauching and corrupting of negroes, and encouraging them to steal and pilfer from their masters and others, and for shewing his children so wicked an example, training them up in the highway to hell. He further observed to him, that he, his wife, and Peggy, then stood convicted of a felony for receiving stolen goods of negroes; and that now nothing remained but to pass sentence to death upon them, and to appoint a day for their execution for that fact; but that it was now determined, that he, his wife and daughter, and Peggy, should also be tried for being confederated in this most horrible conspiracy; that the evidence would appear so strong and clear against them in this particular, that there was little doubt of their being all convicted upon that head also; that it would appear undeniably that he was a principal, and head agent in this detestable scheme of villainy; the chief abettor, together with the rest of his family, of this execrable and monstrous contrivance for shedding the blood of his neighbours, and laying the whole city in ashes, upon the expectation of enriching himself by such an inhuman and execrable undertaking. He therefore admonished him, if he would entertain the least hopes of recommending himself to the mercy of God Almighty, before whose tribunal he must soon appear, that he would ingenuously tell the truth, and lay open the whole scene of this dark tragedy, which had been brooding at his house, and discover the several parties he knew to have been engaged in it; in doing which he would make some atonement for his past villainies, by preventing that slaughter, bloodshed and devastation, which he and his confederates had intended; or the recorder expressed himself in words to this purpose. But hereupon Hughson put on a soft smiling air of innocence upon his countenance, again desiring that he might be sworn, which was refused him, and he then declared, he knew nothing of all of any conspiracy, and called God to witness his protestations, that he was as innocent with respect to that charge as the child unborn, and also his wife, daughter and Peggy, for aught he knew.

Whereupon the Recorder remanded him to jail.

Whether the man was struck with a compunction, or flattered himself with making a merit by his discovery, and thereby recommended himself to mercy, and that he should so save his life; or whether he imagined that if he could be sworn, and then make the most solemn protestations with the sanction of an oath, that this would give such strong impressions of his innocence, as might make way for his escape; what his view was can only be guessed at; but several who were by him in the jail when he expressed his desire of having the opportunity of speaking with the judges, as above mentioned, concluded from his condition and behaviour at that instant, that he was then really in earnest to lay open this scene of villainy; but it was thought that in two or three hours afterwards, his wife or others had got the better of him, and prevailed with him to change his mind, and desist from his former resolution.

SUPREME COURT
Tuesday, June 2.

Present, the second and third justices.

Court opened and adjourned to four o'clock in the afternoon P.M. Present, the second justice.

The king against John Hughson, Sarah his wife, Sarah their daughter, Margaret Sorubiero, alias Kerry.

The prisoners were arraigned upon an indictment for a conspiracy, for abetting and encouraging the negro Quack, to burn the king's house in the fort: to which they severally pleaded, *not guilty*, etc.

Note. This is the first indictment against Sarah, the daughter, and the second against the rest.

Court adjourned to Thursday, the 4th inst. 10 o'clock in the morning.

SUPREME COURT
Thursday, June 4.

Present, the second and third justices.

The king against John Hughson; Sarah his wife, Sarah their daughter, Margaret Sorubiero, alias Kerry.

On motion of Mr. Attorney General, the prisoners were brought to the bar, and arraigned on an indictment for a conspiracy, for counselling, abetting, etc. the negro Cuffee, to burn Mr. Philipse's storehouse, and all pleaded, *not guilty*.

Note. This was the second indictment against the daughter, the third against the rest.

And this being the day appointed for their trials on the former indictments, whereof they had due notice, the court proceeded thereupon as followeth:

The King against the same, on trial upon three indictments.

Clerk in court. Cryer, make proclamation.

Cryer. Oyes! Our sovereign lord the king doth strictly charge and command all manner of persons to keep silence upon pain of imprisonment.

Cryer. If any one can inform the king's justices or Attorney General for this province, or the inquest now to be taken on the behalf of our sovereign lord the king, of any treason, murder, felony, or any other misdemeanor committed or done by the prisoners at the bar, let them come forth, and they shall be heard, for the prisoners stand upon their deliverance.

Clerk. Cryer, make proclamation.

Cryer. Oyes! You good men that are impanelled to inquire between our sovereign lord the king and John Hughson, Sarah his wife, Sarah Hughson the daughter, and Margaret Sorubiero alias Kerry, the prisoners at the bar, answer to your names, etc.

Clerk. John Hughson, Sarah the wife of John Hughson, Sarah the daughter of John Hughson, Margaret Sorubiero, alias Kerry, hold up your hands.

These good men that are now called and here appear, are those which are to pass between you and our sovereign lord the king, upon your lives or deaths, if you, or any, or either of you challenge any of them, you must speak as they come to the book to be sworn, and before they are sworn.

Court. You the prisoners at the bar, we must inform you that the law allows you the liberty of challenging peremptorily twenty of the jurors, if you have any dislike to them, and you need not give your reasons for so doing; and you may likewise challenge as many more as you can give sufficient reasons for; and you may either all join in your challenges, or make them separately.

The prisoners agreed that John Hughson should challenge for them all.

(At Hughson's challenging (among others) a young gentleman, merchant of the town, Peggy seemed out of humour, and intimated that he had challenged one of the best of them all; which occasioned some mirth to those within the hearing of it.)

The prisoners having peremptorily challenged sixteen, the following jurors were sworn:

Edward Man, Robert Benson, Henry Lawrence, Samuel Burdet, Charles Arding, Thomas Wendover, John Lasher, John Troup, Frederick Becker, Francis Roswell, Evert Byvanck, Peter Vergerean.

Clerk. Cryer, make proclamation.

Cryer. Oyes! Our sovereign lord the king doth strictly charge and command all manner of persons to keep silence, upon pain of imprisonment.

Clerk. You, gentlemen of the jury that are sworn, look upon the prisoners and hearken to their charge.

The substance of the three indictments followeth:

The first indictment sets forth, that Hughson, his wife, and Kerry, and also three negroes, to wit, Caesar, Prince and Cuffee, had on the third day of March then last past, entered into a most detestable and felonious conspiracy, combination and confederacy with each other, to set on fire and burn the house of our lord the king, which was then standing and being at the fort within the city, and also this whole town, and to kill and destroy the inhabitants thereof; and that they had feloniously and of their malice aforethought, procured, abetted, counselled and encouraged the said Cuffee, the felony and burning aforesaid, committed and perpetrated, to commit and perpetrate, in most pernicious example of all others in the like cases offending, contrary to the form of the statutes in such case made and provided, and against the peace of our sovereign lord the king, his crown and dignity.

To which three several indictments the prisoners, defendants in each (e) have been arraigned, and thereto pleaded, *not guilty.*

The Attorney General, after opening to the court and jury the charge against the prisoners, proceeded as followeth.

Gentlemen,

I shall in the first place, on the trial of the prisoners upon these indictments, shew you, that the negroes Quack and Cuffee, mentioned in the second and third of them, have already been tried, found guilty, and executed for the felonies

(e) The first of these three indictments for the conspiracy was found against Hughson, his wife, and Kerry, soon after their conviction of having received stolen goods, knowing them to have been such, and some time before the trial of the negro Quack and Cuffee, and before it was discovered that Quack had set fire to his majesty's house in the fort, or Cuffee to Mr. Philipse's storehouse, or that Sarah (Hughson's daughter) was known to be a party concerned in the conspiracy.

and burnings which these indictments charge them to have been guilty of: that they confessed the same at the place of their execution; and that the evidence which Mary Burton gave against them at their trial, was true, in every respect.

In the next place, gentlemen, I am to shew you, what share each of the prisoners at the bar had in these most horrible felonies.

And, gentlemen, as each of these four criminals have acted their several parts in this black, this monstrous and tragical scene, I shall begin with opening the evidence against the three last named, that I may conclude with observations on the charge against Hughson himself, and set him and his most detestable notions in their proper colours before you.

First then I shall prove to you, gentlemen, from full and clear evidence, that these prisoners are all guilty of the whole charge against them. That they entered into a most wicked and hellish plot to set on fire and lay in ashes the king's house, and this whole town, and to kill and destroy the inhabitants as they should come to secure their effects, and extinguish the flames. That this dreadful conspiracy took its first rise at Hughson's house in this city: that it was there formed, set on feet, and carried on; (f) and that the three last named criminals, as well as Hughson himself, were all present at divers meetings of great numbers of negroes, and the rest of the conspirators there for that purpose. That there these three criminals were all sworn into this abominable plot, and at those meetings, joined with Hughson in exciting and encouraging Quack and Cuffee, and the rest of the negroes, and other their wicked confederates, to commit these execrable felonies.

I shall now endeavour to represent to you the part which Hughson himself has acted in this tragedy.

Gentlemen, it will appear to you in the course of the evi-

(f) From what had hitherto come to light, it could be supposed no otherwise, but that Hughson was the principal contriver of this monstrous scheme; but nevertheless, it was there principally hatched and brought to maturity, as may be gathered from the whole of the discovery.

[127]

dence for the king upon this trial, that John Hughson was the chief contriver, abetter and encourager of all this mystery of iniquity; that it was he who advised and procured secret and frequent meetings of the negroes, and the rest of the conspirators at his house, there to form and carry on these horrible conspiracies. That it was he that swore the negroes Quack and Cuffee, with many others, and himself too, into this direful plot. That it was he who devised firebrands, death and destruction to be sent among you. That it was he who received of negroes twelve pounds in money, stolen money, no doubt (and what he could not but know to be so) to buy arms and ammunition, to kill and destroy his neighbours: and that he in pursuance thereof, made a journey on purpose to buy, and did procure arms and ammunition, and hid them in his house, against such time as this unnatural and bloody scheme should be ripe for execution.

Gentlemen, such a monster will this Hughson appear before you, that for the sake of the plunder he expected by setting in flames the king's house, and this whole city, and by the effusion of the blood of his neighbours, he, murderous and remorseless he! counselled and encouraged the committing of all these most astonishing deeds of darkness, cruelty and inhumanity.—Infamous Hughson!

Gentlemen, This is that Hughson! whose name and most detestable conspiracies will no doubt be had in everlasting remembrance, to his eternal reproach; and stand recorded to latest posterity.—This is the man!—this that grand incendiary!—that arch rebel against God, his king, and his country! —that devil incarnate, and chief agent of the old Abaddon of the infernal pit, and Geryon of darkness.

Gentlemen, behold the author and abettor of all the late conflagrations, terrors, and devastation that have befallen this city.—Was not this Hughson sunk below the dignity of human nature! was he not abandoned to all sense of shame and remorse! to all sense of feeling and dreadful calamities he has brought on this city, and his own guilt, his mon-

[128]

strous guilt, be so confounded, as not able to look up, or stand without the greatest confusion of face, before this court and audience; but would openly confess his, and the rest of his wretched confederates' guilt, and humbly ask pardon of God, the king, and his injured country.

Gentlemen, we shall now call, and examine the witnesses, who will prove the crimes charged upon each of the four criminals; and when we have so done, I doubt not but you will find all of them guilty.

Of council for the king, with Mr. Attorney General.—Joseph Murray, James Alexander, William Smith, John Chambers, esquires.

These gentlemen severally assisted in examining the witnesses, taking down their evidence, and remarking such things as they thought most material to be observed upon to the court and jury.

Witnesses for the king.—Mr. George Joseph Moore, clerk in court, and Mr. John Roosevelt called and sworn.

Mr. Moore proved the arraignment and conviction of the two negroes, Quack and Cuffee, for burning the king's house in the fort, and Mr. Philipse's storehouse.

Both witnesses proved the confessions of these two negroes, taken in writing at the stake,

"That they declared, that Hughson was the first contriver and promoter of the plot, and urged them into it; and that they should never have thought of it, if he had not put it into their heads. That Quack said, the plot was to burn the houses."

Mr. Moore proved Cuffee's confession, more particularly taken in writing by him,

"That, as Quack said, the plot was to burn the houses of the town; Cuffee said likewise, that the plot was, to kill the people; and that both of them declared, that what Mary

Burton had given in evidence upon their trials, was true; and that she could name many more (persons) concerned: all which Mr. Roosevelt confirmed." (g)

Court to the prisoners. Have you any questions to ask these witnesses? The prisoners answered, nothing.

Joseph North, Peter Lynch, and John Dunscomb, called and sworn.

North and Lynch proved,

"That there was a cabal of negroes at Hughson's last Whitsuntide was twelve months; ten, twelve, or fourteen of them, which they have intelligence of went down thither in order to disperse them; and when they came there, they went into the room where the negroes were round a table, eating and drinking, for there was meat on the table, and knives and forks; and the negroes were calling for what they wanted; and at their appearance, the negroes were making off as fast as they could, and North laid his cane about them, and soon cleared the room of them: they said, they thought that Peggy was waiting upon them, and had a tumbler in her hand for them to drink in; that they saw the negro who was then hanged in gibbets (h) at that time waiting at the door, in order to get in as they took it: that they had heard frequent complaints of Hughson's entertaining negroes there; they said, that John Hughson was at the door, and as they came away, they reproached him therewith; and he answered them, that he could not help it, it was his wife's fault."

Court to the prisoners. Have you any questions to ask these witnesses?—They had nothing to ask.

Mary Burton called and sworn.—She said,

"That there were many negroes frequently at Hughson's at

(g) See the confessions before annexed to the trials of Quack and Cuffee, 30th May.
(h) Vaarck's Caesar.

[130]

nights, ever since she came to the house, eating and drinking; that she has seen twenty and thirty at a time there, but most of a Sunday; that the negroes used to bring provisions there, particularly Carpenter's negro; (i) that Hughson, his wife and daughter, and Peggy used, at such meetings, frequently to be amongst the negroes; and that they talked of burning the town and killing the people."

(While Mary Burton was delivering her evidence, Hughson and his wife were crying and bemoaning themselves, and embracing and kissing their daughter Sarah; and Hughson the father, intimated what care they had taken in catechizing her, and the rest of their children, and teaching them to read the bible, and breeding them up in the fear of the Lord. And in order (as may be supposed) to move compassion in the court and jury, Hughson's wife brought thither a sucking child at her breast, which was ordered to be taken away.)
Mary Burton further said,

"That at such great meetings of negroes at Hughson's, Caesar (Vaarck's) and Prince (Auboyneau's) negroes (that were hanged) and Cuffee (Philipse's) were usually amongst them.

"That Hughson swore the negroes into the plot, and the Hughsons swore themselves and Peggy; that one of Hughson's daughters carried a bible up stairs, and the Hughsons carried the negroes into a private room; and when they came down again to the rest of the negroes, Hughson said they were all sworn; but the witness said, she did not see them sworn."

(Upon the witness saying, that a bible was carried up stairs, Hughson's wife interrupted and said to her, as if much surprised, now you are found out in a great lie, for we never had a bible in the world; which the audience, considering what her husband declared but a little before, were much diverted with.)
Mary Burton further said,

(i) His mistress was a butcher.

[131]

"That she saw Vaarck's Caesar pay John Hughson twelve pounds in silver Spanish pieces of eight, to buy guns, swords and pistols; and that Hughson thereupon went up into the country; and when he returned, he brought with him seven or eight guns and swords, and that he hid them in the house; that she had seen a bag of shot and a barrel of gunpowder there; that the negroes were sworn to burn the fort first; and that they were to go down to the Fly, and so to burn the whole town; and the negroes were to cut their masters' and their mistresses' throats; and when all this was done, Hughson was to be king, and Caesar (Vaarck's) governor: that the negroes used to say to Hughson, when she (the witness) was in the room and heard them talking of burning the town and killing the people, that perhaps she (the witness) would tell; and Hughson said, no, that she dared not; and the negroes swore that if she did, they would burn or destroy her.

"That the Hughsons often tempted her to swear, and offered her silks and gold rings, in order to prevail with her, but she would not." (k)

(The prisoners asked the witnesses no material questions, such only as seemed rather to imply their guilt; but some of them threw up their hands, and cast up their eyes, as if astonished,

(k) Some time after the trial was entered upon, the town was again alarmed by a fire in the lots behind the storehouses of Messrs. Philipses; a boarded stable was set on fire on the outside, by some brands ends being placed against it, but it was suppressed before it had got to any head, though the incendiary was undiscovered. This was a bold attempt after all that had happened, and was conjectured to be a scheme contrived in favor of the Hughsons, etc. upon a supposition, that the court might be put into so much confusion upon the occasion, that those criminals might thereby have an opportunity of making their escape; or at least the trial be thereby interrupted and postponed: but if these were their designs they were disappointed.—This note rather than it should be omitted, remains here misplaced, as it was at first; because some people had affirmed, that this fire happened upon the Hughsons trial for the conspiracy; whereas upon further inquiry and recollection when the printer had gone beyond it, it was found to have been on the sixth of May, the day the Hughsons were tried upon the felony for receiving stolen goods.

[132]

and said, she was a very wicked creature, and protested all she said was false.)

Arthur Price called and sworn.

His evidence was the substance of his deposition, No. 1, 2, 3, of the third, seventh and twelfth May, as to what passed in conversation in the jail between him and Peggy, Sarah Hughson the daughter, and Mr. Philipse's Cuffee separately; and therefore to avoid repetition, the reader is referred to them.

John Schultz, James Mills, Peter Lynch, Cornelius Brower, and ——— Dunscomb, called and sworn.

Schultz said, "that Cuffee (Philipse's negro) being carried with Quack, immediately after their conviction, into prison, where Hughson and his wife were, as he came in said to Hughson, we may thank you for this, for this is what you have brought us to; and Cuffee owned the next day to the witness that he had said so."

Mills said, "that Cuffee said to Hughson, I may thank you for this, for you have brought me to this."

Brower said, "that Cuffee said, I thank you for this, you have brought me to this."

Dunscomb, Schultz, Lynch and Mills, all said "that last Monday Hughson said, he wanted to speak to the judges and open his heart to them, and they should know more, and was very urgent that somebody should go to the judges to acquaint them therewith."

Court to the prisoners. If you have any questions to ask these witnesses, now is your time to propose them; or if you have any witnesses to produce to your characters, let them be called.

Witnesses for the prisoners.—Eleanor Ryan, Mr. Blanck and Peter Kirby called.

Eleanor Ryan (1) said, "that she and her husband lodged two months in Hughson's house last winter; that she saw no negroes there but Cuff (Philipse's) and the negro that was hung in gib-

---

(1) Wife of Andrew Ryan, a soldier, afterwards charged as one of the conspirators, and committed.

bets, three or four times; that she never saw any entertainments there for negroes, but said that she lay sick in bed in the kitchen almost day and night all that time."

Mr. Blanck said, "he saw Hughson give a dram to a negro, but that he thought him a civil man."

Peter Kirby said, "that he knew nothing of the character of Hughson's house, but he never saw no harm of him."

Francis Silvester called and sworn for the king.

He said,

"That when John Hughson lived next door to him upon the dock, he kept a very disorderly house, and sold liquor to, and entertained negroes there; he had often seen many of them there at a time, at nights as well as in the daytime: once in particular he remembers, in the evening, he saw a great many of them in a room, dancing to a fiddle, and Hughson's wife and daughter along with them. That he often reproached Hughson with keeping such a disorderly house, which very much offended his neighbours; and Hughson replied to him, that his wife persuaded him to leave the country, where he subsisted his family tolerably well by his trade (m) and his farm; but his wife said, they would live much better in town, though then he wished they had returned to the country again, for he found their gains were so small, and his family so large, that they soon run away with what they had got: that his wife was the chief cause of having the negroes at his house, and he was afraid some misfortune would happen to him, and that he should come to some untimely end, or that Hughson expressed himself in words to that effect."

Court to the prisoners. Have you any more witnesses?

Prisoners. Yes sir; we desire that Adam King and Gerardus Comfort may be called.

Adam King and Gerardus Comfort called.

King said "that of late he took Hughson's house to be disor-

(m) He was by trade a shoemaker.

derly; for he saw whole companies of negroes playing at dice there, and that Wyncoop's negro once carried a silver spoon there that was hammered down; that he saw no harm of the man himself."

Attorney General (to Hughson). Have you any more such witnesses as this?

Comfort said "that he saw nothing amiss of him; his business was a cooper, and that he was often abroad, and went very seldom to his house."

Court. Mr. Comfort, you are a next door neighbour to Hughson: you live opposite to him, and surely you must have seen negroes go in and out there often, as the witnesses have testified, that there were frequent caballings with the negroes there; pray what have you observed of the house since Hughson came to live there?

Comfort. I have seen nothing amiss; I have seen no harm there.

Court (to the prisoners). Have you any more witnesses?

Hughson. We have no more, sir.

Court. Then now is the time for you the prisoners, severally to offer what you can in your own defence, that then the counsel for the king may sum up the evidence.

Then the prisoners severally spoke in their justification in their turns, protested their innocence, and declared that all the witnesses said against them was false, and called upon God to witness their asseverations.

Mr. Smith then proceeded as followeth:

May it please your honours, and you gentlemen of the jury,

You have heard the charge against the prisoners at the bar contained in their several indictments, to which they have each of them pleaded *not guilty.* Mr. Attorney has opened the nature of the evidence on the part of the king, and the witnesses on both sides have been heard, and I cannot think that one among you is in any doubt concerning what verdict you ought to give upon the oath which you have taken.

Gentlemen—Scarce any thing can be conceived more hor-

[135]

rid than the crimes charged on the prisoners. A scheme so black and hellish, as the burning of this city, and the murdering of the inhabitants of it, one would hardly imagine, could enter into the thought; much less be harboured in the breast of any human creature; but more wonderful is it, that so great a number should unite and conspire in so detestable a piece of villainy. And yet, gentlemen, there seems nothing wanting to complete the evidence of so barbarous, unjust and cruel a design as has been set on foot; of which we have had in particular demonstration, in the late fires that have been enkindled in divers parts of this city; several of which have been lighted up in one day, to the amazement and terror of the people.

Gentlemen—Though the circumstances attending these fires convinced every body that the most of them did not proceed from accidental causes, but from a malicious and wilful design; yet it was long before any considerable discovery could be made of the authors and abettors of this most wicked and destructive undertaking. Yet at length, by the blessing of heaven, and the uncommon diligence of the magistrates, we trust that some of the principal authors of this mischief, and the ringleader of it are now before you.

Upon this Mr. Smith proceeded to a distinct consideration of the charge, and in observing upon the evidence of the witnesses (which was in substance as before set forth) distinguished the proofs against each of the prisoners; which for brevity sake are here omitted. And then concluded,

Thus, gentlemen, nothing remains to be considered of by you, but the credit of the witnesses, against which I can see no reasonable objection; if they are to be believed, then the prisoners are guilty; and you now behold, at this bar, the authors, abettors, and contrivers of those destructive fires which your eyes have seen; two of the immediate agents of those villainies, have already suffered a deserved punishment and died confessing their crimes. The witnesses declare the principal contriver of those mischiefs to be that wicked man, John Hughson, whose crimes have made him blacker than a negro: the scandal of his complexion, and the disgrace of human nature! whose name will descend with infamy to posterity! who could not be content to live by the gains of honest industry, but must be rich at the expense of the blood and ruin of his fellow citizens! miserable wretch! how has he plunged himself and family into that pit which he had dug for others, and brought down upon his own pate that violent dealing which he contrived, and in part executed against his neighbours! Gentlemen, though the crimes charged on the defendants are such as merit a just indignation, yet in matters that affect life, you ought to have the most convincing evidence: the trial of the fact is your province. In matters of judgment, to condemn the innocent, and acquit the guilty, is equally criminal. If you can, after what you have heard, think the prisoners innocent, you ought to acquit them; but if you find them guilty, you cannot acquit them without the greatest injustice and cruelty to your country and yourselves. Gentlemen, I shall add no more, but leave you to the direction of the court, and your own consciences.

Then the third justice charged the jury as followeth.

Gentlemen of the jury,

It is needless for the court to observe further to you, after what has been said by the counsel for the king, concerning the nature and destructive tendency of so execrable a piece of villainy as this conspiracy, now charged upon the prisoners at the bar: it has been sufficiently and properly enlarged upon; nor is it any more necessary for the court to recapitulate the evidence given in the case; for that has been clearly stated by the gentlemen at the bar.

Now, gentlemen, if you cannot credit the several witnesses for the king, if that can be the case, you will then acquit the prisoners of this charge against them, and find them not guilty; but on the other hand, as the evidence against them seems to be so ample, so full, so clear and satisfactory, if you have no particular reasons in your own breasts, in your own consciences, to discredit them, if that, I say, is not the case, if you have no reason to discredit them, then I make no doubt but you will discharge a good conscience, and find them guilty.

A constable being sworn to attend the jury, they withdrew, and being returned in a short time, found Hughson, his wife, and Kerry, *guilty* of all three indictments; and Sarah Hughson the daughter, *guilty* of the second and third.

SUPREME COURT
Friday, June 5, A.M.

Present, the second and third justices.

Court opened and adjourned till four o'clock in the afternoon. P.M. Present, as before.

Court opened and adjourned till to-morrow morning, ten o'clock.

Examination of Sarah (Mrs. Burk's negro) before the grand jury, No. 3.—She said,

1. "That the company at Comfort's, who were there when they whetted their knives, and said, would burn the house and kill the white people, were, Comfort's negroes, Jack, and Cook, the old man; Niblet's Sandy or Sawney; Chambers' Robin; Old Kip's Harry; a stranger of Dewit's; a tall negro; Peter DeLancey's Antonio; Curacoa Dick; Auboyneau's Prince; Philipse's Cuffee; Roosevelt's Quack; Mr. Jay's Brash; Rowe's Tom (old) Hunt's Warwick; five or six Spanish negroes.

2. "That the following negroes were at Comfort's also, but went away before the talk aforesaid:

Dr. Fisher's Harry, Bagley's Jemmy, Widow Schuyler's tall slender fellow, Abeel's Tom, Clopper's Betty (went with Sarah to the house, and afterwards went with Comfort's Jenny), Comfort's Jenny, Clarkson's Tom, Croesbeck's

*Mink, English's *Patrick, Brinkerhoff's Tom, Ten Eyck's *Bill, Sylvester's Sambo, Kierstede's *Braveboy, Hunt's Jenny, Shurmur's *Cato, Leffert's *Pompey. (n)

3. At the same time brought the following Spanish negroes before Sarah and Sandy:

Filkin's *Joseph or Will, Benson's *Pablo,† Sarly's Juan,† Meanard's Antonio,† DeLancey's *Antonio,† Bosch's Francis,† Wendover's Manuel,† McMullen's Augustine, Dr. Nicol's John.†

(Those with the mark * before their names, Sarah said were there, and the rest not. Those with the mark † after their names, Sandy said were there, and the rest not.)

Said Sarah declared also,

4. "That Curacoa Dick and Comfort's Jack were principal speakers, that they would burn the houses and kill the white people, whetting their knives, and saying they were sharp enough for that purpose.

5. "That Curacoa Dick was the person who asked her to go to Comfort's house; and in going she met Clopper's wench going also, and went in with her.

6. "That Acco, alias Cook (Comfort's old man) cursed her, and wished thunder might strike her if she discovered.

7. "Being asked if Cuffee (Gomez's) was at Comfort's? she said he was not.

8. "That Antonio (DeLancey's Spaniard) seemed very forward when at Comfort's, and talked much to Curacoa Dick. (o)

9. "That the meeting was at Comfort's shop.

10. "That they then there did talk of and resolve in particular, that Quack should put the fort on fire."

(n) Here she differs from her examination, No. 2, before one of the judges, on Monday last, as to the persons she would excuse, by pretending that they went away before the talk of the conspiracy: those marked with an (*) asterisk here were not excepted by her in the last.

(o) It was said Curacoa Dick could talk Spanish, and that Antonio could talk some English.

SUPREME COURT
Saturday, June 6.

Present, the second and third justices.

The king against Jack and Cook (Comfort's); Robin (Chamber's); Caesar (Peck's); Cuffee (Gomez's); Jamaica (Ellison's), negroes.

The prisoners being set to the bar, were arraigned on an indictment for conspiring, combining and confederating with divers negroes, to burn the whole town and city of New-York, and to kill and destroy the inhabitants thereof; and pleaded, *not guilty*: and for their trials put themselves upon God and the country.

Court adjourned to Monday the 8th inst., 10 o'clock in the morning.

SUPREME COURT
Monday, June 8.

Present, the second and third justices.

The king against John Hughson, Sarah his wife, Margaret Hughson (Sorubiero), alias Kerry, Sarah the daughter.

The prisoners being called up to judgment upon their conviction for the conspiracy, and placed at the bar, the second justice proceeded to pass sentence, as followeth:

John Hughson, and you the rest of the prisoners at the bar.

You are now brought before this court to receive that sentence which the law has appointed for your offences; though I cannot say the punishment is adequate to the horrid crimes of which you stand convicted. The Roman commonwealth was established some hundred years before any law was made against parricide, they not thinking any person capable of so atrocious a crime; yours are indeed as singular, and unheard of before, they are such as one would scarce believe any man capable of committing, especially any one who had heard of a God and a future state; for people who

[140]

have been brought up and always lived in a christian country, and also called themselves christians, to be guilty not only of making negro slaves their equals, but even their superiors, by waiting upon, keeping with, and entertaining them with meat, drink and lodging, and what is much more amazing, to plot, conspire, consult, abet and encourage these black seed of Cain, to burn this city, and to kill and destroy us all. Good God! when I reflect on the disorders, confusion, desolation and havock, which the effect of your most wicked, most detestable and diabolical councils might have produced (had not the hand of our great and good God interposed) it shocks me! for you, who would have burnt and destroyed without mercy, ought to be served in like manner; and although each of you have with an uncommon assurance, denied the fact, and audaciously called upon God as a witness of your innocence; yet it hath pleased him, out of his unbounded goodness and mercy to us, to confound your devices, and cause your malicious and wicked machinations and intentions to be laid open and clear before us, not only to the satisfaction and conviction of the court, the grand and petty jury, but likewise to every one else that has heard the evidence against you: all are satisfied the just judgment of God has overtaken you, and that you justly merit a more severe death than is intended for you, having, in my opinion, been much worse than the negroes: however, though your crimes deserve it, yet we must not act contrary to law.

And now I do most earnestly exhort you, and each of you, to a serious and diligent improvement of the little time you have yet to live on this side of eternity, duly and heartily to weigh and consider your past wicked and ill-spent lives, by bewailing, confessing and sincerely repenting of your sins; that thereby you may obtain mercy and forgiveness from our great and just God; for without a sincere, as well as contrite heart, you can neither expect mercy or forgiveness for your manifold offences, both against God and your neighbours.

I must now speak particularly to you John Hughson, and

to you Sarah Hughson: look upon your poor unhappy daughter, now standing by you, of whom you have been the miserable instruments of bringing into the world; after that, to train and bring her up in the school of the devil, and now lastly to the gallows.—I say, consider and set her a good example, in a time when every moment is precious to you, that the great deceiver of mankind may not have the same power over you all in the next world, as he seems to have had in this.

I must now proceed to the duty the law requires of me; which is to tell you, that you the prisoners now at the bar, be removed to the place from whence you came, and from thence to the place of execution, and there you, and each of you, are to be hanged by the neck until you are severally dead; and I pray God of his great goodness, to have mercy on your souls.

Ordered, That the said condemned prisoners be executed on Friday the twelfth day of June instant, between the hours of nine and one of the same day; and that the body of John Hughson be afterwards hung in chains.

The king, against Comfort's Jack and Cook, Chambers's Robin, Peck's Caesar, Gomez's Cuffee, Ellison's Jamaica, on trial upon indictment for the conspiracy.

Jury called, and the prisoners challenging none, the following jurors sworn:

William Smith, Joseph Sacket, John Shurmur, Josiah Millikan, Isaac Van Dam, James Tucker, Daniel Dunscomb, Isaac Twentyman, Sidney Breese, Peter Vandursen, Benjamin Thomas, John Robins.

Of council for the king.—Mr. Attorney General, Joseph Murray, John Chambers, esquires.

The Attorney General, after having opened the indictment against these six negroes, spoke briefly as follows.

Gentlemen, It will, I doubt not, appear to you, upon hearing our witnesses for the king on this trial, that these six negroes are some of the conspirators which combined with those principal incendiaries, Hughson and his family, to set on fire the kings house, and this whole town, and to kill and murder the inhabitants.

But as I have already, upon the trial of the negro Quack, for burning the King's house, and of another negro called Cuffee, for burning Mr. Philipse's storehouse, and likewise on the last trial of Hughson, his wife and daughter, and Kerry, endeavoured to set forth the heinousness of so horrible and detestable a conspiracy, and the dangers this city and province may still be exposed to, until examples are made of all such as have been concerned in this most wicked plot: I think I have no need upon this trial, to say any thing further on either of these heads, not doubting but when you have heard the crimes which these criminals stand charged with, proved against them, you will find them guilty.

Witnesses called for the king, Mr. George Joseph Moore, Mr. John Roosevelt, Mary Burton, sworn. Niblet's Sandy, Burk's Sarah, Wilkin's Fortune, negroes.

Mr. Moore and Mr. Roosevelt proved the confessions of Roosevelt's Quack and Philipse's Cuffee at the stake.

Evidence affecting Comfort's Jack and Cook, one or both of them.—Quack's confession, section 4, 11, 30th May. Cuffee's confession, sections 3, 30th May. Sandy's examination, No. 1, 22d May; No. 2, 25th May; No. 3, 1st June. Sarah (Burk's) examination, No. 2, 1st June; No. 3, 5th June.

Sawney said upon the trial, "Jack was to be a captain; that he asked him to help burn houses, and said as soon as the fort was burnt, they would kill the white men: that Jack swore six Spaniards (Spanish slaves) and the rest were to come next day to be sworn.

"That it was agreed among them that Cook was to be an officer.

"That this meeting was of a Sunday when Comfort was not at home."

Mary Burton said, "Jack and Cook used to be at the meetings at Hughson's, when they were talking of firing the town and murdering the people, and were active and consenting; but that she did not see them sworn.

Burk's Sarah said likewise, "that it was agreed among them that Jack should be a captain."

Evidence affecting Chamber's Robin.—Quack's confession, section 2, 30th May. Cuffee's confession, section 3, 30th May. Sandy's examination, No. 3, section 3, 1st June. Sarah (Burk's) examination, No. 2, sections 1, 3, 1st June; No. 3, section 1, 5th June.

Sandy and Sarah both said, "That Robin was at the meeting at Comfort's (mentioned in both their examinations)."

Sandy said, "Robin had a knife there, and sharpened it, and consented to help kill the white men, and to take their wives."

Mr. Chambers examined the witness against Jack, Cook and Robin, and summed up.

Evidence affecting Gomez's Cuffee.—Quack's confession, sections 2, 7, 20th May. Cuffee's confession, sections 3, 5, 30th May. Sandy's examination, No. 1, section 11, 22d May. Fortune's examination, No. 1, section 6, 22d May. Sandy's examination, No. 3, sections 7, 8, 1st June.

Evidence affecting Peck's Caesar.—Cuffee's confession at the stake, section 5, 30th May. Quack's confession, sections 4, 7, 30th May. Sandy's examination, No. 2, sections 1, 2, 25th May; No. 3, section 8, 1st June.

Sawney said upon the trial, "That Caesar declared, he would kill the white men, and drink their blood to their good healths: this was about a fortnight or three weeks before the fort was burnt."

Evidence affecting Ellison's Jamaica.—Mary Burton's deposition, No. 2, section 4, 13th May. She testified against him further at the trial, "That he used to be very forward at the meetings at Hughson's in talk about the conspiracy; and that particularly once when they (the conspirators) were talking of burning the town and killing the people; Jamaica (being a fiddler) said, he would dance (or play) over them while they were roasting in the flames; and said he had been slave long enough."

[144]

Mr. Murray examined the witnesses against Cuffee, Caesar and Jamaica, and summed up.

There was nothing material in the defence of any of the prisoners; they asked the witnesses now and then a few trifling questions, and denied all that was alleged against them.

The jury being charged, and having withdrawn, and after a short stay, being returned, found the six negroes guilty of the indictment.

Then the court, after admonition to the criminals, proceeded to pass sentence upon them as followeth, viz.—"That Jack, Cook, Robin, Caesar, Cuffee, and Jamaica, should be carried from thence to the place from whence they came, and thence to the place of execution, where the said Jack, Cook, Robin, Caesar and Cuffee, should be chained to a stake, and burnt until they should be severally dead; and that the said Jamaica should be there hanged," etc.

Ordered, that Jack, Cook, Robin, Caesar and Cuffee, be executed on the morrow, the 9th instant, between the hours of one and seven of the afternoon of the same day, and that Jamaica be executed on Friday the 12th instant, between the hours of nine and one of the same day.

The king against Tom Peal, alias Bastian, Francis (Bosch's), Albany and Curacoa Dick, negroes.

The prisoners being placed at the bar, were arraigned on an indictment for conspiring, etc. with divers negro slaves and others, to burn the whole town and city of New-York, and also to kill and destroy the inhabitants thereof, whereunto they severally pleaded *not guilty*, etc.

Court adjourned till to-morrow morning, 10 o'clock.

This evening captain Jack (Comfort's negro) condemned, amongst others, to be executed to-morrow afternoon, had caused to be signified to the judges, that if his life might be spared, he would discover all that he knew of the conspiracy. From the course of the evidence, there was reason to conclude that he had been a most trusty and diligent agent for Hughson; he lived very near him, and his master was frequently absent from home for days and weeks together, which left him too much at liberty; and there was a well in his yard whereto many negroes resorted every day, morning and afternoon, to fetch tea water; and Hughson, no doubt, thought he had carried a great point when he had seduced captain Jack to his infamous schemes, for this gave him the greatest opportunities of corrupting his fellow slaves; and Jack was a crafty, subtle fellow, very well qualified for such an enterprize, and might be captivated with the fine promises and hopes given him of being not only a free, but a great man; a commander in this band of fools, of whom the greatest knaves perhaps (like fools too) projected to make a prey in the end. It was therefore thought proper, as this mystery of iniquity was yet but beginning to be unfolded, so far to accept Jack's offer as to respite his execution, till it was found how well he would deserve further favour.

Jack was examined before the judges this afternoon, and was under examination the next day, when his fellow criminals were carrying from the City-Hall to their execution. He was advised not to flatter himself with the hopes of life, without he would do the utmost in his power to deserve it, and that would be by telling freely all that he knew of the matter, and discovering all the parties concerned, to the best of his knowledge. He was told we were already let so far into this secret, as to persons and things, as to be able to give a good guess, whether he spoke the truth, and he would but deceive himself in the end if he told falsehoods. Jack looked very serious, and at length began to open, but his dialect was so perfectly negro and unintelligible, it was thought that it would be impossible to make any thing of him without the help of an interpreter. There were two young men, sons-in-law of Jack's master, who were aware Jack would not be understood without their aid, and they signified their desire of being by when he was examined, from a supposition that they might be of service in interpreting his meaning, as he had been used to them, having often worked in the same shop together at the cooper's trade, whereby he was so familiarized to them, they could make a shift to understand his language, and they thought they had such an influence over him, that they were persuaded, they could also prevail upon him to make an ingenuous confession; and to do them justice, they were very serviceable in both respects, and the event well answered the expectation they had given. But notwithstanding this assistance, his examination took up as much time of three successive days, morning and afternoon, as could conveniently be spared him from other business.

Several negroes concerned in the conspiracy, having been discovered by Jack in this first sitting, were apprehended the next morning early, pursuant to orders then immediately given, but there was not time to commit his confession to writing this evening, yet it is thought proper to set the same forth as of this day. Jack desired he might be removed from the cell where his fellow criminals, condemned with him, were lodged, and his request was granted.

Examination and Confession of Jack (Comfort's) before one of the judges, No. 1.—He said,

1. "That a little after new year, on a Monday, about four in the afternoon, Ben (p) (Capt. Marshall's) came to Comfort's house to fetch tea water, where he left his keg in the shop, and went to Hughson's house (Hughson and his wife then gone into the country); Ben staid about two hours there, and then returned to Comfort's, and told Jack that he had met there six Spaniards, among whom were Anthony and Wan (q) (now in jail) and said to him, countryman, I have heard some good news: what news said Jack? Ben said there were Spanish negroes at Hughson's, who told him they had designs of taking this country against the wars came; what would they do with this country? said Jack, to which Ben answered, oh! you fool, those Spaniards know better than York negroes, and could help better to take it than they, because they were more used to war; but they must begin first to set the house (i.e. the houses) on fire.

2. "That the Sunday following Hughson and his wife came home, and brought a goods, a quarter of mutton, and a fowl home. That Ben came a little after church out, in the

(p) Jack's description of Ben:—His master live in tall house Broadway. Ben ride de fat horse.

(q) Mr. Peter DeLancey's (see section 28) and Capt. Sarly's.

afternoon, to Comfort's, and told him, brother go to Hughson's, all our company is come down: he went with Ben thither, and went round the house and went in at the back door; when he came there they sat all round the table, and had a goose, a quarter of mutton, a fowl, and two loaves of bread: Hughson took a flask of rum out of a case and set it on the table, and two bowls of punch were made; some drink dram; a cloth was laid:

Quash (H. Rutgers's negro); Caesar (Koertrecht's Powlus, a Spanish negro; Toby, or Cato (Provoost's); Cato (Shurmur's); Cook (Comfort's); John (Vaarck's); York and London (Marschalk's); Ticklepitcher (Carpenter's); Francis (Bosch's); Bastian, alias Tom Peal; Scipio (Mrs. Van Borsom's); Ben (captain Marshall's) were all present, and also six Spanish negroes, among whom were Wan and Anthony, and a negro lately belonging to John Marschalk, the three others he should know if he saw them; Hughson, and his wife, and daughter sat down on one side of the table, and the negroes on the other: two or three tables were put together to make it long; Hughson's daughter brought in the victuals, and just as he came in Sarah brought the cloth and laid it; Mary Burton did not come into the room, but Hughson said she was above making a bed; Peggy came down stairs and sat down by Hughson's wife at the table, and eat with them; when they were eating they began all to talk about setting the houses on fire, and Hughson asked Ben, who would be the head man or captain for to rise? Ben said yes, he would stand for that, and said he could find a gun, shot and powder, at his master's house, that his master did not watch him, he could go into every room: Ben asked Quash, what will you stand for? he said he did not care what he stood for, or should be, but he could kill three, four, five white men before night.

3. "That Quash said he could get two half dozen of knives in papers, three or four swords; and that he would set his master's house on fire, and when he had done that, he would come abroad to fight.

4. "That Marschalk's York said that his mistress had

[148]

scolded at him, and he would kill her before he went out to fight.

5. "London (Marschalk's other negro) said that before he went out to fight, he would set his master's house on fire.

6. "Scipio (Van Borsom's negro) said he would set his mistress's house on fire before he would go out to fight.

7. "Cato (Shurmur's negro) said he would set his mistress's house on fire, and that as the houses stand all together, the fire would go more far.

8. "Cato alias Toby (John Provoost's negro) said he would get his master's sword, and then set the house on fire, and go out to fight.

9. "The Spanish negroes he could not understand.

10. "Caesar (Kortrecht's negro) said he would set his master's bakehouse on fire.

11. "Ben said (when it was proposed to burn his master's house) no, if they conquered the place, he would keep that to live in himself.

12. "That Dick came in just as they had done eating, but victuals enough were left for him, and he sat down and eat: when Dick had done eating, he said every one must stand to his word, and that he would get his master's gun, and after that would set his stable on fire.

13. "He (Jack) being asked to set his master's house on fire, said no, he would set his master's shingles on fire, and then go out to fight.

14. "Hughson said he would stand by what the Spanish and York negroes should do; and he would go before and be their king, and would mix them one amongst another when they came to fight.

15. "Hughson sat the negroes upon this discourse, and design, at the said meeting; on which the Spanish negroes agreed all to join with the York negroes. (r)

16. "That they all swore; some said d——n, some said by G——d, and other oaths; a Spanish negro swear by thunder; Hughson swore by G——d, if they would be true to him, he

(r) See the confessions of Quack and Cuffee, 30th May.

would take this country; and Jack swore by G——d for his part.

17. "That Peggy went away after they had done eating, before they swore.

18. "Mary Burton took away the dishes and plates, and Sarah (Hughson's daughter) took away the cloth; Sarah (Hughson's wife) sat down by her husband, and continued there all the time.

19. "The meeting broke up just after sun down.

20. "Tickle (Carpenter's negro) said, his mistress was cross, and he worked hard, and could get no good clothes; that he would murder his mistress first, because she was not good to him, before he went out to fight.

21. "Bastian alias Tom Peal (Vaarck's) eat at Hughson's; Quash asked him if he would stand to help? he said yes, he knew that, and that was the reason he came there.

22. "Francis (Jasper Bosch's) said, he would set his master's house on fire, before he came out to fight.

23. "Comfort's Cook went with him (Jack) to Hughson's; swore, and said he would set his master's storehouse on fire; and was to go fight too, and could get a penknife or any thing.

24. "Vaarck's Jonneau stood at the door a pretty while, but when the meat ready on table, came in, and sat down at table: York asked him, what will you stand for? he said, he was not able to fight, but he would set his master's house on fire, and then his neighbours, and so on.

25. "Says, they agreed to wait a month and half for the Spaniards and French to come; and if they did not come then, they were to begin at Wenman's, next to Mr. DeLancey's, and so on down the Broadway.

26. "That they waited until this month and half was expired, and then the fort was burnt.

27. "Says, that every negro then present was to do what they engaged to do, on one and the same Sunday, when church was gone in of the morning; and if all was not done in that one day, they were to go on the Saturday following;

and so, if the Spaniards and French did not come, they were to do all themselves.

28. "That at this meeting Anthony, belonging to Peter DeLancey, talked about stuff to put the houses on fire, by flinging it into the house, but heard no other negro but him talk of it; but he mentioned it every time they met, but at this meeting for the first time.

29. "That same Sunday's Monday (the next day) about sun down, all the same negroes came to Hughson's again; some brought money and gave to Hughson for drink and dram; Ben played on the fiddle; Hughson's wife and daughter danced together in one part of the room, and the negroes in another; staid there until about seven that night: that they came there that night to frolick and merry make, and did not talk about fires, for they had agreed upon that the day before.

30. "That then one Sunday passed and no meeting any where that he knows of.

31. "The Sunday after that, there was a meeting at his master Comfort's; some negroes were in the shop, and some in the kitchen; that the kitchen and shop join to each other; the doors into each went out into the street, or into the yard; so that to go from one to the other, you must go either into the yard or on the dock; among whom were Marshall's Ben, Rutger's Quash, Provoost's Cato alias Toby, Shumur's Cato, Marschalk's York and London, Vanborsom's Scipio, Carpenter's Albany, Curacoa Dick, Kortrecht's Caesar, Burk's Sarah, Niblet's Sandy, Chamber's Robin, Gomez's Cuffee, Peck's Caesar, Comfort's Cook, Sleydall's Jack; Anthony and Wan, two Spanish negroes; Vanderspiegle's Fortune, Cowley's Cato, Jay's Brash, Bosch's Francis, Furman's Harry and Powlus: which negroes being met, they began all to talk of burning the town and killing the people; and the general conversation was to the effect of that at Hughson's and the fire to begin as aforesaid; every one being to set his master's house or stable on fire, and then go out to fight.

[151]

32. "Furman's Harry was to set his master's cowstable on fire.

33. "This conversation began, and was most talked of before Sandy came in; Sandy came into the kitchen first, being called in by him (Jack) but was loth to come; Jack asked him to drink a dram, Sandy said no; Sarah (Burk's negro wench) who was then present, said he must drink, and made him drink; and having drunk the dram, Jack asked him if he would stand to, and help them burn houses, and kill the white people? Sandy seemed afraid, they all drank a dram round, and he (Jack) brought in nine clasp knives in a paper; those that had not knives before, took knives from the paper; some went into the shop; and some came into the kitchen, and all the knives were distributed: being asked how he came by those knives, said he asked Powlus, a Spanish negro, about a week before this meeting, to give him a knife; Powlus said he would get some for him, and sell him; Powlus appointed him to meet him the Wednesday before this meeting, at the meal-market, about dusk; that Powlus came, and he gave him two shillings and six pence for them.

34. "When they saw Sandy afraid, they whetted their knives in order to frighten him to say yes, to stand by them; and Jack said, if he did not stand by them he would cut his head off; to which Sarah said, he deserves it if he don't say yes; then Sandy said yes. (s)

35. "The stone they whetted their knives on was a brown stone that lay in the yard by the door. About a week and a half after this meeting, the fort was set on fire.

36. "Soon after Sandy had consented, it growing dusk, they parted.

37. "Says he thought the bargain so sure made, that he did not make any more meetings before the fort fired.

38. "Says that some time after the fort burnt, Sleydall's Jack came to Comfort's house, and told the examinant he had put fire to Mr. Murray's haystack.

39. "That he met Provoost's negro the night that Hil-

(s) See Sandy's examination, No. 2, Monday, May 25.

[152]

ton's house was burnt, and asked him what news? for he had heard that there had been fire at that end of the town; Provoost's Cato alias Toby, said he had done it.

40. "That Gomez's Cuffee set Van Zant's storehouse on fire."

SUPREME COURT
Tuesday, June 9.

Present, the second and third justices.

The king against Bastian, Francis (Bosch's), Albany, Curacoa Dick, negroes.

Upon the motion of Mr. Attorney General, ordered, that the trial of the prisoners, Bastian, etc. be deferred till to-morrow.

Ordered, that the execution of Jack (Comfort's negro) be respited till Friday next.

Court adjourned till to-morrow morning, 10 o'clock.

This day Ben (Capt. Marshall's), Quash (H. Rutger's), Caesar (Kortrecht's), Toby alias Cato (Provoost's), Cato (Shurmur's), York and London (Marschalk's), Scipio (Van Borsom's), and Harry (Furman's) were apprehended upon Jack (Comfort's) examination and confession, and committed.

This day also, the negroes Cook and Robin (Chamber's), Caesar (Peek's), Cuffee (Gomez's) were executed according to sentence.

Examination and confession of Pompey (Leffert's) before the grand jury.—He said,

1. "That Quash (Rutger's) and Quack (Roosevelt's) asked him one Sunday, if he would do as they would do? and Pompey asked them what? and Quash said Quack would tell him; and Quack said they would set their masters' houses on fire, if he would set his master's house on fire, and he agreed he would; and they then told him they would tell him when; and they would be all free, and be free from trouble; he asked what they designed to do? Quack said they would tell him in time, and would not tell him then.

2. "Being asked when he was spoke to, he said it was about a fortnight before Quack was taken up.

3. "That Quash told him, two or three days before he was sent to jail, that Ben (Capt. Marshall's man) knew of it."

Evidence affecting this negro.—Sandy's examination, No. 3, section 8, June 1.—Sarah (Burk's) examination, No. 2, June 1. —Worcester (Varian's) examination, June 22, 30.

Examination and confession of Jack (Comfort's) before the grand jury, No. 2.

He repeated much to the same purpose as in his examination before the judge.

1. But on repeating over the persons who were at Comfort's house, and Hughson's, he observed, "that Cato (Cowley's) was not at Hughson's at that meeting; and that Ben, Quash, and Pablo alias Powlus, were not at Comfort's at that meeting; so that the following is a true list of each company, who was there, who are not executed or indicted:

At Hughson's—H. Rutgers' Quash, John Provoost's Cato, P. Marschalk's York and London, Carpenter's Tickle, capt. Marshall's Ben. Spaniards—Becker's Pablo or Powlus, R. DeLancey's Antonio, Sarly's Juan, McMullen's Augustine, Mesnard's Antonio.

2. At Comfort's—Shurmur's Cato, Cowley's Cato, Marschalk's York and London, Van Borsom's Scipio, Kortrecht's Caesar, Sleydall's Jack, Vanderspiegle's Fortune, Jay's Brash, Furman's Harry, B. Moore's Tom. Spaniards—DeLancey's Antonio, Sarly's Juan."

Upon the close of Jack (Comfort's) two examinations, the judges thought proper to recommend him to his honour, the lieutenant governor, for a pardon.

Wednesday, June 10.

Present, the second and third justices.

The king against Bastian, Francis (Bosch's), Albany, Curacoa Dick, negroes.

On trial on an indictment for a conspiracy to burn the city of New-York, and murder the inhabitants.

Jury called, and the prisoners challenged Ben Thomas. (s) The following jurors were sworn, viz.:

John Dyer, Joseph Sacket, John Shurmur, Josiah Millikan, Isaac Van Dam, Humphry Jones, Daniel Dunscomb, Thomas Bohanna, Isaac Twentyman, Peter Van Dursen, John Robins, Peter Evoutzse.

Of council for the king, Attorney General, Joseph Murray, William Smith, esquires.

The Attorney General, after opening the indictment to the court and jury, proceeded as follows:

Gentlemen,

It will appear to you by the evidence for the king upon this trial, that these four prisoners at the bar, are some of that great number of negroes that frequently met at Hughson's house, where he privately entertained them, and where they confederated with him, and the rest of the conspirators, to carry on this most wicked and dreadful conspiracy to burn the king's house and this town, and to murder the inhabitants. The most horrible and destructive plot that ever was yet known in these northern parts of America, of which Hughson here was the chief contriver and director, with great expectations of enriching himself by the ruin and destruction of his neighbours, as has been made fully appear on the preceding trials; wherefore it may justly be called *Hughson's Plot.* It will likewise appear to you in evidence, that each of these negro prisoners were sworn into this dire-

(s) His house was attempted to be set on fire.

[155]

ful conspiracy, and never to discover it, or that Hughson was any way concerned in it.

Gentlemen, many of the conspirators have already been tried, condemned, and' executed, for the abominable parts they have acted in this execrable conspiracy; and Hughson himself, his wife, daughter, and Margaret Kerry, are under that sentence of death which now awaits their execution, the just demerits of their heinous crimes.

Gentlemen, as all the prisoners at the bar are negroes, the evidence of other negroes is made sufficient against them by a law of this province, which I thought proper to observe to you, because we shall examine several negro witnesses to prove what I have alleged against these negro prisoners; and when you have heard their charge proved against them, I cannot doubt but you will, for your oath's sake, and for your own and this city and country's peace and safety, find the prisoners guilty.

We shall now call the witnesses and examine them before you.

Witnesses for the king called.—Mary Burton, Daniel Burgher, Nicholas Roosevelt, George Joseph Moore, sworn. Sandy and Sarah, negroes. Edward Sherlock, interpreter, Francis being a Spaniard.

Jack (Comfort's) being set to the bar, and asked what he had to say why execution of his former sentence should not be awarded, he produced his majesty's most gracious free pardon, and prayed that the same might be read and allowed of, which being read, was allowed by the court accordingly. The said Jack then proceeded to give evidence against the prisoners.

Evidence against Bastian.—Mary Burton's deposition, No. 2, sections 1, 5, May 13.

She said upon the trial, that she had seen the prisoner at Hughson's, amongst twenty other negroes, and he was consenting with the rest, to burn the whole town and destroy all the people.

Jack (Comfort's) examination, No. 1, sections 2, 21, June 8.

Sawney said, he saw Bastian at the meeting at Comfort's.

[156]

Evidence affecting Francis (Bosch's).—Sawney's examination, No. 1, sections 7, 15, May 22; Jack (Comfort's) examination, No. 1, sections 2, 22, 31, June 8.

Sawney said, he was one of the Spanish negroes he heard talking before Lush's door, when they were talking of burning the town: that he was present and consenting at the meeting at Comfort's.

Mary Burton said, she saw him often at the meetings at Hughson's when they were talking of burning the town and killing the people; and he seemed to be consenting; he spoke a little English, and some other language she did not understand.

Evidence against Albany.—Mary Burton's deposition, No. 2, section 5, 13th May; Jack (Comfort's) examination, No. 1, section 31, 8th June; Confession of Quack, sections 4, 11, 30th May; Confession of Cuffee, section 3, 30th May.—Proved by George Joseph Moore and John Roosevelt.

Evidence against Curacoa Dick.—Sawney's examination, No. 1, section 5, 22d May.—Said he saw him at the meeting at Comfort's, and he consented to burn and kill, etc. Sarah (Burk's) examination, No. 2, section 3, 1st June; No. 3, sections 4, 5, 5th June; Jack (Comfort's) examination, No. 1, sections 12, 31, 8th June.

Witnesses called for the prisoners.—Robert Hogg; Mrs. Carpenter, Albany's mistress; Tiebout, Curacoa Dick's master.

The prisoners' defence as usual with the guilty, turned upon the negative; they asked the witnesses no material questions; and the evidence upon the whole being summed up, the jury were charged and withdrew for a short time; and being returned, found them all guilty of the indictment.

Court adjourned to to-morrow morning 10 o'clock.

SUPREME COURT
Thursday, June 11.

Present, the second and third justices.

The king against Bastian; Bosch's Francis, a Spanish negro; Albany and Curacoa Dick.

Judgment being moved for against these four criminals convicted, they were brought to the bar; and being asked what they had to say, why sentence of death should not be pronounced against them?

Bastian (as was intimated by somebody about the jail he would) confessed his guilt; the rest protested their innocence.

The court then proceeded to sentence against them, which was,

"That they should be chained to a stake, and burnt to death."

And ordered, their execution should be the next day, between two and eight of the clock afternoon.

After sentence passed, the following *confession* was immediately thereupon taken from Bastian in court. He said,

1. "That his fellow-servant Caesar, first acquainted him with it (meaning the plot) and carried him to Hughson's; that Hughson, his wife and daughter were present and swore him; that many negroes were there; Cowley's Cato, DeLancey's Anthony, there: they were to burn the fort and town, and kill the people.

2. "That he threatened Mary Burton, as sworn.

3. "That they were sworn on a bible.

4. "That Hughson was to be the governor or ruler over them.

5. "This meeting was on a Sunday.

6. "That they went there the next night to frolick, and all the negroes who had been executed were in the plot.

7. "Quack burnt the fort, and he has heard him say so.

8. "Hughson was the first encourager.

9. "That Hughson was to have the goods that were stolen from the fire. Caesar was to be king.

10. "This meeting was at Hughson's about a week and a half after new year.

11. "Hughson and his wife and daughter, and Mary Burton there.

12. "Came there about four in the afternoon; a great many negroes there, about thirteen or fourteen; the daughter laid the cloth after he came in.

The king against Sarah Hughson, daughter of John Hughson.

As to this miserable creature under sentence of death, to be executed with her father and mother and Margaret Kerry to-morrow, the judges wished that she would have furnished them with some colour or pretence for recommending her as an object of mercy, but they waited for it hitherto in vain: she was a wretch stupified and hardened in wickedness, and seemed void of all sense of a future state; however it was thought proper to respite her execution to Friday, 19th June, which was ordered accordingly, in hopes that after her father and mother had suffered, she might be molified to a confession of her own guilt, and raise some merit by making a further discovery; or at least, configuring what had hitherto been unfolded concerning this accursed scheme.

Court adjourned till to-morrow morning, ten o'clock.

Examination and confession of Bastian, alias Tom Peal, before one of the judges, No. 1.—He said,

1. "That a little after new-year, Caesar (hanged), his fellow servant, asked him to go along with him down to Hughson's house; this was of a Sunday afternoon before church was out; when he came there he found about fifteen negroes, to the best of his remembrance, in a room with Hughson, his wife and daughter (now under condemnation); Caesar (hanged) was then present, and asked him the examinant (Caesar having a pistol in his hand and clapping the same to the examinant's breast) whether he would join along with them to become their own masters? the examinant asked him, what he would have him join with him in? Caesar answered him in the plot, for that they had designed to take the country, and said they had a parcel of good hands, Spanish negroes, five or six of them (then present) who would join with the York negroes: that they expected that war would be proclaimed in a little time against the French, and that the French and Spaniards would come here, and that they (meaning the negroes present and the Hughsons) would join with them to take the place: at first the examinant answered no, and then Caesar said if he did

[159]

not join along with them, swearing, he the examinant should not go alive out of the house: then he offered the examinant something to drink, and made him drink; and then Caesar said how he had got him; and the examinant being affrighted, and very much daunted upon Caesar's offering a pistol at his breast, was forced to consent; whereupon Caesar said to Hughson, the examinant was but a weak-hearted dog; however set his name down, (v) and I will encourage him up: Hughson answered, he would do it.

2. "Says to the same effect as Comfort's Jack (touching the meeting and entertainment at Hughson's) with this further, that there was veal, ducks, geese, a quarter of mutton and fowls to the best of his remembrance.

3. "That Hughson, his wife and daughter, sat down to eat with the negroes, with this difference, that they sat on one side of the table, the negroes on the other; that the cloth was laid on several tables put together, and some boards laid upon tubs.

4. "That Peggy went in and out of the room but did not sit down with them, but believes she must have heard them discourse about the plot carrying on, and talked of at that meeting.

5. "That after they had done eating, the maid and the daughter helped take the things away; then John Hughson brought a bible and laid it upon the table, then opened the book, and seemed to read something out of it, which was in the nature of an oath, that the first thunder might strike them dead that discovered, or did not stand to their words to perform what they had engaged to do. Hughson swore first, then his wife, then his daughter, and all the negroes present, as well as himself, and all kissed the book; and Hughson pronounced the words they swore to, that is to say, to burn the town, and murder the people, but they were to stay till the Spaniards and French came, about a month and a half; and if they did not come in that time,

(v) It seems Hughson kept a list of the confederates, and used to put them down as they were sworn.

they were to begin themselves, and that they were to begin with the fort first.

6. "That captain Marshall's Ben (whom Hughson and the negroes called captain Marshall) was there when the examinant came in. Jack (Comfort's) came in before the cloth was laid, and after Caesar had clapped the pistol to the examinant's breast. (w)

7. "That Hughson took a flask of rum out of a case and put upon the table, and some punch was made of it, and some drank dry drams, and all the negroes agreed to what was proposed as before.

The negroes then present (at Hughson's) were, Caesar (hanged), Prince (hanged), Philipse's Cuffee, Roosevelt's Quack, Chamber's Robin, Gomez's Cuffee, Comfort's Jack and Cook, Peck's Caesar, Marschalk's York and London, Rutger's Quash, captain Marshall's Ben, Powlus, P. DeLancey's Anthony, Cowley's Cato, Shurmur's Cato, Kip's Harry, Carpenter's Tickle Pitcher, Bosch's Francis, captain Provoost's Cato or Toby, whom they called captain Provoost. "Every one to fire his master's house, and then to fire the fort, and to begin next Mr. DeLancey's; and those that lived at the Fly, to burn Van Zant's storehouse, and begin the fire there: those at the Long Bridge were to fire there.

8. "They broke up about nine of the clock, having made their agreement. At this meeting was the first discourse he heard about the plot.

9. "The Monday night following he went to Hughson's, where they had a frolick, no fiddle, and had the said discourse again, all to stand true to their words, etc. Most part of the same company there again; some he believes could not come out: they had agreed the night before to meet again.

10. "They met at Comfort's about a fortnight after, on Sunday. Jack asked Sandy to come in, etc. Sarah said he was an impudent boy not to do as the captain bid him; Jack fetched penknives, etc.

(w) Compare this examination with Jack (Comfort's), June 8.

Negroes present at Comfort's.—He, Bastian, Curacoa Dick, Sandy, Sarah, Bosch's Francis, Albany, Roosevelt's Quack, Chamber's Robin, Comfort's Cook and Jack, Gomez's Cuffee, Kip's Harry, Peck's Caesar, Marshall's Ben, DeLancey's Albany, Sarly's Wan, Wendover's Emanuel (Spanish negro), Shurmur's Cato, Marschalk's York and London, Sleydall's Jack.

11. "Jack (Comfort's) was to put his masters shingles on fire, etc. to the purpose as Jack said." (x)

Bastian seemed by his looks and behaviour, upon his examination, to be touched with a remorse for his guilt, and was very ingenuous in his confession, insomuch, that he was thought an object of mercy, and would be a witness worthy of credit, therefore it was judged proper to recommend him to the lieutenant governor for a pardon.

SUPREME COURT
Friday, June 12.

Present, the second and third justices.

The king against Bastian and Jamaica.

Ordered, that the execution of the negro Bastian be respited till Friday, the 19th instant.

Some favourable circumstances having been represented with respect to Jamaica, the court thought proper likewise to order his execution to be respited till Friday, the 19th instant.

The King against Quash, Ben, Cato, Fortune, Cato, alias Toby, negroes.

The prisoners being set to the bar, were arraigned for conspiring to burn the whole town and city of New-York, and to kill and destroy the inhabitants thereof, and severally pleaded, *not guilty.*

Court adjourned till to-morrow morning, 10 o'clock.

(x) See Jack's examination, No. 1, section 13, June 8.

Examination and confession of Will, alias Ticklepitcher, negro, taken before one of the judges—No. 1.—He said,

1. "That he was one of the company at Hughson's with a parcel of negroes, when North, the constable, came and interrupted them at a feast.

2. "That on the Sunday following, which was about Whitsuntide twelve months, Tom, belonging to captain Rowe, and Quamino, belonging to the estate of Harris, in Stone-street, asked him whether he would do as they would? the examinant asked them, what was that? old Quamino answered, that they would set fire to both rows of houses in Stone-street, and he would find powder and pistol and ball: the examinant said, he would consider of it, he did not know whether he would or no: then Quamino pulled out a razor and threatened to cut his throat if he did not agree with them, upon, which he was forced to consent.

3. "That about three weeks after last new year, one day about the middle of the week, he (the examinant), Albany, his fellow servant, the above named Tom, and the said Quamino, were at the house of the said John Hughson, and had a tankard of punch, which Hughson brought to them.

4. "That they, the said negroes, together with Cowley's Cato, Vanderspiegle's Fortune, Burk's Sarah, Kelly's London, Varian's Worcester, Kip's Harry, Becker the brewer's Mars, Powlus, Debrosse's Primus, Latham's Tony, another negro (Fortune) belonging to the said Latham, captain Lawrence's tall negro (Sterling), Low's yellow fellow Wan (commonly called Indian Wan), Vaarck's Will and Bastian, Gomez's Cuffee, Groesbeck's Mink, Curacoa Dick, the fiddler, Mrs. Sims's Bill or Will, (in all he thinks between twenty and thirty) were all that he remembers to be present at this meeting at Hughson's.

5. "That the day before this meeting, the negroes above named being all present at Hughson's; he the said Hughson said to the negroes, now was a proper time to make a plot, since there were so many of them together: that is to say, they should undertake to burn the town; to burn the fort;

to burn Stone-street; almost every one agreed, and undertook to burn their master's and mistress's house; and to kill the white people as they came to extinguish the flames: he the examinant was to set his mistress's house on fire: they pitched upon him for it.

6. "Hughson brought out a great book to make them swear; Hughson swore himself and Peggy first, and then swore all the negroes; they putting their right hand every one upon the book; the purport of the oath was, damnation to eternity to the failers, or those that brought out (i.e. discovered) what they had agreed upon.

7. "They were to bring all the goods they could get at the fires to Hughson's house; and after all over, Hughson was to carry them (the negroes) off.

8. "Hughson, to encourage this meeting, promised to give them a barrel of cyder."

The Confession of Jack (Sleydall's) before his master and others—He said,

1. "That some time after Christmas he was at the house of John Hughson, and that there was a supper there; and that captain Marshall's Ben, who sat at the head of the table; Mrs. Carpenter's Albany and Tickle, Comfort's Jack and Cook, Rutgers's Quash, DePeyster's Pedro, Bastian alias Tom Peal, Cowley's Cato, Pintard's Caesar, and several other were there; the cloth being laid and taken away by Margaret Kerry—after supper were dancing, and Mr. Philipse's Cuff played on the fiddle; and that after they had done dancing, they made a bowl of punch; and having for some time drank, they said one to another, let us set fire to the town and kill the white people, and then we will make our escape; and that they all agreed to it, and swore on a book, and kissed the book; and that he the said Jack told them, if they did it, he would try to help.

2. "Being asked if Mr. Jay's Brash was there, he said he was not.

3. "That he the said Jack, on a Saturday night, took some

ashes and coals from his master's house in a little kettle, and put it under Mr. Murray's haystack; (c) that he was told to do it by Mr. DePeyster's Pedro, who said that after the stack was on fire, the others would set other parts of the town on fire."

This day John Hughson, Sarah his wife, and Margaret Kerry, were executed according to sentence.

The under-sheriff had often advised John Hughson, to make a confession about the conspiracy, but he always denied he knew any thing of the matter; said he had deserved death for receiving stolen goods. The wife was ever sullen; said little or nothing, but denied all.

The sheriffs observed John Hughson, when he was brought out of jail to be carried to execution, to have a red spot on each cheek, about the bigness of a shilling, which at that time thought very remarkable, for he was always pale of visage: these spots continued all along to the gallows. Amongst other discourse it seems he had said, he did not doubt but some remarkable sign would happen to him, to show his innocence; concerning which more will be observed upon hereafter. He stood up in the cart all the way, looking round about him as if expecting to be rescued, as was by many conjectured from the air he appeared in: one hand was lifted up as high as his pinion would admit of, and a finger pointing, as if intending to beckon.

At the gallows his wife stood like a lifeless trunk, with the rope about her neck, tied up to the tree; she said not a word, and had scarce any visible motion.

Peggy seemed much less resigned than the other two, or rather unwilling to encounter death; she was going to say something, but the old woman who hung next to her, gave her a shove with her hand, as was said by some, so Peggy was silent.

But they all died, having protested their innocence to the last, touching the conspiracy.

This old woman, as it has been generally reported, was bred a

(c) See Jack (Comfort's) examination, No. 1, section 38, Monday eighth June.

Papist; and Peggy was much suspected of the same persuasion, (d) though perhaps it may seem to be of little significance what religion such vile wretches professed.

Peggy had said several times, as well after her conviction as condemnation for the conspiracy, as the judges were informed by the under-sheriff, that she had sworn falsely against John Romme; which was so gross a prevarication, as discouraged them from taking any further pains with her, since there could be no dependance upon what she should say; the evening before her execution she sent a message to Mr. Justice Philipse, signifying her desire to speak with him; he accordingly went to her; she declared to him, that she had forsworn herself, for all that she had said about Romme and his wife was false, excepting as to their receiving the stolen goods of the negroes.—From the scanty room in the jail for the reception of so many prisoners, this miserable wretch, upon her conviction with the Hughsons for the conspiracy, was put in the same cell with them; which perhaps was an unfortunate incident; for though she had to the time of the their trial screened them from the charge of the conspiracy; yet there was reason to expect, that upon the last pinch, when she found there was no hopes of saving her own life if she persisted, the truth as to this particular would have come out; and indeed it was upon this expectation, that she was brought upon trial for the conspiracy; for her several examinations before set forth, and what Arthur Price had sworn to have dropt from her in accidental talk in jail, had put it beyond doubt, that she was privy to many of the Hughsons' secrets concerning this detestable confederacy; but when she was admitted to the Hughsons, under the circumstances of conviction and condemnation for the conspiracy, they most probably prevailed with her to persevere in her obstinacy, to the end to cover their own guilt, since they were determined to confess nothing themselves; and they might drive her to desperation by subtle insinuations, that the judges she saw after they had picked all they could out of her, whatever expectations she might have raised from her confessions, or hopes she flattered herself with of saving her life upon

(d) See Sarah Hughson's confession, No. 2, section 6, 22d July.

the merit of them; yet after all, she was brought to trial and condemned for the conspiracy, as well as they; and why should she expect pardon any more than they: and by such like artifices it is probable they might stop her mouth, and prevent her making further discovery; and not only so, but then of course prevail with her to recant, as to what she had confessed already.

John Hughson's body was hung in chains according to sentence.

This day also, Albany, Curacoa Dick and Francis, negroes, were executed according to sentence.

The following slaves were taken into custody this day, having been impeached as confederates in the conspiracy:—Groesbeck's Mink, Pemberton's Quamino, Low's Indian Wan, Becker's Mars, DeBrosse's Primus, Rowe's Tom, Kelly's London, Lawrence's Sterling, Ten Eyck's Bill.

SUPREME COURT
Saturday, June 13.

Present, the second and third justices.

The king, against DeLancey's Antonio, Mesnard's Antonio, Pablo alias Powlus, Juan alias Wan, Augustine.

The five prisoners being Spanish negroes, lately important into this city as prize slaves, were put to the bar, and arraigned upon an indictment for the conspiracy, and thereto severally pleaded, *not guilty*, etc.

The king against Quash, Ben, Cowley's Cato, Vanderspiegle's Fortune, Cato alias Toby, negroes, on trial upon indictment for the conspiracy.

Jury called, and the prisoners making no challenges, the following jurors were sworn, viz.:

Cornelius Clopper, Roger French, Coenradt Ten Eyck, Jacobus Keirstede, Lawrence Garner, Henry Vandewater, Charles Beekman, Elbert Herren, William Bartlett, John Brewer, Richard Cook, James Jarrard.

The attorney general having opened the indictment, proceeded as follows:

[167]

Gentlemen, I shall shew you by the witnesses for the king upon the trial of these five negroes, that they, with many others, frequently met at Hughson's house, where they entered into a confederacy with and were sworn by him, to carry on this most wicked and villainous plot, and not to discover it, or that Hughson had any hand in it; and that they agreed to bring all their booty to him, to enrich him and make him great. Thus were these stupid wretches seduced by the instigation of the devil, and Hughson his agent, to undertake so senseless as well as wicked enterprize; which must inevitably end in their own destruction, as now too late they find; and that in the snares they laid for us, they themselves are taken. Gentlemen, it cannot be imagined that these silly unthinking creatures (Hughson's black guard) could of themselves have contrived and carried on so deep, so direful and destructive a scheme, as that we have seen with our eyes and have heard fully proved, they had prepared for us, without the advice and assistance of such abandoned wretches as Hughson was—that never to be forgotten Hughson, who is now gone to his place, as did Judas of old to his.

Gentlemen—These negroes being drawn into this abominable conspiracy by others, does not give them the least umbrage of excuse; they are equally, as guilty as if they themselves had devised it, by consenting to it, taking oaths to proceed in it, and in the mean time to keep it secret.

Gentlemen—The number of the conspirators is very great; for besides these five negroes, fourteen others, and four white people, which I have been concerned in the several trials of, have already been convicted, and received sentence of death, and we have still daily new discoveries of many more; but have now, God be thanked, encouragement to hope that we shall soon reach to the bottom of this mystery of iniquity.

Gentlemen—Be pleased to observe, that all the prisoners now to be tried being negroes, the evidence of one negro against another, is, by a law of this province made sufficient, which I thought necessary to put you in mind of, because

[168]

several negro witnesses will be examined against these five negro prisoners; and when you have heard their charges clearly proved against them, I doubt not but you will, for your own sakes, your oaths sake, and for the future peace and security of this city and province, find these negroes guilty.

Witnesses for the king.—Mary Burton sworn. Comfort's Jack, Sawney, alias Sandy, Ticklepitcher, alias Will, Leffert's Pompey, Sleydall's Jack, Bastian, negroes.

Bastian being placed at the bar, and asked what he had to say why he should not suffer death according to the sentence pronounced against him? he produced a pardon, which he prayed might be read and allowed; and the same being read, was allowed of accordingly.

Of counsel for the King, with Mr. Attorney General, Mr. Murray, Mr. Chambers, who examined the witnesses against the prisoners.

Mary Burton said she had seen captain Ben, Quash, Cato (Provoost's), and Cato (Cowley's) amongst the conspirators at the meeting at Hughson's, and that they were all four consenting and as forward as the rest for burning the town and killing the white people. She did not remember that she had seen Fortune at those meetings, but thought she knew his face.

Jack (Comfort's) said he saw captain Ben, Quash, and Cato (Provoost's) at the meeting of the conspirators at Hughson's, on the Sunday, and that there they talked of burning the town and killing the white people and, that they were consenting and as forward and busy as the rest; and that Fortune, Cato (Cowley's) and Ben were at the great meeting at his master's house about ten days before the fort was burnt, where they had the same talk of the plot as at Hughson's, and they were all consenting. Jack said he brought nine knives, and distributed amongst them at this meeting, with which they were to cut their master's and mistress's throats; that he met Cato (Provoost's) in the street on Saturday evening, who told him he had done business to-day; that he had set Ben Thomas's house on fire.

Sandy said that he saw Fortune and Cato (Cowley's) at Comfort's, at the great meeting there about a fortnight before the fort burnt, and that they agreed amongst the rest, to burn the town and kill the white people.

Bastian confirmed Mary Burton's evidence, and likewise Jack (Comfort's) that Ben, Cato (Cowley's), and Quash, and also Fortune, were at the great meeting on a Sunday at Hughson's, when they were talking of burning the town and killing the people. And further, that they were all sworn to do it, and to keep secret; that he likewise saw Ben, Cato (Cowley's) and Quash, at Comfort's on a Sunday, about a fortnight before the fort burnt, and the talk was the same amongst them there, and they all consented. He said there were two rooms full of negroes there; the kitchen and the shop, as he was told, but he was only in the kitchen.

Will alias Tickle or Ticklepitcher, said he was at Comfort's at the great meeting about a fortnight before the fort burnt, and he there saw Fortune, Ben, and Cato (Cowley's) and spoke as to what passed there, as the foregoing witnesses Jack, Sandy and Bastian; and further, that Cato (Cowley's) went to the pump to wash his hands, and Fortune pumped the water for him.

Pompey (Leffert's) against Quash, said the same as in the examination and confession 9th June, and that Quash was to burn his master's house, and he and Quack (Roosevelt's) were to kill the white people, and that they prevailed upon him to consent to do so too.

Sleydall's Jack said he was at the great meeting of the negroes at Hughson's, on a Sunday about a fortnight before the fort burnt, where they were talking of burning the town and killing the people; and that Quash, Ben, and Cowley's Cato were there, and that they agreed and were sworn.

Note. These are all the minutes of the evidence that were taken at the trial.

See the negro evidence more fully in the respective negro witnesses examinations and confessions, as followeth.

Evidence particularly affecting Captain Ben.—Jack (Comfort's) examination, No. 1, sections 1, 2, 11, 29, 31, 8th June; Bastian's examination, No. 1, section 2, 11th June; Jack (Sleydall's) examination, 12th June; Tickle's examination, No. 1, section 11, 12th June.

Evidence particularly affecting Quash.—Jack (Comfort's) examination, No. 1, sections 2, 3, 21, 31, 8th June; Pompey (Leffert's) examination, No. 1, 9th June; Bastian's examination, No. 1, 11th June; Jack (Sleydall's) examination, 12th June.

Evidence particularly affecting Cato alias Toby.—Jack (Comfort's) examination, No. 1, sections 2, 8, 31, 39, 8th June; Bastian's examination, No. 1, 11th June.

Evidence particularly affecting Cato (Cowley's).—Sandy's examination, No. 2, section 1, 25th May; No. 3, section 8, 1st June. Jack (Comfort's) examination, No. 1, section 31, 8th June. Bastian's examination, No. 1, 11th June. Tickle's examination, section 4, 12th June. Jack (Sleydall's) examination, 12th June.

Evidence particularly affecting Fortune.—Sandy's examination, No. 2, sections 1, 2, 25th May; No. 3, section 9, 1st June. Jack (Comfort's) examination, No. 1, section 31, 8th June. Tickle's examination, No. 1, 12th June.

Witnesses called for the prisoners as to their characters.—Mr. Vanderspeigle (Fortune's master); Mr. Lodge; Isaac, Mr. Vanderspeigle's servant.

The prisoners asked the witnesses no material questions, but upon their defence denied all that was testified against them.

Then Mr. Murray summed up the evidence against Ben, Quash and Cowley's Cato.

Mr. Chambers summed up the evidence against Fortune and Provoost's Cato.

Then the jury being charged, withdrew for a little time; and being returned, found them all guilty of the indictment.

Court adjourned to Monday morning 10 o'clock.

This day DePeyster's Pedro, Latham's Fortune and Tony, Gabriel Crooke's Prince, negroes, were apprehended and committed.

Confession of Gabriel Crooke's Prince, negro, taken before one of the judges—No. 1.—He said,

1. "That on the day that Cuffee and Quack were executed, he the said Prince and York (Marschalk's) were at the execution, and whilst they were looking on them in the flames, York said to him (Prince having first taken notice of the great number of white people present) that then was a

[171]

fit time for them (the negroes) to rise; to which he
(Prince) answered, that he did not think so, for as there
were a great number of the people, perhaps they might only
kill one or two, and then they should be taken and hanged
for it, that it was not a right time to begin now, there was
too much trouble in the town; and York said no more."

Ticklepitcher's examination and confession before the grand
jury—No. 11.—Being asked who brought him into the conspiracy, and when he went to Hughson's?

1. "He said, he was carried there by Albany last Whitsuntide was twelve months; and the second time was about
three weeks after Christmas, when several negroes present,
Hughson, wife, daughter and Peggy, when Hughson administered the oath on the book, of damnation to eternity to
them who failed or discovered.

Persons there (negroes) were all sworn.

Vaarck's Will, Caesar (hanged), Carpenter's Albany
and himself, Kelley's London, Varian's Worcester, Sleydall's
Jack, Rowe's Old Tom, Pemberton's Quamino, Lowe's Wan
(Indian), Burk's Sarah, Vanderspeigle's Fortune, Benson's
Mars, Debrosse's Primus, Latham's Tony and Fortune,
Curacoa Dick, Gomez's Cuffee, Kip's Harry, Cowley's Cato,
Lawrence's tall negro Sterling.

2. "He said that the following persons were one Sunday
evening at Comfort's.

Comfort's Jack and Cook; De Lancey's Antonio; five other
Spanish negroes, whose names not known; Groesbeck's Mink;
Breasted's Jack; Niblet's Sawney; Burk's Sarah; Sleydall's Jack;
capt. Marshall's Ben; Comfort's Jemy; Cowley's Cato; Lawrence's tall negro (Sterling); Todd's Dundee.

"That the talk there was the same as at Hughson's, of
setting houses on fire, stealing of goods, and carrying them
to Hughson's, who was to carry them off.

3. "They all pulled out their knives, whetted them, etc.
as described by Sandy, and took notice of Sarah's threatening
Sandy, etc.

4. "That they were sworn at Comfort's, that is to say, those who were not sworn at Hughson's, the oath was given by Ben, something of thunder.

5. "That Rowe's Tom was to be a drummer, to give notice on firing the houses, to kill the people and plunder.

6. "Being asked to tell us more of the names of the negroes who were at Hughson's and Comfort's, he said he does not now remember their names; there were several more.

7. "Says the Spaniards had black stuff to set houses on fire.

8. "That the tall man, Antonio, and Sarly's Juan had of it, and that Juan owned to him in company at Comfort's, that he set fire to the house of Ben Thomas.

9. "That Gomez's Cuffee told him, he had done what he promised, he had set Van Zant's storehouse on fire, and on which Tickle said, you should not have done it till we were all ready.

10. "Being asked if ever he had seen at their meeting at Comfort's and Hughson's, Mr. Moore's Cato, English's Patrick, Todd's Dundee, Pintard's Caesar, Jay's Brash, capt. Lush's negro, and the governor's Danby; he answered he never saw any of them there but Dundee; heard English's Patrick's name called over at Comfort's, for they had a list of them on a paper.

11. "And being asked who had the list? he said Ben had it, and that there was a list of them at Hughson's, as well as Comfort's."

SUPREME COURT.
Monday, June 15.

Present, the second and third justices.

The King against Rutgers' Quash, Marshall's Ben, Cowley's Cato, Vanderspeigle's Fortune, Provost's Cato alias Toby, negroes.

The criminals being placed at the bar, were asked what they had to say why sentence of death should not be pronounced against them, they offered nothing but protestations of their innocence.

Then the third justice proceeded as followeth.

You, the criminals at the bar, hearken to what is now said to you.

You, Ben, by the course of the evidence, appear to have been a principal ringleader in this most horrid and devilish conspiracy, this master-piece of villainy.

You, no doubt, were esteemed amongst these infernal confederates, a deep politician, and was therefore fixed upon to be an officer, nothing less than a captain, a commander of a hundred at least.

And so exact a man were you in your business and trust, that it seems you kept a list; you say you cannot read, but so active and forward have you appeared in this villainy, that a list of this black band was committed to your care, as appeared in evidence; and you gave sufficient reasons for gaining entire credit with them; for you insinuated yourself in their opinions, by showing them how useful a person you could be to them, from your master's great indulgence and entire confidence in you: you could go into any room in his house; you knew where his guns and other arms were, and could come at them, a considerable number, no less than thirty, were stored in a room in an outhouse; you rid and used your master's horse oftener than he did himself, as you said upon your trial; and therefore could, no doubt, the sooner muster your company, visit your confederates, and make despatch: these were some particulars of your merits to recomment you to these assassins, these murderers.

Thou vile wretch! how much does thy ingratitude enhance your guilt! and your hypocritical, canting behaviour upon your trial, your protestations of innocence, your dissimulation before God and man, will be no small article against you at the day of judgment, for ye have all souls to be saved or to be damned; your spirits are immortal, that is to say, they will live forever, be either eternally happy or eternally miserable in the other world; and be not deceived,

God will not be mocked, he will not be baffled withal, he knows all your thoughts, and sees all your actions, and will reward every one according to their works; those that have done good shall go into everlasting rest and happiness, that is to say, into life eternal; and they that have done evil, and die hardy and impenitent, shall be thrown into the infernal lake of fire and brimstone, together with the devil and his accursed spirits, where the worm never dieth, that is, the biting, gnawing worm of conscience will forever be upbraiding you, and the fire will never be quenched, but in this torment you must remain under the most bitter weeping, wailing and gnashing of teeth, time without end.

If you would not have this your portion, then let us tell you and admonish you in compassion to your wretched miserable souls, immediately to confess your guilt, your horrid sins, before God and man, and discover your accomplices, that you may prevent all further mischief which may otherwise happen from this your hellish conspiracy; sincerely and heartily bewail your heinous and crying sins, and entreat forgiveness of God Almighty; for upon these considerations only, can you entertain any rational or well grounded hope of being received into the arms of his mercy.

And now what is the end of all these your most wicked, detestable and horrible devices? why, you have succeeded so far as to put part of your accursed scheme in execution; you have burnt down and consumed the king's house and buildings at the fort; the house of Van Zant, and have made attempts to burn several others, which God Almighty in mercy and his wonderful and gracious good providence has prevented, by suffering the flames to be timely extinguished; the villainies of these diabolical confederates have been detected, many of them have already met with their deserts, and are gone to their long homes, whither your are in a few hours to follow them, for you are now also delivered into the hands of our laws, and in this world you must have justice, and you are left to the mercy of God in the next.

What has already been said, is applicable, most of it, to every one of you.

And in as a particular manner, Quash, may you be upbraided with the like reproaches for your ingratitude, for as we have been informed, you have likewise had a very indulgent master, who has put great trust and confidence in you, it may be presumed from your having better sense than the rest of his negroes: how vilely then have you abused his indulgence! in return for kindnesses, you wretches would imbrue your hands in the blood of your masters and their families; you that would destroy without mercy, with what face can you expect mercy at the hands of God, unless you acknowledge every one his guilt and bewail it with hearty sorrow and sincere tears of repentance, and beseech his forgiveness, laying open the whole wicked scheme, and discovering your several confederates and accomplices, all the parties concerned, so that an effectual stop may be put to all further mischief: upon these conditions only can you expect mercy at the hands of God Almighty.

As to you two Catoes, and you Fortune.

You appear indeed to have been inferior agents, but your hearts as corrupt and ripe for mischief as any of the rest; you have all alike taken that hellish, execrable oath, and equally bound yourselves in that villainous engagement, not only to burn and consume your master's substance, but to murder and destroy their persons and families; you were as willing and ready as the ablest of them to act your parts in this bloody scheme.

It is a very irksome task to pronounce that sentence which the law requires of us, for we delight not in any man's blood; but the law adjudges you unfit to live.

Therefore the sentence against you, is

That you, each and every of you, be carried from hence to the place from whence you came, from thence to the place of execution, where you Ben and Quash, are to be each of you chained to a stake and burnt to death.

And you Cato (Mr. Provost's) you Cato (Mr. Cowley's) and you Fortune, are each and every of you to be hanged by the neck until you be severally dead.

And the Lord of his infinite mercy, have compassion upon your poor wretched souls.

[176]

Ordered, that the execution of Cowley's Cato, Fortune and Cato alias Toby, be on the morrow the 16th instant, between the hours of nine and one of the same day: and

That the execution of Ben and Quash be on the morrow the 16th instant, between the hours of three and seven o'clock of the afternoon of the same day.

The king against De Lancey's Antonio, Mesnard's Antonio, Sarly's Juan alias Wan, Becker's Pablo alias Powlus, McMullen's Augustine, slaves.

This being the day appointed for the trial of these prisoners as slaves upon an indictment for the conspiracy, on which they were arraigned on Saturday last, they were brought to the bar in order to proceed thereon: but they complained (as it is supposed they were advised) that they had great injustice done them by being sold here as slaves, for that, as they pretended, they were free men in their own country, and gave in their several surnames.

The indictment was grounded upon an act of the assembly (i) which enumerated several offences; and conspiracies amongst the rest, and made one slave evidence against another, so that this fetch might probably be calculated to take off the negro evidence: the prisoners all protested they could not speak English, and as Mary Burton was the only white evidence against them, and should it be credited that they could speak only in a tongue which she did not understand, how could she tell what passed between them in conversation at Hughson's? Thus their advisers might think they would stand the best chance for the jury to acquit them.

The court deferred their trial till Wednesday the 17th instant.

Court adjourned until to-morrow morning 10 o'clock.

Examination of Fortune (Latham's negro) before the grand jury.—He said,

"That about five months ago being at Comfort's on a holiday, he met there Comfort's Jack and Cook, and Furman's

(i) 4th Geo. II. For the more effectually preventing and punishing the conspiracy and insurrection of negro and other slaves, etc. before mentioned on trial of Quack and Cuffee, 29th May.

[177]

Harry, and Comfort's old negro woman; that Jack and Cook went out of the house and left him with Harry, who asked him if he would not be concerned with them in helping them to kill the white people? which was all that passed at that time; and he never had any other meeting with them afterwards, nor did any of them ever after talk with him on that subject; and that this is all he knew of the plot."

Evidence affecting this negro.—Tickle's examination and confession, section 4, 12th June.

SUPREME COURT.
Tuesday, June 16.

Present, the second and third justices.

The King against Marchalk's York amd London, Kip's Harry, B. Moore's Tom, Shurmur's Cato, Groesbeck's Mink, negroes.

The prisoners being put to the bar, were arraigned on an indictment for the conspiracy, etc. and York, London, Harry and Cato pleaded *not guilty*; and Tom and Mink pleaded *guilty*, and submitted themselves to the mercy of the court.

Court adjourned till to-morrow morning nine o'clock.

This day the negroes Cowley's Cato, Vanderspeigle's Fortune, Cato alias Toby, Ben and Quash, were executed according to their respective sentences.

SUPREME COURT.
Wednesday, June 17.

Present the second and third justices.

The king against DeLancey's Antonio, Mesnard's Antonio, Becker's Pablo, Sarly's Juan alias Wan, McMullen's Augustine, Spanish negroes.

The prisoners being set to the bar, were arraigned upon a second indictment, for counselling and advising the negro Quack, to burn the fort, etc. by the names of Antonio de St. Bendito,

Antonio de la Cruz, Pablo Ventura Angel, Juan de la Sylva, Augustine Gutierez; whereto they severally pleaded, *not guilty*, etc.

Then the court proceeded upon their trials on both indictments.

Jury called, and the following jurors sworn, viz.—John Bell, Robert Provost, Charles Jandyne, Andrew Jereau, John Dyer, Evert Byvank, Tobias Stoutenburgh, Cornelius Bogart, Stenwick Deriemer, George Burnet, Charles Beekman, jun., Samuel Dunscomb.

Of council for the king, Joseph Murray, James Alexander, John Chambers, esquires.

Mr. Chambers opened the indictment.

Mr. Gomez sworn interpreter.

Witnesses for the king called.

Mary Burton sworn. She said that she had seen many meetings of the negroes at Hughson's, and especially about new-year, and that it was the common talk among them and the Hughson's, that they would burn the town and murder the people, that Hughson swore the negroes to be true to him, and to each other, and not to discover; that they were to burn the fort, then the Fly, and murder the people: that Hughson said they would burn Lush's house, and tie Lush to a beam and roast him like a piece of beef: that there were several great meetings there, and that she had seen Anthony (DeLancey's) often there at nights, that he was there when they talked about fires, and some of them said, the Spaniards could fight well; that she thought the said Anthony was there about new-year, but was sure she saw him there often in March, and that he often spoke to her in English, and that she heard him say, while the York negroes killed one, the Spaniards could kill twenty: that he used to come upon the shingles and get into Peggy's window: that she had seen all the prisoners at Hughson's, when they were talking about the plot, and they were consenting.

Sawney said he knew Mr. DeLancey's Antonio, and heard him say, with five other Spaniards, pointing to captain Lush's house, d——n that son of a b——h, if he did not carry them to their own country, they would ruin the city and play the d——l with him; that they spoke English, and this happened near captain

Lush's house; and captain Sarly's negro (Juan) said, he would first burn captain Lush's house, and then his master's; that one of them rolled something black in his hands, and broke it and gave to the rest, which was to be thrown on the houses, to set fire to the shingles in several places; that the brewer's negro (Pablo) was also there; that this was the first time he heard any thing about the plot; that one Sunday, going for tea water, he saw Mr. Philipse's Cuff at his master's storehouse, and he swore that if he was hanged or burnt, he would fire the storehouse; that he then went to Comfort's, where there were many negroes, and six Spanish negroes, amongst them McMullen's Augustine and Mesnard's Antonio; that they made him (the witness) drink rum, and they whetted their knives and said they were sharp, and would cut the white men's heads off; and they agreed to burn the fort and their master's houses, to kill their masters and take the white women for wives, and they swore upon the thunder to be true to each other; that this was on a Sunday evening, about a fortnight before the fort was burnt; that what he heard near Lush's was about the middle of last summer; that he heard McMullen's Augustine and Wilkins' Fortune agree each of them to burn his master's house, which was near Mr. Smith's, the tavern keeper, before the fort was burnt.

Mr. George Joseph Moore, called and sworn. He proved the confessions of Quack and Cuffee at the stake.

He said, that they declared the Spanish negroes were most of them concerned in the plot; that they did not name any names but referred to Sawney, who, they said, could name them all.

Jack (Comfort's negro) said, that after new year there was a great company of negroes at Hughson's on a Sunday evening; that he went with captain Marshall's Ben thither, and he supped there, and all the prisoners were present, which was in February; that all present agreed to burn the town, and they were all sworn.—That ten days before the fort was burnt, they had a meeting at his master's (Comfort's) and there they all swore to burn the town, and kill the people; that they were first to begin at Mr. DeLancey's and so to go to the fort; that they sharpened their knives, and he let nine have knives that had none; that he bought the knives of Pablo for half a crown; that there was only two Spaniards there, to wit, Antonio (Mr. DeLancey's) and Pablo (Becker's) and that Mr. DeLancey's negro said, he had stuff to throw on the houses to make them get fire, which Hughson had talked about before: that they were to stay a month and a half for the Spaniards, and if they did not come, to begin themselves.

Ticklepitcher said, that about three weeks after new-year, he saw all the prisoners at Hughson's on a Sunday evening with one Spanish negro more; and Mr. DeLancey's negro (Antonio) had something black, which he said was to throw on houses to set them on fire; and he cut it in pieces and gave to several of the negroes: that he (the witness) did not then stay at Hughson's, so did not hear what they talked of. That afterwards there was a great meeting of the negroes at Comfort's, and he saw Juan and Augustine there; and it was agreed by those present to set the town on fire, and kill the white people; and there they sharpened their knives: that Mr. Niblet's Sawney was also there, and Burk's Sarah, who told him that they were making a plot to kill the white people, burn the houses, and to steal the money and goods and go off; there were two rooms full of them, some were in the kitchen and some in the shop.

Bastian said, he knew all the prisoners, and had known them ever since the meeting at Hughson's, which was a little after new-year, where the prisoners all were; that it was on a Sunday afternoon that Caesar and Hughson took him aside, and Caesar asked him if he would do as they did; which was to endeavour to be their own masters; that upon his refusing, Caesar put a pistol to his breast and threatened him, and then he consented: that then they went in the room to the rest of the negroes, where it was agreed to burn the fort first, then by Mr. DeLancey's, then in the Fly, and each to set fire to their own master's houses, and they were to murder the white people: that this meeting was three or four weeks before the fort was burnt: that Quack was pitched upon to set fire to the fort: that they were to wait a month and a half for the French and Spaniards, and if they did not come they were to begin themselves. That Hughson put his name on a paper, when he consented: that afterwards they had a meeting at Comfort's where they ground some clasp knives.

[181]

That Sawney came there, and Comfort's Jack called him in and gave him a dram, and at last, after threatening him, Sawney agreed to be concerned in the plot: that the prisoners Antonio (DeLancey's), and Pablo (Beeker's Spanish negro) were then there, and consented: that at Comfort's some were in the kitchen, some in the shop: that Mr. DeLancey's negro Antonio had something black in his hand, which he cut and gave to other negroes to throw on houses to set them on fire: that Hughson proposed burning the fort before any thing else; because at a former rising, the white people run into the fort; he said if that was set on fire it would blow up the powder, etc.

Richard Nichols, esquire, deputy register of the admiralty, sworn.

He said, that the nineteen negroes and mulattoes, taken and brought in by captain Lush, were libelled in the court of admiralty, as Spanish slaves, and condemned as such in May, 1740; and Pablo (Beeker's) was condemned as a slave taken by captain Kierstead.

John Cruger, esquire, vendue-master.—He said, that he afterwards sold Antonio, DeLancey's; Antonio, Mesnard's; and Juan, Sarly's, at vendue.

Captain John Lush sworn.—He said, that Juan, Sarly's, could speak English, and Antonio, DeLancey's, could speak a little so as to be understood.

William Douglass, sworn.

He said he was taken in captain Hinman's vessel with Mr. De-Lancey's Antonio's brother; that they were carried into the Havanna, and that a gentlemen there brought Antonio's brother as a slave, and said he knew him and his family at Carthagena, and that they were slaves.

Mr. Benson, partner with Mr. Beeker, Pablo's master, sworn.

Being asked whether he had any such clasp knives as Jack (Comfort's) had described, and said he had bought of Pablo? he answered, that he had had a parcel of clasp knives, but whether he had sold them, or whether he had them still, he could not say; but that he would go home and see, if the court pleased; and he going accordingly and being returned, said that upon search he found that he had none of those knives left but one;

that his wife told him that they had brought but three of them when they came to Becket's. He said that Pablo talked very broken English, but he could make a shift to understand him.

Witnesses for the prisoner Antonio (DeLancey's).—Mr. Peter DeLancey, merchant, said that his negro went to his farm in the country last fall, and did not return till two days after the fire at the fort; that he was not there all the while himself, but was frequently there, and saw him lame, his feet being frozen, and he did not think he could have been in town in that time.

Abraham Peltreau said that Mr. DeLancey's negro went up with him to the farm before Christmas, and came down with him after the fort was burnt, and that his feet were frozen after the first great snow, and does not know that he was in town all the winter; that his feet were well some time before he came down.

Witnesses for Antonio (Mesnard's).—Dr. Depuy, senior, said that Antonio (Mesnard's) feet were frozen, and that he dressed them during December and January last.

Dr. Depuy, junior, said that the latter end of November and December last, this negro was ill, and he saw his toes in December, and then they were bad, so that he could not walk, but he did not know whether he was able to walk in February or not: that he (Antonio) came to his father's house the beginning or middle of March, the time he could not exactly say, but it was before the fire at the fort.

Gilbert Budd said that he dressed this negro from the middle of November to the 5th or 6th of March last; that he thinks Mrs. Mesnard told him that he came down stairs about the latter end of February, when his feet grew bad again, for they had been better before.

Francis Dupuy said he thought the negro was not able to walk in February, but believed he came to his father's house to be dressed while Mr. Budd was in Philadelphia, which was between the 6th and 11th of March. That this negro spoke to him in broken English.

Mrs. Mesnard, this negro's mistress, said he was not down stairs from November till the 17th of March, and she believed it was not possible for him to be abroad at that time.

[183]

Witness for Juan.—Captain Jacob Sarly, his master, said that when the fire was at Mr. Thomas's, Juan, his negro, first discovered it to his wife, as she told him, and that he never had a more faithful servant, and when he was home, the negro could not be out after nine at night. That one Don Juan told him by an interpreter, that he heard that his negro was free. Further, that he was not always at home himself, but he did not believe his negro had been out.

Witness for Pablo.—Frederick Beeker, Pablo's master, said that his negro was brought into this country by captain Boyd, in January last, and was sick in his house till some time in March.

Witnesses for Augustine.—McMullen, his master, said that his negro was sick all the winter, and did not know that he was abroad all the winter. In February he had an ague, as the Doctor said, that he kept his bed most of the time, but not constant but about a week: that he always behaved very well, and captain Warren gave him a very good character: that he was brought by capt. Warren into this country, who offered to sell him to him for 70 pounds but they did not agree.

William Quinland said he lived at Mr. McMullen's, and that this negro behaved very well; that he did not know that he had been out all the winter till Easter.

Thomas Palmer said to the same purpose.

The prisoners, upon their defence, denied all in general that was alleged against them, and made great protestations of their innocence, and most of them pretended to have been sick or lame, so that they were incapable of going abroad from new year to the time of the fire at the fort (the eighteenth of March), neither could they speak English.

Antonio (DeLancey's) said in particular, that his master and the overseer could prove that he had been lame, and was in the country all the winter, and that his master had him to town a little after the fort burnt, and that he had not kept company with any negroes since he came to the country.

Augustine said he had been sick ever since he came here; that he knew no negroes; kept no company but McMullen's apprentices.

Pablo or Powlus, said that he kept no company with negroes

since he came here; he had not been used to keep company with negroes (or slaves) in his own country.

Juan or Wan spoke much to the same purpose; he did not use to keep company with negroes (or slaves.)

Antonio (Mesnard's) was sick and lame, etc.

Act of assembly read, 4th Geo. II. for the more effectual preventing and punishing the conspiracy and insurrection of negroes, etc.

Act of parliament read, 4th and 5th Ph. and Mary. Ch. 4.

Mr. Chambers summed up the evidence against Antonio (DeLancey's), Antonio (Mesnard's), and Pablo.

Mr. Murray summed up against Augustine and Juan.

The court charged the jury as followeth:

Gentlemen of the jury,

The prisoners at the bar stand charged upon two several indictments, for conspiring to burn and destroy this city, and murder the white people.

The one indictment is grounded upon an act of assembly of this province, supposing them to be slaves, by which act the testimony of one negro slave shall be legal evidence against another.

But it has been made a question, whether these prisoners, now before us, are slaves or not; and the prisoners themselves pretend to be free subjects of the king of Spain, with whom we are now at war, from whom they have been taken and made prize, and have been condemned and adjudged as such in the court of admiralty here, without any plea being offered there, or so much as any claim or pretence of the prisoners being entitled to any privilege, as being free subjects of Spain; and surely there never could have been a more proper time and season for them to have set up such pretence, as when their case was depending before the court of admiralty, where they should have offered it by way of plea; especially considering, that by their neglect of that opportunity, they must well know the consequence would be, their being adjudged as part of the goods and chattels of the subjects of Spain, would be condemned as lawful prize, and

[185]

would also be sold as slaves; but if this pretence had been offered there, (as was not) and they could not have proved the truth of the plea it would not have availed them, but they must have been adjudged to be slaves.

But they have made that pretence in this court, and what has been offered in support of it? Why there has been several witnesses that have spoke to the point; and what is the amount of their testimony? Why, it is no more than the hearsay of an hearsay of a person, who imagined or believed, that they or most of the Spanish negroes taken by capt. Lush, were freemen; but which of them were or were not, he could not say, nor does it appear that the prisoners at the bar, or any of them, are such of capt. Lush's prize-prisoners, as that the said Spanish gentlemen imagined were free; for it was no more than his imagination, as to any of them being such.

You have heard the adjudication and decree of the court of admiralty read, by which it appears, they were condemned as prize, and that they were sold as slaves, has been proved by the vendue-master; therefore for what appears now before the court, it should seem that they really are slaves; and as nothing appears; no sufficient or proper evidence appears to the contrary, then if you take them upon these considerations, to be slaves, all the negro evidence which has been given upon this trial against them, is legal evidence, and so you are to consider of that testimony, and let it have its full force; and if you should have sufficient reason in your own consciences to discredit them, and that notwithstanding the weight of that evidence, you can think them, or any of them, not guilty, you will then say so and acquit them, or such of them as you think innocent as to the charge of this indictment, upon the act of assembly.

Gentlemen, the prisoners having started this pretence, of being free subjects of the king of Spain, in case it should have happened upon this trial, as we think it has not, that there should be sufficient evidence to shew that the prisoners were freemen, if we could take them to be such, is it fit that persons guilty of so atrocious and enormous crimes (let them be free or bond) such execrable villains should miss of their deserved punishment and escape the justice of the law? Surely that would be very unbecoming, that such wickedness should be suffered with impunity in any well regulated government or society: therefore be they freemen, or be they slaves, the main question before you is, whether they, or any, or which of them are guilty of the charge against them, in the second indictment, of conspiring with other slaves and persons to burn the house in the fort, to burn the town and murder and destroy the people.

To prove the charge in this indictment, there was the testimony of Mary Burton: I must observe to you, that her testimony, as to the charge in this indictment, is single, there is no other witness; but nevertheless gentlemen, one witness is sufficient, and if you give credit to her testimony, you will no doubt discharge a good conscience, and find them guilty; if you should have sufficient reason in your own minds to discredit her testimony, if you can think so, you must then acquit them: the prisoners seem all to be equally involved by her testimony, in this unparalleled and hellish conspiracy, and there is no room to make any difference between them; therefore you will either acquit them all, or find them all guilty.

Then the jury withdrew, and in about half an hour returned, and found them all guilty.

The king against Sarah Hughson, and Jamaica, a negro.

The judges having advised with his honour the lieutenant governor, ordered, the execution of Sarah Hughson and Jamaica, be further respited until next Friday seven-night; though with respect to Sarah this was a mere act of mercy, for she yet remained inflexible.

Court adjourned to Friday, the 19th instant, 10 o'clock in the morning.

Thursday, June 18.

Confession of Mink, negro of John Groesbeck, before the grand jury.—He said,

[187]

"That in the winter Hughson met him in the woods, and carried him to his house, and gave him and asked him to join in the conspiracy, and he consented and was sworn by Hughson on a book, that thunder and lightning might strike him dead if he did not comply, etc.

"He said he was there in all three times, and named a few (negroes) who were executed (that were there) but none else."

Evidence affecting this negro.—Sarah (Burk's negro wench) examination, No. 2, 1st June; Tickle's examination, section 4, 12th June; York (Marschalk's) examination, section 6, 20th June.

Confession of Tom, Ben Moore's negro, before the grand jury. —He said,

1. "That Cuffee, Philipse's, was the first man that engaged him in the conspiracy, that he went with him to Hughson's where he treated him with punch; this was about the beginning of the winter, when the cold weather was coming in, on a Saturday, and the first time of his being at Hughson's house; at which time nothing was said or done remarkable.

(2.) "That about a week after he went there again on a Sunday, with the said Cuffee, Auboyneau's Prince, and Vaarck's Caesar, that soon after they got to Hughson's Caesar and Cuffee went out of the house, and Prince asked him (Tom) if he would be concerned with them in what they were going about to do? On which he asked what that was? to which Prince replied that he should know it when Caesar and Cuffee returned.

3. "That soon after Cuffee and Caesar came in, and then the same question was asked him again; to which he answered as before, by asking of them what they were going about? Cuffee then replied that they were going to burn houses, that he (Cuffee) would burn his master's house, where there was money enough, that he (Tom) should have a share of it.

4. "That he refused to be concerned with them, saying that he durst not do it, for the white people would play the devil with them; but Cuffee answered that he needed not fear that, for that he had got people enough to stand by them; and then he (Tom) told them he would consider on it, and then they broke up; this being the second meeting at Hughson's; at which neither Hughson nor any other person was present.

5. "That about four or five days after, he met Caesar in the street, who told him that if he would go down yonder (meaning to Hughson's) he would come to him, that he went down, and soon after Caesar came to him, and called for some punch, that when they had drank, Caesar asked him if he would be concerned with them in what they were going to do; that he answered he would not, for he did not like it: Caesar took the punch and drank to him again, and when that tankard was out, he called for another, and drank to him again, and then asked him why he refused to be concerned with them, telling him that at their last meeting he said he would consider of it; on which he (Tom) being heated with liquor, said he would join with them, and then Hughson was called on, who came with a book and swore him; the purport of the oath being to be secret and true to one another.

6. "That the next day after, he went to Hughson's in the evening himself; but finding none of the rest there, he returned speedily, and to the best of his remembrance this was the last time that he went there.

7. "That some days after he met Cuffee in the street, who asked him when he would go down again to Hughson's? that he answered him he would go there no more, that he was sorry for what he had done, for what they were going about was a very great sin; that Cuffee then called him a fool, and told him that if he thought it a wrong thing, or a sin, there was a man that he knew that could forgive him; that while they were speaking Caesar came to them, and then Cuffee told him, that he (Tom) was going to leave them, on which Caesar cursed him, and said if he did, or

[189]

spoke a word of what had passed among them, he had a pocket pistol and would be the death of him; but Caesar as well as Cuffee told him that if he was in any pain about what they were going to do, as a sin, there was an old man in town who they knew, that could forgive them.

(8.) "That some time after, Caesar came to him on Bayard's wharf and threatened to throw him into the river if he fell off from them, or informed any body what they were going to do; that he (Tom) was afraid, and told him that he would be true to them, and so they parted; and that ever after that he shunned them, and never was at any time in company with them, neither at public or private meetings.

9. "That one Sunday he had a mind to disclose this design and conspiracy to Mr. Ogilvie, and went to him for that purpose; that he told him, that he had something to tell him, which was a very great sin and would surprize him; but Ogilvie answered that he was going to church, and bid him come when church was out and he would hear him; that he did not go to Mr. Ogilvie after church was out, nor did he ever say any thing to him about it."

Evidence affecting this negro.—Sandy's examination, No. 3, section 8, 1st June; York (Marschalk's) examination, section 6, 20th June; Pompey (DeLancey's) examination, section 5, 22d June.

SUPREME COURT
Friday, June 10.

Present, the second and third justices.

The king against Marschalk's York and London, Kip's Harry, and Shurmur's Cato, negroes, on trial upon indictment for the conspiracy.

Jury called, and the following jurors sworn, viz.—Lawrence Garner, Joseph Sacket, John Saver, John Smith, Charles Arding, Peter Evoutse, John Van Gelder, Thomas Grigg, John Bogart, James Charlton, Isaac Van Hook, Johannis Roshe.

Of council for the king, Mr. Murray, Mr. Chambers.

Mr. Chambers opened the indictment, and then both proceeded to examine the witnesses.

Jack, Comfort's negro, told his whole story of the plot, from Ben's first mentioning it to him at Comfort's; said that London, York and Cato were at the great meeting and entertainment at Hughson's; and that after the cloth was taken away by Hughson's daughter, and the knives and plates by Mary Burton, Hughson began to talk to the negroes, and said, that negroes could do as well as white people, and now was a good time to make a plot; others say no, stay one month and a half until the Spaniards come, and if they did not come then they would try for themselves: that they all present swore to the plot; all to set fire to the houses, and kill the people: some agreed to begin with their masters' and mistress's houses. That Cato told him that he put Ben Thomas's house on fire, and that he struck fire with a steel to do it: that York said, he would kill his mistress before he came abroad. (k) York was to be a captain, and London to be an officer under him: that a week and a half after this the negroes had a great meeting at his (i.e. his master's) house: that he did not see Harry at Comfort's or Hughson's. That York said at Comfort's, he had no occasion for a knife, he would get a sword; and London said at Comfort's, he did not care what he did, or what became of his master or mistress.

Bastian said, he saw York and London at the two great meetings at Hughson's and Comfort's, each on a Sunday; and that the negroes all present agreed to burn their master's houses, and to kill the people; to burn the fort first, then to fire by Mr. De-Lancey's: Ben swore them all. That by direction of Caesar (hanged), Hughson put the witness's name down in a paper, as a person engaged in the conspiracy; Caesar said, he (the witness) was a faint hearted dog, but he would spirit him up. That London said, his master would trust him in the house more than York, and he could easier get into any room and murder him. That both York and London ground their knives at Comfort's;

(k) As the negroes told their story, they were first to kill their masters and mistresses, and then to come abroad, (i.e., out in the streets) to fight.

one had a knife of his own, the other took one of Jack's: that he saw Cato and Harry at the great meeting at Hughson's, where it was agreed, that the negroes were to get their master's arms, to burn their houses, and to murder them: that this meeting was three or four weeks before the fort was burnt, the meeting at Comfort's was the Sunday after: that he saw only Harry at Comfort's; he took a knife of Jack; the negroes all whetted their knives, and some said they were sharp enough to cut the white men's heads off. This witness gave an account of the treatment of Sandy at Comfort's, that upon Sandy's denying Jack to be concerned in the plot, and telling him, that if they wanted to fight, they might go and fight with the Spaniards, and not with their own masters and mistresses; that thereupon Sarah (Burk's negro wench) told Sandy that he was very impudent to talk so to capt. Jack, and that he deserved to have his head cut off.

Tickle, a negro, said he was at the great meeting at Hughson's on a Sunday; that Hughson said to the negroes, now there was so many met together, it was a good time to make a plot; and he proposed to them, that they should set fire to the houses, steal as many goods as they could and bring them to him, and as the people came out of their houses they were to kill them, so to fire the houses all around the town; that he saw Harry at Hughson's, and he agreed to set his mistresses house on fire, and to kill the people; that Hughson swore all the negroes of the plot at that meeting, and then put their names down on a paper; that he saw Cato, the prisoner, at the meeting at Comfort's.

Sandy, a negro, gave the same account as on former trials concerning the negroes meeting at Comfort's, and what passed there: saw Harry (Kip's negro) at the meeting at Comfort's, but did not remember to have seen any of the other prisoners there.

Mr. George Joseph Moore and Jane Lovell sworn.

Mr. Moore proved the confessions of Quack and Cuffee at the stake the 30th of May, and said that both the criminals did there declare, that Harry (Kip's) was concerned in the conspiracy.

Jane Lovell said that the day Mr. Philipse's storehouse was on fire, Mink (Groesbeck's negro) was coming from his master's rope-walk with a coil of ropes; and he and the prisoner Cato stopped by her house, and she said to them, that all this trouble was occasioned by them; to which Mink answered, he wished all concerned were tied to a stake and burnt; whereto Cato replied, he was a fool; if he knew as much as he did, he would hold his tongue.

These were all the notes that were taken upon this trial. See the several negro examinations and confessions affecting the prisoners.

As to London.—Jack (Comfort's) examination, No. 1, sections 2, 5, 31, June 8; Bastian's examination, No. 1, sections 7, 10, June 11.

As to York.—Jack (Comfort's) examination, No. 1, sections 2, 4, 24, 31, June 8; Bastian's examination, No. 1, sections 7, 10, June 11; Prince (Crooke's) examination, June 13.

As to Harry.—Cuff (Philipse's) confession at the stake, section 3, May 30; Quack (Roosevelt's) confession at the stake, section 2, May 30; Sandy's examination, No. 3, section 8, June 1; Sarah (Burk's) examination, No. 2, 3, June 1 and 5; Bastian's examination, No. 1, June 11. Tickle's examination and confession, section 4, June 12.

As to Cato.—Sarah (Burk's) examination, No. 2, June 1; Jack (Comfort's) examination, No. 1, sections 2, 7, 31, June 8; Bastian's examination, No. 1, June 11.

The prisoners upon their defence stifly denied all that had been testified against them.

Act of assembly, 4th Geo. II. For the more effectual preventing and punishing the conspiracy and insurrection of negro and other slaves, etc. read.

Then the counsel summed up the evidence against the prisoners; and the court having charged the jury, they withdrew, and, after a short stay, returned and found the prisoners *guilty*.

The lieutenant governor having this day issued a proclamation with the advice of his majesty's counsel, the same was read in court, taking notice of the conspiracy which had been set on foot, abetted, encouraged and carried on by several white people in conjunction with divers Spanish negroes brought hither from the West-Indies, and a great number of other negroes within this city and country, for the burning and destroying this whole city, and murdering the inhabitants thereof; to the end that mercy

[193]

might be shewn to such as might merit the same, his honour thought it necessary, and did thereby in his majesty's name, offer and promise his majesty's most gracious pardon, to any and every person and persons, whether white people, free negroes, slaves, or others, who had been or were concerned in the said conspiracy, who should on or before the first day of July then next, voluntarily, freely and fully discover, and confession make, of his, her or their confederates, accomplices, or others concerned in the said conspiracy, and his, her and their part or share, actings and doings therein, so that the person or persons making such discovery and confession, were not thereof before convicted, arraigned, or indicted for the same.

The king against Furman's Harry, Pemberton's Quamino, Lowe's Wan (Indian), Kelley's London, Varian's Worcester, negroes or slaves.

The prisoners were arraigned upon an indictment for the conspiracy, whereto Harry, Quamino and Worcester pleaded *not guilty*, and Wan and London *guilty*.

Court adjourned to Tuesday the 23d instant, ten o'clock in the morning.

Confession of Wan, Indian man of Mr. Lowe, before the grand jury.

1. "He said that about twelve months ago he met at the water-side, John, a free Indian, late of Cornelius Cosine, who carried him to Hughson's, where they drank a mug of beer, and paid for it: when John went away, but Hughson stopped him (Wan) and told him a law was made to sell no liquor to slaves, bid him not tell: Wan said he would not; then Hughson bid him swear on a book he held to him, to do what he should tell him, and Wan said he would; and he put his hand on the book and swore after what Hughson said, to burn his master's house, and to kill his master and mistress, and to assist to take the town.

2. "That Ticklepitcher and Bastian were there when he swore; and being asked if any one else? he said none.

3. "That John, the Indian, met him afterwards, and seeing him melancholy, asked him what was the matter? He

[194]

(Wan) told him what he had done, on which John said it was good for him.

4. "That Cuffee (Gomez's) and Francis (Bosch's) told him, they were to set their master's house on fire, and one day asked him if he was ready, and he told them yes.

5. "That being asked what they were to do when they took the town? he answered, they were to kill the white people, the men, and take their wives to themselves."

Evidence affecting this slave.—Tickle's examination, section 4, June 12.

Confession of Primus, Debrosse's negro, before the grand jury.
—He said,

1. "That a week before Christmas he met Ticklepitcher and Kelly's London, on a Sunday at his master's still house, and gave them some punch, and they took a walk, and they carried him to a house on the north river, and called the man (Hughson) for liquor, and they drank, and the man of the house took them down below, and the man told him (Primus) that he must help them to rise to kill the white people, and must steal his master's gun, and must fight and kill his master and mistress first: he said he would help them, but cared not to kill his master and mistress, as they were kind to him, and the man put his hand on a paper, which he told him was a list of the names of those who were to rise, and swore him to be true to come and help them, or the devil fetch him.

2. "That he soon after fell sick, and was sick all the winter.

3. "That when the fire was at Van Zant's, his master sent him out for some things, and he went to the fire and helped as well as he was able, for he was weak, and then went home with his master.

4. "That about two or three days after he went out and met Peck's Caesar, who told him that he (Caesar) and Gomez's Cuffee had set Van Zant's storehouse on fire.

5. "Being asked, if he was at any other time at the white man's house? he said no."

Evidence affecting this negro.—Tickle's examination, No. 2, section 1, 12th June; Caesar (Pintard's) examination, section 4, 22d June; London (Kelly's) examination, 2d July.

Saturday, June 20.

Yesterday evening Mr. Marschalk sent to one of the judges, to inform him that his negroes York and London, convicted that day, had signified that they would make a confession, and withal that he was desirous of being by when they were examined; and accordingly the following confession were taken in his presence this morning.

Confession of York, negro of Marschalk's.—

1. "He acknowledged that what the witnesses said on the trial yesterday was true.

2. "That he went one Sunday morning early about two years ago, to Hughson's house with Kip's Samuel, who has been dead two years, and bought a quart of rum, and went with it to Mr. Bayard's.

3. "That Comfort's Jack, about Christmas last, informed him first of the plot: Jack met him by his gate and told him of it, and appointed him to meet him at Hughson's, that he went to Hughson's; was there the Sunday the feast was, as mentioned by the witnesses in court.

4. "Has been twice at Hughson's and once at Comfort's.

5. "Was to be a captain, and was sworn; that many negroes were present, and all sworn and consented.

6. "Agreed to the circumstances told of the plot in general; Spanish negroes were there; Furman's Harry, Moore's Cato, all the prisoners who were tried with him were there; Ben Moore's Tom and Mink there, Gabriel Crooke's Prince there, Ben and Quash there.

7. "Hughson, his wife and daughter swore first, then

those who were at the upper end of the table, near Hughson, swore upon the book, and the others at a distance without book, by thunder, etc.

8. "He agreed to set his master's house on fire, but said he would not do it until he saw somebody else begin, and then he would; he was to kill his mistress: went to Hughson's just after church out.

9. "That he believed that meeting was about six weeks before the fort burnt.

10. "London (his fellow slave) was to be a private man under him.

11. "Comfort's meeting was two weeks after this: at Comfort's he and Kip's Harry were in the shop, about twenty there; Gabriel Crooke's Prince there, London there, Marshal's Ben there, Hermanus's Quash; Jack went backwards and forwards from the shop to the kitchen, Furman's Harry there.

12. "Hughson proposed to them to get as many other negroes in as they could.

13. "Mr. Moore's Cato, Shurmur's Cato, at Comfort's; he did not go into the kitchen, but heard that a great many were there.

14. "Hughson told him at his house, that the Spaniards knew better than York negroes how to fight, and they were all to stand by one another and assist the French and Spaniards, they were to wait for them sometime, if they did not come, they were to do all themselves.

15. "Every one in the shop (at Comfort's) had knives, and they were sharpening of them; and they where to cut white men's heads off."

Confession of London, negro of Marschalk's.—He said,

1. "That what was said against him at the trial yesterday, was true.

2. "Captain Marshall's Ben came to him and told him, that his master's negro York, wanted him at the white man's house (Hughson's) by the waterside, he went there,

this was of the Sunday that they eat; Moore's Cato, Pintard's Caesar, etc. six Spanish negroes there, the room full of negroes, when they had done eating, the white man bring the book to swear; the table was not big enough for them all to sit down at, so that some forced to stand; the Spaniards sat altogether next to Hughson: when they had done eating, Hughson said the country was not good, too many gentlemen here, and made negroes work hard, they must set fire to their masters' houses, and when they came out they must get their guns, swords and knives, in two or three weeks the Spaniards and French would be here.

3. "That when the business was done, he would put them in a ship, and carry them into their own country.

4. "Those that stood next to Hughson put their hands on a book, swore and kissed it; those who were on the other end of room did not swear on the book, but swore without.

5. "That Hughson said he must set his master's stable on fire, and he consented and agreed to do it; and York told him he must kill his master, to which he said yes; York told him, that his master love him (London) better than him (York.)

6. "That one or two weeks after he was at Comfort's, York, a little young negro belonging to a shoemaker in Pearl-street, near opposite to Mr. Breastead's, and Crooke's Prince were there; that Ben came to his (London's) house one morning between four and five, and took a coal of fire out of the bakehouse, and said he would go and set his master's stable on fire, and bid him (London) fire his master's house; this a week after Philipse's storehouse set on fire.

7. "York was in the shop, and he in the kitchen at Comfort's; Jack brought the knives; but he said he had a knife and could get a sword: Jack looked like a gentlemen. Jack told him he bought the knives of a Spanish negro.

8. "The general talk at Comfort's was to the same effect as that at Hughson's, viz.—to burn the houses and kill the people; they said they agreed, and swore to do this as long as the white man stand by them.

9. "Did not see Sandy; saw five or six Spanish negroes there."

[198]

Monday, June 22.

Confession of Pompey (Mr. Peter DeLancey's) before one of the judges.—He said,

1. "That Sam, negro belonging to Mr. Courtlandt at Yonkers, some time last fall, carried him to Hughson's to drink some punch; when they came there, Sam asked him, before Hughson, whether he would join with them about what they designed to do? he asked them what that was? he answered, when you say yes, I will tell you what it is; then he said yes; then Sam said they intended to burn the houses and kill the white people; he told them he would stand to it: then Hughson fetched the book and made him put his hand on it, and he said, he wished he might never stir from the place if he did not stand to help them, and the d——l d——n him if he did not.

2. "That before he put his hand on the book, Hughson told him there was a great many negroes concerned in this plot, and that they intended to burn the fort first, then Gerardus Comfort's house, and so round the town, and to kill the people.

3. "That Hughson asked him if he could get guns, swords, or pistols from his master; and he told him no, his master locked up all those things; Hughson then said, if he could not get any, that he would find him some.

4. "That Curacoa Dick told him, that the Spaniards could fight better than the York negroes.

5. "That Rutgers's Quash, Pintard's Caesar, colonel Moore's Cato, Shurmur's Cato, Lowe's Sam, Albany, Tickle, Auboyneau's Prince, Philipse's Cuffee, Vaarck's Caesar, Ward's Will, captain Lush's Will, all spoke to him about the plot, and B. Moore's Tom, Breastead's Jack, and English's Patrick all told him they were concerned in it; and Jay's Brash, upon his (Pompey's) asking him whether he had heard what the negroes were about, answered that Pintard's Caesar told him of it.

6. "That he (Pompey) asked Soumain's Tom whether he would be concerned; told him (Tom) that he had been

down at Hughson's with Sam, Courtlandt's negro, and that Hughson and the negroes were going to burn the town and the fort, and to kill the white people, and that he himself was sworn in the plot; and Tom consented that he would be concerned, but he never talked to Tom any other time about it, and knows not whether he was ever sworn, or spoke to any body else about it; this discourse between Tom and him was a fortnight before Christmas.

7. "That Mrs. Stillwell's Pero spoke to him about it last winter; Hermanus Rutger's Jacob likewise.

8. "Othello, chief justice's negro, spoke to him about it last winter, and said he was concerned.

9. "That he spoke to Pompey, Mr. Samuel Bayard's negro, and told him he was concerned in the plot, and was sworn at Hughson's, and Bayard's Pompey told him that he would be concerned.

10. "He spoke likewise to Mrs. Gilbert's Pompey about it, and he agreed he would be concerned; likewise to Mr. Cruger's Deptford, and he said he would be concerned; and Mr. Henry Cruger's Hanover, and he agreed.

11. "Chief justice's Othello said he would be a captain.

12. "That he likewise spoke to Cato, the new brewer's negro, at the other end of the town, and he agreed to be concerned but don't know whether any of those went to Hughson's, and were sworn."

Col. Cortlandt's negro Sam, was immediately apprehended, and confronted with Pompey, but he denied all, and was committed.

Confession of alderman Pintard's negro Caesar, before one of the judges.—He said,

1. "That last fall, soon after the Cuba men were gone, Vaarck's Caesar carried him down to Hughson's, and there asked him in the presence of Hughson, Rutgers' Quash, Marshall's Ben, Kip's Harry, Tickle and Albany, whether he would join along with them to fight the white people, and Hughson asked him whether he would burn his master's

house? to which he answered, he would help to fight the white people, but he would not burn his master's house; Hughson replied every negro had engaged to burn his master's house, as well as kill the white people, and why could not he do as well as they; but he told Hughson he would not set any man's house on fire, that he would only fight and kill the white people.

2. "That then Hughson brought a book like a common prayer book, and swore him that he should not speak of what they had agreed upon to any one but those concerned with them, and that he was to do what he had engaged himself to, upon pain of damnation forever; Hughson all the time holding the book in his hand, and made him kiss it.

3. "That Marshall's Ben, Vaarck's Caesar, and Hughson were to find guns and swords.

4. "That Hughson, after his swearing, put his name down on a piece of paper, and told him he must get as many more negroes as he could; but said he never spoke to any but Brazier's Tony, York (shoemaker's in Pearl-street), Provost's Cato, Cowley's Cato, both hanged, Vaarck's Bill, who told him he had sworn already, Gabriel Crooke's Prince, Van Horne's Bridgewater, Teneyek's Bill, whom he carried to Hughson's and saw him sworn, captain Roger French's London, whom he also carried to Hughson's and saw him sworn, Vanderspeigle's Fortune, hanged, Wyncoop's London (Indian), Curacoa Dick, Peck's Caesar, Benson's Mars, Breasted's Jack, DeBrosse's Primus, Roosevelt's Quack, another negro of Peck's.

5. "That those beforenamed, which he did not carry to Hughson's to be sworn, he carried to Comfort's, on the Sunday of the general meeting of the negroes there, about a fortnight or three weeks before the fort burnt, and there they all swore to fire the town, some to burn their own master's house, and all to kill the white people, they all swore before Comfort's Jack, and he made report to Hughson, who put their names down in a list.

6. "That he knew Mr. Moore's Cato was concerned in the plot about a week before the supper at Hughson's; Cato

was at the entertainment; he was to have been there himself, but was stopped by the watch as he was going.

7. "That he carried Jack, Comfort's to Hughson's to be sworn."

Evidence affecting this negro.—Peggy's examination, No. 1, May 9; Sawney's examination, No. 3, section 8, June 1; Jack (Sleydall's) examination, section 1, June 12; Pompey (DeLancey's) examination, section 5, June 22.

Confession of Cato, colonel Moore's negro, before one of the judges.—(He said,)

1. "That the first that spoke to him about the conspiracy, was Hermanus Rutgers's Quash and Ben, by capt. Marshall's stable, about a fortnight after Christmas, of a Sunday morning; they asked him to go down to Comfort's with them after church out in the evening, for that there was to be company there.

2. "That they told him that the negroes were going to rise against the white people, and asked him to join with them? he told them at first he was not willing, he had no occasion for it, for he lived well: Quash made answer, that he himself lived as well or better than he; and Ben said so did he; but it was a hard case upon the poor negroes, that they could not so much as take a walk after church-out, but the constables took them up; therefore in order to be free, they must set the houses on fire, and kill the white people; and Ben asked him to set his master's house on fire; he told him he was not willing to do that: they asked him to come down to Comfort's after church in the evening, which he did; there was rum there, and he drank a dram; but he did not see Jack this first time: the negroes he then saw at Comfort's were Ben, Quash, Chambers' Robin, Peck's Caesar, Cook, Marschalk's York and London, Shurmur's Cato, Crooke's Prince, Shoemaker's York, Crooke's York, Lowe's Sam, widow Fortune's Cuffee, Van Horne's Bridgwater, Bound's Scipio, Cowley's Cato, Vanderspeigle's Fortune, Provost's (hanged) Cato, Kip's Harry. The same sort of talk

passed there as above mentioned; but they did not all very well agree at that time.

3. "That about a fortnight afterwards, on a Sunday, he went with Pintard's Caesar, in order to meet with Albany, Tickle, Curacoa Dick and Bosch's Frank, and they went down to Hughson's one after another; when they came there, they went into a room where were Hughson, his wife and daughter, but the latter did not stay in the room; Hughson brought them drams, which they paid for; and he talked to them about the plot for burning the houses of the town, and killing the white people; and told them there were several companies of negroes to be made up, and asked if they would be concerned; and some agreed at that time; but he and Pintard's Caesar did not, they came out of the house together after staying about half an hour.

4. "That the Sunday after this, he went to Hughson's again with Albany, and Hughson carried Albany and him up stairs, and swore them upon a bible, after having told them that there were a great many concerned in this plot; that they had agreed to rise against the town, to murder the people; some to murder their masters and mistresses, and to burn their houses, and proposed to him to do the same, and destroy the whole family; which he was unwilling to agree to at first, but at last consented, and then he was sworn and kissed the book; and Albany consented to kill his mistress and the rest of the family, and to burn her house; and was sworn in the same manner: that the purport of the oath was, that they were to keep all secret, and to perform what they had severally engaged to do; and if they failed therein, they were to be damned forever.

5. "That on another Sunday evening about a fortnight or three weeks after that, he went to a supper at Hughson's according to his invitation.

6. "That the last time he met Marschalk's York by Mr. DeLancey's, as he was going; when he came there there were a great number of negroes, he believes forty or fifty, among which were Fortune's Cuffee, Lowe's Sam, Bound's Scipio, Cha. Crooke's York, Van Horne's Bridgwater,

Ward's Will, G. Crooke's Prince, Kortrecht's Caesar, Horsefield's Guy: that he did not sit down at the table where Hughson, his wife and daughter sat, but at a side-table with several others: after supper Hughson talked to them about the plot; they were all to be true to one another, to keep secret, and to perform what they had engaged to do: and Hughson had a book, and swore several upon it, and made them kiss it; but those that were at a distance, swore without book.

7. "That the Sunday fortnight after that, he went to Comfort's, where were, he believes, about forty negroes, where they talked of the plot to the same purpose, and swore. There were Quash, Ben, Fortune's Cuffee, Wyncoop's Indian London, captain French's London, Brazier's Tony, Horsefield's Guy, Duane's Prince.

8. "That Vaarck's Caesar (hanged) told him David Provost's Low was concerned in the plot, and that he was at Hughson's, at that supper on the Sunday, but don't remember he saw him there."

Evidences affecting this negro.—Peggy's examination, No. 1, May 9. Sawney's examination, No. 1, section 12, May 22; No. 3, section 8, June 1. Sarah (Burk's) examination, No. 2, section 5, June 1. Caesar (Pintard's) examination, section 6, June 22. York (Marschalk's) confession, section 6, June 20. Pompey (DeLancey's) confession, section 5, June 22. Jacob (Rutgers') confession, June 24. Dundee's confession, section 9, June 24.

Confessions of several negroes, before one of the judges.—

Harry (Furman's) said Ben (alderman Bayard's) that goes to sea, was concerned in the plot; that Jack was shaving Harry at Comfort's, and said he could set his master's bakehouse on fire, and might be at work in it, and his master would not know he did it; he say no; his master do him good: that Jack said he would cut his throat if he did not agree to it; then Harry said if he would set his master's house on fire first, then he'd set his.

Evidence affecting this negro.—Jack (Comfort's confession, sections 31, 32, June 8; Fortune (Latham's) confession, June 15; York (Marschalk's) section 6, June 20.

Quamino (Pemberton's) said he was sworn at Hughson's by

him; he clapped his hand upon a book; there were present, Rowe's Tom, Albany, Ticklepitcher, Vaarck's Caesar; John (Van Dam's) was in the house when he came, but immediately went away.

Evidence affecting this negro.—Tickle's confession, section 2, June 12; Tom (Rowe's) confession, July 2.

Varian's Worcester said that Leffert's Pompey first spoke to him to be concerned in the plot about Christmas last; that he was at the supper at Hughson's, and was then sworn; Hughson, his wife and daughter swore first, and then the negroes, and he consented that he would join with them in burning houses and killing the people; Hughson told him, after the negroes had killed the white men, they were to marry the gentlewomen.

Evidence affecting this negro.—Quack (Roosevelt's) confession at the stake, section 4, May 30; Tickle's confession, section 4, June 12.

Upon the several confessions taken this day, the following negroes were apprehended and committed to jail:

Lowe's Sam, Brazier's Tony, Van Horne's Bridgwater, French's London, Provost's Low, Wyncoop's London, Crooke's York, Widow Fortune's Cuffee, Bound's Scipio.

SUPREME COURT
Tuesday, June 23.

Present, the second justice.

The king against Furman's Harry, Pemberton's Quamino, Varian's Worcester, negroes.

The prisoners desired leave of the court to withdraw their plea of *not guilty,* and to plead *guilty;* leave was given accordingly, and they pleaded *guilty,* and submitted to the mercy of the court.

Court adjourned to ten o'clock to-morrow morning.

Deposition.—This day Stephen Evan, of Westchester county, made oath before one of the judges,

"That being at Jamaica, on Long-Island, about a year ago, a negro man called Will, belonging to Johannes Hardenbergh,

[205]

Robin (Justice Willet's), and Jack (Dorland's), negroes, were at a house where he (the deponent) was, and that he heard Will say to Robin, what think you of Corlaer's Hook (n) or of the plot? D——n it, replied Robin, I'll have nothing to say to it; if they burn their backsides, they must sit down on the blisters, but said further, let them go on and prosper.

"That the deponent urged very hard to know what they meant; one of them (he thought it was Robin) said it was a plot, and that if it went on, he (the deponent) should hear more of it; and could do no less than hear of it, but would then say no more about it, for fear of bringing himself in."

Confession of Sterling (Mr. S. Lawrence's negro) before one of the judges.—He said,

1. "That he was one concerned in the plot for burning and destroying this city and murdering the inhabitants, and that Hughson swore him upon a book, and made him put his hand upon it and kiss it; and the purport of the oath was, that he should not tell any white people of it, and that he was to do what he promised to do, that is to say, to fire his master's house, and kill his master and mistress, etc. Hughson's wife was in the room when sworn.

2. "That Albany and Tickle carried him thither and there opened the plot to him, Hughson put a flask of rum upon the table, and after making him drink, asked him if he would not help to kill the white people and burn the town? he answered yes; then Hughson swore him, and put his name on a paper.

3. "That Abrahamse's Scipio came down there the same time, and he saw him sworn; this was about Whitsuntide was twelve months.

4. "That Albany told him, that they were to wait, until

(n) A point of land at the east end of the city of New-York, almost opposite Long-Island Ferry.

the winter almost over, and then the wind blew hard, they were to begin to set fire and burn the fort.

5. "That when the governor had forbid Quack coming to the fort last summer, Quack declared that he would burn the fort; Quack and Comfort's Jack came into Hughson's the same day after he (Sterling) was sworn, and there he heard him say this before Albany, Tickle, the said Comfort's Jack, and Hughson."

Evidence affecting this negro.—Tickle's examination and confession, 12th June.

The following supposed to be calculated for a confession, was found amongst the papers, indorsed June, without the particular day; and it is thought to have been after the proclamation of the 19th; because as we understood, Quack until that time strongly denied that he knew any thing at all of a conspiracy, therefore it is here placed.

The confession of Walter's Quack (negro) by an unknown hand—No. 1.

"That about fourteen days before Roosevelt's Quack came to prison, he and Hermanus Rutgers' Quash were in the woodyard, and called a negro man (of a Sunday morning) in, belonging to Mr. Leffert, named Pompey; they asked him if he would do as they would do? he answered, what is that? if you will do as we will, we will tell you: he would.

"Quash proposed if he (Pompey) would set his master's house on fire, that he (Quash) would set his master's house on fire, and Quack was to set his master Mr. Roosevelt's house on fire, likewise Mr. Vanderheul's house. Pompey said they might do as they would, if they did it he would not tell, and likewise said he would set his master's house on fire. They Quack and Quash promised him (Pompey) if he would do as he had promised (that is to set fire to his master's house) they would assist him to escape, and be the means of making him free."

By this confession, if it may be so called, Quack steers clear of charging himself with any privity to the general conspiracy; he

[207]

intimates no more by it, than he overheard this discourse be-tween the three negroes he there mentions, importing a conspiracy between them to set those particular houses on fire; Quack does not say he was in company with them, nor where he was. If this was his own inditing, Quack was no fool; if it was provided for him, he was not very wise that furnished him with it.—But Quack was for coming off as cheap as he could.

This day the following negroes were apprehended and committed upon the foregoing confessions and examinations, viz.—Bayard's Pompey, Gilbert's Pompey, Soumain's Tom, Cruger's Deptford, Benson's Cato, Rutgers' Jacob.

SUPREME COURT
Wednesday, June 24.

Present the second and third justices.

Court opened and adjourned to four o'clock in the afternoon. P.M. Present, as before.

Court opened and adjourned till 10 o'clock to-morrow morning.

Confession of H. Rutgers' Jacob (negro) before one of the judges.—He said,

"That some time before Christmas last he was carried to Hughson's by Roosevelt's Quack, where he gave him a dram, and told him that they were about a plot, they were going to kill the white people and burn the city, and asked him if he would be concerned? that he was frightened at first, but Quack bid him not be afraid there was no body should hurt him; and by that time they had drank out half a pint of rum, he agreed to join with them, and he swore to Quack that he would not tell any body of it, but that he would do as he said. He did not see Hughson or his wife, only a young woman in the house, which he took to be his daughter; but he did not go into the house.—Has talked to

Mr. Moore's Cato about the plot, but no body more, and knows of no other persons concerned."

Evidence affecting this negro.—Pompey (DeLancey's) confession, section 7, 22d June.

Confession of Todd's Dundee (negro) taken by a private hand. No. 1.—He said,

1. "That for three summers past he had fetched water at Comfort's; that in the winter, by his master's order, he fetched it from the fort; that some time before the officers arrived for the Cuba expedition, he was at Comfort's for water, in the afternoon; that Jack asked him to come into the house to play papa; Jack, Cook, Jenny (Comfort's negroes) and he (Dundee) played about two half-hours, that Jack won about two shillings in pennies of him, that after Jack had won the money he asked him to go and drink, and carried him to Hughson's, when they came there Jack called for a pint of rum, which Hughson's wife brought and Jack made punch; that he (Dundee) got almost drunk, and Jack helped him up with the water, and that he heard nothing that time about the plot.

2. "The second time, being the next afternoon, he was at Hughson's, in company with Jack and Cook (Comfort's negroes) that he called for a half pint of rum, that Hughson brought it, that Mrs. Hughson came in and asked Jack whose boy that was? Jack told her Mr. Todd's, and said never fear him, he is a good boy; Hughson then asked him (Dundee) his name, he told him Dundee, Hughson said stay a little while till I fetch a book, that Hughson was gone about two minutes before he brought the book, that he did not tell him it was a bible; Hughson asked him his name a second time, to which he answered as before; that Hughson and Jack told him he must lay his hand on the book, he asked them for what? they told him he must swear to help them set fire to houses, and that he would tell no body of it; that he swore the d——l fetch him, and the d——l d——n

[209]

him if he did; that then he asked what he was to do? they told him, he must set his master's house on fire, that the fort was to be burnt first, and that Quack was to do it, that he must help burn the rest of the houses and destroy the people, to all which he consented; that Jack was to be head captain, and he (Dundee) lower captain, that he was to cut his mistress's throat, in the night, because she scolded him when he stayed of an errand, or if he did not mind his business.

3. "That Comfort's Jack was to kill Mr. Todd, because he once followed Dundee to Comfort's house when he went for tea water, and made a noise at him for staying.

4. "Jack told him he must bring wine in the cask as often as he came there for water, he answered he had no opportunity, or else he would.

5. "Jack told him there were too many guns in the fort, so they were to burn that first; that they were to burn the fort on St. Patrick's day, and Dundee was to fire his master's house the same evening after the fort was destroyed, but was afraid lest he should be catched and hanged.

6. "That when the whole city was on fire, they were all to meet together, and destroy the people as fast as they came out; they were to have penknives to cut their throats, which Jack was to provide for them; that Jack offered him a knife, but he said he would buy one.

7. "That the third time he was there, Patrick (Mr. English's negro) was with him; Patrick said to Cook, you have not forgot what I told you of; no, says Cook, I hope not yet. Dundee overheard their discourse.

8. "That Jack was at work in the shop, but his young master was there, and so they could not speak together.

9. "That the day the fort was burnt, Patrick, Dundee, and Mr. alderman Moore's Cato was on the mount; that Dundee said he was sorry the governor's house was burnt; Patrick said he was not, but that he wished the governor had been burnt in the middle of it; that Cato was not present then, but came just after, and said by and by this

will be put in the news that the fort's burnt, and then the Spaniards will come and take us all."

Confession of London, (Mr. French's negro) taken before his master by a private hand.—

1. "He said that when the forces were raised to go to Cuba, he worked on board captain Bayard's vessel; that he was sent ashore for water, and that he went to Comfort's; that Jack asked him if he would be one of them? The prisoner asked him, one for what? Jack told him that the negroes were going to rise in a body to take this country, to fire the houses and kill the people; he answered, he was going to sea with his master, and that he could not; Jack told him if he would consent, he would set his name down with the rest; he answered, that if he did not go to sea, he would help them to do what they proposed. Jack asked him to swear, which he did; which oath was, that he wished thunder might strike him down if he did not help them, in case his master did not go out to sea.

2. "That the prisoner fetched sand some where near Comfort's this spring, and again saw Jack, who asked him if he remembered his promise, and would stand to it? he answered yes; Jack told him they were to set fire in the Broadway, and that he (the prisoner) should set his master's storehouse on fire in New-street, which the prisoner consented to.

3. "That Jack told him there was a house near by where they would provide arms, and what was necessary, and that he find for him what he wanted.

4. "That when the city was on fire, the negroes were to meet at the end of the Broadway next to the fields."

Evidence affecting this negro.—Caesar (Pintard's) confession, section 4, June 22; Cato (Moore's) confession, section 4, June 22.

Intimation having been given for some time past, that there had of late been Popish priests lurking about the town, diligent inquiry had been made for discovering them, but without effect; at length information was given, that one Ury alias Jury, who had lately come into this city, and entered into partnership with Campbell, a school-master, pretending to teach Greek and Latin, was suspected to be one, and that he kept a private conventicle; he was taken into custody this day, and not giving a satisfactory account of himself, was committed to the city jail.

Confession of Jack (J. Tiebout's negro) before alderman Bancker.—

"He declared that in Easter holidays, Ward's negro Will desired him to drink a dram with him at Mrs. Wendall's, and also desired him to make him two or three sticks of about three foot long, and an whole of about twelve inches bored in them, which was to make a light that no body should see it, because Mr. Van Horne would not allow a candle: and afterwards he was company with him again, and then told him Mr. Van Horne would not allow him to come to his wife, but before it was long he would shew him a trick, and that the negroes here were cowards; for that they had no hearts as those at Antigua: and that Mr. Pintard's negro was a fool, for that he had undertaken a thing which he could not go through with; for that he had given him the gun (that was found under the market) to take care of. (o) When Mr. Philipse's storehouse was extinguished, he said to him (Jack) he would sooner see all the houses burnt down to the ground, before he would lend a hand to it.

SUPREME COURT
Thursday, June 25.

Present, the second and third justices.

The king against Jamaica, a negro, and Sarah Hughson.

(o) There was a gun found under the market by a soldier, not long after the fort was fired, and no owner for it discovered.

Ordered that the execution of these two criminals be respited until to-morrow seven-night.

The king against Wendover's Emanuel, English's Patrick, Jay's Brash, Breasted's Jack, Vaarck's Will alias Bill, Lush's Will, negroes.

The prisoners having been indicted for conspiring, etc. to burn the whole town and city of New-York, and to kill and destroy the inhabitants thereof, were arraigned, and pleaded *not guilty*.

The king against Peck's York, Duane's Prince, Van Borsom's Scipio, Latham's Tony, Provost's Low, and Ward's Will, negroes.

The prisoners having been arraigned on the same indictment, York, Scipio and Will pleaded *guilty*, and Prince, Low, and Tony pleaded *not guilty*.

The court adjourned till to-morrow morning 9 o'clock.

Deposition of Mary Burton, taken before one of the judges. No. 4.—Mary Burton being duly sworn, deposed,

1. "That the person yesterday shewn to her in prison, lately taken into custody on suspicion of being a Roman Catholic priest, is the same person she has often seen at the house of John Hughson; that to the best of her recollection she saw him there first, some time about Christmas last, and that then for a fortnight together he used to come there almost every night, and sometimes used to lie there, but was always gone in the morning before she the deponent got up, but she well remembers he used to go by different names, but whether by the name of Jury or Ury, or Doyle, she cannot now depose positively, but to the best of her remembrance, some of his names consisted only of one syllable, and believes she heard him called by all the said three names.

2. "That after the said fortnight, she believes the said person did not come to Hughson's for about a week, that then he used to come again frequently almost every night, until the time of the stealing of Hogg's goods; he used to strip himself and go to bed as if he was to lie there all night,

but was always gone in the morning when this deponent got out of bed.

3. "That when he came to Hughson's he always went up stairs in the company of Hughson, his wife and daughter, and Peggy, with whom the negroes used to be at the same time consulting about the plot; and that she has often heard Hughson, the rest of the white people, and the negroes talk in the presence of the said Jury about setting fire to the houses and killing the white people of this city, and has often, when such conversation was going on, seen the said Jury alias Ury, whispering to Hughson, his wife, etc. and the negroes, which she understood to be joining in the conspiracy with them, she thought it looked very like it, though she cannot say she ever heard him speak out, but said she esteemed his actions and behaviour to signify his approbation and consent to what was carrying on by the company, touching this conspiracy, and this not one time in particular, but a great many.

4. "That the conspirators before mentioned generally went into a room above stairs to hold their consultations, and the deponent (being a servant in the house) used often to go into that room to carry such things as they wanted, and often came in upon them at such seasons, when (as she believes) they would rather have excused her appearance, for she has observed that her coming in has sometimes made Jury uneasy, that they used generally to call up Mary Hughson the daughter, to bring what they wanted; but when she was out of the way, the deponent used to go up. She believes the said Mary was likewise in their secrets; never heard her say any thing of the plot, but has heard the rest talk of it often before her the said Mary.

5. "That Hughson, his wife, daughter Sarah, and Peggy, and the said Ury, when this deponent has come into the room amongst them to bring what they wanted, have several times turned out all the negroes present, and then have all joined in tempting this deponent to take an oath; but upon her asking them for what? they would not tell her, but said she must swear first, and then they would tell her, but

this she absolutely denied over and over; at which refusal they were angry, and turned her out of the room, and Ury said to her, had not you better swear and go fine, than go as she did; for they all (the Hughsons, Peggy and Jury, had when they proposed to swear her) offered her silks, and a deal of fine things, if she would comply with their requests, and Peggy said she was a great fool if she did not.

6. "That about a a fortnight or three weeks before Hogg's goods were stolen, she has observed Campbell (with whom she has heard Jury used to keep school) come to Hughson's of a Sunday, sometimes one Garrit Van Emborough with him, and that Campbell used to go into the room below with the Hughsons, Peggy, and Caesar, Prince and Cuffee (negroes) and when these were met, the Hughsons used to turn the deponent up stairs; but she cannot say she ever heard them talking of the plot before Campbell, but she strongly suspected that he knew of it, from his keeping company with the Hughsons, and the said three negroes, whom she looked upon to be the principal heads of the negroes in the conspiracy.

7. "That during the time there was snow upon the ground all last winter, she has often known Hughson to go out of town a days, upon the pretence of fetching firewood from the commons, with his sleigh; and that he has not returned home till eight, nine, ten or eleven o'clock at night, at different times, and has brought negroes to town to his house, and that he has carried them back again in his sleigh after midnight, one, two or three o'clock, and has not returned home again sometimes till seven or eight o'clock in the morning.

8. "That she has several times seen Mr. Peter DeLancey's Spanish negro Antonio at Hughson's, when he (Hughson) has come home late out of the woods, and that she has seen him many times get into Hughson's sleigh late in the night, and that Hughson has not returned home till six, seven or eight the next morning; but at that time this deponent did not know where the said Spanish negro lived, whether in town or country.

8. "That one day at Hughson's, some of the negroes had behaved rudely towards her, and being in a passion, she was provoked to swear at them, in the presence of Jury alias Ury, above mentioned, and upon recollecting herself she said, God forgive me; whereupon the said Jury answered her, that was a small matter; he could forgive her a great deal more sins than that; that was nothing.

10. "That at another time when the negroes had provoked her, she wished those black toads at the devil; oh, said Jury, let them be black, or what they will, the devil has nothing to do with them; I can forgive them their sins, and you yours too."

Confession of London, a Spanish Indian (Wyncoop's) before one of the judges.—

1. "He said that last Whitsuntide was twelve months, on the Monday afternoon, he went out and met in the street, Peter Low's Sam, Obadiah Hunt's Warwick, Mrs. Ellison's Billy; that they asked him to go and drink beer at a house, and Billy said he would carry him to a house that belonged to his mistress, and that he carried them all to Hughson's; that they called for beer and cider; that Hughson himself brought it; that himself and two others had but three pence a-piece about them; that Billy told them he would make up the rest; they had four mugs; that the prisoner was almost drunk; that he had drank rum at a house before he came there; that Hughson sat down and drank with them, and talked for some time, and that he went out for a book which he brought; that he told them they must keep secret that he sold liquor to negroes; that they must not tell any thing they saw or heard at his house; that if they would swear to keep secret his proposal, they should always have liquor at his house; that they had better suffer death than tell any body; that they all agreed to what Hughson said, and did swear and kissed the book; that Hughson had a list on which he set their names; that Hughson was to provide guns, swords and knives; that he told them the fort should

[216]

burn first, and that when they saw that all the negroes should set fire to their master's houses, and that as fast as the people run out, they should stab the first they met with, and kill as many as they could.

2. "That some time after the prisoner was at Comfort's, Jack asked him, whether he knew not what some negroes were going to do? yes, yes says the prisoner, I know well enough. Jack told him he must be sure not to tell any body, nor make any talk about it: for said he, they know it as well as we. The prisoner has talked with Sam and Warwick about it in the street sometimes when he met them. The prisoner was to burn his master's house, and to shoot or stab his master before he came out. Hughson was to find guns, powder, balls, knives, and every thing they wanted; Hughson told them he was to be governor."

Evidence affecting this negro.—Confession of Pintard's Caesar, section 4, June 22. Confession of colonel Moore's Cato, section 7, June 22. Confession of Ten Eyck's Dick, June 30. Confession of Hunt's Warwick, July 1.

Confession of Brash, Mr. Peter Jay's negro, taken before one of the judges.—

(1.) "He said, that about this time twelve months, he and his old master's negro (Ben) had been down at the north river, handing up timber from the waterside, in order to be carried to his master's garden there; and John Hughson had been helping them a little; and when he and Ben came to the garden, Ben told him that Hughson had bid him ask him (Brash) to come to his house and drink.

2. "That they went to Hughson's; and when they came there they were both carried up stairs, and there Hughson told them that about three days afterwards he was to have a large company of negroes, and would give them a supper; that they were going to rise against the town, to burn the houses and to kill the people; and Hughson asked them if they would be concerned with them? and after having drank, they both consented; then Hughson brought a book,

[217]

and told them they must both swear that they would set their master's houses on fire, and murder their masters and mistresses; to which they both consented; put their hands on the book and kissed it: Hughson told them they must not tell it to any body but those that were concerned, who were to be there at night; that they were all to begin together; and Hughson said he would tell Ben, and Ben was to tell him; but he told Hughson he could not come to supper; nor did he go.

3. "That a day or two after this, he and Mr. Murray's Jack went for tea-water to Comfort's, and he (Brash) carried Jack to Hughson's, and Hughson carried Jack up stairs, and swore him of this plot, who laid his hand upon the book and kissed it; and Jack agreed to burn his master's stable, his house, and to murder his master and mistress.

4. "That he was at the great meeting at Comfort's on the Sunday about three weeks before the fort burnt, and was in the shop, where he saw Marschalk's two negroes, London and York, and many others; and Toby belonging to Breasted the cooper, next door to Kortrecht's.

5. "That Hughson told him, if he could get any negroes to come in, he should bring them down to him; and that besides what before named, that he carried thither Fortune belonging to Mr. David Clarkson, Jack (mistake for Tom), young negro of captain R. Livingston, Cajoe belonging to Mordecai Gomez, and Tom belonging to Hyer the cooper in Stone-street, and he saw them sworn.

6. "That when Ben and he (Brash) were sworn at Hughson's, Hughson gave Ben a pistol to be carried to the gunsmith's to be mended, and told him, if any should ask whose it was, he should tell them it was his master's.

7. "That Hughson told him and Ben, that they should get what guns, swords and pistols they could from their master's, and bring them to his house; but if they could not get any, that he could furnish them with them himself.

8. "Confesses that he had a knife from Comfort's Cook, but he took it upon account of Ben, instead of pennies due from Cook to him, which Ben desired him to ask for."

[218]

Evidence affecting this negro.—Peggy's examination, No. 1, May 9; Sandy's examination, No. 3, section 8, June 1; Sarah (Burk's) examination, No. 3, June 5; Jack (Comfort's) examination, section 31, June 8; Pompey (DeLancey's) examination, section 5, June 22.

This day the following negroes were apprehended and committed as confederates in the conspiracy, viz.:

Ellison's Billy, Mr. Clarkson's Fortune, Mr. Murray's Jack, Abrahamse's Scipio, Breasted's Toby, Hunt's Warwick, Meyer Cohen's Windsor.

SUPREME COURT
Friday, June 26.

Present, the second and third justices.

The king against Wendover's Emanuel, English's Patrick, Jay's Brash, Breasted's Jack, Vaarck's Will alias Bill, Provost's Low, Lush's Will, Duane's Prince, Latham's Tony, negroes.

The seven first of the above negroes desired leave of the court to withdraw their plea of *not guilty*, and to plead *guilty*, which being granted, they pleaded *guilty*, and submitted to the mercy of the court.

The court then proceeded to the trial of Prince and Tony, upon the indictment for the conspiracy.

Jury called, and the following jurors sworn, viz.—Isaac Van Dam, Cornelius Clopper, Josiah Milliken, Humphry Jones, James Tucker, Edward Man, Peter Fresneau, Patroclus Parmyter, Daniel Dunscomb, John Hunt, John Robins, John Van Gelder.

Mr. Murray and Mr. Chambers of counsel for the king.

Mr. Chambers opened the indictment, and proceeded to examine the witnesses.

Mary Burton called and sworn. She gave an account of the great meetings of the negroes at Hughson's, and the conspiracy carrying on there, as upon former trials; that arms were to be provided and kept by Hughson; that the fort was to be first burnt, and then the Fly and the whole town, and the people were to be murdered, and that this was the common talk betwixt the Hughsons and the negroes at such meetings, and they were to begin to set fire about the time that Hogg's goods were stolen; that she has seen the prisoner, Tony, there several times at those meetings, but cannot say she particularly heard him talk about the fires; that he had been above stairs and came out of Peggy's window; that she had seen the prisoner, Prince, there several times, and had heard him and other negroes together talk about the plot, to which he consented, and promised to do what he could to help them.

Caesar (alderman Pintard's negro) said that he was to have been at the great supper at Hughson's, but was prevented by the constables; but that he went there the next day, when Hughson told him Mr. Duane's Prince was there at supper, and was sworn, and was to burn his master's house, and that he had put him down.

Cato (Colonel Moore's negro) said he was at the great supper at Hughson's, when the prisoner, Prince, was there and was sworn, and he was to burn his master's house and kill his master; that he was at the great meeting at Comfort's on a Sunday, saw Tony there amongst the negroes talking about the plot, and Tony consented.

Sandy said he was at Comfort's at the great meeting on a Sunday, when he saw Prince, the prisoner there, and he was sworn (amongst the rest) of the plot; this was about a fortnight before the fort burnt.

Tickle said he was at the great supper at Hughson's; that the prisoner, Prince, was there and was sworn of the plot amongst many others; and that Tony and his fellow servant, Fortune, were to kill their master, burn his house, and bring the goods to Hughson's.

Jack (Sleydall's) said that he was at the great supper at Hughson's after Christmas, and saw the prisoner, Tony, there, and he was sworn of the plot, and agreed to burn the houses and kill the white people.

The prisoners asked the witnesses no material questions; upon their defence they only denied what had been testified against them.

And the evidence being summed up, and the jury charged, they withdrew, and soon returned and found the two prisoners *guilty*.

Court adjourned till four o'clock in the afternoon.

SUPREME COURT
Friday, June 26.

Present, the second justice.

The king against T. Horsefield's Guy, Thompson's York, Low's Sam, Bound's Scipio, C. Crooke's York, Brazier's Tony, Wyncoop's London, Horsefield's Caesar, negroes.

The prisoners having been indicted for conspiring to burn the town, etc. were arraigned, and all severally pleaded *guilty*, and submitted themselves to the mercy of the court.

The king against Soumain's Tom, H. Rutgers's Jacob, Gilbert's Pompey, J. Cruger's Deptford, Benson's Cato, S. Bayard's Pompey, Courtlandt's Sam, negroes.

The prisoners Tom, etc. having been indicted for the said conspiracy, were brought to the bar and arraigned, and Tom, Jacob, Pompey (Gilbert's), and Deptford pleaded *guilty*, and Cato, Pompey (S. Bayard's), and Sam pleaded *not guilty*.

Court adjourned to Monday morning 8 o'clock.

Confession of Soumain's Tom, by a private hand.—He said,

1. "That some time last summer after the Cuba forces were gone from York, he went in company with Mr. Rutgers's Quash and Mr. Roosevelt's Quack to Hughson's, that it was on a Sunday morning, and that Quack and Quash called for liquor, and that Hughson brought three half-pints of rum, and sat down and drank with them, but said nothing to him at that time, except to tell him, that he must come there again the next Sunday.

2. "That the next Sunday morning he went again, and met with the same company, that they again called for rum, which Hughson brought, that he sat down in company with them, and after they had drank their liquor, Hughson asked

the other two whether he (Tom) would join with them? the prisoner asked for what? Quash said to rise and burn down the town and kill the white people, that Quack said I myself intend to have the fort down before long, that they put a book upon his breast and forced him to swear, that Hughson told him he must wish the thunder to strike him down if he ever discovered it, that he repeated Hughson's words and kissed the book.

3. "That Hughson asked the prisoner whether his master had guns, swords or cutlasses? he answered no, but that his master had sword blades, but said that he never carried any there.

4. "That Hughson told him he must kill his master and all the family, and that he must burn the house; that he said his master was too good to kill, but consented to kill any body else, and to do what other mischief he could.

5. "That Hughson told him he must do this when he saw a great many houses on fire in the night, and great hurry and noise of the people, that he should come and join with the rest, that he must get a knife; to which he answered he would get a sword blade which would do better; that Hughson told him if he would come in the afternoon he might see a great number of negroes who were concerned. Said that he could not go out in the afternoon.

6. "That he went a third time of a Sunday morning with the same company as before, and that they again drank rum, and had much the same discourse as the former, that Hughson was very earnest in the affair.

7. "That once since he heard something of the negroes rising by Mr. DeLancey's Pompey, who came to Mr. Soumain's door and asked the prisoner whether he had heard any talk of the negroes rising? he answered not I; why, have you?

8. "That Hughson told him, Quash and Quack, that after they had conquered, then they would know what it was to be free men, and then he would tell the prisoner what post he was to have."

Evidence affecting this negro.—
Examination and confession of Jack, Mr. Murray's negro, before one of the judges.—He said,

1. "That soon after new-year holidays he went to Comfort's to fetch tea-water, and as he was coming from thence he saw Vaarck's Caesar standing at Hughson's door, who called to him to come thither, and when he came to the house he saw John Hughson in the entry, who asked him to come in, and he went in, and Caesar followed him; and Hughson asked him to set his keg of tea-water down and stay there a little, but he (Jack) said that he could not stay; Hughson then told him that he had better carry his keg of tea-water home, and then return again and bring a gun and powder and bullets, and some negro with him, and then asked him to drink some punch, and he drank a small draught and was then going, but Hughson made him promise to come back, and said when he returned they would talk about a plot, and so he went away: there were present in the room at this time, Hughson, his wife and daughter, and Peggy, Vaarck's Caesar, Walter's Quack, Pintard's Caesar, old Mr. Jay's Ben, Auboyneau's Prince, Philipse's Cuffee, and the Chief Justice's Othello, and three Spanish negroes.

2. "That as he was going home with the tea-water he met Adam, his fellow servant by old Mr. DeLancey's house, and he told Adam where he had been and what had been talked of, and what company was at Hughson's, as before mentioned; Adam thereupon ordered him to set his keg down, which he did, and gave it in charge to one of Mr. DeLancey's negro wenches, and said they would go down there and drink some punch, and they went accordingly.

3. "When they came to Hughson's, they found the same company Jack had left, and the cloth was laid and the supper getting: he heard them talking when he came into the entry, of burning the houses and killing the white people, and of taking all the gentlewomen for their wives.

[223]

4. "That when Adam and he came into the room, Hughson asked them whether they would do as they were going to do; which he said was to set the town on fire and to kill the white men and to keep the white women for their wives, to get all their master's guns and swords and pistols, and when their masters came to put out the fires to kill them all? Adam answered he would do the same, and he (Jack) said he would do the same: then Hughson carried Adam and him up stairs, and brought a book to swear them, but he (Jack) would not swear by the book, but kissed his hand and said he would stand to it, but Adam put his hand upon the book and kissed it, and said he would stand to it; then Hughson produced a paper, and said it was an agreement of the blacks to kill the white folks, and he put his (Jack's) and Adam's names down in it, as he (Jack) understood him.

5. "That after this they went down stairs again to the rest of the company, and there they found two negro men a fiddling to them, before whom Hughson and the blacks talked of the like discourse: one fiddler belonged to Holt, named Joe, the other Kiersted's Braveboy; the negroes shook hands with Adam and him, and wished them joy, and Hughson did the like to them up stairs; and they all said they must keep every thing secret and stand to their words.

6. "They said they expected the French and Spaniards here, and then they would fire and plunder the houses and carry all to Hughson's, who was to carry them off into another country, and make them a free people, but they were to stay about two months before they began to set fire, and then all of them were to begin at once.

7. "That he (Jack) and Adam staid and eat some supper and drank some punch, and as soon as they had supped went home together, and left the rest of the company behind: this meeting was of a Sunday evening.

8. "That he (Jack) went afterwards to Hughson's several times as he went to fetch tea-water, and was there twice afterwards with Adam; that they always talked with Hughson

and the negroes present about the plot, and when was the time to begin.

9. "That Jay's Brash carried him (Jack) once to Hughson's, and another time Pintard's Caesar; and that it was usual for them at such by-meetings to swear without book, that they all stand to their words and keep all secret.

10. "That on Easter Sunday he (Jack) and Adam went down to Hughson's after church in the afternoon; he (Jack) was to go to Comfort's for tea-water; Adam went in before, and he (Jack) went to Comfort's and left his keg there, and soon followed him thither after he had filled his keg, and there they met with Walter's Quack, Pintard's Caesar, Ward's Bill, Jay's Ben, Philipse's Cuffee, Auboyneau's Prince, Brash, Vaarck's Caesar, Mrs. Sims's Billy, Albany, Othello, Hughson, his wife, and daughter Sarah; and then John Hughson proposed to all the negroes last mentioned, and to him (Jack) and Adam, that they should meet at Mr. Murray's house that night, that he (Jack) was to be in the kitchen, and to open the back gate whereat all those negroes were to come in, and Adam and he were to come down stairs to them, and they were to proceed to set fire to the house, murder his master and mistress, and the white people in the house, but he was interrupted by Mrs. Dimmock's (q) accidentally coming down into the kitchen and sending him up to bed.

11. "That after Mrs. Dimmock discovered him in the kitchen and sent him up to bed, a second time he came down again, went into the yard and opened the back gate, and staid in the yard half an hour, expecting the aforesaid negroes coming according to the appointment aforesaid; and they not coming after his waiting so long time, he (Jack) went up to Mr. Cruger's (the Mayor's) corner, and there saw Quack (Walter's) and the other negroes who had engaged to come to his master's house as before mentioned, but they said they could not come then, for they must go

(q) Mr. Murray's house-keeper.

down to Hughson's; and he (Jack) returned home and went in at the kitchen window and there slept, and staid till the first cock-crowing, and then opened the kitchen door and fetched in wood to make the fire, intending thereby to make the family believe that he got up early and came down stairs to make it.

12. "That Hughson at the same meeting proposed to the said negroes, that they should destroy Mr. Murray, Mrs. Murray and all the family with knives, and Hughson asked them all if they had got knives? and they all said they had, and pulled them out of their pockets; and Adam pulled out a long knife, and all the rest had long knives; but he (Jack) had a short one, which he calls a pen-knife, a clasped-knife which he eats his victuals with; he had seen Adam's before, he was whetting it one day upon the broad stones in the yard, and made it very sharp, and eat meat with it in his master's kitchen before all the servants; but he observed he generally kept it in his chest, and it was the same knife which was found upon the general search for stolen goods. (r)

13. "That when the snow was upon the ground, about Christmas last, he was at Hughson's, having been at Comfort's for tea-water, and Caesar (Vaarck's) standing at Hughson's door, called him in to drink; Prince (Auboyneau's), Cuffee (Philipse's), Quack (Walter's), and Bill (Sims') were in the entry; Hughson called him (Jack) aside, and told him, after he (Jack) and Adam had murdered the whole family, that he (Jack) should steal the plate out of the beaufets, the kitchen furniture, wearing apparel, linen, guns, swords, and every thing that was of value, and bring them to his (Hughson's) house; that the aforesaid negroes should assist him to bring them, and that they should bury them under ground; Hughson and his wife were both together with him (Jack) when he received these directions. Jack was unwilling at first, but at length consented to undertake it.

(r) There was such a knife found in Adam's chest upon the general search.

14. "That Adam was to kill his master and mistress, Mrs. Dimmock and her daughter; and that he (Jack) was to kill Caesar, Congo and Dido (s) and after that they were to take the above mentioned goods and carry them to the place appointed, after which they were to return to the house and set fire to it, then go down again to Hughson's and make ready for the general attack.

15. "That this proposal last above said was made by Hughson, before that of the Easter Sunday before mentioned, (t) and that Adam was not present."

The following negroes were apprehended and committed upon the examination of yesterday and this day, viz.:

Adam, captain R. Livingston's Tom, Heyer's Tom, and Gomez's Cajoe.

This day also, Judy Pelham made oath before John Haight, esq. one of his majesty's justices of the peace for the Manor of Cortlandt, in the county of Westchester. That she heard Thomas Plumstead, a soldier, say about three months ago, that there would be bloody times in York before harvest, and that he must be in the middle of it, and that there would be no time granted to take leave of wives or children.

This the justice certified in a letter to a gentlemen in this place, but the fellow was not found.

Saturday, June 27.

Examination and confession of Adam, negro of Joseph Murray, esquire, taken before one of the judges, No. 1.—

1. "He said that about last new-year was three years, there was a match of cock-fighting at the house of Adolph Philipse, esquire, in the evening, amongst the negroes, at which John Hughson (who then lived upon the dock next door to Silvester the cooper) was present, and the following negroes, viz.:

(s) Three other of Mr. Murray's negroes.
(t) See section 10, of this confession.

[227]

Philipse's Cuffee, Vaarck's Caesar, Auboyneau's Prince, Pintard's Caesar, Duyckinck's York, Chief Justice's Othello, and Ventour (Mr. Philipse's old negro man), and the old wench were in the cellar-kitchen, but saw them all there.

2. "That the company broke up about eight o'clock, and as they were all going out of the gate, Hughson stopped him and asked him if he would join with him and the negroes, in what they were going about? Adam asked Hughson what that was? Hughson said they were going to set fire to the houses of the town, and to kill the white people; he answered that he would be concerned with them; then Hughson asked him to come to his house, and talk further upon it.

3. "That accordingly he went to Hughson's house two or three days afterwards, and drank a bowl of punch with him there; Hughson having carried him up stairs, over their liquor the conversation ran upon the intended plot, and Hughson asked him several times, whether he would engage in it? and he as often answered him yes; but Hughson seemed to distrust him, and brought a book, which he took to be a common prayer book, and would have had him swear to it, but he refused to swear to it at that time, and went away in half an hour: Hughson told him at the same time, that Vaarck's Caesar, Philipse's Cuffee and Auboyneau's Prince, and a great many more were to be concerned with them. (t)

4. "That he used afterwards to go to Hughson's house whilst he continued to live upon the dock, and Hughson and he used to talk now and then about the intended plot, and Hughson used to say, he would find arms and powder, but desired he would get some too; to which Adam answered, he had no money to buy them. Hughson thereupon advised him to steal some for that purpose.

5. "That about four or five days after drinking the bowl

(t) If what this negro says is true, this hellish plot was some years a brooding before they attempted the execution of it: and those negroes last mentioned were some of the heads and principals of their colour that were concerned in it.

[228]

of punch as aforesaid, he met Cuffee (Philipse's) who said that Hughson had informed him that he (Adam) had engaged in the plot; Cuffee said that he had a key of his master's things, and he could come at what he pleased, and he could get some of his master's swords and guns; but he (Adam) being in haste, heard no more at that time.

6. "That he has often seen Cuffee and Prince have plenty of money about them, silver and gold; Cuffee had once two doubloons, and offered to fight a cock for one of them; and Prince had once eight or nine Spanish dollars about him.

7. "That soon after Hughson removed to his house at the north river, (u) he, Adam, used to resort thither, and upon his inquiry concerning the plot, Hughson told him that several white men were concerned with him in it, and a great many negroes, and that he kept a list.

8. "That soon after new-year holidays last, of a Sunday afternoon, (church just going out) he (Adam) was walking by old Mr. DeLancey's, and met Jack, his fellow servant, coming from Comfort's with a keg of tea-water; they stopped, and Jack told him he was just come from Hughson's, and that there was company there; Adam asked Jack to go back with him to drink a dram there, and they went there together; and when they came into the house, he saw there in company, Hughson, his wife and daughter, and four or five white people more, (whose faces he believes he should remember if he saw them) and the following negroes, that is to say, Caesar (Pintard's), Caesar (Vaarck's), Prince (Auboyneau's), Brash (Jay's), Pompey (P. DeLancey's); Hughson carried him and Jack into another room, and his wife and daughter came in there; Hughson swore him and Jack, and made them put their hands on a book, which he took to be a common prayer book, and made them

(u) He removed thither in May, 1738. This house was more out of the way, private and fit for Hughson's purposes on all accounts, for caballing and entertainment of negroes, and with respect to receiving stolen goods; it was said to be built with such privacies in the several rooms and cellars as might conceal run goods.

kiss the book: the purport of the oath was, that they were to be true to those concerned in the plot; that they were to keep all secret, and perform what they had engaged to do; and if they discovered to any body, that they might be split with thunder and lightning: they were to murder their masters and mistresses, kill all the white people, and to burn the houses: after they were sworn, Hughson shook them by the hand and wished them much joy. (w)

9. "That when Hughson first proposed the swearing, he was scrupulous about being concerned in the plot, and thought it was a great sin to do any such thing; but Hughson told him there was a man that he knew that could forgive him all his sins; whereupon he took the oath. And when Jack and he had drank their dram out, they came away together.

10. "That after this meeting at Hughson's, he saw a little short man (x) four or five times at Hughson's, who used to teach school at Campbell's, who has just now been shown him in prison, who Hughson told him was one of the two priests who could forgive sins; that he saw him twice in the room at Hughson's, whispering and talking with him, when many negroes were present; and he, Adam, then suspected that the little man knew of the plot, and was concerned in it; but does not remember that Hughson or the negroes talked out concerning the plot when that man was present: (y) Duane's Prince and Latham's Tony were there at the same time, and Cowley's Cato.

11. "That he has heard Hughson and the negroes met at his house, talk of the plot when John Romme was present: that the first time Hughson proposed it to Romme to be concerned, as Cuffee (Philipse's) told him (Adam), Romme seemed to decline it; but afterwards he promised to join with them, and seemed very forward for it.

(w) This agrees with Jack's account in the preceding examination, sections 2, 3, 4, 5, and these negroes were examined apart, and had no opportunity of being or talking together after they were committed.

(x) John Ury the priest.

(y) This agrees with Mary Burton's deposition concerning Ury, No. 4, section 3, Thursday, June 25.

[230]

12. "That he saw Holt, the dancing master, at Hughson's about new-year holidays, at a meeting of the negroes, and another white man belonging to him, whom they called doctor (z) and lodged at Holt's, whose name he knows not: there was likewise Holt's negro Joe with them; and the discourse amongst them was about the plot; and he, Adam, took Holt and the other white men to be concerned. At last he saw Hughson bring a book to swear them, and they laid their hands upon it, and Hughson pronounced the following words, or something to the same effect, that they should be true to one another, and aid and assist in the plot, and not discover any secrets; and then they kissed the book: and then Holt's negro Joe was sworn to the same purpose and in the same manner; and Holt commanded Joe that he should set fire to the play-house at such time as he should tell him: Holt's Joe had before this been telling him (Adam) that his master was concerned, was to be one of them, and would go down such a night to Hughson's to be sworn; and he asked him (Adam) to go down to see him sworn; which was the reason that carried him to Hughson's that night.

13. "That Holt told Hughson, that he had guns of his own, and powder he said he had not enough: Hughson answered, he need not make himself uneasy about that, he had seven or eight barrels.

14. "That Holt promised his man Joe to give him pistols, and asked him (Adam) whether his master had any arms? he, Adam, answered, he had some pistols; Holt advised him to get some, and he said he would, but powder he said he could not get: but both Hughson and Holt promised to supply him therewith.

15. "That one of the four or five white men before mentioned to have been seen by him one time at Hughson's, was one of Hughson's brother's, a boatman (as he now recollects) he had a boat there; and he saw John Hughson give him a small box to put into it, to carry up the river.

16. "That some time last summer, he, Adam, helped

(z) Hamilton, a pretended doctor who lodged at Holt's.

Quack (Walter's) ride his master's coach-horses out; and they came down to Hughson's and went into the house; and Hughson carried them up stairs, and swore Quack of the plot in the same manner, and the oath to the same purpose as Holt, etc. He, Adam, only went down there in order to drink a dram; and Hughson asked Quack to be concerned in the plot; and he directly answered yes, and was sworn as before; Hughson told him, that they were to burn the houses and kill the white people; and Quack then undertook to burn his master's house and cut his throat; and that Quack was as great a rogue as any of them.

17. "That Holt's Joe told him (Adam) not once, but an hundred and an hundred times, that he, Adam, need not be afraid, for that his (Joe's) master was concerned in the plot; and that he had spoke to Hughson for the biggest room he had there, to hold a free mason's lodge. (a)

18. "That he has heard of the great feast of a Sunday evening at Hughson's, but was not there; but believes it was a month or six weeks before the fort was burnt.

19. "That he, Adam, was at a meeting at Comfort's, which he believes was about a fortnight after that at Hughson's last mentioned; where were met a great number of negroes in the kitchen and shop; he, Adam was in the shop: this was also of a Sunday afternoon church just out; and there were present, his fellow servant Jack, Marschalk's Diego, P. DePeyster's Pedro, Othello, Caesar (Pintard's), Cato (colonel Moore's), Patrick (English's), Ben (Marshall's), Albany, and Kierstede's Braveboy: there they all talked about the plot; but he, Adam, stayed but a little time.

20. "That he had been acquainted with Quack (Walter's) from their childhood, used to play marbles together; and that he has often talked with him about the plot, before the frolic in the Bowery-lane which Curacoa Dick told him of; and he always seemed to be as active and forward in it as any body.

(a) Holt it seems was a free-mason.

21. "That one Sunday morning last summer, he and Pompey (P. DeLancey's) were taking a walk, and they met at a well by the new Dutch Church, Othello and Braveboy, who were both very drunk; and Adam asked them where they had been? they said they had been frolicking in the fields (he understood they had been at some free negroe's house in Bowery-land) at which frolic Othello said, that Robin and Sussex (Mrs. Bickley's negroes) were present, and Tiebout's Curacoa Dick.

22. "That the same Sunday morning he afterwards met the said Curacoa Dick, who said they had been dancing at the said frolic, and he fiddled; and that Sussex paid him therefor two pieces of eight, which he called Dutch dollars; he told him so before Mr. Cruger's coachman Hanover; and the said Dick called him aside from Hanover, and told him that they had been talking there about the plot, and said that Quack (Walter's) was there; and he, Adam, saw Quack (Walter's) leading a horse into a stable near the new Dutch church, a little before he met Curacoa Dick, and he believes Pompey saw him also, but he and Pompey were parted before he, Adam, met Curacoa Dick; he (Adam) and Pompey being going to their respective master's stables: he, Adam, observed that Quack was very drunk; just turned his master's horse into the stable, and shut the door and went away.

23. "That when he met Curacoa Dick, he said, mate, we wanted you very much last night at a frolic out of town; that they had a free dance and were very merry; and he pulled two Dutch dollars out of his pocket, which Sussex had given him for fiddling, and shewed them to him; and said nobody else had given him any thing: he leaned upon the post and shook his head when he, Adam, came up to him; and he, Adam, said, Dick you have some ill thoughts in your head: Dick answered, he was not afraid to tell him; he would tell him the truth; he then said, that Othello and Quack (Walter's) both knew of the plot; and that at this frolic they all talked of it; and that there were present at that meeting the negroes following, Othello, Quack

[233]

(Walter's), Braveboy, Robin, Sussex: this Dick told him before Hanover, Mr. Cruger's coachman.

24. "That Cuffee (Philipse's) told him, that he used often to talk to John Romme about the plot; and that he had promised him a great while to get an old sword or two for him (Romme) and this he said when he, Adam, met him carrying an old sword under his coat to Romme's; and he knew that Cuffee used frequently to go thither.

25. "That it was a great while ago since Quack (Walter's) told him that Othello was concerned in the plot; that he has frequently talked to him about it; and he was to do the same that he and Jack were to do; that is to say, to kill his master and mistress and the rest of the family; and he, Adam, and the rest of them who were to murder Mr. Murray's family, were to assist in murdering the chief-justice. (b)

26. "That he recollects that he, Adam, spoke to Othello about the plot, a few days after Hughson had proposed it to him at the cock-fighting at Mr. Philipse's house; and he (Adam) asked him to be concerned; he (Othello) said he would, and laughed, and seemed by his behaviour to have known of it before.

27. "That since the fires began to break out after the fort burnt, he once said to Sussex, at Mr. Murray's, how came the fort to be fired? Sussex answered, Lord have mercy upon us! what will become of us all? Adam replied he did not know.

28. "That Jack his fellow servant and he (Adam) have been very intimate ever since Mr. Freeman's time, and that soon after his coming to town after Mrs. Freeman's death, he (Jack) mentioned the plot first to him (Adam) and told him that Walter's Quack first mentioned it to him (Jack) and asked him to be concerned.

29. "That on Easter Sunday last, he and Jack his fellow servant went down to the North river together, Jack was to fetch tea-water at Comfort's; he went to Hughson's house, and Jack left his keg at Comfort's and followed him to

(b) See Jack's examination, June 26, section 10.

[234]

Hughson's, when they came there, they found in one room, John Hughson, his wife and daughter Sarah, and Peggy, and the following negroes viz.—Walter's Quack, Othello, Pintard's Caesar, Ward's Bill, Philipse's Cuffee, Auboyneau's Prince, Brash, Vaarck's Caesar, Mrs. Sims's Billy (now Ten Eyck's) and Albany; and John Hughson then proposed to the said negroes, in presence of the said white people, that they should meet at Mr. Murray's house that night, and that Jack was to be in the kitchen, and open the back gate, where all those other negroes were to come in, and he (Adam) was to come down stairs to them, and then they were to proceed to set fire to the house, murder his master and mistress, and all the white people in the family; and he (Adam) was to murder Congo, and Jack to murder Caesar (two other of his master's negroes) and then all the said negroes were to go out and kill all the white people that should come to extinguish the fire; the murder was to have been committed with knives, and the knife found in his (Adam's) chest upon the general search, was kept for that purpose, but the negroes so appointed, did not come that night, though they all agreed and promised Hughson so to do, and upon which Hughson gave them a bowl of punch. (c)

30. "That he and Jack have always been very intimate; they never talked any thing before Congo or Caesar, their fellow servants; they always talked by themselves, and do not believe they know any thing of it, nor ever heard Jack say that they did; he believes that if Jack had spoke to them about it, to be sure he would have told him of it.

31. "That when Jack returned from fetching water at Comfort's he was generally drunk, and from that suspected that he had been at Hughson's."

Evidence affecting this negro.—Jack (Murray's) confession, 26th June. Tom (Livingston's) confession, No. 2, section 4, June 28.

This negro, Adam, was very willing to lay hold of the benefit

(c) See Jack's examination, sections 10, 11.

of the proclamation before mentioned, but would entitle himself to it by saying as little as possible to enlarge the discovery of the confederates in this dark scheme: he was under examination several hours, several days running; the information that he gave came from him slowly and by piece-meals, which was very tiresome, and gave so much trouble that he was several times remanded to jail, and told that what he said would do him little service, but as the constable was taking him away he would beg to stay, and say he would tell of all he could recollect.—While he was under examination this day, it was told before Adam, that the chief justice's negro Othello was brought from Rhode-Island, and carrying to jail, and hearing that, he immediately said Othello was concerned in the plot, as if naturally concluding that some body else had impeached him, for till this accident, he had not mentioned his name. This Adam had a general acquaintance amongst the negroes, and idle time enough for doing any mischief, and it was supposed that he must have known most of the negroes concerned, though he mentioned very few but what we were apprized of before, and had already been either executed or apprehended.

It was observed by several in Mr. Murray's family, some time before Adam's commitment, that his behaviour was such as betokened strong symptoms of guilt, he appeared very uneasy and disturbed in his mind, and much more so when Jack his fellow servant was taken up as one concerned in the conspiracy, for the next morning he came several times into the clerk's office, with a seeming intention to disclose some secret; the young gentlemen at last took notice of it, and shutting the door too, asked him, whether he knew any thing concerning the plot? he denied he did, but said he was afraid some dog or another would owe him a spite, and bring him in, for that people talked a great deal of him.

In the afternoon, Mr. Murray having been present and assisting at his negro Jack's examination, upon his return home found Adam running backwards and forwards like a distracted creature, he called him into his study and charged him as one concerned in the conspiracy, which he absolutely denied, and protested his innocence; his master endeavoured and used many

[236]

arguments to prevail with him to confess if he was guilty, but to no purpose, and then he delivered him to the constable.

In the evening two of Mr. Murray's clerks went to see Adam in the jail, to try how far they could prevail upon him; and as soon as he knew they were come, he desired leave to speak with them privately, which being granted, he began with exclamations and protestations of his innocence, declaring it was nothing but damned lies that brought him there, and that he knew who was the author of them, and would be revenged if he died for it: the young gentlemen reasoned with him, telling him if he was innocent to insist upon it, and not be afraid, for he might be assured of having justice done him; but if he was guilty, his denying of it would signify nothing, for that they knew as much about the plot as they that were concerned in it, and the only way to recommend himself to favor, was by making a full confession; he then considered awhile, and desired to know his accuser, they told him they believed it was Jack, which as soon as he heard, he said then I am a dead man, striking his head against one of the beams of the jail; and said further, he was afraid the dog would have served him so. Then he gave the young gentlemen his shoe and knee-buckles (being silver) and some other things desiring they might be delivered to his brother Caesar (another negro of Mr. Murray's.) In this manner they parleyed with him a full hour, till at length tired with his obstinacy, they concluded to leave him, but he pressed them to stay, still giving them some hopes of his confession; they told him they had no occasion to stay to hear him repeat the same things over again: he then asked them what they would have him say? upon which they told him they would have him speak sincerely, whether he was guilty or not: why then said he to speak sincerely, I am guilty.

Confession of Harry, Kip's negro, under conviction, before one of the judges.—He said,

"That all the witnesses testified against him in court on his trial was true: Bastian was the first that told him of it; he went to Comfort's for tea-water, saw a great many negroes there, talked about the conspiracy, he drank drams and consented to burn the houses and kill the people; he

[237]

was only in the kitchen which was very full, and they soon made him drunk, and said he must burn his mistress' house, which he consented to; Derrick Cook's negro was there, Moore's Cato was there, Starling, Mr. Lawrence's negro there, Dick, Mr. Ten Eyck's by Coenties-market there."

Confession of Cato, Mr. Shurmur's negro, under conviction, before one of the judges.—He said,

1. "That all the witnesses who spoke against him at his trial, spoke the truth.
2. "Comfort's Jack was the first who told him of the plot, and said Cato if I tell you any thing, will you stand to it? he said he would; Jack then told him there are great companies to be made up to take this town; Cato then asked him where they must come to consult of it? Jack told him he must come to his house, and if he did not find him at home, he must go to Hughson's; this was last summer.
3. "York, Marschalk's London, and he went to Hughson's, and called for a half-pint of rum, Hughson not at home, but saw the wife and daughter there, Jack was not there, and so they went away again.
4. "Talked with Jack several times in the street about it afterwards.
5. "He was at the great meeting at Hughson's, when they had the great supper, about four or five weeks before the fort burnt, and there the plot was talked of, as mentioned by the witnesses; (f) they swore; that some when they were there went down into the cellar, forty or fifty negroes there, the room not big enough to hold them all, and some in the yard, nor could all sit down to table; he did not see any book there, but they all swore to do as engaged, which was to burn the fort first, and then all the houses in the town, every one to fire either their master's houses or some other houses, and kill the people: He was to set the neighbour's houses on fire, and not his master's. (g)
6. "That he met Gomez's Cuffee, and told him he had

(f) See Jack (Comfort's) and Bastian's evidence on the trial.
(g) His master lived in Ben Thomas' neighbourhood.

promised Jack to set the neighbour's house on fire, (h) and asked Cuffee if he had his tinder-box about him? (for he knew he smoked, and had a new one, and he, Cato, had none) he said he had one; Cato then told him if he would go and set fire to Ben Thomas's house, he would give him half a pint of rum; he agreed to do it, and said he would watch his opportunity when no body saw him; that he (Cuffee) did go and do it, and returned and told him so, and immediately fire was cried out; he gave him the rum. That evening he, Cato, met Comfort's Jack, as witnessed against him, and told him he, Cato, had done the business, (i) concealing that Gomez's Cuffee had done it, lest Jack should blame him for not doing as he promised. Furman's Harry he saw at Comfort's, Ward's Will (a watchmaker) at Hughson's, and (he Will) swore; Peter DeLancey's Pompey (lives sometimes in town and sometimes in country) at Comfort's, (he) swore, a knife in his pocket; Kortrecht's Caesar at both houses, and (he) swore.

7. "It was agreed at Hughson's, that the fort was to burn first, and that Quack should do it, because he had a wife there; then they agreed after that was done, they should all set fire as they could.

8. "That when they went about the swearing, Hughson told the negroes present, that they must not attempt to draw in any one that was not their countryman; that if they met with any countrymen, they must tell them so; and if they found they were likely to come in, then they might tell them of the plot; and those that were willing, they were to bring to Hughson's to be sworn." (k)

Now many negroes began to squeak, in order to lay hold of the benefit of the proclamation; some who had been apprehended

(h) Probably at the great meeting at captain Jack's; for all the negroes present, it seems, promised him to do something; see Jack (Comfort's) confession, section 31.

(i) Meaning the setting fire to Ben Thomas' house.

(k) These two last confessions should have been placed the 20th June; for they were then taken, being the next day after the conviction of these two criminals; but being mislaid, and not coming to hand before the printer had got beyond that day, occasioned their being inserted here.

but not indicted; and many who had been indicted and arraigned, who had pleaded *not guilty*, were disposed to retract their pleas and plead *guilty*, and throw themselves on the mercy of the court; so that confessions were like to be numerous, and business to multiply upon our hands, which made it necessary to call in some gentlemen of the law to our assistance upon the occasion, who very readily undertook the task.

Before the issuing of the proclamation of the 19th instant, for the encouragement of the conspirators to come in, and make voluntary and free confession and discovery, etc. there were betwixt sixty and seventy negroes in jail, who had been already impeached, many of whom after publishing the proclamation, not only confessed their own guilt, in order to entitle themselves to the benefit of it, as may appear by the foregoing examination, but also discovered many of their accomplices who were at large; who were thereupon immediately taken into custody by order of the judges, or grand jury, as the case happened before whom such confessions were made; so that between the 19th and this day, there were upwards of thirty slaves more added to the former, insomuch that the jail began to be so thronged, it was difficult to find room for them; and we were apprehensive that the criminals would be daily multiplying on our hands; nor could we see any likelihood of a stop to impeachments, for it seemed very probable that most of the negroes in town were corrupted.

The season began to grow warm, as usual, and it was to be expected that the heat would be increasing upon us daily; so that the judges found there was a necessity of bethinking themselves of taking such speedy measures, as should upon deliberation be thought most adviseable, for ridding the jail of such of them as should be their confessions be thought most deserving of recommendation of mercy; for it was feared such numbers of them closely confined together, might breed an infection, and they must needs have been very offensive to the poor debtors imprisoned in the city-hall, which from the necessity of the case, could not have been prevented or remedied; therefore the judges associated to them the several gentlemen of the law that were in town, viz.—Messieurs Murray, Alexander, Smith, Chambers,

Jamison, Nicholls and Lodge, in order to consult about this matter, and come to some resolution upon the emergency.

The result of the meeting was, those gentlemen unanimously agreed to bear their respective shares in the fatigue of the several prosecutions, and settled among themselves the part each should take: Messieurs Murray, Alexander, Smith, and Chambers, were to assist in their turns, as counsel upon the several trials, as it should best suit their respective convenience, and Messieurs Nicholls and Lodge, to take the negroes confessions, and abstract them and the other evidence into briefs, for the counsel upon the trials. (Mr. Jamison being high sheriff of the city, had other sufficient business upon his hands.)

The gentlemen thus assigned for taking the confessions, having attended most of the trials of the conspirators already passed, and likewise several examinations of criminals, were well acquainted with the account of the plot, according to the course of the evidence concerning it which had hitherto been brought to light; and as it was to be expected, they would have their hands full of that kind of business, it was necessary that some scheme should be settled for the more ready despatch of it: accordingly a method was proposed, and approved amongst us; a draught with several columns, viz.—one for the name of each negro; another for his respective owner; another for the matter or substance of the confession; another for the negroes they accused, and two others for the place where sworn at, viz.— Hughson's or Comfort's; for Jack, Comfort's negro, was a principal agent for Hughson, and (as may already have been observed from the course of the evidence) had corrupted many negroes, and administered the conspirators' oath to them.

The negroes in general that came to a confession, agreed in the impeachment of Hughson and his family; that the drift of the plot was to burn the town and destroy the inhabitants; that they were sworn into the confederacy at Hughson's, or by Hughson, or some person intrusted by him for that purpose.

As this was already discovered to be the execrable purpose of the conspiracy, these gentlemen (considering the great number to be examined) for the sake of despatch, dropped what was at this time least material, and only minuted down the persons accused, the matter affecting them, where and by whom sworn, and what else came from their examinant which they judged to be most significant; which is the reason that the examinations and confessions taken by those two gentlemen are so concise.

But further, in order to save room, and avoid drawing out this journal to an unnecessary length, which of itself is likely to spin out to a degree beyond patience, the compiler chose not to set them forth in the same manner they were taken, but made them yet shorter, by incorporating the substance of the several columns into the form in which they now appear.

Confessions taken this day by Mr. Nicholls and Mr. Lodge, of the fourteen following negroes:

No. 1. "*Jack* (*Breasted's*) said that Vaarck's Caesar (hanged) carried him to Hughson's; that Hughson told him he must join with them in a plot they were making, and swore him to set his master's house on fire, and to cut his mistress's throat."

Evidence affecting this negro.—Pompey (De Lancey's) confession, section 5, 22d June.

No. 2. "*English's Patrick* said that Moore's Cato listed and swore him at Mr. Moore's garden, to be his boy, and to go a frolic with him; that it was after the fort burnt."

Evidence affecting this negro.—Peggy's examination, No. 1, May 9. Sandy's or Sawney's examination, No. 1, section 12, May 22, and No. 3, section 8, June 1. Sarah (Burk's) examination, No. 2, June 1. Tickle's examination, No. 2, section 10, June 13. Pompey (De Lancey's) examination, section 5, June 22. Dundee's examination, sections 7, 9, June 24.

No. 3. "*Provost's Low* said that Hughson gave him the book to swear to stand by them to overcome the city."

Evidence affecting this negro.—Col. Moore's Cato's confession, section 8, June 22.

No. 4. "*Peck's York* said that Hughson swore him, and promised to furnish him; that Hughson's daughter was present when he was sworn."

Evidence affecting this negro.—Caesar (alderman Pintard's) confession, section 2, June 22.

No. 5. "*Horsefield's Guy* said that Quack and Albany swore him at Hughson's."

Evidence affecting this negro.—Quack's confession at the stake, section 4, May 30. Cambridge's confession, June 30.

No. 6. *"Lush's Will* said that Albany asked him to go and sup at Hughson's, where they went; that Hughson brought him punch and drams; that he swore him (Will) and told him he would furnish him with a gun."

Evidence affecting this negro.—Sandy's examination, No. 4, section 4, June 22. Pompey (De Lancey's) confession, section 5, June 22.

No. 7. *Second confession.*—*"Groesbeck's Mink* said that Hughson swore him into the plot, in February last. (See before 18th June, notes of evidence affecting him, adjoined to his first confession.)

Evidence affecting this negro.—Mars (Benson's) confession, June 29.

No. 8. "Captain Brown's Jeffery said that last January Hughson swore him unto the plot, and that the first of April the whole company was to be murdered."

No. 9. *"York (Thompson's)* said that some time last winter, Furman's Harry carried him to Hughson's with Woolf's Dick, and told the prisoner of the plot, and not to tell any body; that London (A. Van Horn's) was told by the prisoner of the plot, and he agreed to be one; there were present at the same time at Hughson's, besides the before mentioned, Jack (Comfort's), and Warwick (Hunt's)."

No. 10. *Second confession.*—*"Tom (Soumain's)* said, that Hughson told him he must fire his master's house, and kill his master. There were present at Hughson's at the same time, Quack (Roosevelt's), and Quash (Rutgers's)."

See notes of evidence affecting this negro adjoined to his confession, June 26.

No. 11. *"Scipio (Abrahams's)* said, that he was at Hughson's at the great Supper; that Hughson swore him to burn the houses and kill the people."

Evidence affecting this negro.—Starling's confession, section 3, June 23.

No. 12. *First confession.*—*"Livingston's Tom* said, that last summer he met Schuyler's Lewis in the fields; that Lewis told him, he must kill his master and mistress, and carried the prisoner to Hughson's; that Hughson swore both of them, and to keep it secret; and that he afterwards wanted to fight Lewis for not doing what Hughson bid him."

See evidence against this negro referred to under his second confession, June 28.

No. 13. *"Cruger's Deptford* said, that De Lancey's Pompey, and Pintard's Caesar, first engaged him to be concerned in the conspiracy, and Ward's Will afterwards."

Evidence affecting this negro.—Pompey, De Lancey's confession, section 10, June 22.

No. 14. *"Gilbert's Pompey* said, that Hieldreth's Diego engaged him first to be concerned, and to burn his mistress's house, and to get a gun to kill the white people; and pressed him to go to Hughson's. That afterwards he was at Hughson's and drank beer, and saw many negroes."

Evidence affecting this negro.—Delancey's Pompey, confession, section 10, June 22.

No. 15. *"Gabriel Crooke's Prince* said, that Mrs. Stilwell's Pedro carried him to Hughson's, and Hughson swore them to stand by him, to kill the white people and fire the house. (m)

2. "That Marschalk's York, when the first negroes were burning, told Prince, that now it was a fit time to kill the white people; but Prince answered, no, there were too many whites to attempt it.

3. "That Titus (Mr. Phoenix's negro) was one day last fall on the dock with the prisoner, at one Myers's a gun-smith; that Titus asked Myers to sell him a gun to shoot partridges with; but Myers would not sell him one; that afterwards he saw Titus and asked him what he wanted to buy a gun for? that Titus told him he had been at Hughson's, and they were to rise and kill the white people.

4. "That some time before the fort was burnt, he was at Mr. Masterton's; that Cataline, Mr. Masterton's negro was drunk, talking to himself in the yard, that the negroes were fools to do

(m) This in the negroes dialect signifies houses, i.e. the town.

here as they had done in the hot country; for they all burnt and hanged for it in the hot country. (n)

5. "That there were present at the same time at Hughson's, York of Gabriel Crook, Titus of Phoenix, Mr. Moore's Cato, Kip's Harry, and Furman's Harry."

Evidence affecting this negro.—Pintard's Caesar's confession, section 4, June 22. Colonel Moore's Cato's confession, section 2, 6, June 22. Marschalk's York's confession, section 6, June 20. Marschalk's London's confession, section 6, June 20.

Confessions of the four following negroes taken by Mr. George Joseph Moore:

No. 1. *"Walter's Quack, second confession.*—Mr. Walter's Quack said, that one Wednesday or Thursday he was at Hughson's, between five and six of the clock in the afternoon, he went with Vaarck's Caesar and Philipse's Cuffee and Prince, and Van Dam's John; they called for a tankard of egg-punch; they drank it, and Caesar asked him if he (the prisoner) would conclude along with them to set a great many houses on fire? and Caesar said, then they would make their escape, for he had an opportunity to go: the prisoner then told him he believed he would, but would consider of it, and give him an answer."

No. 2. *"Bridgwater (Mr. David Van Horn's)* said, that a little before Christmas, on a Sunday morning, Cowley's Cato called to him as he stood at Mr. Van Horn's door, and asked him to drink a dram; he, the prisoner, went with him to Hughson's; a white woman gave them a dram; Hughson was gone out; they came from Hughson's and went to the new dock; Cato there said, countryman, will you help? help what? said the prisoner; he answered, to set houses on fire and kill white folks; the prisoner said that could not be done, and it was wrong; to which Cato answered, there are a great many that will help; who are they? Cato answered, there are many Spanish negroes, Cook, Francis; to which the prisoner said, if you have so many, I will be one, and try what I can do. In the afternoon Cato called again on the prisoner, and asked him to go to Comfort's; he went to see Jack;

(n) Probably alluding to the conspiracy at Antigua, for which many negroes were executed four or five years ago.

Jack was not at home; Cook asked him, what are you come to help too? he answered yes; it is very well, said Cook; he went away; and this is all he knows."

Evidence affecting this negro.—Caesar (Pintard's) confession, section 4, June 22. Cato (Moore's) confession, section 2, 6, June 22.

No. 3. "*York* (*Ch. Crooke's*) said, that on the second day of Christmas he took a walk to the meal-market; met with Comfort's Jack, who called to him and asked him to go and drink a dram; went with him to Hughson's house; Jack had told him there the negroes were going to rise; he had got guns, powder, knife, but said they wanted hands, for they had not got many yet; to which York answered he would be one; Hughson asked him to drink a dram; the prisoner said thank you, and drank; Hughson said, boy, will you stand by it? to which the prisoner answered he would; Hughson said, if he would not be true, he would stick him with a sword, and pointed to one in a corner of the room; Hughson said, boy, if you stand by it, you must kiss the book; the prisoner did, and said he would stand by it, and would not be a coward; Hughson then said, if you will, you shall be always welcome to my house, come at any time. This was in the kitchen, Jack, Hughson, and he, only present. Hughson made him so drunk he could not stand; several negroes were in another room, does not know them, for he did not see them, only heard their tongues.

2. "Had been at Comfort's very often, and talked of it with Jack and Cook; saw Sam, Low's negro there, Marschalk's two negroes, Cowley's Cato, colonel Moore's Cato, Peck's Caesar. Hughson said, stand by it boys to fight and take this place. Jack told him at his master's shop one day, that he must get a knife; the prisoner said that his master had got knives enough, and he could get one.

3. "Knows no more; never was at Hughson's afterwards; Hughson asked him to stay supper there, and eat a mouthful; York asked for bread, butter, and cheese, Hughson fetched him some. He kept out of the way ever afterwards."

Evidence affecting this negro.—Cato (Moore's) confession,

section 2, 6, June 22. London (Marschalk's) confession, section 6, June 20.

No. 4. "*Caesar* (*Horsefield's*) said, that Roosevelt's Quack, about new year, of a working day, met him in the meal-market, and told him he must go with him to some company on the North river; he went there and drank, and Quack asked him to stay supper; he consented; they supped; had a goose and some mutton; the supper on the table before they went there. Albany and Caesar (Vaarck's) were there."

Being asked several questions about this meeting, and not answering so as to be believed, nor making out any thing, he seemed very much concerned, and said, he understood that Roosevelt's Quack had used his name at the fire, and therefore thought he should be condemned, but declared what he had before said he did because he was afraid of his life, and that he should die if he did not say something, but could not tell what to say, not knowing any thing at all of the plot.

Evidence affecting this negro.—Quack's confession at the stake, section 4, May 30. Cambridge's confession, June 30.

Confession of Emanuel, a Spanish negro belonging to Thomas Wendover, taken by a private hand.—He said,

1. "That about new year last he went to walk behind the English church by the water-side, on a Sunday evening, when the drum was beating at the fort, and there he met with Rutgers' Quash and another negro; that they asked him to go to Hughson's, that he did go, and saw a great number of negroes there, among whom were Wan belonging to captain Sarly, Wan whose master is dead, who was a sail-maker (Peter Van Rantz;) that he talks English very well.

2. "That Hughson asked Quash, whose negro he, the prisoner, was? Quash told him Wendover's, that Hughson asked whether he was a good boy? Quash answered yes; that the negroes were all at supper at a long table, that he saw Hughson amongst them, but no woman, that captain Marshall's Ben sat at the corner of the table, which was very long, and

[247]

Hughson at the other end with a book by him; that he did not go into the room but only looked in at the door, and that the room was so full that several of the negroes stood.

3. "That Quash told the prisoner to come in and eat, that Hughson said don't you see the room is too full already, let him stay there. The prisoner saw Comfort's Jack and Cook there; that Quash brought him punch, and some bread and salt pork, that he eat and drank what Quash gave him.

4. "That he saw another room, but the door was shut, and does not know whether there was any body in the room.

5. "That the prisoner told Quash he must go home and give victuals to the cow, Quash said stay a little, that he Quash came out to the door to him, and told him the negroes were going to rise and cut the white people's throats with knives, that when he had done his business at home he must come back, and then Quash was to tell him a great deal, and to give him a knife, and that he must be sure to tell no body of it.

6. "That the prisoner agreed to kill the white people, and not to discover, but told him he must go home, and he would come back directly.

7. "That his master when he came home would not let him go out again.

8. "That he went there early the next morning, but the doors being shut he returned home, and that he never went there afterwards.

9. "That he has met Quash in the street several times afterwards, who asked him the reason why he did not come there, and he told him his master would not let him go out; Quash told him he must come, for they wanted him very much, for all the negroes he saw there had knives to kill the white people, and next time he went there he would tell him all."

Evidence affecting this negro.—Bastian's examination, No. 1, section 10, 11th June.

[248]

This day the following negroes were apprehended and committed, viz.—widow Van Rantz's John, Mr. Adoniah Schuyler's Lewis, Van Dursen's Diego, Phoenix's Titus, Marston's Scotland, Kiersted's, Mr. Philipse's Frank.

Sunday, June 28.

Confession of Gomez's Cajoe alias Africa, by a private hand.—
He said,

1. "That about August last he went to the house of ——— (p) in company with three negroes belonging to captain Wells, that captain Brown's Jeffery, and James and Frank, three country negroes were there when they went in, that captain Marshall's Ben and his wife came there after him, that Ben said when he first came in, how do ye do, how do ye do, my friends? I hope you will all be my men in a short time.

2. "That they sat down and drank together some time, after which Ben told him that he had some business to do down by the water side, and when he went out said farewell brothers. This is all he remembers to have heard that time, but took on notice of what Ben said as to being his men, not knowing what he meant.

3. "The Saturday after new-year, Mr. Gomez's Cuffee asked him to go down to the North river side, to a house there where there were negroes dancing and fiddling, that accordingly he went with Cuffee into Hughson's, and Cuffee called to Hughson and bid him make a mug of punch, that Hughson brought it, and had, as the prisoner says, put above two thirds of strong rum, and made it so sweet that he did not immediately feel the strength of it.

4. "That Mr. Roosevelt's Quack, Rutgers's Quash, Vaarck's Caesar, Auboyneau's Prince, and Philipse's Cuffee, came there while they were drinking, they all went up stairs

(p) The wife of Jeffery, lived there.

[249]

(where there were negroes dancing) except the prisoner and Cuffee, who sat drinking their punch.

5. "That he does not know who was there except those he saw go up.

6. "That Hughson when they had drank their liquor, asked the prisoner if he would stand his friend; he said what to do? says Hughson you must first swear that you will not discover what I am going to tell you; says the prisoner must I swear to a thing that I don't know what it is? said Hughson come drink about; after he had drank, then Hughson again told him he must swear, that if he did not he should not go out of the house again; Cuffee told him he must swear, but that if he had no mind to do it, that he must tell nobody any thing about it; the prisoner damned his soul to eternity if he ever told any body living; and Hughson read something in a book, which he does not remember, but believes it was an oath, after which he kissed the book; then Hughson told the prisoner he need not be afraid, that he had got a great many hands, and would get many more, and that the prisoner should bring as many there as he could, that they were to rise and burn the houses and kill the white people, and told him he must get his master's small arms and bring them there, and that he might set his master's house on fire and kill any body he could meet with, master first.

7. "That he agreed to whatever they said, in order to get away from them.

8. "After which Hughson brought Ben, and drank good success to their undertaking, which health Cuffee and he drank; after which the prisoner bade them good night, and went away sorry for what he had done. That he never went there afterwards.

9. "Hughson told him the fort was to be burnt first, some time in the spring, and when he saw that, every one must prepare.

10. "That about a week after the fort was burnt, he was going to the post-house, and met with captain Marshall's Ben by his master's door, that Ben told him he must see if

his master had any swords, or guns, or pistols; the prisoner asked him for what? Ben said you see the fort is burnt already, it is now time for every man to prepare; the prisoner said don't be a fool to undertake such a thing, for I will have no hand in it; if you should be found out don't call my name, for I will have nothing to do with you.

11. "That nothing further was said, and nobody else spoke to him after that time."

Evidence affecting this negro.—Brash's confession, section 5.
Confession of Tom, Mr. R. Livingston's negro, before one of the judges, No. 2.—He said,

(1.) "That Lewis, a negro living with Edward Man (q); Tiebout's Venture; Gosport, belonging to Bound the quaker; Abrahams's Jack, Wall-street; captain Walton's Fortune; Mr. Henry Cruger's Hanover; and himself, were at Hughson's last summer, where Hughson talked to them of the plot, he told them they must kill the white people and steal their goods, and bring them to his house, and they must kill their masters and mistresses, which they all agreed to and were sworn, and put hands on book to perform it, and keep all secret; they were not so much as to tell a cat or a dog.

2. "Hughson told them they were to begin to kill about two months after new-year, but they were to come to him first for orders.

3. "That Prince, Kortrecht's negro, told him the day Philipse's storehouse was burnt (as they were screening wheat) that he had been at Hughson's, and was sworn to the plot.

4. "That Murray's Adam told him he had been sworn at Hughson's."

See this negro's confession 27th June, before Mr. Nicholls and Mr. Lodge (No. 12).
Evidence affecting this negro.—Brash's confession, section 5. Dick (Ten Eyck's) confession, 30th June.

(q) Mr. Adoniah Schuyler's.

This day the following negroes were apprehended and committed: Tiebout's Venture, Abraham's Jack, Captain Walton's Fortune, Roerback's Jack.

SUPREME COURT.
Monday, June 29.

Present, the second and third justices.

The king against Dorland's Jack, Hardenbergh's Will, negroes.

John Dorland and Johannes Hardenbergh entered into recognizance for the appearance of Jack and Will, two negroes, at the next court of oyer and terminer and general jail delivery for Queen's county, thereon ordered, that the sheriff of Queen's county do discharge out of his custody the said negroes. (r)

His majesty's ordinance for the further enlarging the present term until Saturday, the 25th day of July next, published.

Court adjourned till ten o'clock to-morrow morning.

Confession of Pedro (De Peyster's negro) by John Schultz.—
He said,

1. "That last fall he went out one Sunday morning with Mrs. Carpenter's negro, Albany; that as they went along the Broadway, they met with Mr. Sleydall's Jack, who was going to Comfort's for tea-water; that at the market near Mr. De Lancey's house they met two other negroes; that Albany asked them all to go down to Hughson's and drink with them; that they first drank cyder, then raw drams; that Hughson sat down and drank with them; that after their liquor was all out, Hughson called Albany aside; when Albany returned, he asked Pedro, Jack, Kid, and Caesar (Dr. Henderson's) if they would consent to become their own masters? they all answered yes; then he told them they must help burn the town and kill the white people, which they consented to readily, having all drank pretty much. Albany told them they must swear to be true to one another, and

(r) See deposition of Stephen Evan.

[252]

not to discover any thing; that Albany had a little book on which they swore; that their oath was, they wished the thunder might split them to pieces on the spot where they first spoke it. Hughson was in the room when they swore, and afterwards told them, that when the time came that they should be wanted, he would take care that they should be sent for.

2. "That Kid told Hughson his master had arms enough, and that he would get some of them, and that he would kill his master and mistress and fire the house, that after that he would go into the street and help kill the people there. Caesar was to act in the same manner.

3. "Jack said his master was too cross, and that he would kill him.

4. "Pedro said he did tell Jack (Sleydall's) to set Mr. Murray's house on fire, which he promised to do, but afterwards fired the hay-stack.

5. "That the reason why they provided knives and cutlasses, was, that the report of a gun would immediately alarm the people, and they thought they might stab many before they were found out."

Evidence affecting this negro.—Jack (Sleydall's) confession, section 1. Adam's confession, section 19.

Confession of Jeffery (captain Brown's) and Mars (Benson's) negroes, before the grand jury.

1. "Jeffery said, that about Christmas last he went for tea water, and called for a dram at Hughson's, when Hughson desired him to swear he would do what he desired him, but at that time he would not.

2. "Some days afterwards (24th January) he went there again, and at length was persuaded by Hughson to swear to do what he asked him, and to keep it secret, and he did swear; and upon it Hughson told him he was to take the town, and told him of negroes concerned, and that they were to meet the first day of April, viz.—to kill the people and take the town.

[253]

3. "Persons there were—Vaarck's Caesar, Auboyneau's Prince, and Albany, and were to be concerned.

4. "That Holt's negro told him his master was to be concerned. Mr. Benson's Mars said, that he heard Gomez's Cuffee and Peck's Caesar say, that Jeffery above was concerned."

Confession of Scotland (Mr. Marston's negro) before one of the judges.—He said,

1. "That a little before Christmas last he met with Marshall's Ben, and he asked him to take a walk, and he carried him down to Hughson's, where they drank punch; Hughson fetched water and rum, and sugar was upon the table; Ben made the punch; Ben asked him whether he would do as they were going to do? he asked him what that was? Ben answered they were going to rise (meaning the negroes) and to kill the white people; he, Scotland, replied that the white people were too strong for them, they could not do it; so they drank out their punch, and nothing further passed between them at that time. Hughson went in and out of the room all the time he, Scotland, and Ben were there, but whether he attended to or heard their discourse, he cannot say. This was of a Sunday afternoon, church out, and no other negroes there at Hughson's as he saw.

2. "The Sunday after this, Ben and he went again to Hughson's and drank punch there; Hughson was at home, and after Ben had talked of the plot to him, and the liquor had made him drunk, he consented to join in it, that is to say, to help burn the houses and to fight the white people; Hughson brought the book in order to swear him, and Ben told him he must put his hand on the book; he asked Ben how far he must swear? Ben said he must wish that the first thunder that came must split him to pieces if he told him any thing of it, or did not stand to his word; and he put his hand on the book and took the said oath, and then they went away, and he never went there again, nor had he ever any more discourse with Ben about it."

This day the following negroes were apprehended and committed, viz.—Gosport (Bound's); Caesar (col. Moore's); Hanover (Mr. Cruger's); Tony or Tonio (Mr. Courtlandt's); Hereford (Myers Cohen's); Kid (Mr. C. Van Horn's); Caesar (Dr. Henderson's).

SUPREME COURT.
Tuesday, June 30.

Present, the second justice.

Court opened and adjourned till to-morrow morning, ten o'clock.

Confession of Braveboy, (Mrs. Kiersted's) before one of the judges.

1. "He said that some time last summer, Carpenter's Albany came to his mistress's house to bring meat, and called him into the yard, saying he wanted to speak with him, and then asked him whether he would join with them? saying they were going to have a small fight, and if he would be on their side, he should not lose by it, and that they would have him, because he was a fiddler, and he must then be sworn to join with them; and he swore that he wished the devil would fetch him away if he did not join with them and keep all secret. Then Albany told him, he would help him to a gun to kill his master; at which he was so struck, that he did not know whether he stood upon his head or his heels, and said, in the names of God, if you are going upon such business, you may do it by yourselves, for he would have no concern in it: upon which Albany made him promise to keep secret what he had said to him, and not tell it to black or white.

2. "That Albany had told him at the same time, that Prince (Auboyneau's), Cuffee (Philipse's), and Caesar (Vaarck's) were concerned in this design.

3. "That about a week after Albany had spoke to him as above, Prince carried him to Hughson's, of a Sunday after-

noon in church time: Hughson was at home, and in company with Caesar (Vaarck's) Cuffee (Philipse's) and Albany; Hughson at coming in gave him a dram, and then went out of the room and brought in a book, and asked him to swear upon it? but he refused to swear, telling Hughson, that he had already been sworn by Albany, and upon that hasted away, Hughson calling him back, and charging him to keep all secret, and said if he did not, he would fare the worse for it; but he did not return, nor had even been there since, or talked to any one about it.

4. "Braveboy's account of the frolic at the Bowery. (w) That he was at a free negroes (the negro man and his wife Isabella present) at a house between Mr. Bayard's land and Greenwich-land.

"Present—Men.—Mrs. Bickley's Robin and Sussex, Cruger's Fortune, both Mr. Haine's slaves, one a mulatto the other a negro; Othello, Walter's Quack, Curacoa Dick, who played on Braveboy's fiddle.—Wenches—Mr. Frank's Lucena, Mr. Richard's Quack's wife, Maria, Sarah and Hannah, three free negroes. Mr. Henry Curger's Neptune came there late, about eleven at night, but the wenches turned him away."

Evidence affecting this negro.—Sarah (Burk's) examination and confession, No. 2. Jack (Murray's) examination and confession, section 5. Adam's examination and confession, No. 1, section 19.

Confession of Samuel Myers Cohen's negro Windsor, taken by John Schultz.

1. "He said, that about two years ago, when the corn was ripe, he had been of an errand to Greenwich, in company with a negro belonging to Alexander Allair, who is since dead; that they, when they came back, went into Hughson's, and the other negro called for rum; that Hughson brought a whole case bottle full, and told them they might

(w) Mentioned by Mr. Murray's Adam in his confession.

drink as much as they pleased: Windsor offered Hughson three pence, but he told him he would take no money, that he was welcome: Allair's negro told Hughson, this is the man I promised you, he is a good marksman: that Hughson liked him very well, and got up and took a book off a shelf and laid down on a table by him; that he (the prisoner) put both his hands on it; that Hughson then told him, the negroes were to rise and set the town on fire, and kill the white people; that he must set his master's house on fire, and kill his master and mistress before he came out, which the prisoner refused, saying he could not do it; that he did not care to set fire to any house, but would help them to fight.

2. "Hughson told him, it is to be done in the spring; that Mr. Allair's negro should tell him the time; and that if he would come to him, he would find him a gun and sword; that he must swear to secrecy, which he did by force; that Hughson put a book upon his breast, and swore some words which he has forgot.

3. "That as they came back, the negro of Mr. Allair told him, that Mr. Valet's Tom, and Mr. Nicholas Bayard's Phaeton, formerly belonging to Mr. Valet, Mr. Jay's Brash, Mr. Pintard's Caesar, Mr. Auboyneau's Prince, Mr. Philipse's Cuffee and Mr. Vaarck's Caesar, were all sworn and belonging to one company.

4. "That he has been at Hughson's three or four times along to drink, and once with Mr. Allair's negro, which was the first time when he was sworn."

The *Confessions* of the seven negroes following, taken by Mr. Nicholls and Mr. Lodge.

No. 1. "*Varian's Worcester* said, that in Christmas holidays Leffert's Pompey carried him to Hughson's, where were many negroes at supper; that they had punch, etc. and after supper, Hughson, his wife, and daughter, swore to a plot against the white people, and that he (Hughson) swore most or all of the negroes then present, among whom the prisoner was sworn; that some swore by one thing, and some by another: there were pres-

don, Carpenter's Tickle and Albany, and Bastian."

Evidence affecting this negro.—Quack's confession at the stake, section 4. Tickle's confession, section 4.

No. 2. "*Codweis's Cambridge* said, that on Christmas Sunday evening, Baker's Cajoe carried him to Hughson's, who swore them both in the plot in the presence of a white girl: that he, Cambridge, afterwards asked Horsefield's Caesar and Guy about it, who both confessed they had been sworn at Hughson's, and told him, when the work was going forward at York, they would give the prisoner notice, and take him over with them in a canoe to assist them; (x) and Cajoe told them they were to kill such of the negroes as would not assist them."

Evidence affecting this negro.—Quack's confession at the stake section 4.

No. 3. "*Bayard's Pompey* says, that Mr. De Lancey's Pompey came to his mistress's to fetch her to Mrs. De Lancey's lying-in; that he and Pompey got gaming together, and then Pompey told him of the plot, and asked his consent to be one among them, and that he consented to it: that afterwards he went to Mr. Peter De Lancey's, where he saw the said Pompey, Pintard's Caesar, Moore's Cato, and a Spanish negro of captain Cunningham."

Evidence affecting this Negro.—De Lancey's Pompey's confession, section 9.

No. 4. "*Widow Breasted's* Toby said, that Christmas holidays Comfort's Cook carried him to Hughson's, where he saw Mr. Jay's Ben, captain Marshall's Ben and some others, who all supped there; that he saw Hughson, his wife, etc. there: that Jay's Ben prevailed on him to kiss the book; that he accordingly did kiss it; that thereupon Ben said he was his man, and should stand to him, but did not tell him for what; but seeing him afterwards, he told him he had swore to fight the white people, and stand by him: that the prisoner promised, and Ben bid him bring him a pistol to Mr. Jay's garden, and told him that they

---

(x) The masters of these two negroes were butchers who lived over the water on Long Island, opposite to this city.

[258]

had bought some arms already, and by and by they would rise. The negroes then present (besides) were Comfort's Cook, Cowley's Cato, Philipse's Cuffee, Roosevelt's Quack."

Evidence affecting this negro.—Brash's confession, section 4.

No. 5. *"Ten Eyck's Will* said, that Albany carried him to Hughson's; that Albany there talked of the number of Cuba men gone off, and said he believed an hundred and fifty men might take this city; and after some discourse, told him of the plot, and swore him by the thunder and lightning to join in the plot and burn his master's house; that Caesar had given Hughson money to buy arms and powder to furnish the negroes with and to appoint the time for the enterprize. The negroes then present were Albany, Bastian, and Vaarck's Jonneau."

Evidence affecting this negro.—Burk's Sarah's examination, No. 2. Pintard's Caesar's confession, section 4. Tickle's confession, section 4. Jonneau's confession.

No. 6. *"Phoenix's Titus* said, that going one day for yeast to Mr. Rutgers's, Quash swore him to burn his master's house and kill his master and mistress; that he agreed to burn the house but refused to kill his master and mistress."

Evidence affecting this negro.—Gab. Crooke's Prince's confession, section 3, 5.

No. 7. *"Ten Eyck's Dick* said, that Carpenter's Albany carried him to Hughson's, where he was sworn into the plot: that Wendover's Toby afterwards informed him of the plot, and asked him to be engaged: that the negroes then present, were Wendover's Toby, Livingston's Tom, Sleydall's Jack, Ryker's Frank, Carpenter's Albany, Wyncoop's London."

Upon the several examinations taken this day, the following negroes were committed this evening.

Valet's Tom, Bayard's Phaeton, Baker's Cajoe, Wendover's Tom, Ryker's Frank.

Minutes of Othello's examination and confession, taken before one of the judges, the 29th and 30th June.

June 29.—1. "He said that at a meeting of several negroes at Coenties-market about this time twelvemonth, present, Albany, Cuffee (Philipse's); Prince (Auboyneau's); Adam,

[259]

and Pompey (De Lancey's); Adam and Albany mentioned the plot to him, and he agreed to join to burn and kill, etc. and swore. Rutgers' Quash, Cowley's Cato, concerned. Hanover, belonging to Mr. John Cruger, from Curacoa, Albany said he was concerned.

2. "Othello was at a feast at Hughson's with a parcel of negroes, when North the constable came and drove them away; present then, Albany, Quamino, Pemberton's, and many others.

3. "Othello being asked, why he so positively denied on Saturday, that he knew any thing about the plot, though he was warned of the proclamation, and that the time therein limited for the confederates to come in and make voluntary confession and discovery, would expire as to-morrow, and notwithstanding he was told that there was full and clear evidence against him, why he did not take the recorder's advice, and confess then what he had done now? He answered with a smile, 'why, sir, I was but just then come to town.'" (y)

June 30.—4. "Othello was at a frolic in the Bowery last summer, at which were present, (z) Walter's Quack, Braveboy, Curacoa Dick, Mr. Haines's Ancram (mulatto), Pompey, Ben Moore's Tom; a white young man who married a mulatto girl, Braveboy can tell best; a free negro, lives at Kip's-Bay, Braveboy knows his name; Mr. Richard's Cato, Mr. Searle's Pompey, Mrs. Jenny's, Mr. Faviere's Cajoe."

SUPREME COURT.
Wednesday, July 1.

Present the second and third justices.

The five Spanish negroes convicted of the conspiracy on the seventeenth of June last, were this day called up to judgment,

(y) i.e. He was willing to spy the land first, to see how it lay, to inform himself how matters stood, what had been doing, and to consider whether there could be room for his escape.

(z) See Adam's confession, sections 21, 22, 23. Braveboy's confession, section 4.

viz.—Mr. De Lancey's Antonio, Mesnard's Antonio, Becker's Pablo, Sarly's Juan or Wan, M'Mullen's Augustine; and having nothing to offer in arrest, but protestations of their innocence, Mr. Gomez (a) was directed to interpret what the court delivered.

The third justice proceeded as followeth:

Mr. Gomez, pray tell the prisoners at the bar, that the court observes, 1st. That they were taken with some Spaniards by an English privateer, were brought into this port, and condemned as lawful prize, being supposed to be slaves belonging to the subjects of the king of Spain; and nothing appeared to the court of admiralty (which is the court to which jurisdiction concerning things of this nature does properly belong) to shew that they were freemen, and they have made no pretence or claim in that court to be such, they were therefore adjudged to be slaves.

2dly. That the court of admiralty having so adjudged them to be slaves, they had been severally sold and disposed of, by which means they were discharged from confinement in prison, and thereby have had the opportunity of caballing with other wicked, mischievous and evil disposed persons, as well white men as slaves, and have confederated themselves with them, in a most diabolical conspiracy, to lay this city in ashes, and to murder and destroy all the inhabitants; whereas had they appeared to have been freemen, they would have been prevented this opportunity of venting and gratifying the rancour of their hearts, by being closely confined as prisoners of war.

3dly. If notwithstanding they were freemen, they ought in all reason to have waited the event of the war, and suffered patiently under their misfortune; and when peace should have been concluded, they might have made the truth of their pretensions appear, and then justice would have been done them.

But now, as they are found guilty of this most horrid and

(a) He had been interpreter upon the trial.

villainous conspiracy, by the laws of our land, nothing remains but to pronounce sentence of death against them. Accordingly they were sentenced to be hanged.

The king against Duane's Prince, Latham's Tony, Shurmur's Cato, Marschalk's York, Kip's Harry, negroes.

The prisoners having been convicted of the conspiracy, were brought to the bar, and having nothing to offer in arrest of judgment, the court passed sentence on them to be hanged: and ordered their execution to be on Friday the third instant, and that the body of York should be afterwards hung in chains on the same gibbet with John Hughson.

The king against Sarah Hughson.

This criminal continuing inflexible, it was ordered she should be executed, according to her sentence, on Wednesday the eighth instant.

The king against Benson's Cato, S. Bayard's Pompey, negroes.

These prisoners having desired leave of the court to withdraw their plea of *not guilty* and to plead *guilty*, it was ordered accordingly; and they pleaded *guilty*, and submitted to the mercy of the court.

The king against Bound's Jeffery, Breasted's Toby, Clarkson's Fortune, Hunt's Warwick, Meyers Cohen's Windsor, Ellison's Billy, negroes.

The prisoners were brought to the bar and arraigned on an indictment for conspiracy, and Jeffery, Toby, Warwick and Windsor pleaded *guilty*, and Fortune and Billy, *not guilty*.

The king against Murray's Jack, Gomez's Cajoe, Hyer's Tom, Schuyler's Lewis, Tiebout's Venture, Bound's Jasper, Abrahams's Jack, Walton's Fortune, negroes.

The prisoners were arraigned on an indictment for the conspiracy; and Tom, Venture, Jasper and Fortune, pleaded *not guilty*, and the two Jacks, Cajoe and Lewis, pleaded *guilty*, and submitted to the mercy of the court.

Court adjourned till to-morrow morning 10 o'clock.

The two following negro *confessions* were this day taken by Mr. Nicholls and Mr. Lodge:

[262]

No. 1.—"*Hunt's Warwick* said, that London, Wyncoop's negro, went with him to Hughson's about two years ago, that Hughson swore him in the presence of his daughter, to kill his master and mistress, that he ordered the prisoner to steal what money he could and bring it to him, to buy arms and powder, that he (Hughson) had three barrels of powder but wanted more, that he (Warwick) was there (at Hughson's) last Christmas, at the great supper, but did not see all the negroes that were there, he being in the cellar and in liquor."

Evidence affecting this negro.—Sarah (Burk's) examination, No. 2, section 1. London (Wyncoop's) confession, section 1.

No. 2.—"*Mr. Adoniah Schuyler's Lewis* said, that on a Saturday afternoon, Mr. Roosevelt's Quack and Rutgers's Quash carried him to Hughson's, that they drank punch there, that he heard nothing of the plot at that time, but Quack engaged him to come to him the next day, which he did, at Mr. Rutgers's brew-house, where Quack swore him to fire his master's house, and kill his master and mistress; that he afterwards set fire to some beading, but it being green, would not take fire. Knows of no others concerned."

Evidence affecting this negro.—Tom (Livingston's) confession, No. 1, 2.

Confession of Sam, negro of colonel Frederick Courtlandt, before one of the judges.—He said,

1. "That some time last fall, being at the house of John Hughson, he asked the examinant whether he would be concerned with him to burn the town, and kill the white people? that the examinant consented; that thereupon he gave the examinant a dram, and told him he expected he would be as good as his word, he answered yes.

2. "That about a fortnight after he met with Pompey (Mr. P. De Lancey's negro) and carried him to Hughson's, and when they were there, they and Hughson drank a mug of punch, after which Hughson asked Pompey whether he would consent to stand on his side against the white people, etc. which he consenting to do, Hughson swore the said

[263]

Pompey, in presence of the examinant and Hughson's wife, to be true; (b) that the examinant told Pompey he had drank a dram to bind him, which was as good as swearing.

3. "That the examinant never spoke to any other negro about the plot, nor has any other negro at any time spoke to him about it."

Evidence affecting this negro.—Pompey (De Lancey's) confession, section 1, 6.

Deposition, No. 1.—John Schultz made oath,

"That whereas by the judge's orders he took a confession in writing from the mouth of Pedro, belonging to Pierre De Peyster, wherein he accused two negroes, the one belonging to Cornelius Van Horn, called Kid, the other to Dr. Henderson, called Caesar, that they Kid and Caesar, with some other negroes and him the said Pedro, were sworn at Hughson's, and there agreed to set fire to houses and destroy the people inhabiting this city: and whereas the said Pedro did, on the 30th day of June 1741, acknowledge voluntarily to the said John Schultz, Francis Barrow being present, and likewise in the evening of the same day, John Schultz, Pierre De Peyster and Stephen Courtlandt being present, that the words which he spoke relating to himself and the others which he had said were present and all sworn at Hughson's, viz.—Kid, Caesar, etc. was not true, and that Will, a negro belonging to one Ward, a watch maker, being in the same prison with him, had told him that he understood these affairs very well, and that unless he the said Pedro did confess and bring in two or three, he would either be hanged or burnt, and did likewise name the aforesaid as proper ones to be accused, and he the said Pedro did say, that Will was the cause of his making that false confession, which he can prove by four negroes which are in the same prison with him."

Deposition, No. 2.—John Schultz made oath,

(b) Compare Pompey's confession with this.

[264]

"That a negro belonging to Henry Breasted, called Jack, did, after he had made confession, send for him to the prison, and told him, he had recollected two more negroes, viz.—Hereford, belonging to Samuel Meyers Cohen, and Tonio, belonging to counsellor Courtlandt, which were afterwards committed by order of the judges, for being concerned in the conspiracy. And whereas it was desired by the master of the said Hereford, that he should be examined, which he afterwards was by the said John Schultz and Samuel Meyers Cohen, and did declare his innocence of what he was charged with, and the said Hereford being a young boy, did give the aforesaid Schultz a suspicion that he was impeached wrongfully, for which reason he the said John Schultz did again go to the prison, and in the presence of Lancaster Green and Catharine Mills did ask the aforesaid Jack, whether the said Hereford had certainly been concerned? that he should take care not to accuse any one unjustly, and if he had so done, to declare it then, to which the said Jack made answer, that he had told a lie about Hereford, and that he was innocent, as far as he knew, and repeated before Lancaster Green what he had said when he accused them."

SUPREME COURT.
Thursday, July 2.

Present, the hon. James De Lancey, esq. chief justice; the second and third justices.

The king against Jamaica, a negro.

Upon the former favourable circumstances concerning this criminal, the court ordered his execution to be further respited for fourteen days.

The king against Will, Ward's negro.

This negro being set to the bar to receive judgment, and there having been credible information that this criminal has, within a few years past, been concerned in two conspiracies in the West Indies, the first at St. John's, the last at Antigua, in the year

1736, where (as it was said) he became an evidence, and from thence was shipped to this city, from hence to Providence, but returned hither again, and was here sold: wherefore it was thought high time to put it out of his power to do any further mischief; and having pleaded *guilty* upon his arraignment as before, the court sentenced him to be burnt at a stake, on Saturday, the 4th inst.

The court adjourned till ten o'clock to-morrow morning.

The eight following negro *confessions* were taken this day by Mr. Nicholls and Mr. Lodge.

No. 1. "*Bound's Scipio* said, that last Christmas holidays, Comfort's Jack carried him to Hughson's, where there were a great number of negroes, near thirty; that they all supped there, and after supper Hughson got a bible, and told them there was a plot going forward against the white people of the town, that the French and Spaniards were expected, and then would be a fair opportunity; that those that would swear to him to be of his side, should be his men; that they might be all free men; that he, Hughson, swore himself, his wife and daughter, and afterwards swore several of the negroes: that he heard Spanish talked among the negroes, but knows not what negroes they were; that he swore them all to secrecy, and said he would provide arms for all of them; that he, Scipio, was to kill his master and mistress. That he was afterwards at Comfort's, and saw Jack there sharpening knives, which he said were to be used to kill the white people; that several negroes were there, and afterwards Jack told him there was to be a general feast at Hughson's; that when he supped at Hughson's, the daughter of Hughson took the cloth from the table."

Evidence affecting this negro.—Cato's (colonel Moore's) confession, sections 2, 6.

As soon as Scipio was brought before Mr. Nicholls and Mr. Lodge to be examined, he was asked who his master was, and what was his name? he answered, master, don't you know me? I am Scipio, belonging to Mr. Robert Bound, and formerly belonging to Dr. Nicols; and it being then demanded of him, how he came to be concerned in the conspiracy? (he being a fellow that did not want sense, and had had a better education than most of his colour) he answered, it is true, sir, I ought to have known better; my first master, Dr. Nicols, brought me up from a child, sent me to school, and had me taught to read; he intended to give me to his son, who was bred a merchant, for which reason he put me to a cooper to learn that trade, but his son going to live in the country, he had no use for me in that business; my old master therefore sold me to my present master, Bound, who has likewise been very kind to me; but it was with me as it is with all my colour, who are never easy till they get a dram, and when they have one want more; this was my case on my meeting with Comfort's Jack, who carried me to Hughson's, where from drinking one dram I drank more, till I was bewitched with it, etc. as in the examination above.

Those gentlemen declared this fellow seemed to be the most sensible of any they examined, and appeared very penitent and sorry for what he had done; he had, when examined, his bible in his bosom, which he said he read in jail as often as he could.

No. 2. *"London (Kelly's)* said, that last Christmas he went with Carpenter's Tickle and Desbrosse's Primus to take a walk; that they went to Hughson's, drank punch and beer; that after they had drank, Hughson told him now was the best time to do something, if they intended to do it, it being war time; that London asked what? that he said he should swear, and got a book and swore him not to tell any body of what he would tell him, and then told him the negroes were going to rise to kill the white people, and that he would find guns for them.

"That ten or fourteen days after, Fortune acquainted Ludlow's York, Le Roux's Quash, and Judah Hay's Jack of the design, and asked them if they would be concerned in the plot? and they said they would with all their hearts, but does not know they went to Hughson's."

Evidence affecting this negro.—Tickle's confession, section 1. Primus (Desbrosse's) confession. Worcester (Varian's) confession.

No. 3. *"Tony (Brazier's)* said, that last summer captain Marshall's Ben carried him to Hughson's, where they drank rum, and Ben there told him he must burn his mistress' house, but he said nothing to it, but went away."

Evidence affecting this negro.—Caesar (Pintard's) confession, section 4. Cato (colonel Moore's) confession, section 7.

No. 4. "*Tom (captain Rowe's)* said, that Whitsuntide last year he was at Hughson's with Albany and Pemberton's Quamino; that after they had drank beer and rum, Hughson got a book and swore him and Quamino not to tell any thing about what he would tell them; and then told them that the negroes did intend to rise against the white people, and that he had some white people in the country that would help him and the negroes; that the town was to be set on fire, and when it was, Tom, being an old fellow, should run to him to be a drummer, not being fit for any thing else."

Evidence affecting this negro.—Sarah (Burk's) confession, No. 2, 3. Tickle's confession, section 2. Quamino (Pemberton's) confession.

No. 5. "*Fortune (Mr. D. Clarkson's)* said, that some time about Christmas last, he was going to Comfort's for tea-water, where he saw captain Marshall's Ben, Mr. Rutgers' Quash, and Mr. Vanderspeigle's Fortune on the hill at Comfort's; that they carried him to Hughson's, where they had one or two bowls of punch; that Hughson drank with them and told them they should never want for liquor whether they had money or not; that after they had drank, Hughson made him swear and kiss a book, and say, d——n my soul to h——ll if I tell any body; and told him he must fire his master's house and kill the family, or else he would kill him; then he promised he would.

2. "That he has been at Hughson's three times since, and once heard Hughson say, they were to get some white people out of the country to help them."

Evidence affecting this negro.—Brash's confession, section 5.

No. 6. "*Kortrecht's Caesar* said, that last Christmas he went with Comfort's Jack to Hughson's; that he was in the shop, and much in liquor; that he saw a room full of negroes eating and drinking, but does not know who they were, being the whole time in the shop; that Comfort's Jack coming out with the pris-

[268]

oner, told him, the Spaniards were coming here, and the negroes were going to rise, and would help the Spaniards; that he offered him (Caesar) a knife to fight with against the white people, but he refused it, having one in his pocket; that then Jack swore him to be one among them, and he promised them he would."

Evidence affecting this negro.—Colonel Moore's Cato's confession, section 6. Comfort's Jack's examination, sections 2, 10.

No. 7. "*Jonneau* said, that last fall he met Vaarck's Caesar, Philipse's Cuffee and Albany, and they went to the house of Frans, a free negro, to drink a dram; that Caesar took him aside and told him the negroes were to rise and take the town, and asked him to be one; that he then declined it, but afterwards he met with those three, who carried him to Hughson's, where they drank much liquor; and then Caesar again asked him to be concerned, that the thing might be done, and he would provide arms, powder and shot; that he then consented; and Caesar swore him into the plot and secresy: that he has afterwards seen Ten Eyck's Billy sworn there on a book by Hughson, with another negro he knew not, but he was a drummer and wore a laced hat: that they were at the free negro's; he does not know whether the free negro could overhear the proposal Caesar made to him when he took him aside."

Evidence affecting this negro.—Mary Burton's deposition, No. 2, section 7. Comfort's Jack's confession, No. 1, sections 2, 24.

No. 8. "*Abraham's Jack* said, that a little before Christmas, Comfort's Jack and Cowley's Cato carried him to Hughson's, where they drank punch; that then Hughson asked him, whether he would be concerned with him to kill the white people? that he consented, and then Hughson told him he must swear and got a book, and swore the d——l take him if he told any body white or black; that when he should hear fire cried at night, he should kill his master and mistress, and come to him, and he would give him a gun and cutlass: that there was a woman at the fire smoaking that saw him sworn, but did not know whether she were Hughson's wife or who else."

Evidence affecting this negro.—Livingston's Tom's confession, No. 2.

This day the grand jury recommended the following negroes to the judges to be discharged, they finding no sufficient evidence against them whereon to found an indictment, viz.:

Van Zant's Tom, Cornelius Van Horn's Kid, Myers Cohen's Hereford.—And they were discharged accordingly.

SUPREME COURT.
Friday, July 3. A.M.

Present the second justice.

Court opened and adjourned to four o'clock in the afternoon.

Present, the second and third justices.

The king against Pintard's Caesar, Todd's Dundee, Kortrecht's Caesar, Ten Eyck's Will or Bill, Rowe's Tom, Lawrence's Sterling, negroes.

The prisoners being arraigned upon an indictment for the conspiracy; all pleaded guilty, and submitted to the mercy of the court.

The king against Mars, French's London, Debrosse's Primus, Bridgewater, Lefferts's Pompey, negroes.

The prisoners being arraigned upon an indictment for the conspiracy; all pleaded guilty, and submitted to the mercy of the court.

Court adjourned to Monday the sixth instant ten o'clock in the morning.

Todd's Dundee's confession—He said,

1. "That the first time he was at Hughson's, he, Jack and Comfort's Cook drank a pint of rum together, and the rum they bought at Hughson's with the money he had lost (at play.)

2. "That the next time the prisoner bought an half pint of rum and drank it with the same Cook and Jack; and then doctor Hamilton and Hughson called Jack, and asked him what boy that was? Jack answered, Todd's; then the doctor and Hughson called the prisoner and asked him to swear upon a book, which he refused, and Jack told him he must

do it; and that he did swear; the doctor held the book and Hughson read something out of it; and after he had sworn, the doctor took his name down upon a piece of paper; that the doctor, Hughson, and Jack, told him not to tell any body of it; and Jack told him to kill his master and mistress; and that the doctor told him, he should be under captain Jack; that then he asked to go, and they told him he might.

3. "That after he had left Hughson's house, he asked Jack what it was he had sworn? Jack told him it was to burn the town and to begin at the fort first; and that Roosevelt's Quack was to set fire to the fort; and then he went home.

4. "That when the fire was in Smith's fly, Mr. English's negro Patrick told him, the fires in the town were not half done yet; upon which the prisoner asked Patrick why he said so? he said because he knew it."—See his confession before.

Evidence affecting this negro.—Arthur Price's deposition, No. 2, section 2. Sandy's examination, No. 3, section 8. Burk's Sarah's examination, 2, section 1.

The three following negro *confessions* were taken this day by Mr. Nicholls and Mr. Lodge:

No. 1. "*Mars* said that some time about Christmas last, Cuffee (Gomez's) and Peck's Caesar, informed him of the plot behind old Het's on the dock, and told him they were to burn the houses in the town, and fight with the white people; and asked him if he would join with them? that they swore him by the thunder, not to discover any thing about it; that after the fort was burnt he saw Caesar (Peck's) and Cuffee (Gomez's) and they told him one job was done."

Evidence affecting this negro.—Tickle's confession, No. 1, sections 3, 4. Caesar (Pintard's) confession, No. 2, sections, 4, 5.

No. 2. *Second confession.*—"*Primus* (*Debrosse's*) said that Sunday before Christmas, Tickle (Carpenter's) and London (Kelly's) carried him to Hughson's, where they drank, and Hughson asked him if he would stand by him to kill the white people of the town; that the French and Spaniards were coming, and would take the town, and they would help the Spaniards; he told him yes; and then Hughson swore him, the d——l fetch him if he told any body, or did not help them; he said yes: that Hughson told him that when he heard a noise in the town, he must steal his master's gun, and come to his house, and that he should kill his master and mistress; but he said he would not.

2. "That two or three days after Van Zant's storehouse was a fire, he met Peck's Caesar, who told him he had set the storehouse on fire."—See his confession before.

Evidence affecting this negro.—Tickle's confession, No. 2, section 1. Caesar (Pintard's) confession, section 4. London (Kelly's) confession.

No. 3. *First confession.*—"*Sam* (*Low's*) said, that on Easter holidays was a year, he went to Hughson's with Comfort's Jack, where he saw Mr. Philipse's Frank and Hyer's Tom; that Frank was drinking beer; that Hughson carried him into another room, and asked him if he would be concerned with them in taking the town? he said he would, if it could be done; that Hughson told him it could, and then he swore him, and told him that when the houses were on fire, he should come to him, and he would furnish him with arms."

Evidence affecting this negro.—Pompey (De Lancey's) confesion, section 5. Cato (colonel Moore's) confession, sections 2, 6. London (Wyncoop's) confession, sections 1, 2.

Deposition.—William Nail, servant to Thomas Cox of the city of New-York, butcher, being duly sworn upon the holy Evangelists of Almighty God, deposeth and saith,

"That he, the deponent, having discourse with one London, a negro man slave belonging to Edward Kelly, butcher, concerning negroes that were taken up on account of the plot, heard the said London swear, by G——d, that if he, the said London, should be taken up on account of the plot, he would hang or burn all the negroes in York, whether they were concerned or not." (c)

(c) It is not improbable but he might know that most of them were concerned.

This day Duane's Prince, Latham's Tony, Shurmur's Cato, Kip's Harry, and Marschalk's York, negroes, were executed at the gallows, according to sentence; and the body of York was afterwards hung in chains, upon the same gibbet with John Hughson.

Some few days after this the town was amused with a rumour, that Hughson was turned negro, and Vaarck's Caesar a white; and when they came to put up York in chains by Hughson (who was hung upon the gibbet three weeks before) so much of him as was visible, viz.—face, hands, neck, and feet, were of a deep shining black, rather blacker than the negro placed by him, who was one of the darkest hue of his kind; and the hair of Hughson's beard and neck (his head could not be seen for he had a cap on) was curling like the wool of a negro's beard and head, and the features of his face were of the symmetry of a negro beauty; the nose broad and flat, the nostrils open and extended, the mouth wide, lips full and thick, his body (which when living was tall, by the view upwards of six feet, but very meagre) swelled to a gigantic size; and as to Caesar (who, though executed for a robbery, was also one of the head negro conspirators, had been hung up in chains a month before Hughson, and was also of the darkest complexion) his face was at the same time somewhat bleached or turned whitish, insomuch that it occasioned a remark, that Hughson and he had changed colours. The beholders were amazed at these appearances; the report of them engaged the attention of many, and drew numbers of all ranks, who had curiosity, to the gibbets, for several days running, in order to be convinced by their own eyes, of the reality of things so confidently reported to be, at least wondrous phenomenons, and upon the view they were found to be such as have been described; many of the spectators were ready to resolve them into miracles; however, others not so hasty, though surprized at the sights, were willing to account for them in a natural way, so that they administered matter for much speculation.

The sun at this time had great power, and the season as usual very hot, that Hughson's body dripped and distilled very much, as it needs must, from the great fermentation and abundance of matter within him, as could not but be supposed at that time, from the extraordinary bulk of his body; though considering the force of the sun, and the natural meagreness of his corpse, one would have been apt to imagine that long ere this it would have been disencumbered of all its juices. At length, about ten days or a fortnight after Hughson's mate, York, was hung by him, Hughson's corpse, unable longer to contain its load, burst and discharged pail fulls (d) of blood and corruption; this was testified by those who were near by, fishing upon the beach when the irruption happened, to whom the stench of it was very offensive.

Those who were inclined to account in a natural way, for what was by some esteemed almost miraculous, by all very surprising, observed, that by the written evidences of witnesses, both black and white, information was given of poison being distributed amongst the conspirators (e) and of the use their principals intended should have been made of it; Harry, a negro doctor, was to bring the negroes poison to use (if they were discovered and taken) before they were executed; Kane had seen him give poison, as they called it, to Walter's Quack for that purpose, in papers; Quack said he should not be suspected, he might go to the prison to carry victuals, and so could give the poison to those that were condemned, to prevent their execution; (f) Kane saw doctor Harry give a large quantity of it to Hughson.

Mary Burton speaks of their having poison amongst them (g); she says she had seen three or four papers of poison in Hughson's drawers, which she understood he had of some negro.

It has been related already that Hughson when he was brought out of jail to be carried to his execution, had a red spot

(d) Which may be understood to mean a surprizing quantity.
(e) See William Kane's examination, section 16.
(f) This office we may suppose was to be administered by Quack, without the knowledge of the patients (and he speaks as if they had a confidence in him) in order to despatch them, and prevent their telling tales: for when they found themselves in jeopardy, there might be danger of their speaking the truth and discovering their principals, in hopes of saving their own lives by it.
(g) In her evidence upon trial of eight negroes, 15th of this month, viz. —her testimony against doctor Harry.

in each cheek, about the bigness of a shilling, which at that time was by some thought very remarkable, because he was always pale of visage, and the sheriffs (who observed it) did not believe from the care that had been taken, he could have drank any strong liquor in jail, which was an additional reason why they took so much notice of it.

Upon the supposition that Hughson had taken poison, it has been made a question whether that might not have occasioned the swelling of his corpse to so amazing a bulk? Nay his arms, legs and thighs, were enlarged in proportion to the body; this is submitted to the consideration of the curious and connoisseur in physic.

As to the change of complexions in Hughson and Caesar, some imputed it to the influence of the sun; but to that it was objected, it would be strange indeed that the sun should have two such different effects as to turn Hughson (a white) black, and Caesar (a negro) whitish.

As to Hughson's taking poison, that by some was thought very improbable, for as it is said in the account of his behaviour at, and going to his execution, his actions were observed to be such as betokened his expectation of being rescued, he held up his hand as high as his pinion would admit of, and seemed to beckon with his finger as one expecting deliverance, and if that was his persuasion he would not have taken poison, which was certain death; and besides if he had taken any, he would have taken a sufficient quantity, and time enough to have answered the design of it, which it must be supposed to be to destroy himself to prevent his execution.

To this was answered, that though he might be determined to take poison to destroy himself, and did take some, yet he might do it with so much reluctance, as not to take the quantity prescribed sufficient to answer the end, which though he might not be aware of, but expect certain death from it, yet the nearer he approached the gallows, the more his thoughts might be confused, and nature prevailed; as long as there is life, there is hopes, and his deliverance might be uppermost in his mind; he would willingly have avoided the infamy of hanging, and stand the chance of saving his life in the bargain.

[275]

Whatever were the causes of these changes, the facts are here related, that every one may make their own conjectures upon them.

But Hughson it seems let the worst happen to him in all events, declared as he was going to mount the cart which was to carry him to execution, that he did not doubt but some remarkable sign would happen to him, to shew (or signify) his innocence; and if his corpse becoming monstrous in size, and his complexion (for once to use a vulgar similtude) as black as the d——l, can be deemed remarkable signs or tokens of his innocence! then some may imagine it has happened according to his expectation.

Saturday, July 4.

The jail being now thronged with negroes committed as confederates in the conspiracy, many whereof had made confessions of their guilt, in hopes of pardon in consequence of the proclamation, and others who were pardoned and turned evidence; it was feared, considering the season of the year, that such numbers closely confined might be apt to breed an infection; therefore the judges thought it was proper to examine the list of them, and to mark out such as should be thought proper to recommend to his honour the lieutenant governor, to be pardoned, upon condition of transportation to be therein limited by a short time, and to distinguish which of them who had been made use of as witnesses, might be necessary to reserve for some time; and for this purpose they associated to them Mr. Nicholls and Mr. Lodge, by whose assistance the following list was accordingly settled, which the judges reported to his honour, and submitted to his consideration.

A list of negroes recommended this day by the judges to his honour the lieutenant governor, for transportation.

Pemberton's Quamino, widow Breasted's Toby, Ten Eyck's Will or Bill, Hunt's Warwick, Soumain's Tom, Crugers's Deptford, Lush's Will, Peck's York, Van Brosom's Scipio, Horsefield's Guy, Benson's Cato, widow Brazier's Tony, Bound's

Scipio, Kortrecht's Caesar, Abrahams's Jack, Todd's Dundee, Lawrence's Starling, Crooke's York, Van Horn's Bridgwater, French's London, Becker's Mars, DeBrosse's Primus, Rutgers' Jacob, Groesbeck's Mink, Phoenix's Titus, Schuyler's Lewis, Vaarck's Jonneau, Marston's Scotland, Varian's Worcester, Ellison's Jamaica, English's Patrick, Abrahams's Scipio, Clarkson's Fortune, Pintard's Caesar, Wilkins's Fortune, Moore's Tom, Leffert's Pompey, Marschalk's London, Low's Wan, Vaarck's Will, Latham's Fortune, Burk's Sarah.

This day Will, Ward's negro, was executed according to sentence, and made the following confession at the stake:

1. "He said that William Kane, a soldier belonging to the fort, knew of the plot, and he heard the said Kane say, he did not care if the fort was burnt down; that since the plot was discovered he told Kane he would make a discovery, on which Kane gave him three pounds in bills and told him not to discover; part of which money his young mistress found in his chest.

2. "That his mistress lost a silver spoon, which he, Will, stole and carried to Kane's wife, who gave it her husband in his presence, and he sold it to Peter Van Dyke, a silversmith, and gave him, Will, eight shillings of the money.

3. "That Kane and Kelly (i) asked Quack to burn the fort, and said if that was done, they (the soldiers) would have their liberty; and Kelly said you must do it with wet cotton, and that will make no smoke.

4. "That he has talked of the plot with Kane and Kelly often, and has been at Kane's house, and has heard that other soldiers were concerned, but does not know them; that he has seen Walter's Quack there, Ryndert's Tom, Governeur's Jack, Cuyler's Pedro, (j) and Van Zant's John, went round, who received some money in his hat, collected at a meeting at Kelly's, which money was to be paid to Hughson.

(i) Both soldiers belonging to the garrison, and reputed papists.
(j) This negro not apprehended.

5. "That Goelet's Quack and Tiebout's Will drew him in; and called on their names to the last.

6. "That DePeyster's Pedro is innocent for what he knows.

7. "That Moore's Cato advised him and Pedro to bring in many negroes, telling Pedro that he would be certainly burnt or hanged if he did not confess; but that if he brought in a good many it would save his life, for he had found it so himself, and must say he was to set his master's house on fire, which would make the judges believe him. (k)

8. "That Pintard's Caesar said much the same, and Comfort's Jack advised Cato; but that Jack was a true evidence."

The pile being kindled, this wretch set his back to the stake, and raising up one of his legs, laid it upon the fire, and lifting up his hands and eyes, cried aloud, and several times repeated the names, Quack Goelet and Will Tiebout, who he had said first brought him into this plot.

This evening William Kane, soldier, Goelet's Quack and Tiebout's Will, negroes, were apprehended and committed.

After we had several of the fires mentioned in the introduction to this journal, Goelet's Quack was had up and examined before the magistrates for some suspicious words overheard to be uttered by him to another negro, which seemed to import strong hints as if he had been privy to the occasion of them; but nothing could be made of it, and was therefore discharged. But this was long before we had the least intimation of a conspiracy.

Sunday, July 5.

Examination of William Kane, soldier, taken before the chief and third justices, No. 1.

(k) Pedro, by Schultz's deposition of the 1st inst. charges Will himself with giving that advice: but these are Will's dying words in the midst of flames, and may be supposed to come from him upon a question put, whether he had not advised Pedro so? So rare it is to get the truth from these wretches!

1. "He said that he was born in Athlone in Ireland, had been in this country four and thirty years, aged about forty.

2. "That he never was at Hughson's house, nor did he know where it was.

3. "That some time last summer, when the Cuba men (1) were here, his wife brought home a silver spoon out of the fields, which she had of one of the Cuba men; this was about the time of their embarking; that he believed his wife could tell the name of the man.

4. "That he carried the said spoon to Van Dyke the silver-smith, to sell; the spoon was battered up, and he told Van Dyke he believed it was a stolen spoon, but he answered he would buy it for all that; his son endeavoured to open the spoon, to see if he could discover the name, and broke it to pieces; Van Dyke bought it of him, and gave him a milled Spanish piece of eight, and he thinks, to the best of his remembrance, seven or eight shillings in pennies. It was about fourteen days time between his wife's bringing the spoon to him, and his carrying it to Van Dyke.

5. "Never was at Kelly's the soldier's house, in his life.

6. "Had no acquaintance with John Romme; never was at his house at the battery in his life.

7. "That he never was in company with Jury alias Ury, now in jail, nor had he any acquaintance with him; nor was he ever at any congregation or meeting where the said Jury alias Ury, either preached or prayed.

8. "That he has no other acquaintance with Connolly, now in jail, than common for one brother soldier with the other; never was at his house in his life.

9. "Professed himself a protestant of the church of England, and said that he never was at any Roman catholic congregation in his life.

10. "That he has heard Thankful Spotten, wife of James Spotten (both lodgers at his house) say, that she once saw a large company of negroes at Kelly's house, dancing to a

(1) Meaning the soldiers raised in this province for the expedition to the Spanish West Indies.

fiddle; she said she then lodged at Kelly's; came home about eight of the clock at night, and one of the negroes (a tall one) asked her what business she had there? and threatened to kick her into the fire, if she did not go away: Kelly's wife asked her to go up stairs, and see the negroes dance; then she was going down stairs, and she met Mr. Kennedy's mulatto coming into the room, who huffed the negro fellow, and bid her sit down again."

While Kane was under examination, the under-sheriff came and informed the judges, that Mary Burton had declared, that she had often seen him at Hughson's, amongst Hughson, his wife, etc. and the negroes, when they were talking of the conspiracy, and that he was one of the confederates: whereupon she was ordered to be brought in, and being confronted with Kane, she immediately declared to the effect in the following deposition. The Chief Justice, who was a stranger to the transactions concerning the detection of the conspiracy (having been absent attending the execution of his majesty's special commission at Providence) he thought proper to admonish the witness in an awful and solemn manner, concerning the nature of an oath, and the consequences of taking a false one, more especially as it affected a man's life: she answered, she was acquainted with the nature of an oath very well, and that she would not take a false one upon any account, and repeated the same charge against Kane over and over, and persisted in it, that what she said was truth; all which Kane as positively denied: whereupon she was sworn, and the following evidence taken.

Deposition No. 5.—Mary Burton being duly sworn and produced before William Kane, soldier, said

"That she had seen the said Kane at Hughson's very often, talking with Hughson, his wife and daughter, Peggy Salingburgh alias Kerry, Caesar, Vaarck's; Galloway, Rutgers'; Prince, Auboyneau's, and Cuffee, Philipse's, negroes; and the discourse amongst them was, that they would burn the town, the fort first, the governor and all his family in it, and kill all the white people, and that she heard the said William Kane say, that he would help them all that lay in his power."

Then Mary Burton was ordered to withdraw, and Kane was apprized of the danger he was in, and told he must not flatter himself with the least hopes of mercy, but by making a candid and ingenuous confession of all that he knew of the matter, or to this purpose: but he still denied what had been alleged against him by Mary Burton, till upon most solemn admonition, he began to be affected; his countenance changed, and being near fainting, desired to have a glass of water, which was brought him, and after some pause, he said he would tell the truth, though at the same time he seemed very loth to do it; but after some hesitation began to open, and several hours were spent in taking down heads of his confession, which were afterwards drawn out at large, and distinctly read over to him, and being duly sworn, he made oath that the same was true, and (not knowing how to write) he put his mark to it.

Further *examination* and *confession* of William Kane, the same day—No. 2.

1. "He said there was one Jerry Corker, who tended in the governor's stable, near before Christmas last, when he was sentry at the governor's door, he came out, and he, Kane, being dry, asked him for some beer; he said he would get some, and had rum in his pocket, and would make flip, which he did in a copper pot with loaf sugar; that he, Kane, drank a draught, and when he was relieved at nine at night, Corker came into the guard-room, and asked him if he would go to Croker's at the fighting cocks, where there was to be a christening by a Romish priest? When they were there the people did not come that night; they stayed till past ten: the next night they went again, and they were not there; the third night they went to New-street, to the house of one Coffin, a pedlar; there they had a child, and christened it, and three acted as priests, and handed the book about.

2. "That about four days after, Corker and he were upon

guard, and Corker said, by G——d I have a mind to burn the fort. Corker went away some time after the fire at the fort, to work in the country; he believed about the White-plains.

3. "That he had heard Corker, John Coffin and Daniel Fagan talking about burning the town, before they went away.

4. "One of those who acted as priest, was a little man that lodged at Corker's. (n)

5. "That Fagan, Corker and Coffin drew him, Kane, behind the church to a meeting, and would have had him to rob houses with them and go off.

6. "That he was at two meetings at Hughson's about the plot; the first was the second day of Christmas, and the second the last Sunday in February, before the fire at the fort: (o) Corker, Fagan and Coffin were at the first meeting; at the second he, Kane, was sworn to secrecy by Hughson; the first who discovered it was to be hanged at low-water mark, his privy-parts were to be cut out and thrown in his face, his belly ripped open, and his body eaten by the birds of the air: Hughson's father and three brothers, and an old white woman they said was crazy, (p) were present: at the second meeting he, Kane, and those men, and Sarah Hughson the daughter, were sworn together: they were to burn what they could of the city, and get what money and goods they could and carry them (to) Mr. Alexander's house, which was to be reserved for Mr. Hughson: we were to kill the principal people.

7. "That if any people came from the country or West-Indies to conquer them; they were to kill the people belonging to the vessels here, and go to Spain: their design was to wait for the French and Spaniards, whom they expected; and if they did not come in six weeks, then they were to try

(n) Ury lodged there until he removed to Campbell's, to keep school with him.
(o) This agrees with the negro account of the great meeting there.
(p) Probably Luckstead, Hughson's mother-in-law, who pretended to tell fortunes.

what they could do for themselves (q) most of the negroes he believed would join them if they were like to succeed: this he learnt from Hughson and Corker. Hughson was to be king, and Vaarck's Caesar the chief among the negroes.

8. "That he has heard several negroes say, that Chief Justice's Othello was concerned; Comfort's Jack said so since the fire at the fort, and since the Chief Justice went to New-England.

9. "That Corker, who attended the plumber the day the fort was burnt, was at Hughson's several times before he, Kane, was there, and brought him there. The priest, the little man that lodged at Corker's, was several times at Hughson's, and many negroes were christened there by him: he had endeavoured to seduce him, Kane, to the Romish religion (r) at Coffin's house; he, Kane, was asked whether he could read Latin? he said no; then whether he could read English? he said no, then Coffin read, and told him (Kane) what a fine thing it was to be a Roman; that they could forgive sins, and should not go to hell; he (Kane) answered, he would not believe that on any man's word; and there happened a squabble, and he (Kane) went away, or else he don't know but they would have seduced him, the priest and Coffin pressed him so. He has not heard the priest say any thing of the conspiracy; but from Corker's account, he (Kane) believes he knew it.

10. "That Connolly, on the Governor's Island, has owned himself to have been bred a priest, to him (Kane) and was often in company with Jury; Kelly is a Roman; Connolly and he were intimate.

11. "That Kelly asked him (Kane) about new-year, if he would go to Hughson's? he asked for what? he (Kelly) said something was to be done there: he (Kane) asked what? he (Kelly) said something you have heard of before; he (Kane) asked what is that? he (Kelly) said, don't you know what Jerry Corker said to you before Christmas about burn-

(q) This also agrees with the negro account. See Comfort's Jack's confession, section 25.
(r) And it is said Kane was always reputed a papist.

[283]

ing the fort? What said he (Kane) is that in agitation still? Yes, said he (Kelly) and ever shall be till the fort be burnt down.

12. "That Campbell had an opportunity to come to him (Kane) yesterday in jail, and said, though he could pay the debt he was in for, yet he believed they would not let him out, on account of the priest (Ury) that lodged at his house.

13. "That he had seen Holt's Joe at Hughson's at the two meetings, and he said he would do his endeavours with the best.

14. "That Holt (t) had (the year he left Mr. DeLancey's house, before he left it) whipt his negro Joe very severely, and Joe meeting him (Kane) the next day, when he, Kane, told him of his whipping; he said that cursed dog my master, is the greatest rogue in the world, he would burn all the town to get money; if you knew what was between him and Hughson it would make you stare: and this he repeated the next day.

15. "That Walter's Quack has often said he would ride in the coach after he had destroyed his master; he was sworn by thunder and lightning, G——d's curse and hell fire fall on them that first discovered the plot, which was the negro oath.

16. "Some black stuff was cut among the negroes, which he did not know, but heard it was to set fire to the roofs of houses in dry weather, he has seen one Harry a negro doctor that lives on Long-Island bring that stuff, and has seen him several times at Hughson's, and at the two meetings: he, Harry, was to bring the negroes poison to use (if they were taken) before they were executed; he, Kane, had seen him give poison (as they called it) to Walter's Quack for that purpose, in papers, which he, Harry, took out of his pocket; Quack said he should not be suspected, and he might go to

(t) Holt, a dancing master, he came to this country from South Carolina about four or five years ago, of what religion we know not, but soon after the fire at the fort he thought proper to ship himself off to Jamaica, where he soon after died, and spared the hangman labour.

the prison and carry victuals, and so could give the poison to those that were condemned, to prevent their execution: he, Kane, has seen doctor Harry give a large quantity to Hughson.

17. "That Niblet's Sandy was at Hughson's at the first meeting; he (Kane) never was at Comfort's, but has seen the negroes there of Sundays, and come to Hughson's; and has seen three Spanish negroes at Hughson's, but does not know whose they are, except one of captain Sarly's, he should if he saw them know them again.

18. "That at the second meeting he was at Hughson's about the plot, there was present about eight negroes, viz.— Walter's Quack, Vaarck's Caesar, Philipse's Cuffee, Auboyneau's Prince, Carpenter's Albany, Chambers's Robin, Comfort's Jack, and Niblet's Sandy, (v) he saw all the negroes sworn, and the following ceremony was used: there was a black ring made on the floor about two feet and a half diameter, and Hughson bid every one pull off the left shoe and put their toes within the ring, and Mrs. Hughson held a bowl of punch over their heads as the negroes stood round the circle, and Hughson pronounced the oath above mentioned, and every negro severally repeated the words after him, and then Hughson's wife fed them with a draught out of the bowl.

19. "That Corker told him (Kane) that Hughson and he had designed to burn the English church last Christmas day, but that Ury the priest said they had better let it alone until better weather, that the roof might be dry and a larger congregation.—Their full design was to burn the English church; they had a greater spite against that than any other, especially this Jury.

20. "That at the time that the eight negroes last mentioned were at Hughson's, he saw several other negroes in the house.

21. "That at the first meeting that he was at Hughson's, about the plot, he saw Galloway there, and Galloway was

(v) Though Sandy always denied he ever was there.

[285]

very talkative, and active about the plot, and said he would lend a brave hand, he would take care of his master, and soon make him breeches. (w)"

The above examination having been distinctly read over to the said William Kane, he being duly sworn, made oath, that the same was true, and signed his mark for his name.

SUPREME COURT
Monday, July 6.

Present, the honourable James DeLancey, esq. chief justice, and the third justice.

Court opened and adjourned till to-morrow morning, ten o'clock.

This day John Coffin, pedlar, was apprehended and immediately brought before two of the judges, who examined him concerning the charge against him as one of the confederates in the conspiracy, the fellow seemed to be under terrible apprehensions, trembled and cried, but denied every thing alleged against him by Kane, particularly he protested that he did not know, nor was any wise acquainted with John Hughson, or ever saw him until he was hanged: that he never had any acquaintance with Kane, nor was ever in his company but once, and then he drank a mug of beer with him at Eleanor Wallis's. Coffin was committed.

Le Roux's Quash, Judah Hays's Jack, negroes, were this day discharged by the third justice, pursuant to the recommendation of the grand jury, who did not credit the evidence of the negro London (Kelly's) which impeached them.

Evidence affecting these two negroes.—London (Kelly's) confession, section 2.

This day also doctor Harry, a negro, was apprehended and committed.

(w) He formerly belonged to a leather-dresser and glover.

SUPREME COURT
Tuesday, July 7.

Present, the chief justice, the second and third justices.

The king against Phoenix's Titus, Vaarck's Jonneau, Marston's Scotland, Wilkins' Fortune, Latham's Fortune, Burk's Sarah, negroes.

The prisoners having been indicted for the conspiracy, were thereupon arraigned, and pleaded *guilty*, and submitted to the mercy of the court.

The king against Sarah, Burk's negro.

The prisoner having pleaded guilty, the court passed sentence upon her to be hanged.

Ordered, that the said Sarah be executed on the morrow, between the hours of nine and one of the same day.

Court adjourned till Thursday, the 9th inst. ten o'clock in the morning.

The reason of the resolution for executing the negro wench Sarah, was that upon the trial of Gomez's Cuffee, Chambers's Robin, Peck's Caesar, Comfort's Jack and Cook, and Ellison's Jamaica, six of the negro conspirators, she was found indorsed upon the indictment as a witness against every one of them, excepting only Jamaica, and when she was called to give her evidence she prevaricated grossly, and differed so widely from what was penned down from her in her several examinations, that the court could give no further credit to her evidence, so that she deservedly drew the rope about her own neck.

Examination and confession of Adam, before one of the judges, No. 2.—He said,

(1). "That he saw the negro doctor Harry at the house of John Hughson, about a week before Christmas last, there were present at that time, Hughson, his wife and daughter, Peggy, and Mary Burton; the doctor was then sworn of the plot, his hand upon the book and kissed it, he was to do as the rest, kill the white people and burn houses; that he had seen doctor Harry at Hughson's four or five times since.

2. "That of a Sunday afternoon he saw the said Harry

cross from the City-Hall down the Church-street, and so round the English church yard down to Hughson's, and he (Adam) went down to Hughson's and saw him there.

3. "That he has seen him once in town about three weeks before the fort fired, and once going down to Hughson's, since the fort burnt. That he had heard he came over in a little canoe. (x)"

Doctor Harry was sent for by two of the judges; and being charged with what was alleged against him as one of the conspirators, he stiffly denied all, and declared that he never was at Hughson's, nor had he been in town since he was ordered out by the magistrates.

Then he was confronted with Kane and Adam, who severally repeated the substance of what they had before declared in their examinations concerning him; but the doctor was stout, denied all, and was remanded.

The doctor was a smooth soft spoken fellow, and like other knaves affected the air of sincerity and innocence, but was of a suspicious character, well known to the magistrates of this city, had a few years before been forbid the town for mal-practice in physic, upon the penalty of being severely whipped if he was seen here again.

Examination of Sam, P. Low's negro—second confession—He said,

"That last Easter was twelve months he went with Jacob, and Abrahams's Scipio to Hughson's house, that when he went in he saw judge Philipse's Frank and the widow Hyer's Tom drinking a mug of beer, that he did not speak to Frank nor to Tom at that time, that he does not know they ever had been told of the plot by either white people or negroes, and that they never mentioned the plot to them, nor they to him; but confesses that he (Sam) was sworn as one of the conspirators; the rest he refers to his former examination. (y)"

(x) He lived upon Nassau, alias Long-Island.
(y) The 3d July.

[288]

A list of the negroes recommended this day by the judges to his honour the lieutenant governor, to be pardoned in order for transportation—

English's Patrick, Vaarck's Will, Varian's Worcester, Ellison's Jamaica, Abraham's Scipio, Pintard's Caesar, Clarkson's Fortune, Wilkins's Fortune, Ben. Moore's Tom, Leffert's Pompey, Marschalk's London, Low's Wan, Latham's Fortune.

Wednesday, July 8.

The sentence of Sarah Hughson the daughter, having been respited for upwards of three weeks since the execution of her father and mother, and she in that time often importuned to confess what she knew of the conspiracy, did always peremptorily deny she knew any thing of the matter, and made use of many wicked imprecations in order to excite compassion in those that moved it to her, after the manner of her parents, whose constant practice it was, whenever spoke to about the plot: And this being the day appointed for Sarah's execution, she was this morning brought up to Mr. Pemberton, who came to pray by her, and after all his admonitions still denied her guilt, and being carried back to her dungeon where was the negro wench Sarah, under sentence also to be executed this day; Sarah Hughson at last owned to her, that she had been sworn into the plot. This negro wench (thinking as may be supposed to make a merit of it) soon after, told what had passed between them to the under-sheriff, who acquainted the judges with it, and they sent for Sarah Hughson, who confessed before them her knowledge of the conspiracy, whereupon the execution of both criminals was further respited.

Examination of Sarah Hughson under condemnation, before the chief justice, second justice and others.—Sarah Hughson being examined said,

1. "She saw William Kane sworn (z) one Sunday eve-

(z) Meaning into the conspiracy, which was the subject matter she was examined upon.

ning, some time before Christmas, she cannot tell exactly; that he threatened to kill her if she discovered, and the negroes threatened her the same; her father charged her to say nothing about it: They were first to begin with burning the fort with a good wind, after that they were to begin at the upper end of the town with an east wind, so as to burn the whole town; to destroy the whites, and after, to keep the town and send notice to the Spaniards that they might come and hold it, so that it could not be taken from them again: she thinks her mother knew of it.

2. "The first time she saw Jury (the priest) was with Campbell, about a fortnight before May day, when they came to see the house, there were several negroes there concerned: Walter's Quack, Philipse's Cuffee, Vaarck's Caesar, Comfort's Jack, Bastian, negroes, used to come after dark; she cannot remember them, but should know them if she saw them; has seen a middle sized white man that called himself a doctor with black hair always cut, of a short chin (c) often talking with the negroes and drinking with them; Peggy used to say that Walter's Quack was her sweetheart, and she thought him the handsomest among them; thinks she has heard the name of one Coffin, he is a fresh coloured long haired man, who was often at Hughson's among the negroes."

This confession was so scanty, and came from her after much difficulty, with great reluctance, that it gave little or no satisfaction, and notwithstanding (it was said, after she returned to jail) she retracted the little said, and denied she had any knowledge of a conspiracy: so that after all the judges thought themselves under a necessity of ordering her execution, as the last experiment to bring her to a deposition to unfold this infernal secret; at least so much of it, as might be thought deserving a recommendation of her, as an object of mercy.

(c) Probably meaning Schultz, whom the description seems somewhat to suit.

Present, the chief justice, the second and third justices.

The king against Scipio, Fortune, negroes.

Scipio and Fortune being brought to the bar, desired leave to retract their plea of *not guilty;* leave was given, and they pleaded *guilty,* and submitted to mercy.

The king against Quamino and forty-one other negroes.

The following negroes having been severally convicted of the conspiracy, were put to the bar, viz.—Pemberton's Quamino, Breasted's Toby, Ten Eyck's Will, Hunt's Warwick, Soumain's Tom, Mayor's Deptford, Lush's Will, Peck's York, Van Borsom's Scipio, Horsefield's Guy, Benson's Cato, Brazier's Tony, Bound's Scipio, Kortrecht's Caesar, Abrahams's Jack, Todd's Dundee, Rowe's Tom, Lawrence's Starling, Crooke's York, Van Horn's Bridgwater, French's London, Benson's Mars, Debrosse's Primus, Phoenix's Titus, Schuyler's Lewis, Vaarck's Jonneau, Marston's Scotland, Varian's Worcester, Ellison's Jamaica, English's Patrick, Abrahams's Scipio, Clarkson's Fortune, Pintard's Caesar, Wilkins' Fortune, Moore's Tom, Leffert's Pompey, Marschalk's London, Low's Wan, Vaarck's Will, Latham's Fortune, Grosbeck's Mink, H. Rutgers' Jacob; and being asked what they had to say, why sentence of death should not pass against them according to law? they all pleaded his majesty's most gracious pardon upon condition of transportation, and prayed that the same might be read and allowed, and the same was read and ordered to be allowed; and that the masters of the said negroes or some one for them, do enter into recognizance before one of the justices of the court, in the penalty of fifty pounds each, to transport their negro according to the proviso in the pardon mentioned; and that the said recognizance be entered into before such negro be taken out of jail.

Court adjourned till to-morrow morning, ten o'clock.

Examination before one of the judges—No. 3.

"William Kane being duly sworn says, that he knows Edward Murphy, now in jail; has seen him several times at

Hughson's, and knows he was concerned in the late conspiracy to burn the fort and town, and kill and destroy the inhabitants, and has heard the said Murphy say, some time before the fort burnt, when the negroes were talking at Hughson's about the conspiracy, d——n him, if he would not lend a hand to the fire as soon as any body."

Deposition before one of the judges—No. 6.

"Mary Burton being duly sworn saith, that she has often seen Edward Murphy (now present) at the house of the late John Hughson, on Hudson's river; that she has often seen the said Murphy among the negroes at the said house, whilst they (the negroes) were plotting and conspiring to burn this city, and to kill and murder the inhabitants thereof; that she hath heard the said Murphy say, that he would help the said negroes and Hughson, to burn and destroy this city and inhabitants, and would give them, the said Hughson and negroes, all the assistance in his power." —Confirmed upon examination before the grand jury.

Deposition before the chief justice—No. 4.

"William Kane being duly sworn, saith, that he hath often seen David Johnson, hatter, (now shewn to him) at Hughson's, particularly since last Christmas, when there were several negroes present; that he was called from the company that came with him, into a room by Hughson and Jury the priest, and stayed in the room a considerable time, and Jerry Corker told him the day the town was to be fired; that Johnson said, damn him if he would not be as ready as any other, and do his endeavour; and that the said Corker told him, that he had said so to Johnson; that the fire was to be on St. Patrick's night, if they could get their hands together."

Deposition before the chief justice—No. 7.

"Mary Burton being duly sworn, saith, that Andrew Ryan lodged at Hughson's some time last winter, and she has seen him with Hughson, some white folks, Caesar (Vaarck's), Cuffee (Philipse's) and other negroes, when the discourse was of the plot, and heard him say he would help them all he could."—Confirmed before the grand jury.

Deposition before the grand jury—No. 8.—Mary Burton further deposed.

1. "That of white people who used to frequent Hughson's, were Holt, the dancing master, a little man (as she believes is him) has seen him in court on the trial of the negroes.
2. "John Earl said to her, when Hogg's goods were found, he had rather have given twenty pounds than it was known, and threatened to kill her if she discovered about the fire.
3. "That Murphy once brought six or seven gold rings, and a gold locket or two, and gave them to Hughson's wife.
4. "That she had seen about seventeen soldiers at Hughson's with John Earl, and used to go up stairs and be with the negroes.
5. "That John Coffin used also to be there."

Examination of William Kane, before the grand jury—No. 5.

"At the christening, the priest, a countryman, Coffin, another man, three women and Corker; the priest sprinkled the child, and had salt on a plate, and rubbed the child's mouth with it. Ury, Coffin, and the other man acted as priests.

"That Coffin last Saturday on the dock meeting him, asked him if he would not go on board the privateer, for all would come out. To which Kane answered, that not he; for no one would tell, unless some blabbing rascal might.

"Walter's Quack handed a knife to the priest (Ury) half unclasped, who took it into the room with him, and afterwards returned to Quack."

[293]

Friday, July 10.

Present, the chief justice, the second and third justices.

The king against Sarah Hughson.

Ordered, that Sarah Hughson be executed on the morrow, according to her former sentence, between the hours of nine and one of the same day.

The king against Sarah, Burk's negro.

Ordered, that the execution of Sarah (Burk's) negro, be respited till Saturday the 18th instant.

The king against Walter's Quack, Othello, Livingston's Braveboy, Rutgers' Galloway, Mizerall's Harry.

The prisoners having been indicted for the conspiracy, were arraigned, and Othello, Quack and Braveboy pleaded *guilty*, and Galloway and Harry, *not guilty*.

The king against Codwise's Cambridge, Henderson's Caesar, Ryker's Frank, H. Wendover's Toby, negroes.

The prisoners were arraigned on the same indictment, and pleaded not guilty.

The king against Walter's Quack, Othello, Livingston's Braveboy, negroes.

The prisoners having pleaded guilty, were set to the bar, and the court proceeded to pass sentence; which was, that Quack and Othello should be burnt, and Braveboy hanged.

Court adjourned till to-morrow morning ten o'clock.

Deposition taken before the Chief Justice—

"John Schultz maketh oath, that a negro man slave, called Cambridge, belonging to Christopher Codwise, esquire, did on the ninth day of June last, confess to this deponent in the presence of the said Mr. Codwise and Richard Baker, that the confession he had made before Messrs. Lodge and Nicholls, was entirely false, viz.—that he had owned himself guilty of the conspiracy, and had accused the negro of Richard Baker, called Cajoe, through fear; and said, that he had heard some negroes talking together in the jail, that if they did not confess, they should be hanged; and that was the reason of his making that false confession: and that what he had said relating to Horsefield's Caesar was a lie: that he did not know in what part of the town Hughson did live, nor did not remember to have heard of the man until it was a common talk over the town and country, that Hughson was concerned in a plot with the negroes. (d)"

(d) A criminal confesses himself guilty at his own peril: it may be the only chance he has for saving his life; if he denies all, and the crime is proved upon him, his case becomes desperate; but when once he confesses his guilt, it will be standing evidence against him.—The remark upon negro recantations once for all, is that one can scarce be thoroughly satisfied when it is that they do speak truth, unless what they say be confirmed by concurring circumstances; and the very sight only of their masters may make them change their notes at any time, if they give them not advice and instruction with respect to their conduct, which there was too much reason to believe some of them did; and perhaps many of these wretches buoyed themselves up with the notion, that their masters would at all hazards save them from the gallows, or transportation, if they could; especially such of the slaves as had been bred up to trades or handicrafts: they might flatter themselves that the want of them would be a great prejudice and damage to their owners; as if for their sakes, vile wretches, the whole town must run the risk of their houses being fired about their ears, and having the inhabitants butchered; but their having once confessed their guilt, a recantation and denial of it afterwards, will scarce be thought an argument of sufficient force to prove their innocence.—The commissioners who tried the negro conspirators upon the detection of the plot in Antigua, in the year 1736, in the report of their proceedings to their governor, have the following clause apropos to the aforegoing observations, section 20, say they, "there were some steps not of a common kind taken by us in the course of our inquiry, which possibly might have been excepted to; two particulars, one the trying the criminals privately, excluding all white persons (more particularly the masters of slaves) excepting the constables guarding the prisoners, and excepting twice or thrice where some gentlemen of figure (not masters of any slaves under trial) were accidentally present;" (the other not being material to the present purpose is omitted.) It goes on— "As to the first, we had experienced the contrary method in the beginning, by trying some of the criminals openly; but the business being of a nature requiring the utmost despatch, we found our proceedings much retarded by the spectators asking many questions of the prisoners and witnesses, and some of them not proper; we soon discovered too (by some things that happened) how much masters were prone to countenance and excuse their slaves, and that slaves were emboldened by their master's presence, and witnesses intimidated; besides we found secrecy necessary, which even oaths of secrecy might not have effectually procured, considering human frailty and forgetfulness, and the common unguardedness of speech most persons are liable to; for sometimes a dangerous criminal might be mentioned by wit-

The *examination* of Sarah Hughson, the daughter, continued from July 8, section 2, before the Chief Justice, the second and third justices, and others.—

3. "She believes the first time she heard of the plot to burn the city and to murder master and mistress, and if they could not prevail to murder, then to burn them up, was when they lived at Ellis's dock, about a year ago; the negroes said they had white people to help them; Kane was there often, and came with several negroes.

4. "Said she had seen John Ury the priest often there when the negroes were there, and speak to them; tell them to keep secrecy, and to be true, and not tell of one another if they were to die for it; that they should burn the town down, and in the night cut their master's and mistress's throats with knives they should get; told her not to discover what he said, if she did he would be the death of her.

5. "He christened Vaarck's Caesar, and others.

6. "She was sworn by Jury (e) when Kane was, of a Sun-

---

nesses as parties accused in the course of the trial, and this might be talked of abroad, and occasion flights and concealments, and other inconveniences not to be foreseen.

In our own case, masters and owners of slaves were admitted as witnesses, which, all things considered, perhaps was too great an indulgence: for it is a known rule of law in civil cases, that a party interested in the event of a suit cannot be a witness; and by a parity of reason it may be concluded, that masters of slaves in criminal cases, should not be witnesses, especially in matters of so much consequence to the public; and if any such like case should hereafter happen, which God forbid, upon the reason of that rule, and the inconveniences which have happened from this indulgence, it may be judged necessary to vary from that practice.

(e) Meaning again, into the conspiracy; at the beginning of her examination on Wednesday, the 8th inst. she only says she saw (William) Kane sworn one Sunday evening; and now this agrees with Kane's examination, No. 2, section 6, who says, they were sworn together, at the second meeting, which was of a Sunday; and she could scarce know that he had given such information, for he had done so but two or three days before, and his examination was not out of the judge's or grand jury's hands; Kane and Sarah were confined in cells separate and distant from each other; but though her owning to the negro wench that she was sworn into the conspiracy, was the occasion of the respite of her execution, and her being sent for and examined by the judges, yet she owned no such thing upon her first examination, but now she does it with such circumstances concurring with day night, as things were generally done on Sunday nights.

7. "Did not know that Andrew Ryan was concerned, or David Johnson.

8. "Had seen Murphy often at the house since Christmas, when Vaarck's Caesar, asked him to drink a dram.

9. "Had often heard the negroes, when they stood round a circle made with chalk (f) say the devil fetch him and burn him that discovered.

10. "Walter's Quack, swore several times; the negroes swore without book; the whites swore by a bible. (g)

11. "Jury the priest told her and her father, he could forgive their sins, if they did not discover. (h)

12. "Peggy (executed) was sworn, and was a Roman.

13. "Jury told us all, that he could forgive sins, if we did any misdemeanor; and said if she would confess to him, he would forgive her all her sins, which was done; and he could forgive all of them, what they were to do in this business of the plot; and thinks he made her father and mother papists. He used to christen negroes at several times.

14. "Negroes said they went to him, and said he prayed for them.

----

other evidence, as puts the truth of the matter beyond doubt, and thereby adds credit to the rest of her confession.

(f) Kane's examination, No. 2, section 18, gives an account of this ceremony of swearing the negroes, in a circle drawn upon the floor; Kane there indeed, calls it a ring, a black ring, and with him agrees Mary Burton in her evidence upon Ury's trial, the 29th of this month, who (as she had done at some of her examinations before) spoke of a black ring or circle upon the floor, with a circumstance attending it which at first seemed to be trifling, and not worth notice, therefore was not taken down. See hereafter note upon her evidence at Ury's trial.

(g) This the reader may observe so many witnesses agreeing in, that reference to the particular places would be endless; not but that many instances also may be noted of the negroes swearing upon a book, according to the legal ceremony; which if not a bible, no doubt was intended to pass for one: but perhaps that formality was used with such of the negro confederates only, as had education and learning; as for the illiterate and ignorant, no doubt these infernal politicians were of opinion, their swearing by thunder and lightning (which are terrible oaths commonly used among themselves) would as effectually engage them to their hellish purposes.

(h) But if they did discover. . . . So that according to this diabolical system, no oaths are available to hold their votaries, but such as bind themselves in a curse to do iniquity.

15. "Jury said, if they discovered all their sins to him, he could forgive them; she said that none but God could, if they prayed to him; he said a priest could as well as G——d.

16. "John Coffin being shewn to her, she said she had not seen him before."

Saturday, July 11.

Sarah Hughson being brought before the chief Justice, Mr. Justice Philipse, and Mr. Chambers this morning, in order for further examination, she denied all she had confessed and was taken down from her, as before on the 8th and 10th inst. she said she had seen negroes at her father's house, but did not know of a plot; she being immediately thereupon exhorted by those gentlemen to speak the truth, then declared every particular in the foregoing examination (except the retraction which was minuted upon it) to be true, as the same was distinctly read to her by Mr. Chambers, and the question particularly put to her.

SUPREME COURT

Present, the second justice.
  The king against Sarah Hughson.
  Ordered, that the execution of Sarah Hughson be respited till Friday next. (i)
  The king against Sam, colonel Courtlandt's negro.
  The prisoner, Sam, desired leave of the court to withdraw his

---

(i) From the untoward behaviour of this wretch upon her examinations, the reader will be apt to conclude there could be little or no dependance on her veracity, or her evidence at best would deserve but very slender credit; and indeed the case would have been so, if her testimony had stood single, and not corroborated by many other witnesses to the same facts, and concurring circumstances attending them; though from her stubborn deportment, it must be owned, very small service was expected from her; for she discovered so irresolute untractable a temper, that it was to be expected she would recall again and again, as she had done already, what she seemed to deliver at times, with some composure and appearance of sincerity.

[298]

plea, and plead *guilty*, which being granted, he pleaded *guilty*, and submitted to the mercy of the court.

Court adjourned till Tuesday the 14th instant, 10 o'clock in the morning.

Yesterday evening and this day, Thomas Hughson, yeoman (father of John Hughson) and his four sons, viz.—Nathaniel, Walter, William and Richard, were taken up and committed to West Chester county jail, being charged as confederates in the conspiracy; one son only out of six standing clear of impeachment upon this occasion.

Sunday, July 12.

Confession of Othello, under sentence of death, before one of the judges—No. 2.—He said,

1. "That about the beginning of last summer, Albany brought meat to his master's house, and asked him to drink a dram with him, which he consenting to, Albany carried him to Hughson's, where Albany called for liquor; and as Hughson did not bring it to them immediately, he (Albany) went into the house and brought out a two-penny dram to Othello in the yard; Albany told him that Hughson desired him (Othello) to stay a little, for he wanted to speak with him; Othello said he could not stay then, but that he would come there in the evening.

2. "He went again about dusk in the evening, and Albany was not there; Hughson and Othello began to talk about the plot, and Hughson would fain have made him swear, but he refused, saying another time would do as well: Hughson told him if he would swear he should never want for liquor, it should not cost him any thing, and desired he would bring his acquaintance with him, and he would make them welcome: he thanked him and went home: was at Hughson's about an hour.

3. "The 30th of October last, Albany brought meat to his master's house, and then asked Othello whether he would go to dinner at Hughson's, the drummers being to have a

feast there that day? (k) he answered that his master was to be at home that day, and that he could not go.

4. "Albany often brought meat there, and would always ask him to go and drink at Hughson's, and as opportunity served, sometimes he went, and sometimes not.

5. "About a year ago he went one evening down to the North river to swim, and there met with Albany; they went into Hughson's and he made them a tankard of punch; Hughson endeavoured again to make them swear, and brought a book to him; he still put it off; then Hughson told him if he would not, he (Othello) must not tell any body what he had been talking about.

6. "He has seen many soldiers at Hughson's at different times, very great with Hughson, but cannot tell whether they knew or were concerned in the plot, but knows that Kane was one of them, (l) and believes he (Kane) can name the rest; Hughson promised Othello to find him a gun and cutlass, and told him if he did any damage he would commit no sin thereby: Othello understood, it would not hinder him from going to heaven.

7. "Vaarck's Caesar told Othello, that Rutgers's Quash was to find arms: Mr. Philipse's Cuffee was likewise spoke to by Othello about the conspiracy, and asked whether he was sworn? Cuffee answered yes, are not you? Othello said no, I have only promised to keep the secret. Said he had not spoke to any one since about it.

8. "Adam told Othello (since their being in the jail) that he (Adam) was to have killed his master and mistress sure enough; and advised Othello to confess that he was to have killed his master and mistress, that that would be a means of getting him off."

(k) The militia drummers, who were negroes, idle fellows no doubt; fiddlers of that colour, many drummers, and other, were tempted by Hughson's great hospitality. It is somewhat amazing! how Hughson, a poor cobbler, with a wife and house full of children and scarce any visible business or means of subsistence, should be able to support such extraordinary generosity.

(l) And Kane it seems knew well that he was.

Confession of Quack, Walter's negro, under sentence of death before one of the judges—No. 3.—He said,

1. "That Philipse's Cuffee, Vaarck's Caesar, Auboyneau's Prince, and himself, went down to Hughson's, that Caesar called for a bowl of punch, they drank it together, and Cuffee, Caesar and Prince, afterwards went out together and talked, while he (Quack) stood upon the threshold of the door, Quack called to them and asked if they would go, for it was almost night? they said they had some business to do; Quack went away: this was last May was twelve months.

2. "That another time he went to Hughson's by himself, and met the three same negroes as before, Cuffee was playing on a violin; they had one tankard of egg-punch, and another of water, sugar and rum, they sat in the parlour; Vaarck's Caesar called for a pack of cards, they played a considerable time, and Quack won two or three bowls of punch, which Mrs. Hughson made, and Peggy paid for: they got pretty merry with drinking; judge Philipse's Frank came in and called for a mug of beer, but did not stay, his boat being at the dock just by; Mr. Van Dam's John came in, and sat a while and drank with them, and afterwards went away; as soon as Frank and John were gone, Vaarck's Caesar said, come Quack I want you for something, but you must swear not to tell it; Quack said I will be curst if I do; they said they did not care to trust Frank or John, nor many others, who were all apt to talk, but if he would agree to their proposal, it would be better for him, and that when he came there he should never want liquor; Peggy was present during the discourse, and went out to call Hughson; Hughson then came into the room and swore Quack; Hughson, himself, Caesar, Cuffee and Prince, swore at the same time, to encourage him to swear, they all kissed a book; they then told Quack of the plot, and Hughson asked him if his master had any guns? Quack answered two, which he could get; Hughson told him he had powder and shot enough, and that he had bought some guns, and had money to buy

more, and told him there were people up the river, and on the other side (the water) that were to come and help: Quack asked whether they were blacks or whites? Hughson said he knew them, and that was sufficient: Quack understood by his discourse they were whites.

3. "Quack remembers to have seen a gun hanging up at Hughson's, likewise a bag of large shot, about five inches high and four broad.

4. "They had another bowl of punch, which Hughson treated with, and at the same time told Quack that if he would bring any company there with him, he would make them welcome. This meeting was in the same month as the first meeting: it was on a Saturday night, he went in about dusk, and stayed till twelve.

5. "Two Sundays after, Caesar, Quack (himself) and one other negro (who he did not know) were at Hughson's, but talked nothing of it at that time.

6. "Captain Marshall's Ben asked him eight or nine times to go to Hughson's with him; but says he never went with Ben any where.

7. "Since new year Albany told Quack, that they had a supper at Hughson's, and that a great many negroes were there present.

8. "Some time this spring Adam sent Jack to invite Quack to come to his master's, that Adam wanted very much to speak to him; Quack being at Mr. Richard's with his wife, refused to go, but knew not what business Adam had with him.

9. "While Quack was in jail, Vaarck's Caesar, who was also in the same jail, told Quack, that Hughson, Peggy, and himself, had had a supper at the house of one Saunders, upon the dock; and from Caesar's discourse, he Quack, understood that Saunders was concerned in the plot. (m)

10. "Caesar likewise told him he had buried money some where near Hughson's, but no one knew of it but himself.

(m) This fellow never apprehended.

Monday, July 13.

The four following examinations were taken this day before one of the judges, Mr. Nicholls and Mr. Lodge present, when the several negroes they affected were passed in review before and picked out by the witnesses.

1. *Examination* taken against Le Roux's Quash—William Kane, Bastian, Tickle, and Sandy, said that Quash was sworn at Hughson's and at Comfort's too, into the plot.

2. *Examination* taken against Valet's Tom—Kane, Burton, and Bastian, said that Tom was often at Hughson's when they talked of the plot, and consented and was sworn there in Kane's presence.

3. *Examination* taken against captain Walton's Jupiter—Kane, Burton, and Bastian, said that Jupiter was often at Hughson's when they talked of the plot, and consented, and was active.

4. *Examination* taken against captain Walton's Dublin—Burton said, that Dublin was at Hughson's when talked of the plot, and that he consented.

Examination of Bastian, negro, before one of the judges, No. 2.

1. "Bastian being further examined, saith, that when he was at that great entertainment at Hughson's, on the Sunday about a month or six weeks before the fort burnt, he heard Hughson call over Quack (Walter's) name in a list, and said that he was to have been there; he also heard Cuff (Jamison's) name twice called out of the list, (n) but he did not appear. Hughson called all the negroes' names over by a list, and the negroes present answered thereto; and whenever Hughson made any particular appointment of a meeting, it was usual for him to call over their names by the list, and those present answered.

2. "That he has seen the said Quack at Hughson's several times, and once in particular, some time last summer, when Hughson, his wife and daughter Sarah, and Peggy were pres-

(n) This negro also escaped us.

[303]

ent and also Vaarck's Caesar; and Quack was complaining to Hughson and them, that he had brought to Hughson's fourteen or fifteen firkins of butter, which Peggy was to receive the money of Hughson for (he being to sell the butter, and as he, Bastian, understood, had sold it to the Cuba vessels) and that he, Quack, was cheated out of that money; and that he had also given Peggy a five pound bill to change, and she had likewise cheated him out of that; and Quack was very angry about it, and Peggy said she had given the money to some of his consorts to give him (to a white man) that he knew very well, but that he was gone off with it.

3. "That he knows one Frans (o) a free negro, a butcher, that lived at Mr. Bayard's farm at Hoboeck, he saw him at Hughson's several times, and particularly he was at Hughson's at the entertainment above mentioned, when they were all talking about the plot, and he joined with them, and talked as much about it as any of the rest, but don't know whether he was sworn of it.

4. "That he has seen Kane the soldier at Hughson's several times when negroes were there, and once shortly after new-year, he saw the said Kane and Hughson a writing in company of negroes, and as far as he could understand, they were copying over a list of the persons concerned in the conspiracy, but said that generally when he came to Hughson's, and the white people were there, he used to go away; but one day seeing Kane at Hughson's, and having seen him there several times before, he asked Hughson's wife what the man did there? she answered that he need not be afraid of him, he would not betray them in any thing.

5. "Has heard Billy (Ward's negro, executed) say, that they (the negroes) had a frolic in the Broadway at a soldier's, where were present, a Roman priest, and Quack (Walter's) amongst other negroes; and that the priest swore the negroes of the plot, and said he could forgive them all the sins that they did.

(o) Nor was this negro ever taken up.

6. "That the negro boy Cato, Mr. Richard's and Neptune, Mr. Cruger's, (as Bill, Ward's, told the examinant) were at the last mentioned meeting."

The following notes were taken upon the *examination* of Mary Burton and William Kane this day, before one of the judges, which in the hurry of business were omitted to be drawn up in form.

1. "Mary Burton said John Earl, who lived in the Broadway, used to come to Hughson's with nine or ten soldiers at a time.

2. "Hughson used to go to Kelly's (the soldier's) house, and has seen Kelly at Hughson's, and used to be amongst the negroes, when they were talking about the fires.

3. "An old man, a very old man, believes not a soldier, in old clothes, sometimes a red jacket, does not know his name, he used to be great amongst the negroes, when talking about the fires.

4. "The white men were to have companies of negroes under them, and Hughson told them they might order their companies as they thought fit; and Jury (Ury) the priest, used to be with them.

5. "A soldier lives at the house behind the English church yard, was concerned in the plot; (p) the soldiers used to come to his house, and Hughson used to go up there and fetch them down to his.

6. "A man by the Mayor's market, lived at the shop where she used to fetch rum from, such another as Kane, and dressed like him, but of a Sunday (q) used to have better clothes; don't know his name, lived in a sort of a cellar opposite the market.

7. "She has gone with Sarah (the daughter of Hughson

(p) This man never taken, though the description of him very circumstantial.

(q) Sunday was generally the day, as the reader may have observed from the course of the evidence, that the conspirators met at Hughson's, which his daughter Sarah confirms in her examination.

meaning) to a house beyond captain Marshall's, a soldier's, for to fetch soldiers down to Hughson's; the old soldier himself, not concerned as she knows.

8. "John Earl, at the time that Hogg's goods were discovered met her in the street, and said he had rather have given twenty pounds than that the discovery had been made of them, but that if she (Mary Burton) discovered any thing about the fires, he would be the death of her. (r)

9. "A doctor that lived by the slip, she took him to be a Scotchman, used often to be at Hughson's since the Cuba men gone.

10. "That she had seen another dancing-master along with Holt and Kane, at Hughson's, talking about the plot, above stairs, and saw several negroes with them. (She stammered at his name, and pronounced a C several times, which she said she believed was the first letter of his name, and though it was known by the judge, and those that were present, whom she must necessarily mean, yet he chose she should recollect the name if she could; at last she said he lived (this being the assembly room, she pointed to the street) in Wall-street; she said she should know his name if she heard it; and we not knowing of any other dancing-master in town, or any that pretended or professed themselves to be such, but this man, who did live in that street she was asked whether his name was Corry? and she readily answered, that was his name, and that she should know him again, if she saw him.)"

Then Mary Burton was sent into the next room, and William Kane sent for.

William Kane being asked whether he knew of any other dancing-master besides Holt (mentioned by him several times before) that was amongst them at Hughson's, when they were talking of the plot? Kane instantly answered, there was Pier's son-in-law, who lived in that street (pointing also to Wall-

(r) This fellow never taken.

[306]

street) who used to be amongst them, and was concerned in the plot. Then Kane was sent away.

Both these witnesses were sworn to the truth of what they declared.

Whereupon a constable was despatched for Corry, who was soon brought, and the following examination taken down, which Corry signed.

Examination before one of the judges.—

"John Corry being examined saith, that he never was at Hughson's house in his life.

"Never spoke a word to Holt in his life, never was in his company. (s)

"S——h he was acquainted with, and has been in his company several times, but never at Hughson's, nor any other place on the North River, within this city."

John Corry.

Then Mary Burton was sent for, and when she came, she shook her head at the sight of the man, and being asked upon the oath she had taken, whether she had seen that man before, and what she knew of him? she declared to his face to the effect of the 9th section of the aforesaid notes of her examination concerning him. But Corry stoutly denied all she said, and declared he had never seen her before, at which the girl laughed.

Then Mary was dismissed, and William Kane sent for, and confronted with Corry, and he charged him with the same he had declared before; but Corry knew him not.

Corry was committed.

The following negroes committed this day, viz.—Walton's Jupiter and Dublin, La Roux's Quash, recommitted, who had been

(s) Though as the proverb is, two of a trade can seldom agree, it is much, very much, that these two dancing masters, living in the same town for four or five years together, should not have had one wrangle, or exchange one word neither in anger or civility, in all that time.—Surely he endeavours to prove too much, for they might possibly have talked together very innocently.

enlarged upon the grand jury's recommendation the sixteenth instant, as not finding sufficient evidence at that time whereon to form an indictment against him.

SUPREME COURT
Tuesday, July 14.

Present, the chief justice, the second and third justices.

The king against Walter's Quack, Othello, negroes.

Ordered, that the execution of Quack and Othello be on Thursday next, the sixteenth instant, between the hours of two and seven of the afternoon of the same day.

Court adjourned till to-morrow nine o'clock.

Examination of John Ury, before the Chief Justice and third justice, apprehended upon suspicion of being a Romish priest, and a confederate in the conspiracy.

> "John Ury, school-master, denies being any wise concerned in the conspiracy for burning the town and killing the inhabitants, says, that he never was any wise acquainted with John Hughson or his wife, or Margaret Kerry, nor did he ever see them in his life, to his knowledge."
>
> *John Ury*

Deposition, No. 9—Mary Burton, before the grand jury, being first sworn; said,

> "That white people that used to come to Hughson's and being in company with those who talked about the fires, etc. were Corry the dancing-master, (and) Alanor (t) an old man. Once he fought with on Butchell there, and the negroes asked him to be concerned, and he said, yes; but she thought he might be in liquor."

Examination before the grand jury—No. 5—William Kane being duly sworn said,

(t) Who this meant is not discovered.

"That Edward Murphy he had seen many times at Hughson's when they were talking of the fires and burning of the town, and that he swore d——n him, if he would not lend a hand to the fire as soon as any body; and that at the same meeting all the company were speaking about killing the white people.

2. "That David Johnson came one evening to Hughson's, with three women, a little (as he imagined) in liquor. That Ury, the priest, took Johnson by the shoulder when he came in, and carried him to another room, where some negroes were: that he (Johnson) came in a short time out of the room, and took the examinant by the shoulder, and said, d——n ye, don't be downhearted, never fear, for we shall have money enough by-and-by, and that immediately he swore, in the room that he came into, in the presence of the company, that he would help to burn the town, and kill as many white people as he could; and that both Murphy and Johnson were that night sworn into the plot; and that old Hughson, and three of his sons were sworn the same night.

3. "That one Corry, a dancing-master, was frequently at Hughson's, and often in company with the priest: that he has heard Corry say, that he would assist to burn the fort; and that he was frequently in company with the negroes, when Hughson and they used to talk of burning the town and killing of the white people.

4. "That Holt, the dancing-master, was frequently at Hughson's, in company with the priest; that he never heard any of them say, that they would assist at burning of the houses and killing of the people; but that both were in the room where some negroes were sworn, and where burning of the town and killing of the people was spoke of in so free and public a manner, that he had reason to believe that both of them heard all that was said on the subject.

5. "That John Coffin, Jerry Corker, Daniel Fagen, John Ury the priest, Thomas Hughson the father, and his three sons, were all in the conspiracy.

6. "That a young gentleman with a pigtail wig, used frequently to come there with Corry, Ury the priest, and Holt;

[309]

but never saw him in company with any negroes, as those other white people used to be when he was absent."

SUPREME COURT
Wednesday, July 15. A.M.

Present, the Chief Justice, the second and third justices.

The king against colonel Moore's Cato, Ten Eyck's Dick, Crooke's Prince, De Lancey's Pompey, Vaughton's Cuffee, negroes.

The prisoners were arraigned on an indictment for the conspiracy, and thereto pleaded guilty; and in arrest of judgment produced his majesty's most gracious pardon on condition of transportation; which was read and allowed of.

The king against Jay's Brash, Bayard's Pompey, Gomez's Cajoe, Wendover's Emanuel, Wyncoop's London, Livingston's Braveboy, Gilbert's Pompey, Courtlandt's Sam, Burk's Sarah, negroes.

The prisoners being brought to the bar, and asked what they had to say, why judgment of death should not pass upon them; they produced, and severally pleaded his majesty's most gracious pardon; which being read, was allowed of.

Court adjourned to three o'clock in the afternoon.

P.M. Present, as before.

The king against Hyer's Tom, Tiebout's Venture, Bound's Jasper, Walton's Fortune, Mizerall's Dr. Harry, Rutgers's Galloway, Ryker's Frank, Wendover's Toby, negroes.

On trial upon indictment for the conspiracy.

Jury called and sworn, viz.—Joseph Sacket, Thomas Willet, Richard Langdon, John Provost, Charles Arding, Adrian Banker, Cornelius Cloppert, Alexander Allaire, John Smith, Peter Evoutsee, Patrick Jackson, Steenwick Deriemer.

Witness for the king—Mary Burton, William Kane, sworn.

Brash, Livingston's Tom, Bastian, Tickle, Ten Eyck's Dick, Adam, negroes.

Witness for the prisoners—Jacob Walton, Fortune's master, Harmanus Wendover, Toby's master.

[310]

Of counsel for the king, Mr. Murray, Mr. Smith, and Mr. Chambers.

Mr. Murray, after the indictment was opened, examined the witnesses against Tom, Venture and Jasper.

Notes taken of the evidence upon this trial.

Mary Burton said that Tom was at Hughson's when they were talking about the fires, but did not remember whether he talked of them; she saw him there twice or thrice; he went up stairs with Hughson once; did not know what he did there.

That she had seen Venture at Hughson's talking about the plot several times; said he would set the houses a fire, and he was to have a pistol.

That she did not know that she had seen Jasper at Hughson's.

Brash said that he went with Tom, and Mr. Jay's Ben to Hughson's, and they went up stairs, and saw Tom sworn of the plot, viz.—To burn the town and destroy the white people; that he (Brash) asked Tom first if he would be concerned, and he said yes; and he (Brash) told Hughson so, and so Tom was sworn.

That he did not know any thing of Jasper or Venture.

William Kane upon his evidence gave a general account how he was let into the plot, about Jerry Corker, and his going to a Romish christening as in his examination of the 5th instant.

Said he had seen Tom at Hughson's, and he was sworn of the plot; had seen him two or three times there; he was sworn to burn the town and kill the white people: he was sworn by thunder and lightning, that if he divulged the secret, that might strike him dead.

That he had seen Venture at Hughson's when they were talking about the plot, and he was to help, but he did not see him sworn; that he saw him several times there since Christmas.

That he had likewise seen Jasper at Hughson's, when they were talking about the plot; he saw him there the last Sunday in February; did not see him sworn; he (Kane) was drinking there; nor did he hear him consent.

Tom (Livingston's) said, he told Venture that the white men wanted him to join to help to kill the white people, and he answered Tom, he would go down to Hughson's; he said this was last spring was twelve months that he told Venture this.

That Jasper (was) talking to him (the witness) about killing the white people, and promised to go to Hughson's to swear to kill the white people, but he did not see him afterwards.

Bastian said he saw Venture at Hughson's several times playing at dice; and he was talking about the conspiracy to set the town on fire, and to kill the white people, and he consented, and was to have a gun of Hughson.

Mr. Smith examined the witnesses against Fortune, Dr. Harry and Galloway.

Livingston's Tom said he asked Fortune to go to Hughson's to see the fun there; he answered he would go if he had time.

Kane said he had seen Fortune at Hughson's when they were talking about the plot, but did not see him sworn, nor did he hear him consent; there was a dozen or fourteen negroes there dancing; Hughson proposed the plot to the negroes present, to kill the white people and burn the town, in the hearing of Fortune, but whether he consented or not, he did not know.

Kane said he saw doctor Harry sworn at Hughson's into the plot; that he swore at all meetings, and he resolved to help the negroes to combustible matter to fire the houses, and did help them to some black stuff for that purpose; he was to furnish them with poison; he gave Hughson some, and some to Quack (Walter's) and the doctor cried, hurrah for Guanas boys, for he had Guanas (v) boys enough.

Kane said that the time appointed among them to set the town on fire, was the 17th day of March, at night, St. Patrick's day.

Kane said Hughson used the ceremony of swearing negroes into the plot, by making a circle on the floor with chalk, or something, and then he made the negroes pull off their shoe off the left foot, and put their toes into the circle, and as a negro was sworn, Hughson's wife fed the negro with a draught out of a bowl of punch.

(v) The name of the place where the doctor lived.

Kane said he had seen Galloway several times at Hughson's, that he said he would lend a hand, d——n him if he would not, to destroy the town and murder the inhabitants, and would make a breeches for his master, that he understood from some negroes, that Galloway was sworn of the plot, but Kane did not see him sworn.

Bastian said he heard Fortune say at Hughson's, before all the company, that he would join in the plot (it was some time soon after new-year, there were fourteen or fifteen negroes there) to set the town on fire and kill the people; Bastian heard him talk to doctor Harry, and tell him there was a particular house where all the negroes concerned in the conspiracy met, and could have victuals and drink for nothing.

That he saw Galloway at Hughson's, and he there promised to help set the town on fire and kill the white people.

Mary Burton said she had seen three or four papers of poison in Hughson's drawers, which she understood he had had of some negro; that she heard Vaarck's Caesar, and Philipse's Cuffee, and Auboyneau's Prince, say that Galloway was sworn in the plot.

Adam said he heard doctor Harry talk to Hughson about poison that he would give him; that doctor Harry consented to the burning the town and killing the people in Adam's hearing, that he saw doctor Harry four times at Hughson's, twice he was in the house with him, and twice he saw him go in; that he saw him sworn the first time by Hughson.

Tickle said he saw Galloway sworn at Hughson's, he was to help set houses on fire, Hughson was to find him a gun, and he was to kill the people.

Mr. Chambers examined the witnesses against Frank and Toby.

Ten Eyck's Dick said he told both Frank and Toby about the plot, and asked them to be concerned, and they say yes, they agree to it, and he (the witness) was to call them to go to Hughson's, but never did; he was to call them to go to Hughson's when the time of the fires was to come.

Mary Burton said she had seen him at Hughson's, heard him say he would help to burn the town and destroy all the people.

That she had seen Toby several times at Hughson's, and he said much the same as the other, he consented to be one of the plot.

Bastian said he had seen Frank at Hughson's several times, heard him say he would help to burn the town and destroy the white people, this at two different times.

Kane said he had seen Frank very often at Hughson's, saw him sworn of the plot, and was with Ury; he was to burn the city, and kill the people; there were several other negroes with the priest: this was last winter, Galloway and doctor Harry were with him at the same time; Frank used to say he would be captain Holland.

Mr. Walton, witness on behalf of Fortune, said that he had one day desired Mary Burton to go up stairs to see his negro, Fortune, and that upon viewing of him, she declared that she had never seen him at Hughson's.

Note—the girl gave no evidence against him, but it was no consequence, that because she had not seen him there, that nobody else did. But this seemed to be made an objection, as if Burton had given some evidence against him.

The several counsel summed up the evidence of the witnesses, which they respectively examined; the prisoners said nothing material on their defense, but denied all alleged against them.

The court charged the jury, who withdrew, and being soon returned, found the prisoners all *guilty*.

The king against John Ury alias Jury.

The prisoner having been indicted for counselling, abetting, and procuring, etc. a negro man slave called Quack, to set fire to the king's house in the fort, in pursuance of which the said house, etc. was burnt: he was brought to the bar and arraigned thereon, and thereon pleaded *not guilty*.

The king against the same.

The prisoner having been indicted a second time, on an act of the general assembly of the province, passed in the eleventh year of king William the third; for that he being an ecclesiastical person, made by authority pretended from the See of Rome, did after the time limited to the said act, come into the province and city of New-York, and there remained for the space of seven months, and did profess himself to be an ecclesiastical person, made and ordained by authority from the See of Rome, and did appear so to be, by celebrating masses, and granting absolution etc. on which indictment he was also arraigned, and thereto pleaded *not guilty.* (w)

The prisoner then prayed a copy of each indictment; but the court refused a copy of the first, and ordered him a copy of the second.

Then Ury prayed the use of pen, ink and paper, which was granted.

Ordered, that the trial of the said Ury be on Tuesday next.

The king against Sarah Hughson.

Ordered, that the execution of Sarah be further respited until Tuesday next.

Court adjourned till Friday morning ten o'clock.

An *extract* taken this day by the grand jury, from Ury, the priest's journal, seized upon his commitment.

"(He) arrived at Philadelphia, 17th February, 1738—At Lundinum (x) 5th March, 1739—To Philadelphia, 29th April, 1739—Began school at Burlington, in New-Jersey, 18th June, 1739—Occulto, (z) Jacobus Atherthwait, 28th July 1739—Came to the school at Burlington, 23d January,

(w) Entitled, an act against Jesuits and Popish priests, by the second clause of this act, it is enacted, "That all and every Jesuit seminary, priest, missionary, or other spiritual or ecclesiastical person made or ordained by any authority, power or jurisdiction derived, challenged, or pretended from the Pope or See of Rome, or that shall profess himself, or otherwise appear to be such, by practising and teaching of others to say any Popish prayers, by celebrating masses, granting of absolutions, or using any other of the Romish ceremonies, and rites of worship, by what name, title, or degree soever, such person shall be called or known, who shall continue, abide, remain, or come into this province, or any part thereof, after the first day of November aforesaid (1700), shall be deemed and accounted an incendiary and disturber of the public peace and safety, and an enemy to the true christian religion, and shall be adjudged to suffer perpetual imprisonment. And if any person being so sentenced and actually imprisoned, shall break prison and make his escape, and he afterwards retaken, he shall suffer pains of death, penalties and forfeitures, as in cases of felony."

(x) London, a town in Pennsylvania, upon the borders of Maryland.

(z) What was done privately or covertly between Ury and him is like to remain a secret.

1740—(He saw) madman—Went to Philadelphia, 19th May, 1740—Went to Burlington, 18th June, 1740—At 6 in the evening to Penefuck (a) to Joseph Ashton,—Began school at Dublin (b) under Charles Hastee, at 8 pounds a year, 31st July, 1740—15th October, 1740—27th October— Came to John Croker (at the fighting cocks) New-York, 2d November, 1740—I boarded gratis with him, 7th November, 1740—Naturo Johannis Pool, 26th December, 1740—I began to teach with John Campbell, 6th April, 1741—Baptized Timothy Ryan, born 18th April, 1740, son of John Ryan and Mary Ryan (c) 18th May, 1741.

"Pater confessor Butler 2 Anni. non sacramentum non confessio. (d)"

This day the following list of negroes were recommended by the judges to his honour the lieutenant governor, to be inserted in a pardon in order for transportation, viz.:

Peter Jay's Brash, De Lancey's Pompey, Livingston's Brave-

(a) i.e. Pennypack in Pennsylvania.

(b) There are two Dublins, Upper and Lower in Pennsylvania, supposed to be so named from Irish settlers.

(c) What family this was we know not, unless the priest is mistaken in the christian names of the father and mother of the child; there was one Andrew Ryan accused by William Kane, as one of the conspirators, which will appear hereafter, who lodged with Eleanor his wife, at Hughson's, all the winter before the conspiracy broke out, whom Kane affirmed to be a professed papist, and it has been credibly reported that Kane was one himself, and always professed himself so, until accused as a confederate in the conspiracy; it was said he would not so much as suffer his wife to keep a protestant book in the house, so great a devotee was he; therefore as he was also of the same persuasion, he could best discover his brethren.—There was another Ryan a married man (at that time also an inhabitant of this town) a professed papist, who has it seems since withdrawn himself, but neither his nor his wife's name answers Ury's minute. But whosoever the infant belonged to, its being kept so long from baptism, in a place where there are so many protestant clergy of many denominations ready at hand, gives umbrage to the conjecture, that this office was reserved for a popish priest.

(d) Who father confessor Butler was, also remains a secret as to us. Suppose some reverend gentleman residing in a neighboring colony. Ury minutes it as if it were something observable, that there was neither sacrament nor confession for two years, i.e. in the popish way of ceremony, as may be presumed.

boy, Gilbert's Pompey, Gomez's Cajoe, col. Moore's Cato, Ten Eyck's Dick, G. Crooke's Prince, Vaughton's Cuffee, Wyncoop's London, Bayard's Pompey, Burk's Sarah, Van Courtlandt's Sam, Wendover's Emanuel, most of which had been made use of as witnesses.

Thursday, July 16.

Quack, Mr. Walter's negro, having been convicted upon his own confession, as a confederate in the conspiracy, and thereupon sentenced to be burnt; great solicitations were made to his honour the lieutenant governor, for saving his life; or at least, if that could not be done, that his sentence might be changed from burning to hanging.

Othello the Chief Justice's negro, being in the same condemnation, his honour, for his further information and satisfaction, directed the other two judges to report their opinions concerning these two criminals.

The judges accordingly reported, that considering the circumstances they stood in before the court, they were of opinion, that they did not come within the intent, nor did they think them entitled to the benefit of his honor's proclamation lately published, offering mercy to such persons, whites or blacks, as were concerned in the conspiracy, who should make a full and free confession of their guilt, etc. by the time therein limited.

SUPREME COURT
Friday, July 17.

Present, the chief justice, the second and third justices.

The king against Othello, Walter's Quack, Negroes.

His honour the lieutenant governor, by and with the advice of the council, having recommended to the judges of the court to change the sentence formerly passed against these criminals, to that of hanging, the court *ordered* it accordingly.

Ordered, that the execution of the said Othello and Quack be

[317]

on the morrow, between the hours of nine and one of the same day.

The king against Hyer's Tom, Tiebout's Venture, Walton's Fortune, Mizerall's Harry, Rutger's Galloway, Ryker's Frank, negroes.

The court proceeded to pass sentence on the prisoners, which was, that Harry should be burnt, and the other five hanged.

Ordered, that the execution of Tom, Venture, Fortune, Galloway and Frank, be on the morrow between the hours of nine and one of the same day; and that the execution of Harry be on the morrow, between the hours of two and seven of the afternoon of the same day.

Court adjourned till Monday the 20th instant, ten o'clock in the morning.

Saturday, July 18.

Schultz, the high constable, having signified to the Recorder, late last night, that Othello had informed him he could make very considerable discoveries relating to the conspiracy, which he had a desire to communicate to him, the Recorder went up early this morning to the City-Hall, and sent for him, and the following confession was taken before him.

Othello's confession, No. 3.

1. "He said, that some time last fall he saw Tom Evans, a soldier, at Hughson's, and also James Obrien, a soldier, at different times, talking to Hughson, and after they were gone, Hughson told him that they were both concerned in the plot, and that there were as many white people concerned as negroes.

2. "That some time after he met Obrien, and he advised him (Othello) to steal his master's waistcoat and breeches, and to bring them to him, and he would satisfy him very well; but he never did it.

3. "That Hughson promised to give him a gun and a cut-

lass, but as to powder, or what quantity of arms or ammunition Hughson had, he never told Othello.

4. "That he does not know of any other whites or blacks that he has heard or knows, of his own knowledge, to have been concerned.

5. "That he did not know that the fort was to be fired, nor when they were to begin to set fire to the town; Hughson said Albany should tell him, who was the first that told him of the plot, and that was the first time he carried him down to Hughson's, in June was twelve months, just about the time the Cuba people came here.

6. "That colonel Philipse's Frank carried him down to Hughson's to drink a dram, his boat lay at Hughson's dock, and he treated him, but nobody said any thing at that time of the plot, nor did he ever speak to Frank about it, or Frank to him, nor does he know that Frank knew of it.

7. "Hughson asked him if he could get some of his master's guns, but he told him that he could not come at them.

8. "That Adam persuaded him, since he came in jail, to say that he had agreed to kill his master and mistress, and that by saying so he would get clear; but this was all false, he never engaged to do any such thing, nor was it ever proposed to him by Hughson or any one else; only Hughson told him he must rise with the mob, and kill the people in general, as the rest were to do.

9. "That he never engaged with any negroes or others, to go to Mr. Murray's house to kill or assist in the killing Mr. Murray, Mrs. Murray, and family. All this he says as he is going to answer it to God Almighty.

10. "That Walter's Quack denied, before Mr. Charlton, that he ever engaged in any such design to kill Mr. Murray, etc. but that Adam sent for him to come and sup at Mr. Murray's that night; (e) but Quack said he was sick and

(e) If this was true, it is much (as Quack pretended to be ignorant of this engagement) that he should remember the very night, and send so rude an answer to a civil invitation, as that he would not come: his pretence of sickness would have been sufficient excuse for a disappointment in a matter of lesser consequence than this intended savage butchery.

would not come. Jack came of the message with a lanthorn for him, and told him there was to be company there and good liquor.

11. "He solemnly protests to God Almighty, that he never talked to Adam, or Adam to him of the plot, nor did he know that Adam was concerned in it till after he came. (f)"

This negro behaved upon this occasion with a great deal of composure and decency, with an air of sincerity which very much affected the Recorder, for from the intimacy he had the honour of with his master, he had frequent opportunities of seeing this negro at his house, and Othello's case could not but move some compassion, but all things considered, when calmly reflected upon, one could not yield entire credit to his protestations, more particularly as to the last article; for Adam and he were well known to be familiar acquaintances, and as they were both, by their own confessions, sworn into this execrable engagement, this diabolical conspiracy, it will scarce be believed but they knew each other were concerned, and not only so, but must have had frequent discourse about it.

Othello being remanded, Quack, Walter's negro, was sent for, and the Recorder asked him many questions, and exhorted him to tell the truth in what he should say, as he was in a few moments to answer for his words and actions before God Almighty; but Quack said he knew nothing more of the matter than what he had already declared in his confessions; so he was remanded.

Evidence affecting Othello.—Pompey (De Lancy's) confession, sections 8, 11. Jack (Murray's) confession, sections 1, 10. Adam's confession, sections 19, 23, 25, 26, 29. William Kane's examination, No. 2, section 8. Othello's own confessions.

Evidence affecting Quack.—Abigail Earle and Lydia George's depositions. Sandy or Sawney's examination, No. 1, section 16.

(f) But this is a great falsity! See minutes of Othello's confession, section 1, June 29, 30. He had forgot, surely, what he had said before, that Adam and Albany had mentioned the plot to him, and that he had agreed to join to burn and kill, etc. and was sworn, it should seem, by Adam and Albany.

Jack (Murray's) confession, sections 1, 10. Adam's confession, sections 16, 22, 23, 25, 28, 29. William Kane's examination, No. 2 and 5, sections 15, 16, 18. Sarah Hughson's examination, sections 2, 10. Quack's own confessions.

As to the circumstances attending these two negroes, as they appeared before the court:

The characters of these two miserable wretches were well known: they had more sense than the common rank of negroes, they had both kind and indulgent masters, they were two of the head negroes in town, both fellows of high spirits, had both general acquaintance and great influence amongst the inferior sort of negroes, their confessions were neither voluntary or free, but came from them very unwillingly, and after much persuasion, nor could the judges look upon them to be full, so that these criminals were deficient in all the particulars required by the proclamation, as essentials in a recommendation to mercy; they indeed acknowledged their guilt in general, by their plea, and by their confessions in a few particulars, thinking thereby, as it may well be inferred, to come off as cheap as they could; for perhaps they might flatter themselves, that by confessing what they did they should save their lives; what they did say was very sparing and of little or no significance, more especially what came from Quack, and there was great reason to conjecture they both had it in their power to make very considerable discoveries.

Quack had been committed upon suspicion, and was in confinement some time before any evidence came to light, which directly charged him as a confederate in the conspiracy, and he held it out stoutly, till the proclamation of the 19th June issued, protesting he knew nothing at all of the matter; it was well known how much idle time Quack had, almost at his own disposal, as if he were his own master; and now at length the proofs that he was one of the conspirators, came out to be strong against him, and he had been impeached for a long while before indicted; what he pretended to call the confessions, were of little avail, as before observed; the first of them, viz.—23d June, charged nothing more upon himself than a bare head-knowledge (to use a modern cant word) that there was a conspiracy on foot, to burn houses, which he by accident as it should seem, overheard negroes talking of, not that he was any way concerned, or had agreed to, and engaged in it: in the second confession, 27th June, indeed he goes a step farther, and says that one day he was at Hughson's, and Vaarck's Caesar asked him if he would conclude along with them to set a great many houses on fire? Quack readily (but it may be observed by the way, in such a manner as if he was no such stranger to the villainous enterprize) told him he believed he would, but would consider of it, and give him an answer. So that yet there was no acknowledgement of Quack's engaging himself, even in the purpose of burning houses only, not the least hint that he so much as knew, or heard of any design to murder and destroy the people.

The liberties Quack took were very notorious, not forgetting his expressions and airs on Sunday, 5th April, in the midst of the many fires that alarmed and terrified us, upon which he was first committed, and then recommitted, after enlargement for some time, and yet he still obstinately insisted on his innocence; but at last, when confessions became fashionable amongst them, and Quack had reason to apprehend himself in jeopardy, and that he had but one chance to save his neck, then comes his third confession of the 12th inst. which pretends to discover nothing but what was well known before, excepting one piece of hearsay, section 9. That Vaarck's Caesar, who was also a prisoner in the same jail, told him that Hughson, Peggy, and himself, had had a supper at the house of one Saunders, upon the dock; and from Caesar's discourse, he (Quack) understood that Saunders was concerned in the plot; (g) but not one negro does Quack impeach, notwithstanding his general acquaintance among them, and notwithstanding what Ward's Will declared to Williams (and Will was very expert at plots, for this was the third time he had engaged in them) he believed there were not ten grown negroes in York but what knew of it. (h) Quack's insolence and ingratitude towards his master were very remarkable, as declared

(g) It is surprising that these deluded wretches did not discover all the white people they knew to be concerned, who had no doubt been the chief cause of bringing them to such untimely end.

(h) It seems most probable upon the whole, that this was the truth.

by William Kane: (i) what virtues he might have had are best known to the family he belonged to if he had any, but it seemed agreed on at all hands, that Quack was always much better fed than taught.

Othello had been waiting upon his master in New-England all this summer, who left this place soon after the fire at the fort, and had been attending at Providence in Rhode-Island government, upon his majesty's special commission: the Chief Justice it seems had many times taken him to task there, after he was informed what had been doing amongst us, and well knowing the nature and disposition of Othello, he concluded if there was a plot he was very likely to have a hand in it, and he took a great deal of pains with him, endeavouring to persuade him to confess if he was any way engaged in it, or knew any thing about it, assuring him at the same time that if he was guilty, and would embrace that opportunity, by making an ingenuous confession, he would use his interest with the governor to save his life: but on the contrary, if he went to New-York and was tried and convicted, he would leave him to justice without mercy: but Othello withstood it all, notwithstanding his master endeavoured several times to prevail with him; and then when the Chief Justice was advised of his being impeached, he took the first opportunity of sending him by water hither, in irons; and immediately upon his arrival he was brought before and examined by one of the judges, who warned him of the proclamation, and that the time limited for making voluntary, free and full confession and discovery, was to expire within two or three days, and admonished him to embrace that opportunity; but nevertheless, he obstinately persisted in protestations of his innocence, and was committed; but the next morning when he had time to inquire of his brother criminals how matters stood, he bethought himself, that it was proper for him to make some confession, and intimated that he would to one of the Chief Justice's brothers, and the day after that, the judge sent for him down, and took the confession Monday, 30th June.

The aptness and alacrity of these two criminals for mischief

(i) See Kane's examination, No. 2, section 15, 5th July.

was monstrously remarkable, as declared in evidence upon the confessions of two of their own colour and accomplices, in the same savage, cruel and bloody purpose; though Quack and Othello denied it to the last. (k) That the scheme was proposed by Hughson to a set of negroes at his house, and consented to by them, of which Othello and Quack were two of the chief; and the very night was fixed upon for being admitted by Mr. Murray's Jack into his master's house: and in conjunction with him, and Adam, his fellow servant, these ruffians were to butcher that whole family in their beds, then to set the house on fire, after they had plundered it, and were to carry the spoils to Hughson's: if this was true, surely the masters of these two bloody villains had nothing less to expect from them in their turns, than a share in the like fate; and certainly it was not fit that two such cannibals, who could coolly engage to embrue their hands in the blood of innocent persons by wholesale, who could never have offended them, should be suffered any longer to breathe, when the justice of the law had overtaken them: the judges could by no means think them proper objects of mercy; and had they recommended them to the governor as such, and his honour had pardoned them, such lenity towards them, might have been deemed cruelty to the people. (l)

(k) See Jack, Mr. Murray's negro's examination, sections 10, 11, 12. Adam's examination, section 29. And the agreement of these two negroes' examinations concerning this particular, as well as many others, upon comparison, seems very remarkable; they did not see one another after they were sent to jail, for they were kept apart till after these confessions were taken; nor could they so much as see one another till there was occasion to make use of them as witnesses.

(l) The other negroes concerned in this horrible undertaking, were likewise of the head or the chief slaves in town, and principal agents, no doubt, amongst the conspirators of their own colour; some, perhaps may object, why were not all, or at least Mr. Murray's own negroes, made examples of, as well as these two criminals, for (may they say) they equally deserved it? —Though one is not always obliged to give an answer to every one that askes a question, yet for once to oblige (if there should be any) such.— It is very true, they all deserved exemplary punishment; but if all the conspirators in town had been executed, perhaps this would have been carrying the argument further than the objectors would have chosen it should, especially if any of their own slaves had been detected: though indeed it were much to be wished, that every negro in town concerned were transported,

[324]

About noon Othello, Walter's Quack, Venture, Frank, Walton's Fortune, and Galloway, negroes, were executed according to sentence.

Othello being asked some questions at the gallows about the plot, answered he had nothing more to say than what he had this morning declared to one of the judges.

Walton's Fortune behaved at the gallows like a mountebank's fool, jumped off the cart several times with the halter about his neck, as if sporting with death. Some conjectured he was intoxicated with rum.

Tom, Heyer's negro, was reprieved.

This afternoon Harry, the negro doctor, was executed according to sentence; in the way from the jail to the stake, there were several endeavoured to persuade him to make a confession; but Harry's heart was hardened, he would discover nothing, as he had no hopes of benefiting himself by it in this world: perhaps he might have been persuaded of having fine things in the next, upon condition of his keeping all secret here: however, at length the terrors of death and the lighted pile affrighted him so, that it seems he let drop some unguarded expressions, from which his guilt might be inferred, and that he could have made some discovery if he had thought proper; so much as was minuted down, as may be thought to have any relation to the conspiracy, followeth.

Minutes of doctor Harry's confession at the stake, taken by Mr. John Sprat.—He said,

---

or the place rid of them almost at any rate; and if so, it is probable there would be very few to trouble us. But more particularly—This black band of ruffians consisted of no less than twelve according to Adam; Jack agrees to all the same persons, and adds one more which Adam had omitted, viz. —Ben (Jay's), who had been sent off to the Madeiras the spring before the plot broke out; and all the rest, excepting Caesar (Pintard's), Brash, Bill (Ten Eyck's), and Adam and Jack, (Murray's) had been executed already: and these last five made large confessions, and considerable discoveries, more especially Caesar (Pintard's), Brash, Adam, and Jack, insomuch that it was judged necessary to make use of them as witnesses: for which reason, considerably the pledge of the public faith, and as they made those large confessions and discoveries, conformable to and relying upon the proclamation for their indemnity with regard to their lives, their escape could not be avoided, though their crimes merited a more severe fate.

1. "James Cosyn's negro told him (Harry) when they had some difference, that he would be soon hanged or burnt.

2. "That he knew nothing of the plot of his own knowledge, that if he did, he would discover it to save his soul.

3. "That he did not remember one negro upon Long-Island, that was concerned.

4. "Being asked about the combustible stuff for burning houses, and about the poison for negroes, he said he knew nothing of it, and that it signified nothing to confess."

SUPREME COURT.
Monday, July 20.

Present, the second justice.

The king against Sarah Hughson.

Ordered, that the execution of Sarah Hughson be respited till Wednesday sevennight next.

Court adjourned till to-morrow morning, 10 o'clock.

A list of negroes recommended this day by the grand jury to the judges, to be discharged; they finding no sufficient evidence to accuse them, viz.:

Colonel Moore's Caesar, Mrs. Bickley's Robin and Sussex, colonel Philipse's Frank, Rip Van Dam's, esq. John, Peter De Peyster's Pedro, John Roerbeck's Jack, Mr. Filkin's Will, widow Van Rantz's John.

And they were discharged accordingly.

SUPREME COURT.
Tuesday, July 21.

Present, the chief justice, the second and third justices.

The king against John Ury.

Mr. Chambers, of counsel for the king in this prosecution, moved to put off the trial of the prisoner, Ury, until the next term.

Ordered accordingly, and that the prisoner have sufficient notice of trial.

Ordered, that the persons indicted for selling spirituous liquors to negroes, and for keeping disorderly houses, do attend the court, on Thursday next, at ten o'clock.

Court adjourned till to-morrow morning, eleven o'clock.

Examination of William Kane, before one of the judges, No. 6.

"William Kane being duly sworn, and asked whether he knew one Thomas Evans, he answered he did not, but that he knew one Griffith Evans, a soldier, who was burnt in the fire at the fort.

"He was then asked whether he knew that James Obrien, a soldier, was concerned in the plot? he answered he did not.

"But at last he said, he recollected one Thomas Evans who was out upon a furlough, but was in town all last winter, and very great with Obrien: he said, if Obrien was apprehended perhaps he might tell."

SUPREME COURT.
Wednesday, July 22.

Present, the chief justice, the second and third justices.

The king against John Ury alias Jury.

John Ury was arraigned on a new indictment, for being an ecclesiastical person, made by authority pretended from the See of Rome, and coming into and abiding in this province after the time limited by the act of assembly made the 11th of William III. etc. as in the other indictment; (in the former indictment there having been a mistake) and pleaded *not guilty*, etc.

Court adjourned till to-morrow morning, eleven o'clock.

The further examination of Sarah Hughson, before the chief justice, No. 2.

1. "She said that she had often seen Ury the priest at her father's house, who used to come there in the evenings and

at nights, and has seen him in company with the negroes, and talking with them about the plot of burning the town and destroying the white people.

2. "That she has seen him several times make a round ring with chalk on the floor, and make all the negroes then present stand round it, and he (Ury) used to stand in the middle of the ring, with a cross in his hand, and there swore all the negroes to be concerned in the plot, and that they should not discover him, nor any thing else of the plot, though they should die for it.

3. "That William Kane used often to come there with the negroes, and once, as she remembers, he came there with Ury the priest, who swore him into the plot, and several negroes, in particular, Vaarck's Caesar, Comfort's Jack, Auboyneau's Prince, Walter's Quack, Philipse's Cuffee, Peggy, and the examinant herself, and her father and mother; that all this was done the last winter, and she thinks before Christmas.

4. "That she saw him, the said Ury, baptize the above named negroes, or some of them, and told them he made them christians, and forgave them all their sins, and all the sins they should commit about the plot, and preached to the negroes; Kane being there also.

5. "That she has heard Vaarck's Caesar, Philipse's Cuffee, and other negroes say, that they used to go to Ury's lodging, where they used to pray in private after the popish fashion, and that he used to forgive them their sins for burning the town and destroying and cutting of the peoples throats.

6. "That Ury afterwards told the examinant that she must confess what sins she had been guilty of, to him, and he would forgive her them; that she told him that she had been guilty of no other sins but cursing and swearing in a passion; upon which he told her, as she had taken the oath to be concerned in the plot, he pardoned her her sins; she replied that she did not believe any body could forgive her sins but God; and he said yes, he and all priests could, if the people did but do what the priests bid them, and followed

all their directions; that Peggy used to confess in private to Ury, and she heard him tell her, if she would confess all the wickedness she had done in the world, he would forgive her, and particularly about the plot, and she says that Peggy has often told her she was a strong papist.

7. "That several of the soldiers used often to come to their house and call for liquors, but she does not know whether they knew of or were concerned in the plot, or not."

Minutes of examinations taken before the grand jury, of negroes not indicted.

Thomson's York said that Wolf's Dick was sworn with him at Hughson's.

Le Roux's Quash is accused by Tickle, Bastian, and Sandy, all three very clear and positive in their evidence, and likewise by Kane.

Walton's Jupiter is accused by Bastian, fully, clearly; and by Kane.

Van Rantz's York, sworn at Hughson's, by the evidence of Livingston's Tom, and to kill the white people.

Kortrecht's Prince was sworn at Hughson and promised to kill the white people, as appears by the evidence of Livingston's Tom.

Abraham Marschalk's Diego, accused by Murray's Adam, who says he saw him at Comfort's, where were many negroes talking of killing the white people, but cannot say that he heard Diego say any thing.

Adam further says, that Murray's Jack told him that he had seen Diego at Comfort's, and Jack, an examinant, denied it.

Bastian says, that the free negro called Franck or Frans, that he accuses, lives at Hoboeck, on Mr. Bayard's farm, and that he has seen him at Hughson's among the rest of the negroes at supper, when they were talking of the plot.

SUPREME COURT.
Thursday, July 23.

Present, the Chief Justice, the second and third justices.

The king against William Whitefield, on an indictment for keeping a disorderly house.

William Whitefield having pleaded guilty to the indictment for keeping a disorderly house, entertaining negroes, etc.

Ordered, that for the said offence, the said William Whitefield be fined eight pounds, and stand committed until he pay his fine.

The king against Stephen Burdett, on the like; the like, and fined forty shillings.

The king against Israel Shadwick, the like, and fined ten shillings.

The king against John Christian, the like, and fined five pounds.

The king against Nicholas Burger, the like, and fined forty shillings.

The king against Michael Breton, the like, and fined five pounds.

The king against Elizabeth Nevill, the like, and fined ten shillings.

The king against Eleanor Cavillier, the like, and fined ten shillings.

The king against Sarah Hales, the like, and fined ten shillings.

The king against Robert Saunders, (m) the like, and fined six pence; and ordered to be discharged out of custody, paying his fees.

The following negroes discharged this day out of jail, the grand jury not finding sufficient evidence to indict them.

John Francois, a free negro, Valet's Tom, Robins's Dick, Walton's Dublin, Goelet's Quack, Tiebout's Will, Courtlandt's Jonio, Abraham Marschalk's Diego, Vandursen's Diego.

(m) This supposed to be the man that Walter's Quack understood from what Vaarck's Caesar said to him, to be concerned in the plot. See Quack's confession, 12th July, section 9, but this not thought of at that time.

SUPREME COURT.
Friday, July 24.

Present, the chief justice, the second and third justices.

Court opened and adjourned till to-morrow morning, nine o'clock.

Deposition before one of the judges—

"Elias Debrosse, of New-York, confectioner, being duly sworn, deposeth, that John Ury, now in jail, said to be a popish priest, came to this deponent's house about three months since, along with one Web, a carpenter, and asked if he had any sugar bits or wafers to sell? (the bits are usually made, as the deponent apprehends, in imitation of Spanish silver coin) this deponent shewed the said Ury some confectionary in imitation of dogs, hawks, owls, lambs and swans, supposing that he wanted them to give away to please children, but told him he had no bits or wafers: then the said Ury asked the deponent, whether the Lutheran minister had not his wafers of him? or whether that paste which the deponent shewed him, was not made of the same ingredients as the Lutheran minister's? or asked the deponent some question to that purpose: then the deponent told him the said Jury, that if he had a congregation, and wanted any such things, that he might get a mould made by any joiner for that purpose: the deponent asked the said Ury (supposing him to be a professor of some particular sect) where his congregation was? and this he asked him two or three times; but the said Ury waived giving the deponent any answer thereto."

A list of seven negroes indicted by the grand jury, who are not to be found, viz.:

Mr. Henry Curger's Hanover, Abraham Van Horn's London, Stephen Bayard's Ben, Richard Stilwell's Pedro, Augustus Jay's Ben, Mrs. Governeur's Jack, Henry Holt's Joe.

Present, the chief justice, the second and third justices.

The grand jury came into court, and being called over, presented (amongst other bills) a bill against Pedro, Pierre De Peyster's negro, for the conspiracy.

Then the grand jury were discharged, with the thanks of the court for the great service they had done their country.

The court adjourned to Tuesday the 28th instant, ten o'clock in the morning, being the first day of the ordinary July term.

Monday, July 27.

Deposition taken before one of the judges—Joseph Web of the city of New-York, carpenter and house joiner, being duly sworn, deposed,

(1.) "That some time last fall, about the latter end of October or beginning of November, to the best of his remembrance, he was at work at John Croker's, at the fighting cocks, and there became acquainted with John Ury; and hearing him read Latin and English to some people in the house, and thinking that he read very well, he inquired of Croker who he was; and he informed him, he was a schoolmaster lately come from Philadelphia, and taught his children to read; that after this, he became acquainted with the said Ury, and asked him if he would teach a child of his? and he said he would, if Croker would give him the liberty of coming to his house, and Croker agreed to it; and he sent his child to him.

2. "That afterwards, this deponent, and Ury growing more intimate, and deponent observing a poor and mean appearance in his clothing, he thought his pocket answerable thereto, and gave him an invitation to his house, and told him he should be welcome to his table noon and night at any time when he saw proper, and Ury accordingly came

to this deponent's house frequently, all the winter afterwards; and in their conversations he understood by the said
Ury, that he professed himself a nonjuring minister; and
that he had been taken into custody in London, for a book
that he wrote and printed, that some critics picked a hole in
it, and construed it treason, which was contrary to his intent and meaning; but by means of some friend (a great
man) who knew his family very well, and had a regard for
him, he had his liberty and got away: and that by leaving
England, he lost a living (as the deponent understood him)
church preferment of 50 pounds a year income.

3. "That the said Ury told the deponent in some of their
conversation, that in the time of the late king William the
third, the said king offered a certain bishop (whose name he
does not now remember) a bishoprick of about nine thousand pounds a year, if he would take the oaths; but that the
said bishop refused to comply therewith; or that the said
bishop was in profession of that preferment, and was ousted
upon refusing to take the oaths; or the said Ury expressed
himself to one or other of those purposes; and that the deponent asked him the said Ury, how they did then, when that
bishop was dead? why said Ury they take it by seniority in a
regular succession: and Ury declared that he himself was ordained by a bishop, who took his bishoprick by seniority
and regular succession, or expressed himself to that purpose,
as the deponent understood him.

4. "That Ury in some of his conversations with him upon
religious topics, expressed himself in such a dark, obscure,
and mysterious manner, that the deponent could not understand him; he would give hints that he could neither make
head nor tail of.

5. "That some time in May last, since the said Ury went
to live at Campbell's, in the house where Hughson lived,
the said Ury asked the deponent, whether he knew of any
confectioner? and the deponent carried him to Mr. De
Brosse; and when he came there he asked De Brosse to
shew him some confectionary; and Ury likewise asked De
Brosse whether the lutheran minister had his wafers of him?

[333]

and De Brosse shewed Ury confectionary in different shapes (that is to say) some lions, some dogs, and cocks (as deponent thinks) but Ury said they would not suit him, and so went away.

6. "That one day the conversation between Ury and deponent was about negroes; deponent having said they had souls to be saved or lost as well as other people: Ury said they were not proper objects of salvation; deponent replied what would you do with them then, what would you damn them all? no says Ury, leave them to that Great Being that has made them, he knows best what to do with them; says Ury, they are of a slavish nature, it is the nature of them to be slaves, give them learning, do all the good you can, and put them above the condition of slaves, and in return they will cut your throats. (n)

7. "That after Campbell removed to Hughson's house, Ury removed thither about a week or ten days after him, and the deponent went thither three times, and heard him read prayers, in the manner of the church of England, but in the prayers for the king he only mentioned our sovereign lord the king, and not king George; the drift of his first sermon was against drunkenness and debauchery of life, and against deists; the first part of his second sermon was much to the same purpose with the former, and the latter part was an admonition to every one to keep to their own minister; they that were of the church of England, to the English minister, those that were of the Lutheran persuasion to keep to that, and those of the Presbyterian to keep to their minister: that he did not propose to set up a society for preaching to them, that he only gave a word of admonition at the request of the family where he was.

8. "That at his third sermon Mr. Hildreth was present, and Ury therein took notice of two ministers that had lately preached in this city, whose doctrine he condemned; the particulars that the deponent remembers he took notice of, were their preaching up, that faith without works were suffi-

(n) Ury seemed to be well acquainted with the disposition of them.

[334]

cient for salvation; he said that this destroyed two grand attributes of God Almighty, his justice and mercy, (as he thinks) and insisted that there must be good works: This was the Sunday before the king's proclamation day, and at the close he warned the persons present, that on the king's proclamation day, at five o'clock in the evening, he intended to preach upon the following words, among others: upon this rock I will build my church, and the gates of hell shall not prevail against it (concerning St. Peter) and these other words, whosoever sins ye remit, they are remitted, and whosoever sins ye retain, they are retained. This is to the best of deponent's remembrance, but deponent has not heard that he preached according to that warning.

9. "That the deponent has heard Ury say, that such a time and such a time was his sacrament day, and that he must receive the sacrament, and he thinks he has heard him say, that he must administer the sacrament but cannot be positive."

The judges of the supreme court having for some time past had under consideration the case of Sarah Hughson, daughter of John Hughson and Sarah his wife, all lately convicted as accomplices in the conspiracy; the circumstances of her misfortune of having been trained up under the influence and evil example of such wicked disposed parents, bore great weight with them; they were therefore inclinable (if she could be prevailed upon to give some colour for it) to recommend her to his honour the lieutenant governor as an object of mercy; and in this expectation, her execution (which by order of the court was proposed to have been at the same time with her father and mother) had been from time to time respited; but after their execution she remained for some time very obstinate, and though there was great reason to expect that it was in her power to give a further insight into this scene of iniquity, yet she remained inflexible after several examinations, and would discover nothing; till at length they were under a necessity of calling her up to sentence, and appointing a day for her execution, proposing this as the last experiment to bring her to a confession, which happened to have the intended effect, and if there could be any dependence upon her veracity in what she had declared (and that she has discovered some truths not before brought to light, they judged from the nature of the conspiracy, so far as it has been unfolded) and if she could be affected with a sense of gratitude for saving her life upon so small merit, and kept to her history concerning John Ury then in custody, and soon to be tried as an accomplice in the plot, and also as a Roman catholic priest, they thought she would be a very material evidence against him: on these considerations they thought fit this day to recommend her to his honour for a pardon, as an object of mercy.

SUPREME COURT
Tuesday, July 28.

Present, the chief justice, the second and third justices.

Court opened with the usual forms.

Grand jury called, and the following appeared and were sworn.

Messrs. Joseph Robinson, James Livingston, Hermanus Rutgers, jun. Charles LeRoux, Abraham Boelen, Peter Rutgers, Jacobus Roosevelt, John Auboyneau, Stephen Van Courtlandt, jun. Abraham Lynsen, Gerardus Duyckinck, John Provost, Henry Lane, jun. Henry Cuyler, John Roosevelt, Abraham De Peyster, Edward Hicks, Joseph Ryall, Peter Schuyler, Peter Jay, merchants.

The chief justice charged the grand jury to prosecute the inquiry for the detection of the conspirators, and to present all crimes and offences from treasons down to trespasses.

A list of eighteen negroes recommended by the judges this day to his honour the lieutenant governor, to be inserted in a pardon, in order for transportation.

Joshua Sleydall's Jack, Henry Breasted's Jack, Thomas Niblet's Sandy, Israel Horsefield's Caesar, (o) Elizabeth Carpenter's

(o) After the secret of the plot had got air, it was observed by several, as they declared afterwards, that the behaviour of many negroes was wild and confused, though the cause of such extravagance was not accounted

Tickle, John Furman's Harry, Edward Kelly's London, David Provost's Low, captain Brown's Jeffery, Thomas Thomas's York, Peter Low's Sam, Samuel Meyers Cohen's Windsor, Mr. Murray's Jack and Adam, Robert Livingston's Tom, Robert Bound's Gosport, Hercules Wendover's Toby, widow Hyer's Tom.

The six following had been indicted for the conspiracy, but their masters agreed to enter into recognizance to transport them forthwith:

Wolf's Dick, Dr. Henderson's Caesar, Cornelius Kortrecht's Prince, widow Van Zandt's York, Charles LeRoux's Quash, captain Walton's Jupiter.

---

for, till those wretches were impeached and taken into custody; all the negroes arraigned upon the indictment for the conspiracy, on the 26th of June, with Caesar, had pleaded guilty; but Caesar was hardy, insisted upon his innocence, and pleaded not guilty. Some endeavour was used by the counsel at the bar, who knew the evidence affecting Caesar, to prevail with him to confess his guilt, but in vain; till at length one of those gentlemen inspecting the indictment, observed colonel Moore's Cato to be indorsed thereon as a witness against him, whereupon he asked Caesar whether he was acquainted with that Cato? at which Caesar seemed confounded, and immediately answered guilty.

TRIAL OF JOHN URY alias JURY.

SUPREME COURT
Wednesday, July 29.

Present, the chief justice, the second and third justices.

The king against Sarah Hughson, the daughter.

This criminal convict being set to the bar, the court demanded of her, what she had to say, why execution of her former sentence should not be awarded against her? she thereupon produced and pleaded his majesty's most gracious pardon, and the same was read and allowed of.

The king against John Ury alias Jury.

The prisoner was brought to the bar, and the court proceeded upon his trial, as followeth.

Clerk in court. Cryer, make proclamation for silence.

Cryer. Oyes! Our sovereign lord the king does strictly charge and command all manner of persons to keep silence upon pain of imprisonment.

Cryer. If any one can inform the king's justices, the king's Attorney General for this province, or the inquest now to be taken on behalf of our sovereign lord the king, of any treason, murder, felony, or any other misdemeanor committed or done by the prisoner at the bar, let them come forth and they shall be heard, for the prisoner now stands upon his deliverance.

Clerk. Cryer, make proclamation.

Cryer. Oyes! You good men that are impanelled to inquire between our sovereign lord the king, and John Ury alias Jury, the prisoner at the bar, answer to your names.

Clerk. John Ury alias Jury, hold up thy hand.

These good men that are now called and here appear, are

those which are to pass between you and our sovereign lord the king, upon your life or death; if you challenge any of them, you must speak as they come to the book to be sworn, and before they are sworn.

(The court apprized the prisoner of the nature and extent of that liberty the law allowed him for making his challenges to the jurors.)

The prisoner challenging none, the court proceeded, and the jury was sworn, to wit: William Hamersley, Gerardus Beekman, John Shurmur, Sidney Breese, Daniel Shatford, Thomas Behenna, Peter Fresneau, Thomas Willet, John Breese, John Hastier, James Tucker, Brandt Schuyler.

Clerk. Cryer, make proclamation.

Cryer. Oyes! Our sovereign lord the king does strictly charge and command all manner of persons to keep silence upon pain of imprisonment.

Clerk. You, gentlemen of the jury, that are now sworn, look upon the prisoner, and hearken to his charge.

The prisoner stands indicted, for that, whereas a negro man slave, called Quack, belonging to John Roosevelt of the city of New-York, merchant, on the eighteenth day of March, in the fourteenth year of the reign of our sovereign lord, George II. by the grace of God, king of Great Britain, etc., at the city of New-York, into a certain dwelling house of our said lord the king, which then was standing and being at the fort in the said city of New-York, and was then in the possession of the hon. George Clarke, esq. his majesty's lieutenant governor of the province of New-York, did enter, and of his malice afore-thought, lighted fire, then and there wickedly, maliciously, voluntarily, wilfully, and feloniously did put, and with the said lighted fire, he the said negro man slave called Quack, the dwelling house aforesaid, and then and there wickedly, etc. did set on fire, and burn, and wholly consume, and destroy, against the peace of our said sovereign lord the king, his crown and dignity: and that John Ury alias Jury, private school-master, on the twenty-second day of February, in the said fourteenth year of the reign of our said lord the king, and divers other days and times, before the felony and burning aforesaid, in form aforesaid, done and perpetrated at

[339]

the city of New-York, of his malice afore-thought, wickedly, maliciously, voluntarily, wilfully, and feloniously, did counsel, abet, procure and encourage the aforesaid negro man slave called Quack, the felony and burning aforesaid, in form aforesaid committed and perpetrated, to commit and perpetrate, in most pernicious example of all others in like case offending, contrary to the form of the statutes in such case made and provided, and against the peace of our sovereign lord the king, his crown and dignity.

Upon this indictment he has been arraigned, and hath pleaded thereunto, *not guilty*, and for his trial hath put himself upon God and his country, which country you are.

Your charge is to inquire, whether he be guilty of the felony whereof he stands indicted, or not guilty. If you find him guilty, you are to inquire what goods and chattel, lands and tenements he had at the time when the felony was committed, or at any time since. If you find him not guilty, you are to say so, and no more: and hear your evidence.

Of counsel for the king—the Attorney General, Mr. Murray, Mr. Alexander, Mr. Smith, Mr. Chambers.

The Attorney General, Richard Bradley, esq. addressing himself to the court and jury, opened the indictment, and proceeded as followeth:

In order to maintain the charge against the prisoner, upon this indictment, we shall produce to you the following evidence, to wit:

That the prisoner was actually concerned in the plot to burn the king's house and this city, and murder the inhabitants.

That he has frequently been at Hughson's house, in company with Hughson, his wife and daughter, and Margaret Kerry, and with divers negroes, talking with them about the plot, and counselling and encouraging them to burn the king's house and the town, and to kill and destroy the inhabitants; that the negro Quack, who burnt the king's house, was present at one or more of those times, when the prisoner counselled and encouraged the negroes as afore-said; that he advised them what would be the fittest time to set the English church on fire; and that the prisoner, as a popish priest, baptized Hughson, his wife and daughter, and Kerry, and also divers negroes, and told them then, and at several other times, that he could forgive sins, and that he forgave them their sins relating to the plot.

That when he was with the negroes at Hughson's house, he used to make a round ring on the floor with chalk, or some other thing, and stand in the middle of it with a cross in his hand, and swear the negroes into the plot, and that they should not discover either the plot or him, or any other person concerned in it, though they were to die for it.

That some time last winter, he (at Hughson's house) swore Hughson, his wife and daughter, and Kerry, and several negroes into the plot.

That he went by several names, and that when he baptized the negroes, or any of the conspirators, he used to tell them he forgave them all the sins they should commit about the plot.

We shall likewise produce to you, a letter from general Oglethorpe to his honour, our governor, whereby it appears, that some time before the plot broke out here, the Spaniards had employed emissaries to burn all the magazines and considerable towns in the English North America, and that many priests were employed, under pretended appellations of physicians, dancing-masters, and such like occupations, and under such pretences to get admittance into, and confidence in families.

This, gentlemen, was their hellish device to set on foot and carry on the late dreadful conspiracy among us; and the prisoner, in conjunction with Hughson (as we now have reason to believe) drew in the rest of the conspirators.

Gentlemen, what I have alleged, and much more, you will hear fully proved against the prisoner, by the witnesses for the king on this trial: but before we enter upon their examination, give me leave to say a few words concerning the hei-nousness of this prisoner's offences, and of the popish religion in general, which I shall speak but very briefly to, as there are several other gentlemen of counsel for the king on this trial, and as I have not had either health or leisure to prepare to say much on this occasion.

Gentlemen, the late dreadful conspiracy to burn the king's house, and this whole town, and to kill and destroy the inhabitants, which the prisoner, as well as Hughson advised and encouraged, and swore many of the conspirators to join and bear their parts in, are crimes of too black and inhuman a nature to need any aggravation, and no doubt, the prisoner's engaging at the peril of his own life, in so destructive, so bloody and dangerous an enterprize, proceed from his being employed in it by other popish priests and emissaries, and his zeal for that murderous religion; for the popish religion is such, that they hold it not only lawful but meritorious to kill and destroy all that differ in opinion from them, if it may any ways serve the interest of their detestable religion; the whole scheme of which seems to be a restless endeavour to extirpate all other religions whatsoever, but more expecially the protestant religion, which they maliciously call the Northern heresy: and to attain this wicked end, their first trick is, by subtle arguments to persuade the laity out of their senses, by shewing them a seeming necessity for their believing as their church believes, if they tender their own salvation; and this, with many more frauds, the church of Rome has artfully devised to get an absolute dominion over the consciences, that they may the more easily pick the pockets of credulous people: witness the pretended pardons and indulgences of that crafty and deceitful church, and their masses to pray souls out of purgatory, which they quote (or rather wrest) scripture for, when no such thing is to be found there; but it is a mere invention and cheat of their own to gull the laity of their money.

Then they have their doctrine of transubstantiation, which is so big with absurdities that it is shocking to the common sense and reason of mankind; for were that doctrine true, their priests by a few words of their mouths, can make a

[342]

God as often as they please: but then they eat him too, and this they have the impudence to call honouring and adoring him. Blasphemous wretches! for hereby they endeavour to exalt themselves above God himself, inasmuch as the creator must necessarily be greater than his creature.

These and many other juggling tricks they have in their hocus pocus, bloody religion, which have been stripped of all their wretched disguise, and fully exposed in their own colours by many eminent divines, but more particularly by the great Dr. Tillotson, whose extraordinary endowments of mind, his inimitable words, and exemplary piety and charity have gained him such universal esteem and applause throughout all the protestant world, as, no doubt, will endure as long as the protestant name and religion lasts, which I hope will be to the end of time.

Gentlemen, when you have heard the witnesses prove to you what I have alleged against the prisoner, I make no doubt but you will, for your oaths sake, and for your own country's peace and future safety, find him *guilty.*

Witnesses for the king.—Mr. George Joseph Moore, clerk in court, sworn,

He proved the arraignment and conviction of Quack, on the twenty-eighth and twenty-ninth days of May last, who set fire to the fort.

Mary Burton sworn.

Mr. Chambers. Mary, give the court and jury an account of what you know concerning this conspiracy to burn down the town and murder and destroy the inhabitants, and what part you know the prisoner at the bar has acted in it: tell the whole story from the beginning, in your own method, but speak slow, not so hastily as you usually do, that the court and jury may the better understand you.

Mary Burton. Why I have seen Ury very often at Hughson's about Christmas and new-year, and then he stayed away about a fortnight or three weeks, and returned again about the time that Hogg's goods came to our house. I have often seen him in company with Hughson, his wife and daughter, and Peggy, and several negroes, talking about the plot, burning the fort first, then the Fly, and then the dock; and upon some of the negroes saying they were afraid of being damned for being concerned in the plot, I heard Ury tell them they need not fear doing of it, for that he could forgive them their sins as well as God Almighty, and would forgive them. They were to burn the whole town and to kill the people: Ury was to be captain of a company of negroes, and he was to begin the fire where he lodged; (p) that when they were once together above stairs, Ury, Hughson, his wife and Peggy, they called Mary, and I went up, but when I came up stairs, Ury had a book in his hand, and bid me go away, and asked me what business I had there, and said they did not call me, they called Mary Hughson, and he was angry and shut the door too again, and I looked under it, and there was a black ring upon the floor, and things in it that seemed to look like rats, I don't know what they were. (q)—That another time I heard him talking with the negroes, Quack and others, about the plot, and turned the negroes out of the room, and asked me to swear? and I said I would swear if they would tell me what I was going to swear, but they would have me swear first; and Hughson and his wife went and fetched silks and gold rings, and offered them to me in case I would swear, but I would not, and they said I was a fool; and Ury then told me he could forgive sins as well as God, I answered I thought it was out of his power. That one night, some time about new-year, I was listening at the door of the room upon the stairs, where there was Ury, Hughson, his wife and daughter Sarah, Vaarck's Caesar, Auboyneau's Prince, Philipse's Cuff and other negroes; and I looked through the door and saw upon the table a black thing like a child, and Ury had a book in his hand and was reading, but I did not understand the language; and having a spoon in my

(p) At Croker's, near the coffee-house, by the long bridge.
(q) See Sarah Hughson's examination, section 9, and note letter (f) thereon. What Mary saw was by looking under the door, which it may be supposed, afforded but an obscure view, and the negroes perhaps pulling their black toes backward and forwards, Mary might be puzzled what to make of them. But Sarah Hughson and Kane agree with Burton, that there was a ceremony used with a ring or circle upon the floor, at swearing confederates.

hand, I happened to let it drop upon the floor, and Ury came out of the room, running after me down stairs, and he fell into a tub of water which stood at the foot of the stairs, and I ran away. When they were doing any thing extraordinary at nights, they would send me to bed.

Prisoner. You say you have seen me several times at Hughson's, what clothes did I usually wear?

Mary Burton. I cannot tell what clothes you wore particularly.

Prisoner. That is strange, and know me so well.

M. Burton. I have seen you in several clothes, but you chiefly wore a riding coat, and often a brown coat trimmed with black.

Prisoner. I never wore any such coat.

Prisoner. What time of the day did I use to come to Hughson's?

M. Burton. You used chiefly to come in the night time, and when I have been going to bed I have seen you undressing in Peggy's room, as if you were to lie there; but I cannot say that you did, for you were always gone before I was up in the morning.

Prisoner. What room was I in when I called Mary, and you came up, as you said:

M. Burton. In the great room up stairs.

Prisoner. What answer did the negroes make when I offered to forgive them their sins, as you said?

M. Burton. I don't remember.

William Kane, soldier, sworn.

Mr. Chambers. Kane, will you give the court and jury an account of what you know of the prisoner at the bar, and of his being concerned in the conspiracy for burning the fort, and the town, and murdering the inhabitants? give the whole account at large.

William Kane. I know the prisoner very well, I have seen him at Croker's, at Coffin's, and Hughson's; and particularly with Daniel Fagan, Jerry Corker, and one Plummer, and several negroes, at Hughson's. Jerry Corker was one of the first that brought me into the plot. One day before Christmas last, I was standing sentry at the governor's door, and Jerry Corker coming out, I being dry asked him for beer; Jerry said he would get some, that he had rum in his pocket, and would make flip, and then he went in and made it in a copper pot, and told me it was with loaf sugar, I drank a draught of it; and when I was relieved at night, Corker came into the guard room, and asked me if I would go to Croker's at the fighting cocks, where there was to be a christening by a Romish priest: we went thither and stayed till past ten o'clock, but the people did not come that night: the next night Corker and I went there again, but the people were not there: the third night we went to New-street, to the house of one Coffin, a pedler, there they had a child and Ury christened it, and read Latin; three acted as priests and handed the book about. Ury put salt into the child's mouth, sprinkled it thrice, and crossed it. That Ury and Corker there endeavoured to persuade me to be a Roman catholic; Ury said it was best to be a Roman, they could forgive sins for any thing ever so bad; I told him I did not believe him, and Corker told me that Ury and all priests could forgive sins. That Ury was present at Hughson's, when John Hughson swore me and his father and brothers into the plot, there was Quack and forty or fifty negroes there at the same time; we were to burn the town and destroy the people. David Johnson was there, and Ury tapped him on the shoulder, and they went into a room together and stayed a quarter of an hour, and when they came back Johnson said d——n me, but we will burn the Dutch and get their money. That by Ury's persuasions that he could forgive sins, many were brought in to be concerned: Ury was near me when I was sworn, and the Hughsons and I took him to be one of the head; Ury wanted to christen me, but I would not, and he would not speak to me, nor before me for a long time, for he could not abide me because I refused to become a Roman, till after he knew that I was concerned in the plot, and even then he did not much care for me: Ury was by when Hughson swore eight negroes into the plot in a ring, and it was then talked among them of burning the fort, and Quack (who was present) was at that time pitched upon to do it, in the presence of Ury who he believed might and did hear it. Jerry Corker told me, that the English church was intended to be burnt on Christmas day last, but Ury put it off, and said that when the weather was better, then there would be a fuller congregation.

Prisoner. You say you have seen me very often, you saw me at Coffin's, you saw me several times at Hughson's, pray what clothes did you see me in?

Kane. I have seen you in black, I have seen you in a yellowish great coat, and sometimes in a straight bodied coat, of much the same colour.

Prisoner. What time of the day have you seen me at Hughson's, and what did I say to you?

Kane. I have seen you there chiefly at nights, and you told me you could forgive me my sins, and there would be no fear of damnation, and you wanted to christen me.

Prisoner. You say you saw me christen a child in New-street, how was the child drest, and what ceremony did I use, and who was present there then?

Kane. The child was not naked, it was dressed as usual; and you put it on your left arm, and sprinkled it with water three times, and put salt in its mouth, and crossed it, as I said before: there were about nine persons present.

Prisoner. Did I use any thing besides salt and water?

Kane. Not that I saw.

Prisoner. Who were present at the christening?

Kane. Eight or nine persons, I think; there was Jerry Corker, Daniel Fagan, Coffin, you, the mother of the child, myself, and two or three more.

Prisoner. You say you saw me at Hughson's several times, what room was I usually in?

Kane. Sometimes in one room, and sometimes in another.

Prisoner. At what time was I there?

Kane. At night.

Prisoner. What habit have you seen me wear?

Kane. A black coat, yellowish surtout, and sometimes a light coloured close-bodied cape coat.

Prisoner. What did I offer in order to induce you to become a Roman catholic?

Kane. Forgiveness of all my sins past, and what I should do in this case; and I said to you, what a fine thing it is to be of such a religion, when a priest can forgive sins, and send one to Heaven.

Mr. Chambers. Call Sarah Hughson.

Prisoner. I except against her being sworn, for she has been convicted, and received sentence of death for being concerned in this conspirarcy, and therefore cannot be a witness.

Attorney General. But Mr. Ury, she has received his majesty's most gracious pardon, which she has pleaded in court this morning, and it has been allowed of, and therefore the law says, she is good evidence. H. Hawk, title pardon. Chap. 37, section 48.

Court. Her pardon has been pleaded and allowed, and by law she may be admitted.

Sarah Hughson sworn.

Mr. Chambers. Sarah, do you give the court and jury an account of what you know of Ury's being concerned in this conspiracy.

S. Hughson. I know him, and have often seen him at my father's, late in last fall chiefly: I have seen him there at nights in company with negroes, when they have been talking of burning the town and killing the white people. I have seen him make a ring with chalk on the floor, which he made the negroes stand round and put their left foot in, and he swore them with a cross in his hand, to burn and destroy the town, and to cut their master's and mistress's throats. He swore Bastian, Vaarck's Caesar, Auboyneau's Prince, and Walter's Quack; he swore them to keep secret, not to discover him or any body else, if they were to die for it. I have heard Ury, and the negroes, talk of burning the fort; and he said, if that did not do, they were to begin at the east end of the town, with a strong easterly wind, and that would go through the whole town. He asked me to swear to the plot, and said that I should have all my sins forgiven, if I kept all secret; and he swore me on an English book, and my parents and Peggy were by; and he swore Peggy too; and I heard him tell her, that all the sins which she had committed should be forgiven her; and he told her, that priests could forgive sins as well as God, if they would follow their directions. That he used to

[348]

christen negroes there; he christened Caesar, Quack, and other negroes, crossed them on the face, had water and other things; and he told them he would absolve them from all their sins.

Prisoner. How did I swear you?

S. Hughson. On a book: I believe it was an English book.

Prisoner. Who was present when I swore you?

S. Hughson. My parents, Peggy, Kane, and others.

Prisoner. You say I baptized several people, pray what ceremony did I use at baptizing? (r)

S. Hughson. When you baptized the negroes, you made a cross upon their faces, and sprinkled water, and you used some thing else, but I cannot tell what; and you talked in a language which I did not understand.

Prisoner. Whom did I baptize?

S. Hughson. Caesar, Prince, Bastian, Quack, Cuffee, and several other negroes. (s)

(r) Since the notes upon the extracts out of Ury's journal were made, it has been discovered, that John Ryan, whose son Timothy, Ury had registered to have been baptized by him, was an Irish servant brought hither the summer before the plot broke out, by col. Cope when he came to embark for the expedition to the West-Indies; which Ryan, it is said, is a professed Roman catholic, still residing in this city. See extracts from Ury's journal, and notes thereon, ante . . . (July 15).

(s) The behaviour of this miserable wretch was, upon this occasion, beyond expectation, composed and decent. She seemed to be touched with remorse and compunction. What came from her was delivered with all the visible marks and semblance of sincerity and truth; insomuch, that the court, jury, and many of the audience, looked upon her at this instant to be under real conviction of mind for her past offences, which was somewhat surprizing to those who were witnesses to the rest of her conduct, since her condemnation and several reprieves. Her evidence, as the reader may observe, was regular and uniform, and agreed with the account of the plot, as to the persons and things she spoke to, and was chiefly confirmed by many concurring evidences; and therefore, for once, it seems but reasonable and just to allow, that she spoke the truth. She was brought this morning to plead her pardon out of the condemned hole, where she had been confined from the time of her condemnation; and when her pardon was pleaded, she was taken from court into a room in custody of the under-sheriff, where she was to be near at hand for call upon this trial, and there she remained till wanted and was sent for: and the witnesses delivered their testimony in the order of time they are here placed, out of the hearing of each other, till each respective person had given their evidence—which is mentioned, that the reader may more particularly observe the correspondence and remarkable agreement between her evidence, Kane's and Mary

Mr. Murray (counsel for the king). If your honours please, I have a piece of evidence, which I would not offer until I have opened the nature of it; it has been hinted at by Mr. Attorney, in the opening; which is a letter from general Oglethorpe to the lieutenant governor, informing him, that a party of Indians had returned to Georgia, on the eighth of May last, from war against the Spaniards, who in an engagement with a party of Spanish horse near Augustine, had taken one of them prisoner, and had brought him to the general; that the Spaniard in his examination before the magistrates of Georgia, had given some intelligence of a villainous design of a very extraordinary nature, that the Spaniards had employed emissaries to burn all the magazines and considerable towns in the English North America, thereby to prevent the subsistence of the English fleet in the West-Indies; and that for this purpose, many priests were employed, who pretended to be physicians, dancing-masters, and other kinds of occupations; and under that pretence to endeavour to gain admittance and confidence in private families.

I only offer this by way of inducement and illustration of what is strictly evidence, and what I think by law I may; it is to shew in general, that there was a plot; (and cited some authorities out of the state trials.)

Court. Mr. Murray, you must prove that signing to be general Oglethorpe's hand.

It was proved accordingly: and so much of the letter read as relates to the present purpose; which followeth:

Frederica, in Georgia, May 16, 1741.

Sir—A party of our Indians returned the eighth instant from war against the Spaniards; they had an engagement with a party of Spanish horse, just by Augustine, and brought one of them prisoner to me: he gives me an

---

Burton's, which must be seen by every one that will be at the pains to make the comparison: and Sarah was under ground before and all the time Kane had been committed, so that there could have been no confabulation between them, nor could Mary Burton have intercourse with either, who was the first white evidence that impeached Kane, and Kane by his confession confirmed her evidence, and now all three confirm each other.

account of three Spanish sloops and a snow, privateers, who are sailed from Augustine to the northward, for the provision vessels, bound from the northward to the West-Indies, hoping thereby to supply themselves with flour, of which they are in want. Besides this account which he gave to me, he mentioned many particulars in his examination before our magistrates.

Some intelligence I had of a villainous design of a very extraordinary nature, and if true, very important, viz. that the Spaniards had employed emissaries to burn all the magazines and considerable towns in the English North-America, thereby to prevent the subsisting of the great expedition and fleet in the West-Indies: and that for this purpose, many priests were employed, who pretended to be physicians, dancing-masters, and other such kinds of occupations; and under that pretence to get admittance and confidence in families. As I could not give credit to these advices, since the thing was too horrid for any prince to order, I asked him concerning them; but he would not own he knew any thing about them.

I am, sir, your very humble servant,
James Oglethorpe.

Superscribed,
   To the honourable George Clarke, Esq.
   Lieutenant Governor of New-York (t)
Court. Mr. Murray, have you any more witnesses?
Mr. Murray. Sir, we shall rest here at present.

(t) What would make one give yet more heed to this piece of intelligence, is, a paragraph in the American newspapers, the winter before this conspiracy broke out, extracted from those of London, viz.—in the Boston Gazette, first December, South-Carolina Gazette, twenty-fifth December, and the Pennsylvania Gazette first of January, the last of which has it as taken from the London papers of the seventh of October, 1740.

In order for the reader to make the most he can of it, it is thought proper also to insert the introduction to it; the whole is said to be an extract of a letter from the Hague as followeth:—

"The Marquis de Fenelon, ambassador from France, continues to exhort the states general to make a common cause with his court for maintaining the treaty of Utrecht, in regard to the possessions of his Catholic Majesty

Court. Mr. Ury, have you any witnesses; for now is your time to produce them?

Prisoner. May it please the King's judges, and the gentlemen of the jury—It is very incongrous to reason to think that I can

---

in America: and for this purpose that their high mightinesses would join a squadron with those of his most Christian Majesty, in order to prevent the commerce in the West-Indies from being interrupted by any power whatsoever: the deputies of their high mightinesses manifested then surprize at the proposition of this ambassador, and told him, that it was not by the English that their merchants, who traffic to the West-Indies, had in the least suffered; but that it was the continual vexations and injurious treatment they had met with from the Spaniards, that they had only cause to complain of; and their high mightinesses had caused representations to be made upon this subject at the court of Spain, and had reiterated their instances, but all in vain; wherefore their high mightinesses had found it very necessary to grant the protections to their subjects and to maintain the liberty of commerce, which treaties concluded in the most solemn manner, had privileged them to do.

The states general looks with a watchful eye upon the designs of the court of France, which are, as it is positively assured, to turn the tables upon the English in America, by exciting revolts and disturbances in their possessions, and by doing every thing in its power to traverse the designs and even to distress the English."

The letter writer best knew what assurances there were concerning this matter; surely these pieces of intelligence could not arise from nothing; whenever there is much smoke, it is a necessary conclusion there must be some fire.

About the time, or soon after, we had the several fires in this city, as related in the introduction, one Luke Barrington an Irishman, a professed papist (who came to live in the county of Ulster some short time before, and set up for a school-master, and kept school at Little-Britain) being in the company with James McClaghry, Peter Mullender and several others; Mullender drank king George's health to Barrington, who taking the bason of liquor into his hand, drank king Philip's, or Philip of Spain's health; McClaghry thereupon told Barrington, it was wrong in him to drink the king of Spain's health in that company, especially as it was war with Spain, and if any would inform against him, he might be hanged on that tree, pointing to a tree near by: to' which Barrington replied, he scorned to dissemble for any body: that king Philip was his king: and if he would come over with his army, he would take up arms for him, and knock all the English on the head. Barrington stayed a day and two nights afterwards in that neighbourhood, and then left it. Of this McClaghry afterwards made oath before one of his majesty's council for this province, living near that neighbourhood, who ensued diligent inquiry to be made after Barrington, in order to apprehend him: but he was not met with at that time; though it was said, he was taken up some time afterwards, and committed to Kingston jail, and from thence made escape.

It seems this school-master came first into those parts the fall before: he

[352]

have any hand or be any way concerned in this plot, if these things be duly weighed; that after the discovery of the conspiracy and the execution of many for it, that I should act such a lunatick part if I were guilty as to continue in this city, join with Mr. Campbell, and not only so, but publicly advertise myself for teaching of grammar (v) yea further, that I should still continue even after the caution Mr. Webb gave me a week and a few days before I was taken into custody he told me Mr. Chambers told him that the eyes of this city were fixed on me, and that I was suspected to be a Roman priest and thought to be in the plot I answered my innocency would protect me I valued not what the world said; again another instance that must free me from this plot is when Mr. Campbell went to take possession of Huson's house his daughter refusing to go out and she swearing like a life guardman I took up the cause Mr. Campbell not exerting himself as I thought was proper at that time and told her if she would not go out quietly I would take another method with her for I would have no such wicked person (as she was said to be) live where I was to dwell now reason must pronounce me innocent for had I been engaged in their scheme of guilt my fears would have forced me to have acted in a very different manner rather to have soothed her and gave her liberty to stay till provided for instead of not shewing her the least countenance and further what corroborates my non knowledge of this plot is that the negro who confessed as it is said that he set fire to the fort

---

was a young man about five and twenty: he pretended to be a minister's son of the church of England, in Ireland; knew many of the Irish gentry, and could give an account of their families; he said he left his father in a pet, had travelled into Italy, and confessed to some that he turned Roman catholic there: and as the neighbourhood talked much of his being an extraordinary scholar, and of his understanding several languages, the consellor several times sent him an invitation to his house but he never went, nor did that gentleman ever see him—But it was said that some time after his arrival there, he chiefly kept company with the Irish servants, of which they have many in that part of the country, and the greatest number of them Roman catholics, and they had frequent meetings together.

So that this is a fourth instance of suspicious school-masters infesting these parts, correspondent to general Oglethorpe's letter of advice. This man, Ury the priest, Holt a dancing-master, and John Corry an Irishman, a dancing-master and professed papist.

(v) There was no name to his advertisement as he remarked.

did not mention me in all his confession doubtless he would not have neglected and passed over such a person as I am said to be namely a priest and if he was bound by any oath or oaths as he confest it shewed he thought it or them of no value and therefore would have confessed and laid open the whole scheme and all the persons he knew concerned in it but more especially the priest as it is said I am and what is still more strong for my innocency is that neither Huson his wife nor the creature that was hanged with them and all that have been put to death since did not once name me certainly gentlemen if I am a priest as you take me to be I could not be so foolish as to engage myself in so absurd a contrivance as to bind myself with a cord for negroes or what is worse profligate whites the scum of this earth superior in villany to the knights of the post to make an halter for me gentlemen as there is a great unknown and tremendous being whom we call God I never knew or saw Huson his wife or the creature that was hanged with them to my knowledge living dying or dead or the negro that is said to have fired the fort excepting in his last moments but put the case I had known Huson's and had been at his house is it to be inferred from thence that I must be acquainted with his villainy or knew his secrets and as he kept a public house which is open and free for all is it reasonable to think that all or any man being seen at Huson's must make him or them culpable or chargeable with his villainy surely no for if so sad would be the case of many gentlemen who in travelling the countries in England who have used bad houses or inns and lit into the company of highwaymen who by their garb and conversation they took for some honest country gentleman or tradesman and yet these have not been in the least suspected but I fear all this trouble of mine springs from and is grounded upon, the apprehensions of my being a Roman priest, and therefore must be a plotter some believing there can be no mischief in a country but a priest (if there) must be in it say they that in the chain of general woes the first and the last link must be tied to the priest's girdle. But gentlemen I must assure you from reading and conversation I believe no priest would hold a confederacy with negroes they are too wise too cunning to trust such sort of gentry it is not men of fortune good sense and learning they care to meddle with or entrust in such affairs as plots excepting they be men of their own kidney of their own way of thinking in religion supposing a priest could be so foolish or become so non compos mentes as to plot in short a priest a joint contriver of firing a fort a celebrater of masses a dispenser of absolutions as it is said I am so long passed by such a particular person forgotten No gentlemen you must think and believe he would have been the next person after the discovery of the plot that would have been brought on the carpet And further what is of great note is that Huson was sworn to be the whole projector and carrier on of the plot and if these witnesses knew me so well as they pretend to how came it about what reason can be assigned why they did not bring me out before what not any thing of me before I came to prison, doubtless they would have been eager to have betrayed me when the scheme was discovered, for being a priest and consequently artful and cunning they would have been afraid of my escaping. No if I had been engaged they would have soon informed thinking to have saved their own lives knowing how this government stands affected to such gentlemen, And as to the second indictment wherein—

Court. Mr. Ury, if you have any witnesses to examine, it is more proper you should do that now, and make your defense afterwards.

Prisoner. If that be the pleasure of the judges, I have several witnesses; I desire Mr. Croker may be called.

Mr. Croker called and sworn.

Prisoner. As I have lodged at your house for some time, you can best give an account of my manner of life and conversation; and pray first inform the king's judges, and the jury, if you ever saw any negroes come after me.

Croker. No, I never saw any negroes come after you.

Prisoner. Pray give an account of what you know of me.

Croker. Mr. Ury came to my house the summer before last, and stayed a week; and then returned to Burlington, and came back last November, and said he was going further; but I prevailed upon him to stay, to teach my son latin, for which I was to give him his lodging and diet. He taught Norwood's children, and col. Beekman's daughter to write and cypher. Some time ago he went to Staten-island, and preached there, and said he was paid for it: he lodged at my house from November till a little before Campbell took Hughson's house; and while he was with me, he kept pretty good hours; sometimes he came home by eight, or nine, or ten o'clock, and sometimes staid out till eleven or twelve at night. He once went to Brunswick this spring, before the fort was burnt, as I heard, or else I do not know that he lay out of my house; that once talking of negroes, I heard him say, he did not think them proper objects of salvation. He used to go up stairs sometimes, light a candle in the day time, and lock himself up in a room alone.

Attorney General. Pray, Mr. Croker, was you in town all the time he lodged at your house?

Croker. No, I have been out for a day or so.

Attorney General. Pray, Mr. Croker what hours did the prisoner usually come home at?

Croker. Sometimes sooner and sometimes later: I have known him stay out sometimes till eleven or twelve o'clock, once or twice later; I asked him why he stayed so late, and where he had been? he commonly told me he had been at Mr. Webb's and sometimes at some other private houses.

Attorney General. When did Ury come to lodge at your house, and when did he leave it?

Croker. He came to my house in November last, and left it a little before Campbell went to live at Hughson's house.

Attorney General. Have you ever heard him preach?

Croker. Yes, once, and he then said he was to preach again the next Sunday; and in his prayer before sermon, he prayed for his majesty king George, and all the royal family. (w)

Joseph Webb called for the prisoner and sworn.

Prisoner. Mr. Webb, I desire you will give an account of what you know of me.

Webb. I have known Mr. Ury since November last, I was then at work at John Croker's, at the fighting cocks, and hearing

(w) Which is beyond what any other witness says, and contrary to Ury's own pretended principles of a non juror.

him reading Latin and English, and thinking he read well, enquired of Croker who he was? he told me he was a schoolmaster lately come from Philadelphia; and from this I became acquainted with him, and I asked him if he would teach a child of mine: and he said he would, if Croker would give him liberty of coming to his house; which Croker agreed to; and I sent my child to him, and he taught him Latin; and after this I recommended him to Col. Beekman, to teach his daughter to write and cypher; and he and I growing more intimate, and I observing a poor and mean appearance in his habit, I thought his pocket might be answerable to it; and I gave him an invitation to my house, and told him he should be welcome at my table noon and night, at any time, when he saw proper; and he frequently came to my house accordingly all the winter: that he used often to stay at my house late in discoursing, sometimes on one subject, sometimes on another; and has stayed there now and then till eleven or twelve o'clock at night, and I have often gone home with him to his lodging at those hours. Mr. Ury told me he was a non juring minister; having asked him who ordained him, he answered me, the senior non juror in England: I have heard him preach, and have heard him say, such a day is my sacrament day, and he must be at sacrament.

Attorney General. Did he say he must take the sacrament, or be at sacrament, or administer the sacrament?

Webb. I cannot be sure, but I remember he said it was his sacrament day.

Attorney General. Was it Sundays or working days he said were his sacrament days?

Webb. I cannot be sure, but I think I have heard him name both.

Attorney General. Do you know any thing of his buying of wafers, or going to a confectioner's?

Webb. He asked me for a confectioner's shop, and I showed him Mr. De Brosse's, where he went along with me; and after he asked for several sorts of sweetmeats, he asked for wafers; which being shown to him, he asked Mr. De Brosse if he made wafers for the Lutheran minister, and he was told he did, but I do not

[357]

remember that he bought any of them: I have heard him pray and preach several times, but do not remember that ever I heard him pray for king George, but in general terms for the king. I am by trade a carpenter, and Ury applied to me to make him up something in Hughson's house, which I have heard since called an altar; that Ury gave me directions for making it, and said it was a place to lay books on to read, or to put a candle or a bottle and glass on, or other such like common uses; it was two pieces of board, which formed a triangle, and was raised against the wall, at the bottom of which was a shelf; on each side there was a place to hold a candle.

Attorney General. Do you think if a man wanted a shelf or other place to lay a book on to read, or set a bottle or glass on, he would make it in that form?

Webb. I can't say; people may have odd humours, but I should not.

Attorney General. Do you know any thing of Ury's being imprisoned in England?

Webb. Ury did tell me that he was imprisoned in England: for he said he had wrote a book there, and that the critics laid hold of it, picked a hole in it, and construed it treason; but if it was, he said, it was contrary to his intentions.

Attorney General. Mr. Webb, in your conversations together, what have you heard him say about negroes?

Webb. We were one day talking about negroes, and I said I thought they had souls to be saved or lost as well as other people: Ury said he thought they were not proper objects of salvation; I replied, what would you do with them then; what, would you damn them all? No, says he, leave them to that Great Being that has made them, he knows best what to do with them; says he, they are of a slavish nature, it is the nature of them to be slaves, give them learning, do them all the good you can, and put them beyond the condition of slaves, and in return, they will cut your throats.

Court. Mr. Ury, would you ask this witness any more questions?

Prisoner. No, sir, I have nothing more to ask.

Court. Have you any more witnesses?

Prisoner. Yes sir, I have some more, I desire that John Campbell and Mrs. Campbell may be called.

John Campbell and his wife sworn.

Prisoner. Mr. Campbell, did you ever see me at Hughson's house before I went there with you, and what passed there?

John Campbell. I never saw him there till I went to take possession of the house at May day last, and then as we were going there together, he said he did not know the way thither, and when we came down, he took Gerardus Comfort's house for it; as for any thing else, I know nothing more of him, for I took him for a grave, sober, honest man.

Prisoner. Mrs. Campbell, will you please to give an account of what you know of me, and what passed between Sarah Hughson and me, when we went to take possession of the house.

A. Campbell. I went with my husband and Mr. Ury, on May day last, to Hughson's, to take possession of the house, and when we came there, Sarah Hughson the daughter was in possession, and we told her she must go out of the house, for that my husband had taken it; whereupon Sarah Hughson swore and cursed at me; Mr. Ury said to her, how dare you talk so impertinently and saucily to an old woman, you impudent hussey! go out of the house, or I will turn you out; Sarah then swore miserably, and said you have a house now, but shall not have one long. I have often heard him pray and sing psalms, and he prayed by a sick woman; I never saw any harm by him; my husband and he were to keep school together.

Court. Will you ask them any more questions?

Prisoner. No sir, I have nothing more.

Attorney General. If your honours please, as the prisoner has been endeavouring to prove he is not a Romish priest, and has already insisted on it as a part of his defence; I shall beg leave to examine a witness or two to that point.

Court. Call them then, Mr. Attorney.

Joseph Hildreth, school master, and Richard Norwood, called and sworn.

Attorney General. Mr. Hildreth, will you give an account of

[359]

what you know of the prisoner, how you became acquainted with him, and what has passed between him and you in conversation from time to time.

Hildreth. What I have to say, sir, I have committed to writing. (and produced a paper from his pocket.)

Chief Justice. You must not read the paper, but you may look into it to refresh your memory.

Hildreth. The way I came to hear of, or know this Mr. Ury, was, that last winter some time in February, I happened to be in company with a friend at Mr. Croker's, and Mr. Webb, joiner, called me aside and asked me what school I had and if I would incline to take a partner, one very well versed in the English, Latin and Greek tongues? I answered what school I had I could very well manage myself, I had no inclination for a partner at all: he said he was a good sober sort of a man, and understood his business very well; and if we could agree, he did not doubt but it would do very well; I answered him I inclined to be master of my own school alone, though it was not so large as if I had a partner. He seeing I had no inclination for him, did not tell me who he was.

Some time after, about seven or eight weeks, I had a little business on board captain Griffiths, where I met with him and Webb in company, which was the first time I ever spoke to him, then after our salutation of each other, he began to ask me some questions concerning my school and method of teaching; after which we stepped in at Baker's and took a serious glass together; at which time he took a small book out of his pocket (English and Latin) and construed (I think) the 117th psalm; then laying the book on the table, I took it up, and was going to look on the title page, but he directly seized it out of my hands, and told me I must not look into it, and put it into his pocket.

Another time at my school, I had some discourse with him concerning Mr. Whitefield's letter in answer to Mr. Wesley's sermon on free-grace, which letter he did not approve of at all, and told me he believed it was through the great encouragement the negroes had received from Mr. Whitefield, we had all the disturbance, and that he believed Mr. Whitefield was more of a Roman than any thing else, and he believed he came abroad

with no good design. Then I asked him what was the signification of a non-juror, as I understood he pretended to be? and he
answered those that would not take the oath of allegiance, as he
did not; I asked him why? says he can you swear one to be a bas-
tard? no; no more can they say king J—— was one; and the difference between we non-jurors and others, in this; we in the
prayers for the king and royal family, mention no names, as they
do; I asked him if they prayed for the pretender? he said, for
him, let him be who he will, that was the king, he mentioned no
names.

At another time, says he, you talk so much against popery, I
believe though you speak so much against it, you will find you
have (or I think will have) a pope in your belly, for says he the
absolution of the church of Rome is not half so bad as that of
the church of England at the visitation of the sick: but says I, I
don't approve of their confessing to priests, etc. says I there is a
deal of wickedness and deceit in it: says he, no, no, for when any
person makes confessions the priest does not know who they be,
for he does not so much as see them, but only hears and ab-
solves them: Then says I, I was mistaken. Oh! says he, they
speak against the church of Rome, but don't know them; their
priests says he, are the most learned of men; the articles of the
church of England were made in distracted times. And I
observed several times he said, we priests. Says he, your Roman
priests will make you believe, and prove by the plain rules of
grammar, that black is white, and white black, and that the
wafer and wine is the real body and blood of Christ.

We were often in company, but the best part of our discourse
was upon salvation by faith alone, which he would not allow,
nor predestination; and he told me he really believed the moon
to be an inhabited planet, and all the stars were inhabited; or
else says he, I would not repeat that part of the nicene creed, be-
gotten of his father before all worlds; and says he, many texts of
scripture confirm it to be so.

I was several times since in his company, but do not remember any thing in particular relating to priests, etc. but the last
time I had any thing of discourse was about two days before I
heard him preach, and then in his room; I seeing the altar placed

in the corner, I asked him what use that was for? first he said only to lay books on, or for a candle to sit and read by; but I told him I could not think it, for I supposed it for the sacrament by its form and odd colour; I begged him to let me know what it was; so after some time he seriously told me it was for the sacrament; and he told me, I think, every saint's day it was exposed, only covered with a piece of white linen, and that he administered on some proper days; and he told me they received the wafer instead of bread, and white instead of red wine: I asked, why the wafer? because, says he, the wafer is more pure; and no bread he thought pure enough to represent the body of our Lord; then going to his small box, says he I will get a piece and you shall taste it if you will, and he brought me a piece, and I took and eat it.

I think he told me, that some time before he had baptized a child in the house, but they used more ceremonies than we; and he talked as if they anointed and washed one another's feet; he told me further, that the time of the celebration, or at what time the sacrament was exposed, they had lighted candles burning to represent our Saviour as the light of the world; and when I came to hear him preach, I accordingly saw it as he told me; for he told me before, that if I came on Sunday evening to hear him, I could see it, for the sacrament was on the altar, covered with a white linen cloth, and there were three candles burning, but not a minute after I came in, he put out the candles, and put his sacrament in his box, and locked them up.

Some time after I became thus acquainted with him, I was informed he kept a private meeting, and made use of the church form of prayer every Sunday evening, at the house of Mr. John Campbell, in his own hired room.

My curiosity led me the next Sunday evening to go and hear him preach, but when I came there he told me he did not make a practice of preaching to any others but those of his own society, and those of his society did not make any practice of running to any of our churches or meetings, for he did not approve of any such thing; and as he was a non-jured minister, so he had a society and members of his own.

Afterwards he told me he had some company from Philadelphia (I think) and desired to be excused; but next Sunday evening, if I would call, he would be glad to see me.

The next Sunday evening I accordingly went, and heard him discourse upon the second chapter of the second epistle of St. Peter, the 1st, 2d and 3d verses; and before he dismissed us, he told us he would preach the next Wednesday following (being the day his majesty began his happy reign) upon the 16th chapter of Matthew, the 18th and 19th verses, adjoining to them the words of our Lord to his disciples, whose soever sins ye remit, they are remitted unto them, and whose soever sins ye retain, they are retained: which discourse I did not hear.

Council. Mr. Ury, would you ask this witness any question?

Prisoner. No sir, I have nothing to ask him.

Attorney General. Mr. Norwood, will you give the court and jury an account of what you know of the prisoner at the bar?

Norwood. I became acquainted with him last fall, and I agreed with him in December to teach my children to write and read; that several times in conversation with him, he talked in such a manner that I suspected him to be a popish priest. He used very often to miss coming to teach my children at the school time, and made frivolous excuses, and at last I was very angry with him and discharged him; that in the evening he used very often to pretend that he must go to pray by a sick persons by the English church, that belonged to his society, or that he must go and pray with his society by the English church: (x) whereupon I once asked him to let me go along with him, but he refused me, and said it was not proper for any one to go there who were not of the society, which occasioned a jealousy in me, and I had often a mind to have dogged him, to have seen where he went, and do not know how it happened, but I never did; that one day I met Campbell, the school master, in the street, who said to me, what do you think? Webb has taken away his son from me, and has put him in a school master that lodges at Croker's; and Campbell said, d——n him, he is a popish priest;

(x) Hughson's was near by it.

[363]

and at last having a bad opinion of him, I discharged him, lest he should inveigle my children, and I told him I would have nothing more to say to him.

Court. Mr. Ury, would you ask this witness any thing?

Prisoner. No sir.

Mr. Murray. May it please your honours, and you, gentlemen of the jury.

That the prisoner is a Romish emissary, sent according to the intimation in general Oglethorpe's letter, I think must be concluded from what has been given in evidence against him; and from the known principles of the Romish religion, it may be judged what inducement the prisoner had to undertake so wicked and diabolical a project. The letter of general Oglethorpe has been offered by way of inducement, and in aid of other evidence in general, to show that there was a plot, and herein I apprehend we are justified by the precedents and authorities in law before cited.

Mr. Smith, addressing himself to the court, proceeded as followeth.

Before the prisoner enters upon his defence, we conceive it will be proper to read to him some passages out of the sundry books that declare the customs and usages of the church of Rome. To which his practices among us, as declared by the witnesses, hear some conformity; and unless he can make it appear that his practices are warranted by the usage of any other church, we conceive they will convince every body that he is a priest of the Roman church, and no other.

And first, as to the use of salt—Peter de Moulin, in his book entitled, Anatomie de la Messe, part 2, p. 94, gives us the form of the priests exorcising salt, in order to prepare it for their superstitious uses, in the following words; which, because the prisoner professes himself a scholar, I shall first read in the original, and then render it into English.

Exorciso te, creatura salis, per Deum vivum, per Deum verum, per Deum sanctum, per Deum qui te per Elisaeum prophetam, in aquam-mitti jussit, ut sanaretur sterilitas aquae; ut efficiaris sal exsorcisatus, in salutem credentium, ut sis omnibus te sumentibus, sanitas animae et corporis, et effugiat atque discedat ab eo loco quo aspersus fueris, omnis phantasia et nequitia, vel versutia diabolicae fraudis omnisque spiritus in mundus adjuratus, per eum qui venturus est judicare vivos et mortuos et seculum per ignem. Amen.

In English thus—Creature of salt, I exorcise thee by the living God, by the true God, by the holy God, by the God who commanded thee to be put into the water by Elisha the prophet, that the barrenness of the water might be healed; that thou mayest become salt exorcised, for the salvation of them that believe; that thou mayest be to all who take thee health of soul and body, and that from the place where thou art sprinkled, may fly and depart every apparition and wickedness or craftiness of diabolical fraud, and every unclean spirit adjured by him who will come to judge the quick and the dead, and the world by fire. Amen.

As to the popish use of salt in baptism, we have a most authentic testimony in their catechism, edited by the decree of the council of Trent, in chapter 9, De Baptisimi Sacramento.

The 66th question is—Cur ejus qui baptizatur, ori sal admoveatur?

Responsio—Accedunt ad exorcismum aliae, ceremoniae, quarum singulae ut quae mysticae sint propriam, atq; illustrem significationem habent, nam cum sal in illius os qui ad baptismum adducendus est, inseritur hoc significari perspicuum est, cum fidei Doctrina et Gratiae dono consequaturum esse, ut a peccatorum putredine liberetur, saporemque bonorum operum percipiat, et divinae sapientae pabulo delectetur.

In English thus—Q.66. Why is salt put to the mouth of the person that is baptized?

Answer. There are other ceremonies added to exorcism, of which some being mystical, have a proper and remarkable signification; for which salt is put in the mouth of him who is to be brought to baptism, it is clear that this is signified, that he shall obtain by the doctrine of faith and gift of grace, a freedom from the corruption of his sins, partake of the savour of good works, and be delighted with the food of divine wisdom.

As to the point of absolution—We have the Jesuits' doctrine concerning it at large, in a book, entitled, Les Provinciales, ou Lettres ecrites par Louis Montalte, a un provincial de ses amis et au R.R.P.P. Jesuits sur la Morale a la politique des ces Peres. Tom.2, lettre 10. I shall only cite one or two passages from this letter page 50, which quotes Le P. Bauni, q.15, in these words:

On peut absoudre celai qui avoue, que l'esperance detre absous l'a porte a pecher, avec plus de facilite qu' il n'eut fait, sans cette esperance.

"Et le P. Caussin defendant cette proposition dit.p.211, de sa Resp. a la Theol. mor. que si elle n' etoit veritable, l' usage de la confession seroit interdit a la plu'part du monde et qu' il n' y auroit plus d'autre remede aux pecheurs qu' une branche d' arbre et une corde."

In English thus—A man may be absolved, says father Bauni, who confesses that the hope of absolution encouraged him to commit sin with the greater ease, which he had not done with out such hope. And father Caussin defending this proposition, says, that if this was not true, the use of confession would be forbidden to the greatest part of the world; and sinners would have no other remedy left but the limb of a tree and an halter.

This is the doctrine of the church of Rome, contrary to that of St. Paul, who says, shall we continue in sin that grace may abound? God forbid.

May it please your honours, this is all that we shall mention at present, that if the prisoner pleases, he may take notice of them in his defence, and shew if he can, that he had another warrant than the church of Rome, for the like practices proved by the witnesses.

Court. Mr. Ury, now is the time for you to make your defence.

Prisoner. May it please the king's judges, and the gentlemen of the jury.

(Here the prisoner read over again that part of his speech which is set forth before, and then proceeded as followeth.)

And as to the second indictment wherein I stand charged with being an ecclesiastic person made by authority from the See of Rome that I have celebrated masses given absolutions and that I have acknowledged myself to be a priest of the Church of Rome all which cannot is not proved. As to my professing myself to be an ecclesiastic of the church of Rome is very improbable if it be considered that no gentlemen who is a priest would be so childish as to tell any person out of communion that he is a priest there must be as I have been informed very good proof that a person is a Roman catholic before a priest will have any thing to say to him and that proof consists in the persons producing a regular certificate from their last confessor and as to my celebrating of masses it is very unlikely if it be considered that if the evidences saw me celebrating of masses they must have seen more, seeing there can be no mass without two at the altar, and by the priest's breviary and directory for celebrating of high mass three priests two officials and at some masses four officials twelve a clock. As to absolution it is well known by the learned that the sacrament of penance must precede which if the evidences are asked what it means I believe they can give no account of   It is not persons professing themselves Roman catholics by going to mass or being brought up in that way that have any thing to say to a priest and as to those who were not born within the pale of that church if not learned that know any thing of her doctrines or worship much less to converse with priests as priests nay before they can partake of any privileges of that church they must be rebaptized and inducted   Now how come these persons to know so much, to be acquainted with priests and their secrets who know not what mass is nor what the difference of a vesper from a compline or a compline from a nocturn nor the hours of mass no more than we were swallows shelter in the winter, but by conjecture; as to my books and writings I cannot be deemed a Roman catholic either a spiritual person or laick I believe it cannot with reason be concluded that a person having a mass book in possession must therefore be a papist. If so a man having the alcoran must be a Mahometan and a presbyterian

with a common prayer must from thence be a churchman but I
believe that will not be allowed by any—The written book was
transcribed from the secret history of Europe and after some remarks I told colonel Beekman it was a very insipid thing and
that if a priest wrote it he was a very foolish one. But now suppose these lines are my own thought does that make me penable
when they were never exposed in print and therefore cannot be
libellous. I remember in the case of Algernoon Sidney who was
beheaded in king James II. reign for writings found in his closet
which were of his own composing and this was thought so
wicked and unreasonable an action that king William and his
parliament took of the attainder of high treason and registered it
murder. And gentlemen I believe you cannot be brought to
think that such a venerable pious and learned gentlemen as Mr.
Comyns could make such a mistake as to take a roman priest for
a non-juring minister not yet the gentleman when he recommended me to ——— as a person worthy their notice and benev-
olence which accordingly took effect for I had my passage paid
and provided for until I could get into business—gentlemen the
mistake the major part of the world lies under is their apprehending that a non-juring priest must be a popish priest whereas
there is no truer protestants for they are far from having any regard to a pretender or for setting on the throne a popish prince
to be head of a protestant church. The doctrines they assert and
stand by is non-resistance and passive obedience which is now as
vigorously maintained as ever it was in any reign. And I believe
that there is no non-juror either clergy or laity but would shew
themselves such true subjects to the present king George as to
take the oaths of allegiance and supremacy I have now no more
to say but hope and pray that what has been offered will be considered with minds unprejudiced minds prepossessed with no
opinions with minds in a diligent search after truth   You
being gentlemen I hope fearing God reverencing conscience hat-
ing partiality lovers of truth and innocency and having a tender
regard to life. (y)

(y) This and the other part of the speech, or defence, delivered by the
prisoner, being taken from his paper, which he read in court, from whose
hands it was obtained the next morning: and being wrote in the prisoner's

[368]

Mr. Smith summed up the evidence for the king, and addressing himself to the court and jury, proceeded as followeth:

Though this work of darkness, in the contrivance of a horrible plot, to burn and destroy this city, has manifested itself in many blazing effects, to the terror and amazement of us all; yet the secret springs of this mischief lay long concealed: this destructive scene has opened by slow degrees: but now, gentlemen, we have at length great reason to conclude, that it took its rise from a foreign influence; and that it originally depended upon causes, that we ourselves little thought of, and which, perhaps, very few of the inferior and subordinate agents were intimately acquainted with.

The monstrous wickedness of this plot would probably among strangers impeach its credit; but if it be considered as the contrivance of the public enemy, and the inhuman dictate of a bloody religion, the wonder ceases.

What more cruel and unnatural can be conceived, than what Rome had contrived; yea what more savage and barbarous, than what popery has attempted, and sometimes executed, for the extirpation of that which the papists call heresy? We need not go so far from home as the vallies of Piedmont, nor rake into the ashes of the ancient Waldenses and Albigenses, for tragical instances of popish cruelty. We need not remind you of the massacre at Paris, nor the later desolations in France, nor mention the horrible slaughters of the duke d'Alva, in the Low Countries. We need not recount the many millions of lives, that in remote countries, and different ages, have been sacrificed to the Roman idol; nor measure out to you that ocean of foreign blood with which the scarlet whore hath made herself perpetually drunk.

No, gentlemen, the histories of our native country will

---

own hand, without stops or pointing, he apologized therefor to the person he delivered it to, and as there were none in the original, the compiler would not risk altering the sense by printing it with any: though it may be remarked, that those who were somewhat acquainted with the man, were of opinion, he was not very capable of making them.

give us a formidable idea of popery; and inform us of the detestable principles of that religion: witness the blood of our own martyrs (who perished in prisons and at the stake) without beginning higher than my lord Cobham, and recounting their number down to the end of queen Mary's reign.

Witness that excerable design to blow up king, lords, and commons, in the gunpowder treason, contrived by the popists: that intestine fire that broke out in the late unnatural civil war, the coals whereof were blown up by them. The bloody massacre of many thousands of protestants by the Irish papists about the same time: the restless spirit of that party, which has broke out in plots in almost every reign since the reformation. The arbitrary and illegal measures that proceeded the glorious revolution; and the unnatural rebellion within our memory: these are all evidences of the destructive tendency of that bloody religion, which, in order to promote its interests, never boggles at the vilest means, can sanctify the most execrable villanies; and to encourage its votaries, will cannonize for saints a Guy Faux and others, some of the greatest monsters of iniquity that ever trod upon the face of the earth!

Gentlemen, if the evidence you have heard is sufficient to produce a general conviction that the late fires in this city, and the murderous design against its inhabitants, are the effects of a Spanish and popish plot, then the mystery of this iniquity, which has so much puzzled us, in unveiled, and our admiration ceases: all the mischiefs we have suffered or been threatened with, are but a sprout from that evil root, a small stream from that overflowing fountain of destruction, that has often deluged the earth with slaughter and blood, and spread ruin and desolation far and wide.

We need not wonder to see a popish priest at this bar, as a prime incendiary; nor think it strange that an Englishman of that religion and character should be concerned in so detestable a design. What can be expected from those that profess a religion that is at war with God and man; not only with the truths of the Holy Scriptures, but also with common sense and reason; and is destructive of all the kind and tender sensations of human nature? When a man, contrary to the evidence of his senses, can believe the absurd doctrine of transubstantiation; can give up his reason to a blind obedience and an implicit faith; can be persuaded to believe that the most unnatural crimes, such as treason and murder, when done in obedience to the pope, or for the service of the holy church, by rooting out what they call heresy, will merit heaven: I say, when a man has imbibed such principles as these, he can easily divest himself of every thing that is human but his shape, he is capable of any villainy, even as bad as that which is charged on the prisoner at the bar.

(Thence Mr. Smith proceeded to observe on the several parts of the indictment, that were necessary to be proved, in order to convict the prisoner; particularly, that Quack did burn his majesty's house in the fort; that the prisoner did counsel, abet, procure and encourage the said negro to commit that felony. He observed, that the three witnesses, Mary Burton, William Kane and Sarah Hughson, had fully proved the fact. He reminded the jury of the caution that the court had taken in favour of the prisoner, so that none of the three witnesses had heard the testimony which was given by those which had been examined before them; the particulars of which evidence is before mentioned, and the observations thereon, are here omitted for brevity sake.)
And then concluded—

Thus, gentlemen, nothing remains to be considered but the credit of the witnesses. Indeed two of them have been concerned in the plot; but we have proved them (under their present circumstances) to be legal witnesses. They all give a consistent account of the fact; and if you believe their testimony, we think you cannot avoid finding the prisoner guilty. You have heard the prisoner's defence; which, we conceive, does not affect the main parts of the accusation: he tells you that he must have been a lunatic to have stayed in town after notice, if he had been guilty: true; and in some sense he must be supposed to have been a lunatic from the time he first concerned himself in this detestable plot. Gentlemen, all wickedness is in some sort madness; and the degrees of it rise in proportion to the enormity of the crime; and when men have filled up the measure of their iniquity, and are ripe for ruin, they are commonly cut off from all the means of escaping it.

As to his rough language to Sarah Hughson at Campbell's, on which he lays some stress; this may be accounted for, as proceeding from other causes than his innocence; either from a personal resentment of a supposed injury to himself, who wanted the room she took up in that house; or perhaps with a design to make a show that he never had been acquainted with her; for priests, he tells us, are very artful and cunning. But be this how it will, we conceive it cannot amount to a disproof of the main charge against the prisoner.

As to what he alleges concerning Quack, Hughson and his wife, and the creature that died with them, not having accused him; we think very little can be inferred from thence in his favour. As to Quack, he accused many in general terms more than he particularly named; and indeed the confession that Quack made was in the hurries of death, after he was fastened to the stake. Hughson, his wife, and the creature that died with them, confessed nothing at all; therefore, nothing can be inferred from their not accusing the prisoner. It seems strange, that Mr. Ury could not give us the name of that creature that died with Hughson and his wife, seeing as Mary Burton says, he was so well acquainted with her as to have had the liberty of undressing himself in her bedroom.

As to the prisoner's appeal to God for his innocence; this we conceive witnesses nothing in his favour, but rather against him; for we often find, that the wickedest of men will attempt to cloak their villainies with the same practice, and good men are ever sparing in their appeals to heaven, even in cases where their innocence is concerned.

He says that it does not follow from his being at Hughson's that he was guilty of the plot: true; but admitting that he had used that house, his pretence to John Campbell, of not knowing it, must have been a piece of craft; and it renders the evidence of his being concerned in the wickedness carried on there, the more probable.

He says a priest is more artful and cunning than to trust negroes, if so foolish or non compos mentes as to plot; but gentlemen, this proves nothing in the prisoner's favour; for supposing a priest to be concerned in this plot, it was too extensive for him to execute it alone, and therefore he must trust part of it to such tools as he could find.

Thus gentlemen, I have replied to the principal part of the prisoner's defence, from which we conceive there appears nothing material for his justification. As to his being a Roman priest, this was only offered as an inducement to the credit of the testimony of the witnesses who were brought to prove his being an accessary to the burning of his majesty's house in the fort; and was allowed by the court to be given in evidence on this trial, upon the authorities which were produced only for this intent—That he is a priest is what he has often confessed and never denied; he has also confessed that he is a non-juring priest, and consequently bears no good will to the present government. But we have no evidence of his having confessed himself a Roman priest. That he was a reputed such, by some of his acquaintance, is clear from what William Kane has told you; that he approved of their practices, seems evident from his conversation with Mr. Hildreth.

You have doubtless, observed that before the prisoner made his defence, we read to him (in Latin) sundry passages, and one of them out of an authentic book of the Roman church, being their catechism, published by a decree of the council of Trent: these passages we translated into English, in his hearing, which shew the usages of that church to be agreeable to the practice of the prisoner in this city. We have shewn from the writings of the Jesuits the Popish doctrines concerning absolution; and to what an extent they carry that imposture and cheat upon mankind: this also has been read to the prisoner (in French) and also translated into English. We urged that the prisoner ought (if he could) to shew that he was a priest of some other communion that maintained these usages, and preached such doctrines; if not, his performing his priest's office in Latin, his baptising with salt, his use of the crucifix, his exposing the sacrament by lighted candles, his preaching upon those texts upon which the papists pretend to found the Pope's supremacy, and his declared power to forgive sins as well as God Almighty, will undoubtedly fix the brand of a Roman priest upon him. To all this the prisoner has made nothing that can be properly called a defence. He says, indeed, that there is no proof of his having confessed himself a Roman priest, nor that he has celebrated mass: he tells us also that non-jurors are not papists, that their principle is passive obedience and non-resistance; and seems willing to screen himself under that denomination.

But, gentlemen, though we have not proved that the prisoner is a Roman priest, by his own confession, or his celebration of mass; yet he has not denied that the instances proved against him, are notorious badges of popery; and such as we conceive will leave it past any reasonable doubt, that if he is a priest at all, he is a priest of the Roman church.

However, gentlemen, as I observed before, the principle point in this trial, is to prove the prisoner was an accessary to the burning of the king's house in the fort; if you find also that he is a Roman priest, then though he is guilty, as the indictment charges him, and has acted a most wicked part in the public and private mischiefs that have troubled us, yet he has acted consistent enough with the principle of that corrupt and apostate church, whereof he is a member; and all that the witnesses have declared against him, is the more easy to be believed.

Gentlemen, I shall add no more; but leave you to the direction of the court, and your own consciences, not doubting but that you will weigh the evidence which has been

[374]

produced, and give such a verdict in the present case as will be consistent with your oath and duty.

Then the chief justice charged the jury, and a constable being sworn to attend them, they withdrew; and having staid out about a quarter of an hour, returned, and found the prisoner guilty of the indictment.

SUPREME COURT.
Thursday, July 30.

Present, the chief justice, the second and third justices.

The king against Murray's Adam, Livingston's Tom, Carpenter's Tickle, Niblet's Sandy, negroes.

The prisoners having been indicted for the conspiracy, were set to the bar, and arraigned, and all of them pleaded *guilty* to the indictment.

The king against Elliston's Billy, negro.

Proclamation having been made, and none appearing to prosecute, the prisoner was discharged.

SUPREME COURT.
Saturday, August 1.

Present, the second and third justices.

Court opened and adjourned to Monday the third instant, 10 o'clock in the morning.

The king against eighteen negroes, viz.—Sleydal's Jack, Niblet's Sandy, Carpenter's Tickle, David Provost's Low, J. Brown's Jeffery, Peter Low's Sam, Murray's Jack and Adam, Wendover's Toby, Breasted's Jack, Horsefield's Caesar, Furman's Harry, Kelly's London, Thomas's York, Meyers Cohen's Windsor, Livingston's Tom, Bound's Gosport, Hyer's Tom.

The prisoners being set to the bar, pleaded his majesty's pardon; which was read and allowed of.

Court adjourned till to-morrow morning, 11 o'clock.

This day a warrant was issued for apprehending the negroes, John alias Jack, and Cambridge, belonging to Mr. Codwise, Caesar, to Israel Horsefield, and Guise alias Galie, to Timothy Horsefield, all of King's county, being charged with being concerned in the conspiracy; and they were all but Jack taken accordingly, and committed to the jail of this city.

SUPREME COURT.
Friday, July 31.

Present, the chief justice, the second and third justices.

Court opened and adjourned till to-morrow morning 11 o'clock.

SUPREME COURT.
Monday, August 3.

Present, the chief justice, the second justice.

Court adjourned till to-morrow morning 11 o'clock.

SUPREME COURT.
Tuesday, August 4.

Present, the Chief Justice, the second and third justices.

The king against John Ury alias Jury.

On motion of Mr. Attorney General, the prisoner was called up to judgment, and being set to the bar and asked whether he had aught to say in arrest thereof, why sentence of death should not be pronounced against him? he had nothing to offer; but requested the favour of the court, that they would allow him as much time as they could before his execution, for the settling his private affairs.

Then the Chief Justice (after taking notice of the heinousness of the offence of which he was convicted, the dangerous and pernicious tendency of the doctrines of the church of Rome, which emboldened her disciples to embark in the most hazardous, wicked, and inhumane enterprizes, which he illustrated from several passages cited from the works of the late archbishop Tillotson) he exhorted the criminal to make a candid and ingenuous confession of his guilt, and an ample discovery of his accomplices in this dark confederacy, and to improve the time the court would indulge him with to the best advantage, in order for his preparation for another world, whither he was soon going to give an account of his actions.

He was sentenced to be hanged next Saturday, the 15th inst.

An ordinance published for enlarging the term of sitting of this court to the first Tuesday in September next.

Court adjourned till Tuesday, the 11th inst. 11 o'clock in the morning.

SUPREME COURT.
Tuesday, August 11.

Present, the Chief Justice.

The king against Juan alias Wan, a Spanish negro.

Ordered, that Juan alias Wan, be executed according to his former sentence, on Saturday next, between the hours of 9 and 1 of the same day.

Court adjourned till to-morrow morning, 11 o'clock.

SUPREME COURT.
Wednesday, August 12.

Present, the Chief Justice.

Court opened and adjourned till Tuesday, the 18th inst. 10 o'clock in the morning.

Saturday, August 15.

This being the day appointed for the execution of John Ury, his honour the lieutenant governor, was pleased, upon the humble petition of the said Ury, to respite the same till Wednesday following.

Juan alias Wan de Sylva, the Spanish negro, condemned for the conspiracy, was this day executed according to sentence; he was neatly dressed in a white shirt, jacket, drawers, and stockings, behaved decently, prayed in Spanish, kissed a crucifix, insisting on his innocence to the last.

SUPREME COURT.
Tuesday, August 18.

Present, the Chief Justice, the second justice.

The court opened and adjourned till Thursday, the 20th inst. 11 o'clock in the morning.

SUPREME COURT.
Thursday, August 20.

Present, the Chief Justice.

Court opened and adjourned till Tuesday, the 25th inst.

SUPREME COURT.
Tuesday, August 25.

Present, the Chief Justice.

Court opened.

The king against John Ury.

The prisoner, John Ury, being set to the bar, and asked what he had to say why execution should not be awarded against him according to his former sentence? and having nothing to allege,

Ordered, that the said John Ury be executed according to the said sentence, on Saturday next, between the hours of 9 and 2 of the same day.

Court adjourned till Monday, the 31st inst.

This day John Ury was executed according to sentence. Being asked by the sheriff whether he had any speech or paper to deliver? he answered he had given one to his friend, or Webb (the person who attended him at the gallows:) he repeated somewhat of the substance of it before he was turned off: a copy of this paper was made in the jail (from one delivered by Ury himself in his own hand writing) from which the following was taken.

The Last Speech of John Ury.

Fellow Christians—I am now going to suffer a death attended with ignominy and pain; but it is the cup that my heavenly father has put into my hand, and I drink it with pleasure; it is the cross of my dear redeemer, I bear it with alacrity; knowing that all that live godly in Christ Jesus, must suffer persecution; and we must be made in some degree partakers of his sufferings before we can share in the glories of his resurrection: for he went not up to glory before he ascended Mount Calvary; did not wear the crown of glory before the crown of thorns. And I am to appear before an awful and tremendous God, a being of infinite purity and unerring justice, a God who by no means will clear the guilty, that cannot be reconciled either to sin or sinners; now this is the being at whose bar I am to stand, in the presence of this God, the possessor of heaven and earth, I lift up my hands and solemnly protest I am innocent of what is laid to my charge: I appeal to the great God for my non-knowledge of Hewson, his wife, or the creature that was hanged with them, I never saw them living, dying, or dead; nor never had I any knowledge or confederacy with white or black as to any plot; and upon the memorials of the body and blood of my dearest lord, in the creatures of bread and wine, in which I have commemorated the love of my dying lord, I protest that the witnesses are perjured; I never knew the perjured witnesses but at my trial. But for the removal of all scruples that may arise after my death, I shall give my thoughts on some points.

First—I firmly believe and attest, that it is not in the power of man to forgive sin; that it is the prerogative only of the great God to dispense pardon for sins; and that those who dare pretend to such a power, do in some degree commit that great and unpardonable sin, the sin against the Holy Spirit, because they pretend to that power which their own consciences proclaim to be a lie.

Again, I solemnly attest and believe, that a person having committed crimes that have or might have proved hurtful or destructive to the peace of society, and does not discover the whole scheme, and all the persons concerned with them, cannot obtain pardon from God: and it is not the taking any oath or oaths that ought to hinder him from confessing his guilt, and all that he knows about it; for such obligations are not only sinful, but unpardonable, if not broken: now a person firmly believing this, and knowing that an eternal state of happiness or misery depends upon the performance or non-performance of the above mentioned things, cannot, will not trifle with such important affairs.

I have not more to say by way of clearing my innocence, knowing that to a true christian unprejudiced mind, I must appear guiltless; but however, I am not very solicitous about it. I rejoice, and it is now my comfort (and that will support me and protect me from the crowd of evil spirits that I must meet with in my flight to the region of bliss assigned me) that my conscience speaks peace to me.

Indeed, it may be shocking to some serious christians, that the holy God should suffer innocence to be slain by the hands of cruel and bloody persons; (I mean the witnesses who swore against me at my trial), indeed, there may be reasons assigned for it; but, as they may be liable to objections, I decline them; and shall only say, that this is one of the dark providences of the great God, in his wise, just and good government of this lower earth.

In fine, I depart this waste, this howling wilderness, with

a mind serene, free from all malice, with a forgiving spirit, so far as the gospel of my dear and only redeemer obliges and enjoins me to, hoping and praying, that Jesus, who alone is the giver of repentance, will convince, conquer and enlighten my murderers' souls, that they may publicly confess their horrid wickedness before God and the world, so that their souls may be saved in the day of the Lord Jesus.

And now, a word of advice to you, spectators: behold me launching into eternity; seriously, solemnly view me, and ask yourselves severally, how stands the case with me? die I must: am I prepared to meet my Lord when the midnight cry is echoed forth? shall I then have the wedding garment on? Oh, sinners! trifle no longer; consider life hangs on a thread; here to-day and gone to-morrow; forsake your sins ere ye be forsaken forever: hearken, now is God awfully calling you to repent, warning you by me, his minister and prisoner, to embrace Jesus, to take, to lay hold on him for your alone saviour, in order to escape the wrath to come; no longer delay, seeing the summons may come before ye are aware, and you standing before the bar of a God who is consuming fire out of the Lord Jesus Christ, should be hurled, be doomed to that place, where their worm dies not, and their fire is never to be quenched. (z)

Note.—This copy differs from that supposed to have been printed at Philadelphia soon after Ury's execution, which perhaps might have been altered and corrected by some of his associates; as also that of his defence made at his trial, which was printed with it; for that in the foregoing trial was taken from a copy literally transcribed from one delivered in his own hand writing, without points; it was therefore printed with Ury's misspellings, and unpointed, that the reader may have a specimen of his scholarship, and from thence conjecture, whether the defence and dying speech were of his own genuine product.

The following account concerning this person, comes from a

(z) See Langhern's dying speech, State Trials, 2d volume.

gentleman who had several conversations with him between the time of his sentence and execution, who says Ury informed him,

That his father was secretary of the South Sea Company, but died when the said Ury was young.

That after the death of his father he was taken care of by a gentleman who bore the character of a non-juror: but who, he had since reason to believe, was a Jesuit.

That he was educated at two universities. But what universities they were, he did not care to tell me.

That afterwards he became a non-juring clergyman; and that the head of their society was one Dr. Clarke.

That while in this character, he was taken up and tried for writing a book against the government; of which he was found guilty: upon this account, a chapel he had of his own, and which brought him in 50 pounds sterling per annum, was seized into the hands of the government, and he himself escaped with his life only through the character and interest of his friends. Being thus reduced to difficult and disgraceful circumstances, he could not bear to stay in a place where he had once lived in honour and credit; and this occasioned his removal into America.

Says the gentleman, I had a great curiosity to know how far this account of himself was true; and he having often told me that he was intimately acquainted with a gentleman of distinguished worth and character in London, with whom I had some correspondence by letters; I wrote to that gentleman, desiring, if he knew any thing of this John Ury, that he would give me a particular account of him and his circumstances.

In answer to my request, he informed me—That John Ury's father was a secretary in the South Sea, but dismissed before the great advance of it in 1720; so that he had no share in those gains: that when he died he left his family in the utmost distress and poverty. This John Ury had been a sort of a shopboy, to carry messages, but educated to no business or profession.

His highest ambition was to be a common servant in a family. He professed great religion, went often to worship with the dissenters, but always communicated with the church of England. He never heard of his writing against the government, nor believed him capable of it, being without education: at last, being disappointed in most of his designs, he fell into distraction. From which time this gentleman heard nothing of him, till the melancholy news from America, which was about the space of three years.

SUPREME COURT.
Monday, August 31.

Present, the chief justice, the second and third justices.

The grand jury being called, and appearing, were discharged.

The king, against John Corry, dancing-master.

John Corry, impeached of the conspiracy, being placed at the bar, and no person appearing to prosecute, was discharged by proclamation.

The king, against Andrew Ryan, Edward Kelly, John Coffin, Edward Murphy, Peter Conolly, David Johnson.

The prisoners, also impeached of the conspiracy, being placed at the bar and proclamations made, and no one appearing to prosecute, they were discharged.

Court adjourned till to-morrow morning, 9 o'clock.

Evidence affecting John Corry.—Notes of Mary Burton and William Kane's examination, 13th June. William Kane's examination, No. 5, sections 3, 6.

Evidence affecting Andrew Ryan.—Mary Burton's deposition, No. 7.

Evidence affecting Edward Kelly, soldier.—William Kane's examination, No. 2, sections 10, 11. See Will (Ward's) negro's confession at his execution, upon which only Kane himself was taken up, sections 3, 4.

Evidence affecting John Coffin.—William Kane's examination, No. 2, sections 1, 3, 5, 6, 9. Sarah Hughson's examination, 8th July, section 2; 10th July, section 16. But his person exactly answered her description in her first examination. Mary Burton's deposition, No. 8, section 5. William Kane's examination, No. 5.

Evidence affecting Edward Murphey.—William Kane's examination, No. 3. Mary Burton's deposition, No. 6, 8.

Evidence affecting Peter Connolly.—William Kane's examination, No. 2, section 10.

[383]

Friday, September 4.

This day his honour the lieutenant-governor, by and with the advice of his majesty's council, issued a proclamation, commanding and directing Thursday, the 24th day of September, instant, to be set apart and observed as a day of public and general thanksgiving to Almighty God, for his late mercies vouchsafed unto us, in delivering his majesty's subjects of this province from the destruction with which they were so generally threatened by this horrible and execrable conspiracy.

Thursday, September 24.

This being the day appointed by his honour the lieutenant governor's proclamation of the 14th instant, to be observed throughout this province, as a day of public thanksgiving, for the deliverance of his majesty's subjects here from the destruction wherewith they were so generally threatened by the late execrable conspiracy; the same was decently and reverently observed accordingly.

Thomas Hughson, (father of John Hughson, executed,) and four of his sons, viz.—Richard, William, Nathaniel and Walter, having been indicted by the first grand jury, as parties concerned in the conspiracy, they still remained under confinement in Westchester county jail, and from thence petitioned the judges of the supreme court this day, as followeth:

May it please your honours,
Our being so long confined in prison, and at this season of the year, has almost reduced our families to become a public charge, and we are likely to perish should we be continued here the approaching winter.

We are innocent of the crime laid to our charge, and hope it would appear, were (we to) be tried: and we humbly pray, that if the law will admit of it, we may be delivered to bail, which we can procure, until you shall think proper to try us.

But if the law will not admit us to be bailed, rather than to suffer here, and our wives and children should perish at home, or be burthensome to their neighbours, we are willing to accept of a pardon, to prevent our being further molested on account of the indictment found against us, and to depart this province, and never to make any settlement any more therein; and we humbly pray your honours to procure the same for us, and in such manner that we may be released as soon as possible; and we remain,

Your most obedient, though distressed, humble servants, Thomas Hughson, Richard Hughson, William Hughson, Nathaniel Hughson, Walter Hughson.

Whereupon, as matters were circumstanced at this time, the judges thought proper so far to comply with the prayer of the petition, as to recommend them to his honour the lieutenant governor for a pardon, upon condition of their leaving the province. And some days afterwards they were let out upon bail, having entered into recognizance with sureties for their appearance at the supreme court on the first day of the next term.

SUPREME COURT
Wednesday, October 21.

Present, the chief justice, the third justice.

The king, against Richard Hughson, Thomas Hughson, William Hughson, Nathaniel Hughson, Walter Hughson.

The Hughsons appeared in discharge of their recognizance, and pleaded his majesty's most gracious free pardon; which was read and allowed of; and they were discharged.

The pardon was upon condition of their leaving the province by a day therein limited.

Upon the return of the vessels that had transported the negro conspirators the last summer, to various foreign parts, many particulars of intelligence concerning the conspiracy, which had dropt from those criminals in their discourse with the captains, passengers and others, were brought hither, from which there was reason to apprehend that this city and people were not yet out of danger from this hellish confederacy, which had been so wickedly and maliciously formed against both; and considering the hints the negroes gave concerning the execrable oath the conspirators had engaged themselves in, it seemed probable that the like attempts would be renewed, notwithstanding the many examples that had been made by executions, and the number of slaves sent out of the province; for the conspirators impiously looked upon the oath to be so sacred, that they thought (as no doubt they were made to believe) that the eternal welfare of their souls depended upon the strict observance and execution of it; for fear (as the cant was, both of whites and blacks) that if they should reveal it, or desist from the execution of the engagements they were laid under by it, they should wrong their own souls.

Many cabals of negroes also had been discovered in diverse parts of the country, since the execution and transportation of the conspirators, which justly caused suspicion that the same villainous scheme was yet in agitation, particularly in Queen's county, on Nassau alias Long-Island; the negroes had there formed themselves into a company about Christmas last, by way of play or diversion (as they would have had it thought) had mustered and trained with the borrowed arms and accoutrements of their masters (or we would rather suppose, surreptitiously obtained) information whereof having been given to his honour the lieutenant governor, he immediately ordered his majesty's attorney general to write to the justices of that county about it, and to expostulate with them upon the occasion, and direct them to inflict due punishment on the offenders.

And the negroes were accordingly chastised for this daring piece of insolence.

There having also been reports about the same time, of several pretended prophecies of negroes, that Charles-Town in South-Carolina, and the city of New-York, were to be burnt down on the twenty-fifth of March next; these circumstances considered, and added to what had been wrote by general Oglethorpe, as before mentioned, that the declared enemies had secretly conspired to burn down and destroy all his majesty's magazines in North America; and considering what a scene of monstrous iniquity had been discovered the last summer, tending to this detestable purpose; there seemed to be too much reason to suspect that these sort of divinations were founded upon a conspiracy still subsisting, as well as in part executed, both here and in South-Carolina.

The lieutenant governor therefore thought it necessary to put the people upon their guard, by writing circular letters to the magistrates of every city, borough and county within this government.

The following letter was sent directed to the mayor, recorder and aldermen of this city.

20th January, 1742.
Gentlemen, after the providential discovery of the late most execrable conspiracy, and the hellish and barbarous designs of a perverse and blood-thirsty people, for the ruin and destruction of the whole province and the inhabitants thereof, and that even at a time when all things were ripe for execution, and the intended desolation was so nigh at hand, one would think our signal preservation could never be forgot, and that no one could be so blind to himself and regardless of his future safety, as to suffer the negroes to have private or public meetings and caballings together; thereby giving them an opportunity of forming new designs, or another conspiracy, knowing them to be a people whom no example can reclaim, no punishment deter, or lenitives appease, yet from the many undoubted informations I have received from diverse parts of the country, the insolence of the negroes is as great, if not greater than ever, and they are not only suffered to have private, but even public meetings, in great

[387]

numbers, without the least molestation or interruption from the magistrates, and in defiance of those laws they ought to be the protectors of, and see put in due execution; thereby suffering them and themselves to be trampled on and insulted, to the endangering the peace of the province: If this practice continues, what may we not fear? for I doubt there are too many yet remaining among us who were of the late conspiracy, and though we have felled the tree, I fear it is not entirely rooted up. I must therefore require you, as you value the peace and safety of this city and province, and your own preservation; and you are hereby strictly charged and required, to see the laws against negroes duly and punctually executed, suffering no meetings of them within your city and county and several districts: and in order that the same may be more effectually done, I do hereby direct you to charge all the constables and other officers to be diligent in their duty, and that they apprehend and bring before you, or some of you, all and every one so offending; as also all such persons as shall be found to harbour negroes, confederate or consort with them, that they may be proceeded against according to law. And in order that every one may have notice hereof, I do direct, that you cause this letter to be read from time to time at your general quarter sessions; and that you give in charge to the grand juries, that they make inquiries concerning the offenders. I doubt not but you will have regard hereto, as it so highly concerns you all, and that you will take such prudent measures as may prevent any future disturbance.

I am, Gentlemen,
Your most humble servant,
GEO. CLARKE

Tuesday, February 2.

At the general quarter sessions of the peace, held this day for the city and county of New-York.

The grand jury being called and sworn, the above letter was

read; and the recorder after observing upon, and endeavouring to enforce the same by his charge, likewise recommended to them to inquire in general concerning tavern-keepers and inn-holders entertaining of negroes at their houses, as a crime of most pernicious and dangerous tendency; and having received information concerning M——— and Whitefield, two tavern-keepers, that they were much suspected of being guilty of that vile practice (notwithstanding the latter was convicted upon an indictment found against him for the like crime, and fined thereupon the last summer) the recorder gave them particularly in charge.

Hereupon the grand jury, as they were about to be discharged, reported, that they had inquired into the respective neighbourhoods of those two persons, and that they could get no sufficient information concerning this matter whereon to found an accusation against them.

But how well grounded the lieutenant governor's apprehensions were, concerning the danger which still threatened us from the conspirators remaining amongst us, may be conceived from what follows.

Monday, February 15.

This morning about six o'clock, it was providentially discovered that some fire had been put in the gutter of a shed adjoining to the house where Walter Hyer lived, next the fence of the old Dutch church-yard; the wind blowing very hard at N. and the gutter lying N. and S. some of the coals were blown into the street, which were accidentally discerned by one Hendricks, a carpenter, who was opening the window shutters of a new house he was about finishing, fronting the end of the street, in order to go to work; whereupon he immediately went to Hyer's house, and called him out of bed; and they found some live coals in the gutter next the shed towards the church-yard, and likewise a brand's end, or the bark of a brand's end, on the other side of the house next Ratsey's. The mayor being acquainted herewith, he summoned the magistrates to meet this morning at the City-

Hall, to consult what steps to take in order to discover the incendiaries; and the magistrates being accordingly met, it was proposed by one of them, as no particular person was suspected, that they should all go and view the house, and inquire what negroes were in the neighbourhood, and their characters, whereby the most suspicious might be laid hold of and examined; it was thought most likely that by this method the truth might chance to bolt out: they went accordingly, and it luckily happened that the first person's negro inquired after, was the widow Bradt's. She kept a bake-house near by, and her yard ran along the rear of Hyer's and Ratsey's houses, up to the churchyard fence, where were an heap of oyster shells lying so near Hyer's gutter, that a middle sized man might easily step up and put fire into the gutter, at the North end of it, and from the same yard as easily throw a brand's end on the other side of the house next Ratsey's: upon the inquiry, it was said that the widow Bradt had only one negro, a sort of a simple halfwitted boy, but however he was ordered to be brought forth; and he appeared upon view to be a lusty well-set fellow, of man's growth, and was afterwards judged, by those that knew him best, and had brought him into the country, to be one or two and twenty years old: his natural countenance was none of the pleasantest, but his appearance upon his occasion betokened symptoms of guilt: it was thought that Baker's servants, from the nature of their business must be up early, and have always a command of fire, which administered some colour of suspicion, which the looks of the fellow very much heightened; and therefore he was without ceremony committed, in order for examination in the afternoon, and likewise some other negroes of the neighbourhood, who were afterwards discharged.

The magistrates being met at three o'clock in the afternoon, and Tom asked, how he came to put fire to Hyer's house, and who advised and assisted him in it? he directly owned that he put the fire in the gutter himself: and being then very particularly examined, his confession was taken down in writing in the presence of the justices, and by them signed.

The confession followeth.

1. "Tom confesseth and saith, that the Sunday before last, he being in the yard of captain Jasper Farmar, a playing for pennies with Jack a negro belonging to said Farmar, a negro belonging to Samuel Dunscombe, a negro belonging to John Tudor called Peter, and a negro belonging to Charles Crooke (Rob), Jack told him (Tom) that his mistress was cross to him, he should take fire and throw it upon the shed or offdackye, (Dutch for a shed) and set them on fire; that if he the said Tom did not do it, he (Jack) would poison him: that Jack told him this in the hearing of Peter.

2. "That Jack told him if he fired the shed, that would fire the house of captain Ratsey, and his mistress's house too, and her in it: that Jack told him (Tom) that in firing the shed, that would fire the whole town, and then the negroes in town with the negroes that were to come from Long-Island, would murder the white people; and that he said this in the presence and hearing of all the negroes above mentioned.

3. "That all the negroes above mentioned said, that when the negroes came from Long-Island, they could do it all at once (that is) murder the white people; and they would assist or help in murdering of the whites, and then they would be rich like the Backarara. (b)

4. "That Jack told him (Tom) to throw fire upon the offdackye early on Monday morning come week; and that he rose very early, about five o'clock, lit a candle, made a fire in the bake-house, heated water to melt the sugar, and then took a lighted coal of fire and threw it upon the roof of the shed.

5. "That immediately after his throwing the coal of fire upon the roof, the coal in falling broke into several smaller coals; that the wind blew the sparks into the little street.

6. "That soon after he heard a knocking at Walter Hyer's door; that he was then still in his mistress's yard, and hearing the knocking, he was afraid to be discovered, and run

(b) Negro language, signifies white people.

into his mistress's bake-house, and sat himself down at the fire side; that being afraid he might be followed, he bolted the side door which leads into the yard."

Taken before the Mayor, Recorder, and several Aldermen.

Tuesday, February 16.

At a further meeting of the justices in the afternoon, the negro Tom (Mrs. Bradt's) further confessed and said,—No. 2—

1. "That being at captain Farmar's house on Sunday afternoon last, with his negro Jack, and going away, Jack followed him to the gate, and then told this Tom, that he should not forget to-morrow morning (meaning to fire the offdackye or shed) says Jack the wind blows hard now, and if it does so to-morrow morning, then you must fire the shed; but if the wind does not blow hard, then he (Tom) should not do it.

2. "That on Monday morning last, about five of the clock, Tom being up, he heard a knocking at his mistress's gate, went and opened it, and found a negro man there whose name he does not well know, unless it be Jack, who told him that Farmar's Jack had sent him to tell him (Tom) to fire the offdackye immediately. That this negro brought with him a piece of wallnut-wood bark which was on fire at one end and not on the other; and that this negro put that fire between the house of captain Ratsey and Walter Hyer's house; and that this negro ran away when the knocking was at Hyer's house, over the church-yard fence."

Taken before the Mayor, Recorder, and several Aldermen.

Thursday, February 18.

Further examination of Bradt's Tom before the justices.—No. 3 —Tom being confronted with Farmar's Jack, charged him with what he had said against him in the two former confessions, and says,

1. "That Michael, (e) Dunscomb's negro, was at Farmar's gate last Sunday, and heard Farmar's Jack tell him, Tom, to remember what he had told him the Sunday before, that is to say, to put fire to the offdackye, etc. and that Dunscomb's negro said thereupon, oh! he, why do you put such a little boy upon putting fire? oh! says Jack he is big enough.

2. "That his mistress called him up last Monday morning early, about five of the clock, to make fire, and melt sugar to make cookies, and that he put fire to the offdackye next the church-yard first; that he had fire in the tongs in one hand, and bark of nut wood on fire in the other, and the fire in the tongs he threw in the gutter next the church-yard, and threw the lighted bark afterwards on the side of Hyer's house next Ratsey's; and this he says was between five and six o'clock in the morning: the coal he had in the tongs he got out of the bake-house, the nut-wood bark he had out of the parlour.

3. "That he put this fire all alone, and nobody was with him or helped him.

4. "That there was a negro came for fire that morning, and took it, having knocked at the gate for that purpose, and then went out at the gate again, and does not know who he was."

Taken as the former.

Thursday, February 25.

The justices being met a fourth time, in order to endeavour to pry further into this mystery of inquity, by examining Tom once

(e) Dunscomb's negro was afterwards proved to have been nine miles out of town, from Saturday until Monday afternoon; so that Tom was at least mistaken as to the Sunday, which is no uncommon thing for negroes to mistake in point of time.

more; for as to what had been drawn from him hitherto one could not give entire credit, as the reader may conclude, excepting as to his being the instrument of putting the fire; and it being intimated by one of the magistrates that Tom's mistress had a strong imagination (one might venture to say a strange one) that she and her son, if the magistrates would permit their attendance, could prevail upon their negro to speak the whole truth. As there were many of us, there was difference in opinions upon this matter. However, at length it was ruled that they should be admitted, and were sent for accordingly. Upon their appearance, Tom was admonished to tell the whole truth, how it was concerning this matter; and he declared himself at first to the same purpose as to the negroes he before accused, and as to the same matter and substance with his examination before set forth; but in the close, as there was great doubt made of his veracity, being strenuously urged by some of the magistrates, and his master and mistress, to be sure that he spoke nothing but the truth, and being asked whether he was sure that what he had said as to these negroes was the truth? he thereupon recanted, and declared what he had before related concerning the negroes he had accused, were all lies; and took the whole upon himself. And being asked what he did it, and how he came to do so? he answered, he could not help doing it.

This fellow having thus prevaricated, no use could be proposed to be made of him as an evidence to convict others, however he might have chanced to change his note afterwards; and it was therefore determined to bring him upon his trial. But it may be proper to observe that in the interval between Tom's first and last examination, the negroes accused by him, were several times closely examined, both separately and face to face, but they all along positively denied every thing alleged against them by Tom concerning the fire, etc. but owned their being together at Farmar's playing at pennies; thought it could scarce be imagined that Tom (who was really no fool, nor any of the wisest) had framed this scheme, and made this attempt merely on his own bottom, which should so correspond with the villanious confederacy of the last year. His recantation was not taken down in writing, but what is above set forth contains the substance of it.

Saturday, February 27.

The justices, pursuant to the direction of an act of general assembly, issued their summons to James Alexander, esq. Mr. David Clarkson, Mr. Robert Livingston, sen. merchants, Paul Richard, esq. and Peter Van Brugh Livingston, merchant, as some of the principal freeholders within this city, thereby, summoning and requiring them to appear at the city-hall on Tuesday the second day of March next ensuing, at three of the clock in the afternoon of the same day, to hear and determine, in conjunction with the justices, whether Tom, a negro man slave, be guilty of conspiring or attempting to kill his majesty's liege people, or of burning the houses of Baffie Vanderwater, or of Andrew Bradford and Cornelia his wife, within this city, whereof he stood accused.

Tuesday, March 2.

City of New-York, ss.

At a meeting this day of the justices and five principal freeholders of this city, pursuant to the summons and directions of an act of general assembly of this colony, made in the fourth year of his present majesty's reign, entitled, an act for the more effectual preventing and punishing the conspiracy and insurrection of negro and other slaves; for the better regulating them, and for repealing the other acts therein mentioned, relating thereto.

Present, John Cruger, esq. mayor, the recorder, justices of the quorum.

William Romme, Simon Johnson, John Moore, Christopher Banker, John Pintard, John Marshall, esqrs. aldermen, and justices of the peace.

Mr. Peter Van Brugh Livingston having been summoned upon this occasion, appeared, and excused himself from serving, as not being a freeholder, and Mr. James Searle was summoned in his room, and appeared.

James Alexander, esq. Mr. David Clarkson, Mr. Robert Livingston, sen. Paul Richard, esq. Mr. James Searle, merchants, principal freeholders of this city.

Tom (d), a negro man slave brought to the bar. And William Smith, esq. having been appointed by the justice, council and prosecutor for the king, he delivered into court articles of accusation against the prisoner.

Before the articles were read, the freeholders were sworn, well and truly to try and judge as directed by the act of assembly; and the recorder warned the prisoner in favour of life, that he need not plead guilty to any of the articles, but, nevertheless, that his several confessions being read to the court, would amount to full proof, so far as they affected himself.

Then the articles were read, and were as followeth,

Tom, a negro man slave belonging to Divertie Bradt of the said city, widow, stands charged and accused,

First, For that he the said Tom, on Sunday the seventh day of February, last past, at the dock ward of this city, did conspire with Jack, a negro man slave belonging to Jasper Farmar, Michael, a negro man slave belonging to John Tudor, and Rob, a negro man slave belonging to Charles Crooke, of this city, and divers other negro slaves unknown, to kill and murder the said Divertie Bradt, Baffie Vandewater, and other his majesty's liege people within the city of New-York.

Secondly, For that he the said Tom, on Monday the fifteenth day of February last past, did wilfully put fire to and burn the shed or outhouse of Baffie Vandewater, and the house of Andrew Bradford and Cornelia his wife, in the dock ward of the same city.

Thirdly, For that he the said Tom, did on the fifteenth day of February last past, at the city and ward aforesaid, attempt to kill

(d) By this act the owners of slaves have it in their choice to try them by a jury, which is attended with some small charge; but this upon the question proposed, Mrs. Bradt declined.

and murder Divertie Bradt and Baffie Vandewater, of this city, by setting fire to their houses, and burning them in the same.

Fourthly, That he the said Tom, on the fifteenth day of February last past, at the city and ward aforesaid, did attempt to burn the outhouse of the said Divertie Bradt and the dwelling-houses of Baffie Vandewater, and Andrew Bradford and Cornelia his wife, situate in the same ward, and to burn the whole town and city of New-York.

To the first article the prisoner pleaded, not guilty. To the second, guilty. To the third, not guilty.

As the prisoner had pleaded guilty to the second article, the court were of the opinion to proceed to judgment upon that; but Mr. Smith moved, that before they proceeded, some witnesses might be sworn, and the criminal's several examinations and confessions taken by the justices, as before set forth, might be read for their further information concerning his guilt, and for the greater satisfaction of the court and audience.

And here it may not be improper to observe, that the prisoner distinguished and pleaded to the three several articles directly, without hesitation; which seems to be a further argument that he had more sense than some people were willing to allow him.

Proclamations for silence and witnesses.

Witnesses for the king sworn, Hendricks and Hyer.

Hendricks said, he discovered the fire to fall out of the gutter as he was looking from a window into the street; and that thereupon he went and knocked at Hyer's door, and called him out of bed, and they searched and found coals on each side of the house; some in the gutter next the shed, towards the church-yard, and some on the side next Ratsey's house.

Hyer said, that the gutter next the church-yard was burnt black in the spot, or part of the gutter, where he found the coals lying.

The criminal's confessions read as before set forth.

And the judges further informed the court, that the criminal at his last examination, though he at the beginning of it persisted in the same story as to his accusation of Jack (Farmar's) prompting and proposing to him to put the fire, etc. and as to the other negroes present at the two meetings at Farmar's house, advising and threatening him if he did not, etc. yet in the close he declared for truth, that all he had said relating to them, were lies, and that he put the fire of his own head; and being asked why he did it, and how he came to do so? he answered, he could not help doing it. And being asked by the court whether he did not make such confessions as had been then just read? he answered, yes. He was then bid to tell the same story over again as he had told to the justices at the three first examinations, and likewise at the first part of the fourth and last; and he repeated the same over again, as it were in the same words: and when he had done, being asked whether what he had then said as to the other negroes was true? he answered, no, it was all lies; and took all again upon himself, and owned his recantation to be the truth.

The audience being ordered to withdraw, the prisoner taken from the bar, and the court-room cleared; the recorder advised with the justices and freeholders; and having taken their opinions, which were unanimous upon that occasion, the doors were ordered to be opened, and the prisoner brought back; and being accordingly brought back, the recorder proceeded to admonition and sentence, as followeth:

You, Tom, the criminal at the bar, hearken to what is now to be said to you.

You stand convicted of wilfully putting fire to and burning the shed or outhouse of Baffie Vandewater (e) within this city. The evidence of your guilt has stood principally upon your own confession before your trial; which you now confirm by your plea: and indeed this is the strongest proof, the highest conviction that can be: for this single fact you deserve death: and though the court proceeds to give judgment against you upon this article, yet your offense is of a complicated nature, *i.e.* consists of many particulars, all tending to one and the same monstrous and execrable purpose; the murdering the inhabitants of this city.

(e) Laid in her name in the articles of accusation, being owner of the house; Walter Hyer tenant.

The hellish scheme you have engaged in, as you have confessed before the magistrates over and over again (I think no less than four several times) was, to set Walter Hyer's house on fire, and (as you concluded and proposed) that would consequently set the next house (Ratsey's) on fire, and that would set your mistress's on fire, and burn your mistress in it; and then that would burn the whole town: then the Long-Island negroes were to come over to the assistance of the negroes here; and they, in conjunction were to murder all the white people of this city: and, in order that your malicious, hellish purposes might effectually take place, the fire was to be put, as it actually was, when the wind blew hard, that in all probability, any attempts made to extinguish the flames, might be in vain.

And such a trusty agent have you been in the devil's service, that in prosecution of this infernal conspiracy, you did actually take the first step proposed, in order to accomplish this diabolical purpose, by putting fire to Hyer's house on both sides of it.

All this that I have said, you have confessed over and over again; and in this we must take your word. It was a merciful act of Providence that your designs were timely prevented, that you were committed upon suspicion only, and that thereupon the truth has thus bolted out from you.

It was rumoured without doors, that you were an half-witted fellow (boy I think they called you, though you are said to be two or three and twenty years old) and indeed one would think hardly any body but arrant fools, or mad folks, would engage in such chimerical, wicked, villanious and dangerous projects, which must most probably end in the confusion and destruction of the wretches concerned; as you found by woeful experience in the many examples of those miserable creatures of your colour that expired in flames, and at the gallows, the last summer, for the like detestable offences: and yet so hardened and stupified are ye in villainy, that no examples though ever so severe, no terrors of punishment can affright ye; but ye will even defy the gallows and commit your bodies to the flames, rather than not risk the chance of gratifying your savage, cruel, and insatiable thirst for blood.

But, nevertheless, to convince one that you are not that half-witted fellow, as some would represent you, you showed some cunning (as it should seem you thought) after your commitment, in providing for your own safety and preservation, by laying this scheme upon and accusing others, as having prompted you to this mischief, hoping thereby, as it must be supposed, to be admitted an evidence against them, and so save your own life. This was a thought too deep for a fool, or half-witted fellow: and indeed, from my observation of you, during the course of your several examinations, I could discover no reason for an insinuation, that you had less sense than those of the common rank of negroes, but that your qualifications for mischief are inferior to none of them: that you have sense enough to distinguish between good and evil; that your own conscience could direct you what was fit and proper to be done, and what not, you yourself, by your own confessions, have given most convincing proofs; for, when (as you all along said, till the last time, when you recanted and declared that what you had told concerning the other negroes was all lies, I say, as you told the story) Jack (Farmar's) in order to try whether you were fit for the undertaking, said to you, Tom, your mistress is cross to you, you must set fire to the offdackye, then that will burn Hyer's house, that will burn Ratsey's house, then that will burn your mistress's house, and burn your mistress in it: your answer to Jack upon this proposal was, No, my mistress no cross to me, my mistress good enough, what should I set fire for? you may do it yourself; or words to that effect: that thereupon Jack insisted that you should set fire, and the reason why you at last agreed to do it, was because, you said Jack threatened he would poison you if you did not. This is what we call natural reason, and shows such a measure of it, or there is such a chain of consequence drawn by it, that supposing it to be your own scheme (as you now take all upon yourself) you can be no fool, or half-witted fellow; and if it was the scheme of others proposed to yourself, your very repetition of it, your telling that story as you have done so often over and over again, almost in the same words, shows that you do not want understanding; but that you have made a very bad use of it, and acted against that light which God Almighty has given you to employ to better purposes: so that here, I say, in these instances of the very proposal and answer, you give convincing proof that you were conscious, *i.e.* that you yourself was sensible and knew, that what you was going to attempt was wrong, was wicked, and what you ought not to do: whether Jack (Farmar's) was the person that proposed the thing to you, we cannot tell; but that somebody did, and that you did not do it altogether of your own head, I am fully persuaded. But if no one but the devil and you contrived it: then so much must be drawn from it as is sufficient to show that you acted against the light of your own conscience, your own reason, by your own way of arguing, and out of your own mouth you are judged. How you came at last to withdraw your accusation against those negroes, you for four examinations running, charged with advising you, and being concerned with you, in this villainous project, I know not; nor can I account for it, without the devil had a mind to leave you in the lurch at last.

You negroes are treated here with great humanity and tenderness; ye have no hard task-masters, ye are not laden with too heavy burthens; but your work is moderate and easy: you say, your mistress no cross to you, she very good, or she good enough; and yet with small persuasion you were prevailed upon to destroy her in flames; such worthless, detestable wretches are many, it may be said most, of your complexion, that no kindnesses can oblige ye; there is such an untowardness, as it should seem, in the very nature and temper of ye, that ye grow cruel by too much indulgence: so much are ye degenerated and debased below the dignity of human species, that even the brute animals may upbraid you; for the ox knoweth his owner, and the ass his master's crib; even the very dogs also will, by their actions express their gratitude to the hand that feeds them, their thankfulness for kindnesses; they will fawn and fondle upon their masters; nay, if any one should attempt to assault them, they will defend them from injury, to the utmost of their power. Such is the fidelity of these dumb beasts; but ye, the beasts of the people, though ye are clothed and fed, and provided with all necessaries of life, without care; in requital of your benefactors, in return for blessings ye give curses, and would scatter firebrands, death and destruction around them, destroy their estates and butcher their persons. Thus monstrous is your ingratitude! But thanks be to Almighty God, that through his wondrous and merciful providence, your hellish devices are discovered, and you are now to reap the just reward for your labours.

And since justice has at last overtaken you, I shall in compassion to your poor soul, which is in the utmost, the greatest danger of being forever miserable, give you a word of advice, in order to prevail upon you to make use of those few moments you have to remain in this world, to the best advantage; for be not deceived, there is another world after this, and there is a God above who has a clear view of all your actions, and knows the very secrets of your hearts, and will require at your hands according to that degree of reason which he has given you: and though your body be consumed in the flames here on earth (a punishment of short continuance) yet your soul will never die; that must survive the body, either to be forever happy or forever miserable, according to your actions here.

What a horrible expectation must yours be then! you that would murder and destroy without mercy, nay without provocation; what reasonable hopes can you entertain of mercy from the hands of the God of justice, who will reward every man according to his words? they that have done good shall be forever happy; they that have done evil shall be cast into a sea of fire and brimstone, to be forever tormented with the devil and his accused spirits, from whence there will be no returning, no coming out again, but there will be bitter weeping and wailing, and gnashing of teeth, time without end.

Now to avoid this dreadful everlasting punishment, the only method for you to take, is to make the best use of the time allowed you between this and your execution, by bringing yourself to a due sense of your guilt, your heinous crying sins; truly to repent you of, and be heartily sorry for your wickedness, and earnestly to pray to God Almighty for forgiveness: and this is not all; but that your repentance may be sincere, you must make that little amends which is in your power, towards us you have designed, and conspired to murder and destroy, by discovering all those persons whom you know to be any ways engaged or concerned in this hellish plot, that you may thereby prevent all further mischief. Upon these conditions only can you have any reasonable or well-grounded hope or expectation of the salvation of your soul, and avoiding that dreadful eternal punishment against which I have forewarned you.

And now it were but just, that the same mischief which you intended for others should fall upon your own pate; but the court has had some regard to your confession, as you acknowledged your guilt upon your first examination, they have adjudged you to be hanged, otherwise you would have been burnt.

And therefore the sentence which I am to pronounce against you is, that etc.

The court then ordered the execution to be on Friday next between the hours of ten and one.

But his honour the lieutenant governor, by advice of his majesty's council, thought proper to reprieve him to the Friday sevennight.

Tom after this condemnation returned to his old story as to Jack (Farmar's) advising him to set fire, etc. and brought in Duyckink's Philip as joining with Jack therein, and in the threatenings to poison or kill him if he did not, but Jack and Philip were several times examined after Tom's condemnation, and confronted with him, and he charged them to their faces, but they could not be brought to a confession. Their examinations follow.

[403]

Wednesday, March 4.

Duyckink's Philip, negro, being *examined*, says,

    1. "That he was at Jack (Farmar's) on Sunday about a month ago; in the afternoon, in church time, he was going by Farmar's house to church, and Jack called him in, and he found in the yard Kingston, Tudor's Peter, Debrosse's York in the square, Bradt's Tom, called amongst them Monkey, to the number of six with Jack and himself: they all played at pennies, and the examinant lost two pence, and then went away just before church out, in order to fetch his mistress's stove from church, and left all the others in the yard.

    2. "That he never was at Jack (Farmar's) any other time, and says he did not hear any talk from any of those negroes about setting fire to the house, or the Long-Island negroes coming over to assist the New-York negroes in killing the white people.

    3. "That there was looking on upon the negroes playing at pennies, a white boy (f) Tudor's apprentice, when he came into the yard, and he left him there when he came away.

    4. "The examinant at last remembers that Mr. Marston's negro Oronoko, was also at Jack (Farmar's) at the same time."

Jack (Farmar's) though he denied it at first, now owns, that Duyckink's Philip and Marston's Oronoko, were at his mistress's in the yard one Sunday, but did not see them play at pennies, but each of them once on different Sundays; and that Oronoko came to his house frequently on a week day.

Both Philip and Oronoko own, they were playing at pennies at Jack (Farmar's) on Sunday three weeks ago.

Bradt's Tom confronted with Jack (Farmar's) and charged him with telling him, that Philip said, he (Tom) should put the

(f) Abraham. He was examined, and said the several negroes mentioned by Tom were at Farmar's, but he heard no such talk amongst them relating to the conspiracy.

[404]

fire; that Philip was by and heard Jack tell him so, and said if he did not he would lick him; and Farmar's Jack said he would poison him if he did not. Tom was likewise at the same time confronted with Philip, and declared to the same purpose to his face.

Saturday, March 15.

The negro Tom was executed. At the gallows he declared, that now he was sure he must die, he would tell the truth, and said that Farmar's Jack, Duyckink's Philip, William Gilbert's Cuffee, and David Van Horne's Corah, were the persons that put him upon setting the fire.

Immediately after Tom's execution, Cuffee, Corah and Philip, were apprehended and strictly examined by the mayor and recorder, but nothing could be got out of them.

Monday, March 15.

A tanner's barkhouse, belonging to one Stevens' was set on fire, in the swamp at the east end of this city, the wind blowing exceeding hard at N. W. The alarm of fire was between 12 and 1 o'clock, which put the people into great consternation; but the tan pit being detached some distance from any dwelling houses, it did no other damage than the burning a few wooden work and bark houses belonging to the tanners there.

Upon inquiry it was found, that two of Stevens' negroes, Sam and Tom, and also his white servant boy, John, had been at work there in the morning, and it being cold, they had made some fire under the window near the work-house, and had inclosed the fire on both sides with two doors or boards, to prevent the eddy wind from blowing the fire about.

At 12 o'clock these servants all left off work, in order to go home to dinner. Negro Sam sends Tom to fetch tea-water at a little distance from the place where they had been at work, and afterwards sends the white boy after him, and Sam undertakes to put out the fire and fasten the doors of the bark house and stable; which done, and Tom and the white boy returned with tea-water, they all go home together to dinner, and towards 1 o'clock this fire was discovered.

The bark house was a new close boarded building, adjoining to a stable and mill house, on the side of the yard opposite to the work house, under the side of which the fire was made by the servants in the yard, and the bark house was at the end of those buildings first mentioned, farthest out of the course of the wind; so that it was most improbable that any coals could have blown thither; and it seemed to be agreed on all hands; that the fire must have been put there on purpose.

Tuesday, March 16.

Examinations taken this day, and several other succeeding days, before the mayor, recorder, and several of the aldermen, concerning the fire at the tan yard in the swamp.

Paul Romme saith, "That being at the tan yards in Beekman's swamp, on Monday, near 1 o'clock, he heard the cracking as of cedar or boards on fire; that looking around him he soon heard the cry of fire, fire, and immediately thereupon perceived a great flame and blaze breaking through the upper part of the roof of the bark house of Mr. John Stevens; that the blaze, fire, and smoke spread in a surprizing manner, and took to the stable, mill house, etc. in a very short time; that when he came to the fire, he found there Hendrick Vandewater, a young man belonging to Dobson, etc. that he does not believe that the fire which broke out of the roof did proceed from the fire that was made in the yard at the side of the work house; believes that it was set on fire on purpose, but does not know by whom."

Hendrick Vandewater said, "That standing at his father-in-law's house with Daniel Van Dursen, he perceived a smoke go out from one of the houses at the tan yards at Beekman's swamp; upon which he desired Van Dursen to look at the place, and said he believed it was on fire; that continuing to look, he found the smoke increase, upon which he ran towards it, and

Van Dursen after him; that when he came to the bark house of John Stevens, he saw a great blaze and fire strike through the upper part of the roof; that this was near 1 o'clock yesterday afternoon; that this fire could not, as he apprehends and believes, proceed from the fire that was in the yard at the side of the work house; but believes it was set on fire by hand."

John Bass, Stevens' white boy, said "That Sam told him to go and help Tom to fill the jug (this John denied this morning, and Sam just now says, that he and Sam shut all the doors together) that when he and Tom did return with the water, they did not find Sam near the place where the fire had been, nor did they stand there with him; that he did not see Sam till he passed the work house, and then Sam stood within five yards of Mr. Bonnett's lime house."

Tom said "When he went for tea water, he left Sam and the white boy at the fire by the work house, and that it was not then put out, nor did he see it put out but that Sam said he had put it out with water; that he did not see Sam stand at the waterhole, nor did he see him till he came to the lime house of Mr. Bonnett, when he saw him stand at the little gate waiting for Tom and the white boy; that the white boy came to Tom after he had filled his jug with tea-water; that he did not stand at the side of the work-house with Sam and the white boy, after his return with the tea-water."

William Rogers said, "That on the 5th inst. being Friday, in the afternoon about 5 o'clock, being at the tan yards in Beekman's swamp, at work for Mr. Bonnett, Sam, a negro belonging to John Stevens, delivered to this Rogers, a piece of gold called a double doubleloon, which was very black, and desired him to get it changed for him into smaller money; that Rogers delivered this gold to Mr. Stevens, who took his negro up stairs and whipped him; that afterwards, being Saturday, said Sam came again to the tan yards, where finding said Rogers, Sam said, well, William, you have occasioned my master's whipping of me, who said he would whip me again, but I will be even with you for it; that said Rogers afterwards acquainted Mr. Stevens with those threatening speeches of his negro, who answered him, don't fear him, he will not hurt you, he is a harmless fellow."

Mr. Bonnett said, "That Mr. Stevens told him he would or had whipped his negro; but understood that he said he had whipped him; that the negro told him that his master had whipped him: this was touching the doubleloon spoken of by William Rogers."

Sam said, "That he shut the back door, that nobody was then with him; that he then came out at the stable door, and shut it, nobody being then with him; that at these times Tom and the white boy were gone for tea-water: that when Tom and the white boy returned, Sam stood where the fire had been, under the side of the work-house; that Tom and the white boy came to him where the fire had been, and stood a little while; that they could see that the fire was put out; that the white boy then said come Sam, let us go home: that Tom and the white boy were gone for tea-water about ten minutes; that after putting out the fire he put the shovel into the stable; that after putting out the fire, and before putting the shovel into the stable, he put the shovel into the water of one of the coops; that Tom did not ask him whether he had put out the fire, nor did he tell him that he had, and the white boy either."

This fire at the tan-pits just brought the year round to St. Patrick's day, the evening whereof the last year (as the reader may have observed from the course of the evidence) was calculated by the conspirators for burning the fort; a place, no doubt, most likely to give them the great annoyance; which, though accordingly attempted, was not however affected till the next day. Why that particular time was fixed upon, from what afterwards appeared in evidence concerning the conspiracy, was no difficult matter to conjecture: for as that was an evening of national rejoicing, according to the custom of some, it were most likely that many would then be incapacitated for giving that assistance which the nature of their duty might require, in time of extraordinary emergency; and therefore it seems to have been a principal aim of the conspirators, to attempt the destruction of the fort at all events, and at that particular time, especially as some of the soldiers themselves were proved afterwards to be of that villainous confederacy, who also knew of what consequence it

[408]

might be to their diabolical scheme, to have that place demolished; and no doubt, these miscreants were engaged and accordingly endeavoured to cheer up their innocent comrades as well as their wicked confederates to such a pitch, under colour of their national festival, as might render the former useless, and the latter desperate: for as the secrets of this infernal confederacy were afterwards unfolded, it is scarce to be doubted, that had the fire at the fort taken effect on St. Patrick's night, there would then have been a general insurrection of the negroes, and the whites their abettors; and much more mischief done, probably many persons, nay families butchered, had not the providence of God most remarkably interposed in our favour, by preventing the fires taking effect that night, as the conspirators purposed it should. (g) But the fire breaking out there the next day about noon, the buildings in the fort were all down to the ground long before night, which was the most suitable season for these assassins to act their intended tragedy; but as was observed in the introduction, a company of militia being under arms in the evening, and continuing so all night, the conspirator's hearts failed them, and thus a stop was happily put to their career, and their wicked machinations afterwards as providentially detected. But soon after the examples had been made of many of the conspirators, by executions and transportations, it seemed as if the people had almost generally composed themselves into a tranquil security; some by discrediting, others (as one would imagine) forgetting that there had been a real conspiracy; though from reiterated accounts still daily arriving by masters of vessels, to this time, of what the transported negroes had in their passages declared concerning it, there seemed too much reason to apprehend there were yet remaining among us, many of the associates in that execrable confederacy, who might yet be hardy enough to persist in the same wicked purposes, and make new attempts; and as an earnest of it, two fresh alarms we have already passed over; and had but the last taken effect, when a strong wind favoured the design, perhaps St. Patrick's day

(g) See negro Quack's confession, section 3. McDonald's evidence.

[409]

might have been an anniversary in our calendar, to have been commemorated by the colony with fasting, weeping and mourning.

But notwithstanding those signal providential disappointments, neither did the malice of the conspirators subside, nor their courage abate.

Tuesday, March 23.

In the dusk of the evening, a bundle of linen, set on fire, was thrown into the gutter adjoining to Benson's brew house, at the east end of the town, and was by the wind blown out thence upon the adjoining shed; which was discovered by a neighbour accidentally coming into the yard; when it came down, as the man declared, it was like a round lighted coal, but burnt to tinder, and upon examination of it, he judged that there had been two stuffed in the middle of it.

Wednesday, March 24.

The magistrates met at the City-Hall, and sent for several of Mr. Benson's servants, and others, and examined them; but no particular person being suspected of the fact, nothing could be made of it.

Tuesday, April 20.

Being the first day of the term, the judges of the supreme court recommended it to the grand jury to inquire concerning the fire at Stevens' tan-pits; but nothing further being discovered, they did not think there was sufficient cause to present the negro Sam, upon the evidence before mentioned, but indicted him for a felony and robbery committed some time before, of which he was now impeached.

No discovery was made about the attempt at Benson's.

But the information of the transported negroes before hinted at, and these fresh instances of fires confirming them, seemed at length to gain attention, and were by many thought sufficient to awaken every one from a supine security, and put them upon their guard against these latent enemies.

Tuesday, August 3.

The daring insolence of negroes, observed by many even at this time, and the countenance and encouragement given by dram shops, was still every day complained of; and yet the difficulty was to detect them, so as to convict the aggressors: however, the magistrates thought it their duty to use all the means in their power towards bringing them to condign punishment. And therefore,

At a general quarter sessions of the peace, held this day for the city and county of New-York, before the mayor, recorder, and aldermen—

The grand jury being sworn, his honour the lieutenant governor's circular letter of the 26th January last, directed to the magistrates of the city, before set forth, being read again; the recorder proceeded to his charge as followeth:

Gentlemen of the grand jury, In order for you to pursue the good intention of his honour's letter, it is necessary that you make diligent inquiry into the economy and behaviour of all the mean ale-houses and tipling houses within this city, and to make out all such to this court, who make it a practice (and a most wicked and pernicious one it is) of entertaining negroes, and the scum and dregs of white people in conjunction; who to support such expense, are tempted and abetted to pilfer and steal, that they may debauch each other upon the plunder and spoils of their masters and neighbours: this gives opportunities for the most loose, debased and abandoned wretches amongst us to cabal and confederate together, and ripen themselves in these schools of mischief, for the execution of the most daring and detestable counterprizes; I fear there are yet (k) many of these houses amongst us, and they are the bane and pest of the city; it was such that gave the opportunity of breeding this most horrid and execrable conspiracy, the effects of which infernal combinations, his honour is thus anxious to prevent.

And notwithstanding the great pains and industry (as it should seem) has been taken to bring the notion of a plot into contempt and ridicule, by some people amongst us of phlegmatic tempers, who have endeavoured to make light of it, dozed themselves into a lethargic security, and have set at naught the evidence of their own senses; for they have seen and heard, and methinks they might have felt too: nevertheless, I shall not forbear expressing my fears and apprehensions also, that the enemy is still at work within our bowels; for surely it would be of little avail, if the same execrable and horrible scheme of villainy is still carrying on among us, and should at length break out again in flames about our ears, and proceed to the murdering and butchering our families; I say it will be of no avail for such stupid, thoughtless and incredulous folk as these to stand aghast at their dreadful conviction, and cry out, Lord! who would have thought it? it will be too late then to call upon God, when the affrontive contumacious behaviour of some among us, who spurn at the mercy of providence, our great and signal deliverance out of the jaws of our enemies; when our own irreverent, impious demeanor may have filled up the measure of our iniquities, fitted us for divine vengeance, and drawn down such a heavy and sore judgment upon us, as delivers us ever for a prey unto their evils.

Let us therefore, gentlemen, think seriously, and take better heed to these things; acknowledge the divine goodness in our deliverance and preservation hitherto, by a suitable deportment, and make proper use of the warning that has been given us, by providing for our own safety and security.

(k) Nine persons were indicted, and fined for keeping such disorderly houses.

And besides what I have already pointed out for your consideration, it will be necessary for you also, and highly becoming in you, to inquire concerning all lodgers that are strangers within this city; obscure people that have no visible way of subsistence; for that the popish emissaries have been despatched from abroad to steal in among us, under several disguises, such as dancing-masters, school-masters, physicians, and such like; whereby, as it is calculated, they may easily gain admittance into families, work under ground like a mole in the dark, and accomplish the works of the devil, and other our declared enemies; if any such obscure persons as I have hinted at, you can discover in the course of your inquiries (and that there have been such, we have had very creditable information) it is your duty to present them to the court, that they may be apprehended, and examined by the magistracy, and dealt with according to the law.

Gentlemen, I doubt not but you will remember, that you are sworn, diligently to inquire, and true presentment make of all such matters and things as shall be given you in charge.

I give his honour's letter to you in charge; and these things I have before mentioned, I give you expressly, and particularly in charge also; and persuade myself of your conscientious discharge of your duty.

In general, you are charged to present all crimes and offences which shall come to your knowledge, from treasons, down to trespasses.

Thursday, September 2.
AT A COMMON COUNCIL

Mary Burton, the evidence who detected the conspirators, having applied to the board for the reward offered by the proclamation, issued pursuant to an order of the common council of the 11th of April, 1741, promising the sum of one hundred pounds to any white person that should discover any person or persons concerned in setting fire to any dwelling houses, store-houses, or other buildings within this city: It was ordered, that the mayor should issue his warrant to the treasurer to pay to Mr. Moore, for Mary Burton's use and benefit, the sum of eighty-one pounds, which with the sum of nineteen pounds before paid by the corporation for the freedom and other necessaries to and for the use of the said Mary, made in the whole the sum of one hundred pounds, in full of the reward offered.

The mayor accordingly issued his warrant, and the money was paid to Mary Burton.

CONCLUSION.

By the course of the evidence, it appears, that a design was conceived to destroy this city by fire, and massacre the inhabitants: that fire was to be put to several quarters of the town, at one and the same time; that the English church was to be set on fire at a time when it was most likely there would be the fullest congregation, and the avenues from the church were to be guarded by these ruffians, in order to butcher those that should attempt to escape the flames; this part of the scheme, it seems, Ury, the priest, had particularly at heart. The winds were consulted which would be most proper to attempt the fires with. They were to begin at the east end of the town with a strong easterly wind, which (as it was projected) according to the course of its situation, would probably destroy the whole town; but the king's fort was first to be burnt, because most likely to annoy these furies when their hellish devices were put in execution. The negro confederates were each of them to set fire to his master's house, and proceed to the assassinating their respective masters and families; and these fires were calculated for the night. St. Patrick's night was the time appointed. Accordingly we find, as a proof that they were in earnest, the attempt upon the fort was made on St. Patrick's night, though, through the providence of God, the fire did not take effect until the next day at noon, when the villain who first put it, had renewed his effort, by blowing up the same brand that he had placed for the purpose the night before. (a)

If it be considered, that many of the Irish catholics, unknown to the captains, runagates, or perhaps purposely sent out, had

(a) See the note upon Quack's confession at the stake.

been enlisted in some of the independent companies posted here, some whereof were detected of being confederated with the conspirators; they could not have pitched upon a fitter season for perpetrating their bloody purposes; for on this night, according to custom, their commemoration of their saint might be most likely to excite in those of the infernal league, boldness and resolution, for the execution of this horrible enterprize, and others innocently partaking of their jollity, might in such an event, be thereby incapacitated for service; so that, according to this device, all (it might seem probably to them) would lie at their mercy. But the fire at the fort happening in the day, contrary to the purpose of the conspirators, and the town having been much alarmed at the misfortune, though not apprehending the treachery; yet, a military watch being kept all the night following, the villains were thereat somewhat intimidated, and stopt their progress for a while: nevertheless, from the nightly cabals of the conspirators, at Hughson's, and the encouragement given by Ury the priest, the night after the fort burnt, who told them, now God had prospered them in the beginning, in burning the fort, they need not fear; we must be resolute and proceed in the work, and no doubt God will prosper us in all; execrable wretch! From hence they took courage again, and it was resolved amongst them, that they should proceed. Accordingly after one week had passed, they did, we see, set fire to several houses within the compass of a fortnight, sometimes many in a day, undiscovered; and made several other attempts, in which they were frustrated, till at length some Spanish prize negroes having been seized and committed upon suspicion, a stop was put to their career. But more than a fortnight passed after the last of these fires, before the least intimation was given touching the occasion of them, that they were the effects of a diabolical conspiracy; till Mary Burton, servant to John Hughson, was brought before the grand jury, as a witness to a different matter, concerning which she had testified before the magistrates; she at first refusing to be sworn to give her evidence in that case to the grand jury, at length rather than go to jail, submitted, but withal bolted out, that she would give no evidence concerning the fires; this hint afforded sufficient handle to the gentlemen of the grand jury, to exert their diligence in sifting out her meaning, and to prevail with her to disclose the secret; which, after much entreaty and persuasion, they effected, though at the same time, the girl disburthened herself with apparent dread and great unwillingness, from the apprehension of the danger she should be in of being murdered by the conspirators for the discovery, as she afterwards declared.

By the evidence of this girl, it appears, that her master Hughson was a principal engine, agent and instigator of these deeds of darkness amongst the slaves here, ever since she came into his service; and by the evidence of others, whites and blacks, it also appears, that he having kept a public house for some years, had long since made it a practice to entertain numbers of negroes, often 20, 30, 40, or 50 at a time, and by degrees deluded them to engage in the conspiracy, upon his promises that they should all be freemen, and that other fine things should be done for them; that upon their consenting, Hughson always bound them to their engagements by horrible oaths, not only to perform what they undertook to do, viz.—to burn and massacre, but also to keep all secret, though they were to die for it; that these oaths were reiterated at all future meetings, in order to confirm them; and for their encouragement, Hughson often swore himself over again, and had sworn his wife and daughter into the confederacy also. That Hughson provided arms and gunpowder, further to convince these deluded wretches how much he was in earnest; but the butchery to be executed by the negroes after they had set fire to their master's houses, was calculated to be done with knives; for those weapons, it seems, they judged would make no noise: this the whole current of negro evidence agrees in, and it is corroborated by whites. That a knife designed for this purpose was actually found in the chest of one of the negro conspirators, and most others of them were provided with knives.

That Hughson employed some of the head negroes as agents under him, to decoy other negroes, and their instructions were, not to open the conspiracy to any but those that were of their own country (as they are brought from different parts of Africa, and might be supposed best to know the temper and disposition of each other) and when they brought a convert to Hughson, or one likely to become such, Hughson always gave them drams till they were intoxicated, and then the conspiracy was proposed to them; and they generally consented without much difficulty, upon his specious promises, and sometimes upon the bare proposal; but if they were unwilling to engage, they were terrified by threats of being murdered, till they complied; then all such were constantly sworn, invited to Hughson's feasts, and these commissioned to seduce others. Many, before they knew any thing of the secret, were invited to Hughson's by himself or others: for, by way of introduction, as well as confirmation, Hughson, it seems, kept open house for the negroes, and entertained them at all times, those that had no money at free cost; he assured them, they should be always welcome to him: these compliments he artfully placed as he judged most proper; for as to such as were his special agents and dexterous fellows, they were to pay in money if they had it, or money's worth, by pilfering and stealing as they could, to raise supplies for carrying on the common cause; and they were to bring all to him: more especially upon the grand catastrophe, when the town should be all in flames, and the negroes had butchered their respective families, the most valuable things easiest to be removed (particularly plate) were to be brought to Hughson's, and it seems they had already carried on so successful a trade, and Hughson's house was become a mart of so great note amongst the negroes, that with them it had obtained the name of Oswego, after the province trading-house. They were likewise enjoined to steal their master's arms, powder, etc. and lodge all in Hughson's custody: he had many barrels of gunpowder at a time. It appears that this hellish project was set on foot here, by agent Hughson, four or five years before it was ripened for execution; and it must needs have been a work of time to seduce so many slaves as have been detected.

The white conspirators were sworn by Ury the priest in chief, and the negroes sometimes by Hughson, and sometimes by Ury in a ring surrounded by them, and he, while the oath administering, holding a crucifix over their heads. They were persuaded that the French and Spaniards were soon to come and join them; and if they did not come in a set time, they were to begin and do all themselves. Further to encourage the town negroes, they were told the confederates had many whites and blacks to come out of the country to their assistance, particularly from Long-Island, and Hughson was to give the word when they were to begin. The negroes were flattered they were to be formed into companies, several officers of them were named for the purpose, captains, etc. and the town was divided into districts. Thus all was to be their own; and if any of them were squeamish, Ury the priest could forgive them all they had committed, or should commit, provided they performed what they had engaged in, and kept all secret to their last breath.

But however true these matters have been found to be, so chimerical, wicked, abominable and inhuman was the device, that those at a distance might have been apt to think it all a dream, or a fiction, were it not for the last proof of a reality, which cannot be withstood, the several fires which did happen in the manner we saw; which consideration was a great motive to this publication. The witnesses, whites and blacks, that gave any evidence, or made any confession at all, agree in the most considerable article concerning it; the design of burning the town, and murdering the inhabitants; and that popish priests were concerned in it; which verified, what is sarcastically cited in Ury's defence as proverbial, that there can be no mischief in a country, but a Roman priest (if there) must be in it; but we may venture to go one step further, and say, if such priests had not been here (and some of capacities much superior to Ury's) there would have been no such plot; for upon this and no other footing can it be accounted for. Let us suppose then (and we shall find just grounds for the supposal) that such priests or monks etc. call them what you please, had conceived a design for such a horrible, detestable purpose, as the devastation of this city, and the massacre of its inhabitants, to be perpetrated by the hands of our own slaves, in conjunction with the most abandoned whites, the dregs and disgrace of their complexion; and that at a critical time, when their successful wickedness would have frustrated the supply of provisions and necessaries to his majesty's fleet, then upon an expedition against his enemies in the West-Indies, upon which perhaps their subsistence was in some measure to rely; and that for the purpose, emissaries of these kind of gentry were despatched into his majesty's colonies in several different disguises, as those of dancing-masters, school-masters, physicians, etc. who under these colourable appearances, might not be likely to gain admittance and confidence in private families, and thereby have opportunities of debauching their slaves, and acquainting themselves of such white people as might be most likely to be seduced to their detestable purposes: who then so seemingly proper instruments to be pitched upon amongst us, by such infernal agents, as John Hughson and such like? for as the way to hell must be trod by gradual steps, and no one commences consummate villain in an instant; so Hughson had already taken some hopeful degrees in the school of wickedness; he had for many years entertained negroes at his house in all hours of darkness; and to support that expense, and promote his own lucre, encouraged them to pilfer and steal what they could from their masters, and he readily received their spoils: this might be thought a promising earnest of his qualifications: sure such a one must be judged by these craftsmen, a hopeful tool to make experiments upon; for he that could consort with slaves in one kind of villainy, would probably make the less difficulty of going some steps further. But then his religion! why truly, from what has already been observed, it might be thought to little purpose to talk about that: but his wife (good woman!) was already a professed papist, as common fame has it; so the business might be near half done; for her persuasion joined to a Roman priest's assistance, artifice and dainty-fine promises, free and full remission, pardons, indulgences, and absolution for sins past, present, and to come, and a passport for heaven on the condition of performing engagements (to do the devil's business) bound with the sanction of reiterated oaths, to keep all secret to the last breath; he might perhaps (as others before him have been) be buoyed up in full expectation of becoming rich and great here, and of a fool's paradise hereafter, and thus be seduced to enter into their abominable measures.

There are some passages of history in a French author or two, which may serve to add light to our own case and are therefore thought proper to insert here.

Mr. Jurieu, in the 6th chapter of his History of Popery, (a) treating of the intrigues of the popes and papists against Elizabeth, queen of England, and William and Maurice of Nassau, princes of Orange, and the league of France, the product of popery; has the following remarkable pieces translated from the French thus,

Pope Gregory XIII, who succeeded Pious the V, (b) entered also into all the schemes and designs of his predecessor; which were to oppress the queen of England, by causing her subjects to revolt; and he had pitched upon one Stukely, an English rebel and fugitive, whom he had created a count and a marquis, and he was to go to Ireland, and cause all the papists of that island to revolt: but this Stukely perished in Africa, in that battle against the Moors (c) (where died also Sebastian, king of Portugal.) His death only put the design in suspence a little: soon after the pope sent to Ireland one James Fitz Morice, with Saunders an Irish priest, (author of the history of schism) in the quality of legate, charged with a banner consecrated by the pope, and plenty of indulgences, to solicit the Irish to revolt. Accordingly Saunders set on foot an army of rebels, who were dispersed by the first shock by the queen's troops, and this legate perished wretchedly with hunger and misery in the woods, whither he was chased with the rest of the rebels, at the head of whom he had put himself. It was about the same time, that the pope established English seminaries, one at Douay, another at Rheims, a third at Rome, and some time after a fourth at Valladolid in Spain, for an inexhaustible store of assassins, conspirators, and traitors; for it is in these seminaries that they breed up English papists in these detestable maxims, that every heretical prince is not a legal sovereign, and that people ought, when occasion offers, to do their utmost endeavour for re-

(a) Quarto edition of his works printed at Amsterdam, Anno 1683, page 352 to 354.
(b) Anno 1572.
(c) Anno 1578.

establishing the catholic religion, where it has been abolished, without sparing the life of any one whatsoever. It was out of these seminaries that they afterwards draughted those parricides, which they scattered throughout all England: for instance, one Somervil, (Anno. 1583) with Hall the priest, and other accomplices: this Somervil was found strangled in prison: which was likely to have been done by his companions, that he should not discover any thing further of the conspiracy.

Amongst these enormous popish conspiracies against the life of this queen, that which they designed to execute by William Parry, is remarkable; wherefore we will report it a little more at large: (f) We have all the pieces of his process in the first volume of the memoirs of the league: (g) In short, this William Parry being affected towards popery (which they call in the Roman stile, zeal for the catholic religion) conceived a design to assassinate the queen of England, and he opened the matter at Venice to a jesuit named father Beneditto Palmio, and to the pope's nuncio, named Campeggio; they both much approved of his design, and by their advice he wrote about it to the pope. This parricide returning to Paris, was confirmed in his intention by Thomas Morgan, and many other English papists. Hannibal Codret, a jesuit, strenuously confirmed him also, confessed him and gave him the sacrament, to fix him in this great undertaking. The pope's nuncio who was at Paris, named Ragazoni, was let into the secret, and took upon him to send William Parry's letter to the pope, whereby he requested to be authorised in this action, and that full and entire remission of his sins might be granted him. The pope answered according to his purpose as favourably as William Parry could have wished.

The cardinal Como, who had commission to answer him, wrote him in plain terms, that his holiness could not but commend and approve the good resolution he had taken for the good of his service, and that of the public; that his holiness

(f) Anno 1584–5. Rapin, 2 vol. folio, page 120.
(g) In France.

begged him to persevere; and to the end that he might be the better assisted by the good spirit, which had brought him to it, his holiness granted him full indulgence and remission of all his sins: and moreover promised him great rewards.

The same author in his 8th chapter, treating of the papist's conspiracies in England, amongst other, of those in the reigns of king Charles the 1st and 2d, and that in Ireland in the year 1642, makes general reflections upon the means made use of by the author of the apology for the catholics, to invalidate the proofs of the truth of them, and accordingly proceeds, page 400.

Neither (says he) do I find these gentlemen have said anything upon the affair of Elizabeth Oxley, Nicholas Stubb, and the priest Maurice Gifford, which however is a matter of no small importance. We find by the deposition of oaths, that the great fire of London happened by a horrible conspiracy of the priests and English papists. The deposition of Bedlow proves also, that in the year 1676, when he was at Paris, the confederates in the conspiracy, among others, a Benedictine would have engaged him to set fire to Westminster, Limehouse, and other places, and that father Gifford had joined himself in the design; in the execution whereof they had actually hired cellars in diverse parts of the city, which they filled with wood, charcoal, and all other sorts of combustibles. The story of Elizabeth Oxford, strongly confirms that deposition. (h) This Elixabeth Oxley was in service at the house of one Mr. Bird, a noted attorney in Fetter-Lane; this girl having dwelt there about six weeks, on the 10th April, 1679, when all the family were asleep, put fire in her master's cabinet, where there were a great many papers, and when she thought that the fire was got beyond extinguishing, she cried out fire, and waked her master and mistress. They happily found means to extinguish the fire; when that was done, it was discovered that this creature had made up a bundle of her own clothes, which appeared to have been packed up at leisure, in very

(h) See Rapin, Folio Vol. 2, page 705.

good order; this, added to many other circumstances, caused a suspicion that this servant had put the fire on purpose; she was sent to prison, and upon examination owned all. She said that about Michaelmas, in the year 1687, she became acquainted with one Nicholas Stubb, an English papist, who had taken a great deal of pains to pervert her and make her change her religion; when he thought he had persuaded her, to fix her and make her sensible that she had chosen the good part as well for this world as the other, he several times said to her, that she would see all the protestants in England destroyed before the end of the month of June, the next year; (i) and that all those who would turn catholics, should live much more happily than otherwise they could, if they remained protestants; that after all it was a meritorious action to kill an heretic; and that all the catholics would have a mark upon their hats to distinguish them, to the end they might not be massacred with the others. After many such like discourses, this Nicholas Stubb having learnt that she lodged at this attorney's house, had often advised her to put fire to her master's house, to burn that quarter, promising her for this action five pounds, that is to say 50 or 60 livres, and gave her half a crown earnest; he assured her also, that they would at the same time set fire in several other quarters of the town. This girl being gained by these promises, promised herself, and did all that they desired.

Upon this confession of Elizabeth Oxley, the justice caused Nicholas Stubb to be taken into custody; at first he denied all with a brazen front, but when he was confronted with the girl, he could not resist the force of the truth; he acknowledged all that Elizabeth Oxley had advanced concerning their dealings and conspiracies. He added he had done it at the persuation of father Gifford, his confessor, who assured him there was no crime in setting fire to the houses of heretics. He said further, that there were two Irishmen concerned with him, the one named Flower, a barber,

(i) See Judy Pelham's affidavit concerning Plummer.

and the other Roger Clayton; that they all three usually met in the dusk of the evening at St. James' in the fields, to consult means for putting their design into execution; and that father Gifford had promised to the accused one hundred pounds for this deed. Afterwards this Nicholas Stubb related a thousand extravagances wherewith Gifford buoyed up their hopes, and supported the promises he made them of a sudden change in England, he told them they would levy a great army in England, there were catholics enough there for that, and they would draw over a succour of sixty thousand men from foreign countries: he added, lastly, that this priest made them take horrible oaths to keep the secret, and threatened to have them murdered, if they discovered what they knew.

I own I cannot conceive what they can say to invalidate facts so important, and so well proved: here are persons taken in the fact, and persons that confess, what would you have more? There is nothing of which the hardiness and impudence of these false devotees is not capable; wherefore there is no doubt but they will desire some new cheat, and suborn fresh witnesses to support some new romance about these frequent combustions. It is a matter beyond example, that a town should be set on fire as it were every year; for since the great fire of London, scarce a year has passed but there has been a hundred fires, of two hundred and six hundred houses: one cannot be persuaded that this was natural. Before we leave this story of Elizabeth Oxley and Nicholas Stubb, I wish it may be observed, that this Nicholas Stubb, taken up upon the fact, and committed as an incendiary, confessed exactly what Bedlow had deposed concerning father Gifford, to wit, that it was he that was the instigator of these fires, that they had made preparation for.—Nicholas Stubb, the prisoner accused, convicted, confessing; could he have taken his confession from the mouth of Bedlow, whom probably he had never seen.

The author of the apology for the catholics, makes great shew of advantage, because the lord viscount Stafford, and the other conspirators who were executed, persisted to maintain their innocence to the last, and denied there had been any conspiracy; wherefore it may be proper to call to mind what Mr. Mezeray says upon the gun-powder plot, in 1606. It is customary in these conspiracies to bind the consciences of those that know these affairs, with horrible oaths. You may read in (the book entitled) *Les derniers effort de L'innocence affligee*, (k) the form of an oath which they oblige the conspirators to take.

(The following translation from the book itself, is thus introduced by way of dialogue.)

It having been objected, as an argument of great weight, that persons executed for these popish conspiracies, persisted to maintain their innocence with their last breath; the protestant lawyer answers:

I am surprised, sir, that you make such a difficulty about this obstinate silence; we see, every day, criminals who, to salve their honour, and to have the pleasure of saying they die innocent, resist the most violent tortures; and you do not conceive, that people who have hardened their courage a long while before, for an enterprize the most hazardous in the world, should have resolution to keep, till death, a secret whereon depends not only their honours, but the preservation of all the Roman catholics in England! If they confess themselves guilty, they must name their accomplices; and in doing so, they would destroy an infinite number of people, and render their religion abominable in the world, by shewing it is capable of inspiring such frightful sentiments, and to cause such frantic designs to be hatched. These considerations are of such force, that they alone are capable of supporting the weakest of men, to prevent their revealing a secret of such importance. When the powder-plot was discovered in 1605, not one of the confederates would confess; and they had known nothing from their

(k) Printed at the Hague, anno 1682. Deuxieme Entretien, 12 mo. beginning page 119.

mouths, without the industry of the judges, who placed Garnet and Hall in two dungeons from whence they could communicate, and in the thickness of the wall there was a place wherein they put two witnesses, who could hear every thing the prisoners said; by which means they were forced to own all. Lastly, would you know the principal reason why these secrets are so well guarded? It is a horrible oath wherewith they bind all those who enter into the like conspiracies. Read Mezeray, in the place where we have just left him open.

The last day of January, eight of these principal conspirators were executed at London, for high-treason. Not one of them accused either the priests or the monks; for they were engaged to secrecy by horrible oaths.

To give you full satisfaction in this matter, I will show you the form of the oath, which they administered to all those who were entered into this conspiracy.

The oath for the conspiracy in England.

I, the underwritten, being in the presence of Almighty God, and of the blessed Virgin Mary, of the blessed Michael the archangel, of the most happy St. John the baptist, of the holy apostles St. Peter and St. Paul, and of all the other saints in heaven, and of you, my spiritual father, (1) declare, from the bottom of my heart, that I believe the Pope, the vicar-general of Jesus Christ, to be the only and sole head of the church upon earth; and that by virtue of the keys, and the power given to his holiness by our Lord Jesus Christ, to bind and to loose, he hath authority to depose all heretical kings and princes, to oblige them to relinquish their thrones, or to kill them; wherefore I will defend this doctrine with all my heart, and the rights of his holiness against all sorts of usurpers, especially against him that they pretend to be king of England; because he has broken his oath made to the agents of his holiness, in not fulfilling the promise made to them for establishing in England the holy Roman catholic religion. I renounce and disavow all sort of

(1) The pious priest or confessor administering this excrable oath!

promise and submission to the said present king of England, and all obedience to his officers and inferior magistrates. And I do believe on the contrary that the protestant doctrine is heretical and damnable, and that all those who do not forsake it, are damned. I will also, with all my might, assist the agents of his holiness here in England, to extirpate and root out the said protestant doctrine, and to destroy the said pretended king of England, and all those his subjects which will not adhere to the holy see of Rome, and the religion which they there profess. Moreover, I promise and declare, that I will keep secret, and will not divulge, directly nor indirectly, by word or writing, nor any other circumstance whatsoever, that which you my spiritual father, or others engaged in the advancement of this holy and pious design, will propose to me, or give me in charge; and that I will be diligent and not cease to advance it; and there shall be no hope of recompence, nor threats of punishment, that shall make me discover any thing concerning it; and that if I am discovered, I will never confess one circumstance about it: I swear all these things by the holy trinity, and by the blessed body of God, which I propose presently to receive; and I call to witness all the angels and all the saints in heaven, that this is my true intention. In witness whereof I do receive the holy and blessed sacrament of the eucharist.

The author of the History of Popery goes on, (see page 402.)

Prance informs us in his deposition, that the priests confessed such miserable wretches often, and gave them absolution; but never gave it them till after they had made them reiterate their oaths, adding always, that there would be no mercy nor paradise for them, if they ever discovered the conspiracy. Is it then any thing surprizing, that people (who on the one hand can hope nothing from their making confession, since they are condemned to death, and who fear on the other hand with the ruin of their religion their eternal damnation) have had the hardiness to suppress and deny the truth to the last moment! We find every day, that criminals who for the pleasure of saying they die innocent, deny their guilt at the gallows; and here they would give us proof from the silence and denial of these people, to which they had persuaded them, that they would be damned eternally if they let the least word escape them. All the world knows that Garnet and Oldcorne, who were convicted of the gunpowder-plot in 1606, persisted in the denial of it; and if it had not been that they deceived them by the means above recited, the jesuits would to this day have had the pleasure of proving their innocence by the same argument by which they prove that of the viscount Stafford, and the other persons executed. It must be observed also, that according to the laws of England, they cannot put criminals to the rack; so that the conspirators did not suffer the least torture. It is then a great marvel, indeed, that the jesuits, priests, and people who had hardened themselves in the resolution of denying all, whatsoever they made them suffer, should have had the power to do that which they had resolved, when we see every day criminals condemned, and who have no hopes at all of life, resist the most cruel tortures, and persist till death, to maintain their innocence. It is the conscience which is to criminals a torture of the greatest efficacy to force them to a confession: so far from the conscience bringing these English conspirators to a confession, on the contrary, it was that that kept them from it; for they had been persuaded that they should commit an unpardonable crime in confessing, and that they would do a good deed by denying the truth to their deaths. It is material to know upon this, certain considerable facts: for example, that the confessors and directors of the consciences of these wretched prisoners and accused, took care to harden them, either in person themselves or by some others; that they supplied with set terms of speeches and protestations of innocence for the gallows, those that were not capable of composing any for themselves. There was one found in the pocket of Lawrence Hill, who was executed for having assassinated Godfrey. The executioner, after Hill was hanged, amongst many other papers, pulled out one from his pocket wherein was written the dying speech, whereof he had recited almost the whole substance. You will find it a studied piece, expressed in handsome and strong terms, whereof Hill was not at all capable; for he was illiterate, and besides of low genius.

It is proper to shew it you entire, that you may judge whether it be the style and sentiments of a vulgar person, or the studied production of a priest and a jesuit.

"I come now to the fatal place where I must end my life; and I hope I shall finish it with a courage becoming mine innocence. I am going presently to appeal before the great judge who knows all things, and judges justly of every thing. I hope it will be happy for me a sinner to suffer so unjust a death. I call God, men and angels to witness, that I am utterly ignorant of the manner, the authors, and time of the murder of justice Godfrey. It is nevertheless for this pretended crime, that by the malice of some wicked people I am brought to this shameful death, which I hope will be a ready passage for me to eternal life. In this hope I die with joy, because of mine innocence, and the benefit flowing from the precious wounds of my blessed Saviour, by whose merits I hope to obtain salvation. I die a Roman catholic, and I desire all those who are of the same religion to pray to God for my soul: and I beseech God in his justice, that he will please to detect the authors of this horrible murder, in order that my innocence may appear; though I heartily forgive my accusers, I summon them notwithstanding to appear before the great tribunal of Divine Justice, as well as those who have put their hands to this bloody plot, to answer for the wrong they have done to an innocent man: I summon particularly the Lord Chief Justice who presided in this judgment, and the brothers of Edmondbury Godfrey, with the jury, the witnesses, and all those who have been concerned in this affair. O Lord, bless and preserve the king; have pity on this poor nation, and lay not innocent blood to their charge. I bid you all farewell in Christ Jesus, into whose hands I resign my spirit."

[430]

That author goes on—"There is a great deal of art in this little speech; but I question whether Hill was in earnest in what he professed. To be more certain that it was not his own perform-ance, the paper was shewn to his wife, who protested it was not his writing; and in truth he had not the use of either pen, ink, or paper, all the time he was in jail. So it is that these gentlemen harden the courage of their people, to lie with their last breath."

The conformity and correspondence our own case bears to the circumstances and practices in those aforecited, is so obvious, that it would be almost needless to remark upon them: but we have a further particular considerable; that to accommodate themselves to our circumstances, these gentry have gone yet one step further; they ransacked ancient Rome, Rome in its state of heathenism, for a fresh instance of barbarity, and have exceeded them in villainy, inasmuch as the meanness of the submission to confederate with negro slaves is the most contemptible. (n)

But for this master-piece they must have very well known, they could entertain no hopes of setting on foot any such con-spiracy amongst us, from the utter abhorrence the generality of people here have to their principles and practice. Our slaves being numerous, from the hopes of their corruption only must they have flattered themselves with a prospect of their babel: and indeed, through their great artifice, cunning and industry, their expectations had like to have been too successfully an-swered, had not the providence of God interposed, confounded their devices, and brought them to shame by a detection, whereby many of their confederates have been delivered into the hands of justice, and suffered their condign punishments.

The confessions of criminals of both complexions, which were very many, agreed we see, minutely in the circumstances of this conspiracy, as well as the principal things aimed at, the burning the town and assassinating the inhabitants, as observed before: It appears by the evidence, that more Romish priests than one had a hand in it. Let us remember general Oglethorpe's letter of intelligence from Georgia, that also of the news-writers, that there were designs brooding in Europe, to excite revolts and dis-

(n) See Tarquin's conspiracy, universal history, p. 480.

turbances in his majesty's possessions in America, from whence it may be inferred, some politicians had flattered themselves, his majesty would have enough to do to divert his attention from other affairs of importance to this majesty's dominions. Could these be dreams, or is it more rational to conclude, from what has happened amongst us, that they were founded on realities? what have these miscreants to say then? why they will wipe their mouths, and have recourse to their old trite artifices which they have always practised on such like occasions, and clamour lustily with brazen fronts, that there was no plot at all, and the witnesses were all perjured! for that Hughson, his wife, Kerry, and Ury denied it, and maintained their innocence to their last breath. And so have criminals we see of their communion often done before. But the witnesses, say they, what were they? Why truly generally such as they condescended to confederate with in these deeds of darkness: for who but villians, and the most profligate, debased and abandoned of villains, devoid of all sense of shame, virtue and humanity, would confederate with murderers? and who should discover them but their confederates?

Here were their associates, whites and blacks, detected, confessing their crimes, some before conviction, some afterwards, others in the torments of their conscience, in prospect of flames; some in the anguish and bitterness of their spirits, exclaiming against that accused oath, which bound them in this detestable confederacy, and destined them to that misery; and yet, as it were, maintaining their innocence to the last, or at least being silent as to their guilt (q) others again under actual suffering confessing their heinous crimes, attesting the truth of what evidence against themselves, and accusing others, to that time unimpeached, who likewise afterwards confirmed their testimony by their confessions.

Though so egregiously infatuated were many of these poor deluded wretches, that they were even persuaded they should wrong their own souls if they made discovery; (r) this seems

(q) This was credibly reported to have slipped from captain Marshall's Ben as he was leading to the stake.

(r) See Margaret Salinburgh alias Kerry's voluntary confession, the only one of the kind sent from jail.

was the opinion of whites and blacks; so artfully and painfully had they been tutored! so fixed and steady were these black disciples in these bloody purposes, that one of them who was yet at large, and attending at the execution of a confederate at the stake, was so far from being dismayed at that affrightful object, that he proposed the present time to proceed to their execution, upon observing how many white people were present. (s)

But we may remember, that the principal witness in this shocking case, and happy instrument of this detection, was Mary Burton, Hughson's indented servant; who (however it was) no one so much as insinuated to have been sworn of the confederacy. As she was the prime cause of the discovery, as before related, their envenomed arrows have been chiefly pointed at her; and no doubt, say they, she must have been the wickedest of mortals, to bring so many innocents to this shameful, miserable and untimely end. And what have they to impute to her, sufficient to invalidate her testimony? Why, one particular, say they, enough to outweigh all: she deposed, in her first examination before the grand jury, that she never saw any white person in company when they (the conspirators) talked of burning the town but her master, her mistress, and Peggy. It is true, she did so; and indeed it was very ill done: but, should that one false step preponderate to invalidate her whole evidence? Much might be said to aggravate this offence, much also in extenuation of it. We cannot expect evidence concerning these deeds of darkness, from witnesses of unblemished characters, free of all exception. Say she was sworn to the conspiracy; though it did not appear that she was so; and if it was true, it were something strange, one would think, that not a criminal under execution, or otherwise, who confessed their own guilt and impeached others, should have declared it; but on the contrary, confirmed her testimony against themselves in the torments of flames, attesting, that "she had spoke the truth, and could name many more," *i.e.* that her account of the conspiracy and conspirators, given at their trial was true; which is the utmost attestation that can be to the cred-

(s) Marschalk's negro, York, afterwards hung in chains by Hughson, proposed this at the execution of Quack and Cuffee, May 30. See Prince's confession.

ibility of any person, as to the matter treated of. And if they had known she was engaged in the conspiracy, from the resentment they must have borne to her as a principal evidence in their conviction, it might have been expected, it would naturally have bolted out from them; nor did Sarah Hughson, the daughter, so much as insinuate it, whose spleen was very inveterate towards her, as the cause of their detection: but perhaps Hughson's daughter was more artfully instructed; for if it came out that Burton was sworn in a party, that might add strength to her testimony, and fix the guilt more strongly upon the parties she accused, by an implied confession of the most material part of her evidence; and if she were not sworn of the confederacy, it might seem strange to some that the conspirators trusted her so much with their secrets.

There are allowances to be made, with regard to the special circumstances this girl was under in this case, and some passions and qualities which seemed natural to her: she came over young into this country, an indented servant, a year or two before her first master, after some service, assigned over her indenture to John Hughson for the remainder of her term, the midsummer before this iniquity broke out, when she was between fifteen and sixteen years of age: the girl thus becoming under the power of Hughson, a stranger in the country, and met a friend to advise with; her situation was surely somewhat deplorable; for, being in the hands and under the influence of so hopeful a family, and held to secrecy by her apprehensions of the danger she was beset with from these assassins, she might think her condition helpless, and that she could only wish for deliverance: she was of a warm hasty spirit, had a remarkable glibness of tongue, and uttered more words than people of her supposed education usually do; such a temper, one might think, could ill brook the ceremony of attending and serving upon slaves, and such a band of black and white ruffians; which, it seems, was the service enjoined her, neither could they think themselves safe with her, unless they could seduce her to their wicked purposes, which they might have hopes they should compass at last; and though at first they might think she was not to be trusted at all adventures; yet it so happened, that by degrees, it seems, the conspirators (as depending upon a master's influence over one in her circumstances, added to the terrors of their threatenings to murder her if she made discovery) flattered themselves they had her sure, and at length became so familiarized and unreserved towards her, that they heeded not saying or doing any thing before her; and thus she might be let into their secrets, upon a persuassion that she durst not tell.

The girl, doubtless, must be under terrible apprehensions when her life was thus endangered, both from blacks and whites, if she made discovery; this must have been matter of great restraint to her, and, in her hurry and confusion of thought, might occasion her to utter that through inadvertency, which, upon calm reflection, she became conscious was wrong, though at the time, it might be an involuntary suppression only of part of the truth, arising from an overhastiness in answering, and want of due reflection: which, therefore perhaps, after making all candid and ingenuous allowance, will not be rigorously construed a wilful and deliberate falsehood.

As to such other white persons as Burton did afterwards accuse, against whom there appeared just or probable grounds of impeachment,—viz. Sarah Hughson, the daughter, William Kane, and John Corry the dancing-master; concerning the two former, her testimony affecting them was confirmed by many negro witnesses separately examined, and far enough apart from each other, who not only agreed in the particulars affecting them, but the most minute circumstances also relating to the conspiracy: and though it may be objected, that they were not legal witnesses (and therefore had not been admitted to give evidence on the trial of any white person) yet surely their testimony thus considered together, not only adds strength to that of Burton, but does also amount to the utmost moral certainty of the truth of the facts testified of. But to put the matter beyond dispute concerning them, this Sarah and Kane confessed their own guilt, and confirmed (amongst other things) particularly what Burton said affecting themselves.

Kane himself was first impeached by a negro, as well as other soldiers, however they became so fortunate as to escape justice; and this was nevertheless true for its coming from a negro; for

Kane confessing his guilt, made also some atonement by further material discovery, which squared with the rest of the evidence; and both Sarah Hughson (the daughter) and Kane confirm Burton's testimony in general, and in particular also that against Ury the priest; and as to Corry the dancing-master, that he was one of the conspirators, Kane examined apart from Burton, testified likewise; so that it may be conceded she only kept back or suppressed, upon her first examination, part of that through dread and distraction of thought and want of proper consideration, which at the same time upon due reflection and remembrance she might have known to be the truth, viz.—that there were other white persons concerned in the conspiracy, besides her mistress, her master, and Peggy, though perhaps they might not all at that instant have occurred to her memory; which, as to Hughson's daughter, Burton afterwards declared, she did not think of her at the time.

Thus far then we may venture to infer Burton's testimony affecting the persons by her impeached (whose guilt was manifested by circumstantial and other direct evidence of witnesses, in conjunction with, and corroboration of hers, and by their own conjunction) was deserving of entire credit.

We may have observed by the course of the proceedings, and these poor negro wretches have been deluded by degrees, and cajoled to interest themselves, and become parties in this detestable enterprize through the artifices of agent Hughson; who (though a mean illiterate fellow) from his vicious propensity and natural acuteness had an aptitude for mischief; which these craftsmen made improvement of, and at length rendered suitable to their abominable purposes. Though we cannot suppose that Hughson really had the folly or vanity to aspire to a kingdom of the conspirators erecting; yet the notion might be calculated and propagated, to captivate the negroes, (for with none but fools and negroes could he take:) and further to please them it seems they were persuaded, there should be a motley government as well as motley subjects; for Caesar (Vaarck's) was to be governor over free negroes, who were to marry the gentlewomen; and Caesar had got his white governess already provided. If these phantasms and delusions could have force sufficient to ensnare these simple creatures (as we find they had) it mattered not how extravagant soever the folly of the means was which seduced them to these bloody purposes, provided they served the turn and designs of our enemies; thereby disappointed the supply of provisions to his majesty's armament in the West-Indies, laid waste this city, destroyed the inhabitants, and prepared the way for an invasion of his majesty's enemies, whether secret or declared, and their making an easy prey of the whole province; neither did it signify how illiterate Hughson was, he approved himself sufficiently to his masters, by his dexterous prosecution of their scheme; he did seduce the negroes in the manner we have seen; he tempted them to frequent visits at his house, by his pitable entertainments, at such an expense as it is incredible he could have supported for such a series of time, as this mischief must have been brooding, merely upon the spoils of a few negroes pilferings, and without other private assistance. It must be allowed he was trusty in his agency, very industrious, and used no small craft to encompass a disciple: in the first instance, if they were not pre-engaged by a deputy, Hughson attempted to make them swear, by forms of oaths accommodated to their own customs, by thunder and lightning, and such like horrible imprecations, as have appeared in the course of the evidence, without telling them what they were to swear to: if they scrupled swearing without further explanation concerning what; then he intimated they were to swear to secrecy, that in regard he kept a public house, and entertained negroes contrary to law, the intent of the oath was, that they should not discover him therein: if they agreed to swear at all, it was easy to add, (as we find he did) neither should they tell of what they saw going forward at his house: then upon the main matter proposed, if they scrupled to engage in the conspiracy, from any qualm arising either from the inhumanity or wickedness of the design; they were flattered they were all to be free men, and it was a meritorious undertaking: if they thought it would be a sin, there was a priest that could forgive sins: if all this would not do, their lives were threatened if they would not engage, or at least if they discovered any thing about it: but so apt pupils were most of them, that the bare proposal of the

[437]

scheme was sufficient to engage them immediately, at all adventures.

Hughson artfully engaged in this infamous project, a neighbour's negro, Jack, (Comfort's) a fellow of most remarkable craft and subtlety for one of his complexion, which qualified him afterwards for a more material witness concerning these deeds of darkness; for Jack had more wit than to be hanged for them. Jack was a dignified man amongst them, a captain of one of these bands of fools, had so well approved his parts and capacity to Hughson and the rest, that he had a deputation for swearing, as it should seem; for he administered oaths, to such converts as he made, either abroad or at home; and in both cases had great opportunities of caballing with negroes; for his master was frequently absent from home for several weeks together, insomuch that captain Jack looked upon the house as his own, and himself as his own master: to his well, every morning and evening resorted negroes from all quarters of the town, for tea-water; which, therefore, afforded him convenient seasons for gaining parties, which he made use of to the utmost; and hereat Jack was so dexterous, that he became the very counterpart of his master Hughson; for when their scheme was grown near ripe for execution, Jack, as well as Hughson, had a list of these black confederates, their devotees; and about a month before the fort was burnt, Jack had as large companies of negroes at his levees, as Hughson usually had at his, and buoyed them up with the same hopes, that at the expiration of that time, the French and Spaniards would be here to join them, and take the place; nevertheless, if they did not come, they were to agree, and did agree, amongst them, to proceed and do all themselves.

We may perceive, that what has been unfolded concerning this mystery of iniquity, came out by slow degrees; the first hint concerning the conspiracy, was given by Mary Burton to the grand jury, on her examination the 22d of April; and for some time after the trial of Hughson, etc. for aught that had appeared, he must have been deemed the projector of it, though it had been whispered that Roman priests had been, and that some were then in town; no one however cared to discover them, so as

[438]

they might be laid hold of, and dealt with as a salutary law of this province directs.

Ury the priest was looked upon with a very jealous eye, soon after this iniquity began to unfold; but no certain evidence was given concerning him, that he was such a one, and at last it was suspicion only that caused him to be taken into custody: some footsteps of others were likewise traced, but they were too artful and cunning, got out of reach, left Ury the dog to hold, and slipped their necks out of that collar, which was afterwards deservedly placed about his; though he pretended to maintain and protested his innocence with his last breath—they, it seems, were not so fond of his kind of martyrdom.

Ury was indicted upon the evidence of Burton and Kane, who corroborated the testimony of each other, and Sarah Hughson, the daughter's evidence, establishes the credit of both, as to what they say concerning him; so that the gentlemen of the grand jury which found the bill against him, weighing matters candidly and ingeniously, saw sufficient cause at that time, to credit Burton's testimony; and to do those gentlemen justice, it was owing in great measure, to their good sense, discretion, and indefatigable labour, that this affair was brought to so happy an issue; and their painful service during the course of about three months daily inquiry, ought to be remembered by this city and country, with the utmost gratitude.

But it so happened that for some time before this grand jury was discharged, there arose great clamour against Mary Burton; for so many negroes being daily taken into custody (though not solely through her evidence, but rather principally upon discovery made by the confessions of their black associates already in custody, and their testimony corroborated with her's) some people began to be afraid of losing their slaves; for, as matters were then likely to turn out, there was no guessing where or when there would be an end of impeachments; every one had reason to fear that their own negro would be sent for next; and indeed all things duly considered, it was most probable there was but few of them that were not in the secret; and the girl had declared, that there were many negroes concerned, whose persons she could or might probably remember, but many whose names she knew not; so that it should seem, at length some masters of these slaves, as well as the conspirators, endeavoured to bring the witnesses, and the notion of a plot, into discredit, if perchance it might put a stop, not only to further prosecution, but further inquiry and discovery also: and these attempts, luckily for some, had such an effect, that several whites, as well as negroes, escaped justice; who, had the same evidence appeared against them a few weeks before, would scarce have been thought objects of mercy; nor, from what we may have observed, would Mary Burton's evidence have stood single against them.

However, when the first grand jury drew near their discharge, they were importunate with Burton, to discover all the persons she knew to be engaged in this villanious design; for about this time she had suggested to some, that there were white people of more than ordinary rank above the vulgar, that were concerned, whom if she told of they would not believe her. This having been intimated to the grand jury, they were very pressing with her to discover all she knew, whoever they were; but the girl stood mute; nor could the grand jury prevail with her to name any, not with threatenings of imprisonment; at length, being tired with her obstinacy, they delivered her over to two of the judges, requesting them to endeavour to sift the matter out; but they could not prevail with her to be explicit. She complained (as it seems she had before done to the grand jury) that she had been very ill used; that her life had been threatened by conspirators of both complexion, and frequently insulted by people of the town for bringing their negroes in question, and that people did not believe what she said, so what signified speaking? or to this purpose she expressed herself. She intimated withal, that there were some people *in ruffles* (a phrase as was understood to mean persons of better fashion than ordinary) that were concerned. At last, having been threatened to be imprisoned in the dungeon, she named several persons which she said she had seen at Hughson's amongst the conspirators, talking of the conspiracy, who were engaged in it; amongst whom she mentioned several of known credit, fortunes and reputations, and of religious principles superior to a suspicion of being concerned in such detestable practices; at which the judges were very much astonished; others again were imperfectly described by her, whose reputed religious profession might square with such wicked designs, concerning whom the girl had long before given broad hints, but said she did not know their names, or what part of the city they lived in; but it came out at last, that one of them was a doctor (a professed papist, as common fame had it) whom she had seen several times afterwards in the streets, and who upon sight of her, always turned another way, to avoid meeting her: however it was, this person had the discretion to remove himself out of this province soon after; and it is said, into foreign dominions; and it were much to be wished, that such others, as were justly liable to impeachment, would act with the same prudence and follow his example, for the sake of their own safety, as well as the peace and security of ourselves. But upon the whole, there was reason to conclude, that this girl had at length been tampered withal; might it not be suggested to her, that the reward offered by proclamation for the discovery, she was already sure of, for she was entitled to it; and might she not be tempted to make further advantage of the affair? upon this supposition, the conspirators could not have devised a more effectual means (if they could but prevail with her) to put a stop to further inquiry, to procure the names of persons to be called in question at last, concerning this scene of villiany, whose fortunes and characters set them above suspicion: they very well knew (for papists or priests as Ury intimated, as "too wise and too cunning") if they could but prevail in this, they would thereby not only put a stop to further discovery, but likewise have some pretence, according to their usual custom, to clamour loudly, there was no plot at all: it was a mere dream! and to serve this turn, they had luckily with them some owners of slaves, who happened to humour this artifice, though upon a different view.

It was fit this matter should be stated in its proper light; that on the one hand the evidence of this witness (but for whom next under the interposition of divine providence, this city would in all probability have been laid waste in ashes, so far as deserving of credit) and on the other hand, that where she may be justly suspected to have executed the bounds of truth, there a step may be made, to consider, and conjecture, how it might have come to past, that she told some things incredible at the winding up of this affair; and weigh impartially also, the whole current of the other evidence, remarking how it appears to confirm and establish her testimony, so far as it has been judged proper and fitting to publish it.

The other white people executed, as well as Ury, like true modern Romanists, pretended to maintain (and did protest) their innocence to their last breath; though Hughson himself, soon after his conviction, seemed to betray strong symptoms of his inclination to confess his guilt, and make discovery; but if he was in earnest to have done so, in hopes of saving his own life, his mind was some changed (as it was conjectured) by the persuasion of his wife; yet Kerry left such proofs behind her of many of the particulars of this conspiracy, and of her own guilt, as add great force to the aforegoing accounts of it; and her recanting afterwards, is another irrefragable instance, how these wretches prevaricate, even in their last moments!

That a plot there was, and as to the parties and bloody purpose of it, we presume there can scarce be a doubt amongst us at this time; the ruins of his majesty's house in the fort, are the daily evidence and moments of it, still before our eyes: if the other frights and terrors this city was alarmed with, to their great consernation, are, as to some amongst us, so soon slipped into oblivion; yet surely others will think we ought once a year at least, to pay our tribute of praise and thanksgiving to the Divine Being, that through his merciful providence and infinite goodness, caused this inhuman horrible enterprize to be detected, and so many of the wicked instruments of it to be brought to justice, whereby a check has been put to the execrable malice, and bloody purposes of our foreign and domestic enemies, though we have not been able entirely to unravel the mystery of this iniquity; for it was a dark design, and the veil is in some measure still upon it!

[442]

APPENDIX

Deposition.—Anne Kannady, wife of James Kannady, of the city of New-York, peruke maker, being duly sworn, deposeth,

1. "That on the Tuesday or Wednesday evening (to the best of her remembrance) after the deponent's husband James Kannady, and several other city officers had been several times in search at John Hughson's, after the goods stolen from Mr. Hogg's shop; Mary Burton, then servant to Hughson, came to the deponent's house to buy a pound of candles for her master; and it being a very cold evening the deponent asked her to come in and warm herself, which she did, and thereupon the deponent took upon her to ask her several questions: first of all she asked her her own name, which she told her as above; for the deponent did not know it, though she had been several times at her house upon the like errands, and she knew that she lived at Hughson's; then the deponent asked her whether that was a black child or a white child which that Irish beauty had, which lodged at their house? and she made answer, that it was as white as any of her children, or any other child; the deponent then told her that she heard that there was a negro who kept company with her and was the father of that child; the said Mary answered there was a negro came thither to her, but he was not the father of that child, she believed; then the deponent took upon her to give the said Mary good advice, she told her she would give her a blessing as a mother would a child, as she was a stranger in the country; the deponent advised her to have no dealings with negroes, and to have

[443]

no hand in thievery, for that would be a means of bringing her to the gallows.

2. "That the deponent then asked her, if she knew any thing of the thievery of Mr. Hogg's goods? and she several times denied that she knew any thing about the matter; the deponent then asked her if she had a mind to be freed from Hughson? if she had and would discover the goods, the deponent would free her, and she should come and live with her; then the said Mary answered, that her husband (meaning the deponent's who had been at Hughson's upon search, as aforesaid) was not cute enough; then the deponent said tell me where the goods are, and I will take you away from him to-night; she answered that she would not tell her any thing to-night, she would tell her to-morrow, but that the deponent's husband had trod upon them. Then the deponent let the said Mary return home.

3. "That after this conversation was over, the deponent went the same evening to Mr. Mills, the under sheriff, and told him what had passed as above; whereupon the said Mills, Mr. Hogg and his wife, and several constables, with the deponent's husband and herself, went down to Hughson's house; and the deponent desired Mills to go into the house first, and bring Mary Burton out to her, but Mills staying a long time the deponent went into the house to him, and found him and his wife and Mary Burton in the parlour, and there she denied all that she had said to the deponent as above: then the deponent charged her home with it, until at last the said Mary said she could not tell them any thing there, she was afraid of her life, that they would kill her; whereupon they took her out of the house, and when they had got a little away from thence, she put her hand in her pocket, and pulled out a piece of silver money, which she said was a part of Hogg's money which the negro had given her; whereupon they all went with her to Alderman Banker's and the deponent informing him what she had promised the said Mary, that is to say, to get her freed from her master, the alderman directed that she should that

night lodge with the under sheriff, at the City-Hall for safety, and the deponent went with the said Mary, and left her at Mr. Mills's accordingly.

4. "That some time after the said Mary Burton was parted from Hughson (to the best of deponent's remembrance, it was after the house in the fort was burnt) she came to the deponent's house, and deponent was talking about the robbery at Hogg's, and about butter, indigo and bees wax, which had been lately stolen from other persons, and Mary said that Hughson, his wife and family had had them and it was plain enough, and that she knew enough to hang and burn them all: the deponent then advised her to tell all that she knew, saying it was a pity such people should go on in their wickedness unpunished.

5. "That some time after this, the said Mary said to the deponent that she was better than ever her mother was to her, that she had relieved her from the hands of her enemies, by being the means of taking her away from Hughson's, and that if ever it was in her power, she would reward her handsomely for it.

6. "That the said Mary Burton further said to this deponent, that if they had not taken her the said Mary from Hughson's the night that they did, she verily believed they (meaning the Hughson's) would either have murdered her, or sent her away in a boat by the next morning."

her
Anne ✠ Kannady
mark.

April 13, 1742.—Sworn before the recorder.

The same day and time James Kannady and Mary Goddard (daughter of said James and Anne) wife of Christopher Goddard of New-York, mariner, having severally heard the before mentioned deposition of Anne Kannady taken and read over in their presence, did severally make oath, that that part of the said deposition which relates to what discourse passed between the said Anne Kannady and Mary Burton, did so pass between them when they (the deponents) were respectively present; and that what therein is deposed is the substance and effect of what was so said between them.

Sworn before the recorder.

Deposition—Rebecca Hogg, wife of Robert Hogg of the city of New-York, merchant, deposeth,

1. "That one Wilson, a boy belonging to the Flamborough man of war, used to frequent her house, upon pretence of acquaintance with two white boys, servants to two gentlemen that lodged there.

2. "That the Thursday before the robbery was committed, the said Wilson came to her house with a man belonging to the aforesaid ship, in order to buy some chequered linen; and the deponent shewed them into the shop, where he (Wilson) bought something of her, and gave her a Spanish nine-penny silver piece in pay, and the deponent unadvisedly opening her desk to weigh it, she pulled out a drawer in view of the said Wilson, wherein were a considerable number of Spanish pieces of eight, whereupon she immediately recollected herself, and shut to the drawer and desk again in haste, thinking she had done imprudently in exposing her money to an idle boy who used to be so often backwards and forwards at her house, and thereupon made an excuse to send the piece of money aforesaid out of the house to be weighed. And on the Saturday night following her shop was robbed.

3. "That the Sunday morning after, this boy (Wilson) came to the deponent's house, as usual, and she was telling him how that she had been robbed, and that as she knew he belonged to the man of war, she thought he might be able to give her some intelligence of it; as there were several sailors who frequented vile houses that were near her; the deponent described some snuff-bones and coined silver pieces, one an eight square piece: whereupon he the said Wilson answered that he had been that morning at the house of one Hughson, by the North river, and there he saw one John Gwin (whom the deponent understood to have been

a soldier of that name a person of vile character, who lived in the deponent's back street; but it turned out to be Caesar, Vaarck's negro) whom he saw pull out of his pocket, a worsted cap full of coined silver; and that Philipse's Cuffee came into Hughson's upon pretence of having his master's shoes mended, and seeing John Gwin have this money, he asked him to give him some, and he counted him out half-a-crown in pennies, and asked him if he would have any more, and pulled out a handful of silver in the presence of the boy, Wilson, amongst which he said he saw the eight square piece so described by the deponent as aforesaid; but the deponent did not then suspect Wilson to have had any hand in it.

4. "That upon this information the deponent told her husband; and he and Mr. Mills went the same Sunday morning to Hughson's, to inquire for one John Gwin, a soldier, and Hughson told them that he was not there, nor did he use the house: but Caesar, the negro who went by that name (as he himself after he was apprehended, and after his conviction, confessed to this deponent) was at the same time standing in the chimney corner, in the same room where Mr. Hogg and Mr. Mills came; whereupon Mr. Hogg returned to his house, and told the deponent that there was no such soldier as John Gwin that used that house, that the boy, Wilson, who was present, thereupon said, it was not a white man, but Caesar, a negro belonging to one Vaarck, a baker, who went by that name.

5. "Upon this Caesar was apprehended the same Sunday about 3 o'clock, and being brought to Wilson, to know if that was the right person he said it was.

6. "That upon her examining the said negro Caesar, in jail several times, as well before his trial as after his conviction of this robbery, he confessed to her as followeth.

7. "That the boy Wilson used to be frequently in company with him (Caesar) Philipse's Cuffee, and Auboyneau's Prince, negroes, at Mr. Philipse's house and at Hughson's; and that he (Wilson) came to Hughson's, where were present Hughson and his family, Caesar (himself) Cuffee and

[447]

Prince, and there he told them where they might have a good booty, and described the deponent's house and shop to them, and told them what money he had seen in the drawer, as aforesaid, and said he believed there must be more by seeing that in one drawer. That Caesar and he did not know where Mr. Hogg lived, but he knew the house if it was where the widow Scott lived formerly; and that so said Hughson, that he did not know Mr. Hogg, nor where he lived: but Caesar further said, that upon this information they contrived it at Hughson's how to commit this robbery, and that he (Caesar) going to see Peggy Kerry, who lodged at Hughson's, on the Saturday evening following, he dropped asleep there, and about 10 o'clock John Hughson came to him and waked him, telling him that he had forgot what he had promised the boy (Wilson), Cuffee and Prince, to go to the house in Broad-street, to get that booty.

8. "That thereupon he (Caesar) went to Mr. Philipse's house (Cuffee's master) and finding nobody there he sat himself down in the cellar kitchen, by the fire; and by-and-by hearing his confederates coming, he feigned himself asleep, and they came in with a large bundle, and had it in a bran-box in the stable or out-house, in the yard, as he discovered by their talk, they thinking him asleep, for they did not attempt to wake him, but went out again in search of further prey.

9. "That when they were gone, he went and took the bundle they had so hid, and carried it to John Romme's at the new-battery, who opened the door for him himself, and let him in, and he (Caesar) threw the bundle in a chair, which was tied up in a large table cloth, which Romme opened and took out a piece of cotton and linen cheque, and a pair of silver knee-buckles belonging to Mr. Hogg, and some other linen things which he could not particularly remember; and after this, he (Caesar) carried the remainder of the bundle to Hughson's, and left them in the room where Peggy was and went to bed; and in the morning when he awaked, he took the snuff-boxes, a child whistle, and ring, and a pair of ear rings, end a locket with four dia-

monds, and gave them to Peggy, with some money; and the linen and chequered shirt he left with Peggy, to distribute as she thought proper, but he bid her give an apron to the girl (meaning Mary Burton) and when he (Caesar) went down stairs he distributed money to Hughson, his wife and their children, and likewise to the servant girl.

10. "That Caesar confessed to the deponent, that when he came to Hughson's with the things, the family was all a-bed; but that they had left open a window, as was usual, and he climbed upon the shed and got into the house, and went to bed to Peggy, as Hughson and his family knew he used to do every night.

Rebecca Hogg.

April 14, 1742.—Sworn before the recorder.

July 15, 1742.

The recorder having been informed by Mary Burton, that she had several times talked to the wife of Daniel Masters, carman, concerning the conspiracy, and what she had heard the negroes and the Hughsons often talk about it, whilst she lived at Hughson's, and this before the fire at the fort; he spoke to Daniel Masters and desired him to send his wife to him, in order, as he told him, to enquire of her about it: within three or four days afterwards Susannah Masters came to the recorder (viz.—this morning) and he examined her upon the matter, and took down what she said in the form of a deposition, consisting of twelve sections or paragraphs, which she signed and swore to, after hearing the same distinctly read over: the recorder being obliged to go out, and pressed in point of time, he did not examine her so fully as otherwise he would have done, but upon reading over the deposition in the afternoon, several other questions occurred to him, which he thought might be proper to interrogate her upon; therefore he then sent for her again, and she came very readily, and freely answered the questions proposed to her; notes were taken at large of the fresh information she gave which she was told were to be drawn out in proper order, and added to her deposition, and the whole to be fair copied, ready to be read over to her the next morning, in order to be sworn and signed; and she promised to come the next morning for that purpose; but it may be presumed she had been otherwise advised, for though her husband had been several times afterwards ordered to send her again, yet she thought fit to decline coming; the recorder did not care to be over solicitous about it, for some reasons, but has ventured to give the public her examination at large, as it was drawn out from his notes, which he does aver, he thinks is faithfully done; and to do the woman justice, she seemed to behave upon the occasion with the greatest sincerity and candour. For distinction, the particular paragraphs contained in her first deposition, which were read over to her, and by her sworn to and signed, are included between inverted commas.

Note, upon the fair copying, some of the paragraphs were transposed, and the words inclosed in the (thus) at the end of section 10, were added upon her second examination.

The *deposition* and *examination* of Susannah Masters, wife of Daniel Masters of the city of New-York. She said

1. "That Mary Burton, late servant to John Hughson (executed for the conspiracy), soon after her removal from her said master (upon the discovery of Mr. Hogg's goods, the last year, which were stolen and lodged at the said Hughson's house) came to live with one Wilson, in the same street with this deponent, with whose family this deponent was well acquainted, they used to fetch water at this deponent's house, and to dry their clothes in her yard; and after Mary Burton came to live with Wilson, she used often to come to the deponent's house upon the same errands, which gave the said Mary frequent opportunities of talking to this deponent; and she said she was glad she was got from Hughson's to the place where she now was, for she was afraid there would be mischief in the town, for that she knew there used to be cabals of negroes at Hughson's whilst she lived there, almost every night at supper, and they used to make her wait upon them; and at such meet-

ings, Hughson and the negroes used to talk of killing the people and burning the town; that the governor's house should be the first, and then they would begin at the Fly, and so go through the whole city; and that Hughson's wife said, that rather than it should go undone, she would lend an hand herself; and when all this was done, it was agreed among them, that Hughson was to be king, his wife Queen, Vaarck's Caesar governor, and Peggy, his mistress, governess."

2. "That Mary said, that the negroes and the Hughsons several times threatened her, that if she discovered any thing out of the house that she heard there, they would certainly make away with her."

3. "That the said Mary had discoursed in this manner to the deponent three several times before she spoke of it to her husband; but it had made the deponent very uneasy, though she could not know how to give credit to it."

4. "That at the times of this discourse, Mary Burton seemed very uneasy, and used to sit down and cry and bemoan herself, and said she was but a young girl, a stranger in the country, and no friends, and she was in danger of her life; the deponent then asked her why she did not go to a magistrate and make a discovery of all this? Mary answered, that if she should tell them what she knew, they would not believe her, as she was a poor girl and a stranger."

5. That upon the girl crying and bemoaning herself so to her, the examinant (considering the circumstances she was under, from the manner of her relating her story) was very much affected, and could not but take great compassion of her, as she had no friends or relations in this country to advise with upon her case, or to protect her, and yet the examinant says, she would at sometimes be cheerful and merry, and laughing at the folly of the conspirators, when she was telling the examinant of some particular odd passages which happened at such nightly meetings, and that she bore up against the difficulties she was under, much better than the examinant could have done in the like circumstances, and that she thought she had very good spirits.

6. "That the said Mary used further to talk, that when Hughson and the negroes had any thing extraordinary to do at nights, the Hughsons would send her up to bed; and the night that Hogg's goods came thither they had sent her up to bed, and she heard when the goods came, and she got up and looked out of the window and saw the goods delivered in, but it being dark she could not discover who they were that brought them, for there were many of them, but she heard and knew the voices of Vaarck's Caesar, Auboyneau's Prince, and Philipse's Cuffee, negroes."

7. "That Mary told the deponent, that the night Hogg's goods were stolen, Caesar was asleep upon the table, that he had been drinking very hard, and John Hughson came to him about 11 o'clock and waked him, and said to him you forget your promise, don't you? Caesar answered no sir, I don't, and thereupon got up and went out; and then Hughson sent Mary to bed, and Mary said that upon this she suspected something extraordinary was to be done, she could not sleep; and she heard the noise when they brought the goods, which she took to be about 12 or 1 o'clock."

8. "That Mary Burton told the deponent, that she saw the goods the next morning, and that Caesar offered her as much speckled linen before Peggy, as would make her an apron, but she said she would not have it, and threw it down upon the floor, and told them she did not want it; that want it she did, but that she would not have it in that manner, that she told them she believed they did not come honestly by it; at which she said they were affronted, but she did not value it, she would not receive any thing of them, if she could but get victuals, drink and clothes as long as she staid with them, that was all she cared for: that Caesar offered her a piece of silver, which she supposed was to engage her to look after Peggy in her lying in, but she said no, she would not take care of her and her black child, but perhaps she might have submitted to have looked after white people's."

9. That at last the deponent told her husband of what had passed between her and Mary, but at first he thought it

was all idle talk in the girl, and could not give any credit to it, and rebuked the deponent for giving an ear to her.

10. "That the said Mary further said, that there were many white people, and some in ruffles that used to come to Hughson's, and go into a private room with Hughson; and if she when she was bid, bought any wine or anything to the door of the room where they were, Hughson used to stand ready at the door and receive it, and send her away again: that these white people in ruffles used to come seldom, but they used to send letters and money in them to Hughson often" (for that she has received several letters brought thither, and has felt money in them, large round pieces which she took to be milled Spanish pieces of eight.)

11. "That the said Mary said, that Hughson had a large parcel of arms, which he hid under ground; but she did not know what became of them."

12. That the said Mary told the examinant, that Kannady the constable's wife (at the time that he had been searching at Hughson's in quest of Hogg's goods that had been stolen) upon Mary's going to her shop upon an errand, advised her, if she knew any thing of Hogg's goods to discover it, or else she told her she might be brought into trouble; and that Mary told her, Ah! said she, the constable in this place were not half cute enough, that they went over them several times, and had poked a stick (or cane she thought she said) into a place where some of them were (the examinant apprehended her, that there was some place in the stairs that was broken that they were so poking at) and Mary said that she could scarce forbear laughing to see how dumb they were, and yet she dared not tell them.

(Hereupon Ann Kannady's preceding deposition being read over to the examinant, she declared,)

13. That Mary Burton told her what had passed between the said Ann Kannady and her the said Mary, which to the best of the examinant's remembrance, was much to the same purpose as is related in the said Ann Kannady's depo-

[453]

sition, and that soon after she came to live with Wilson as aforesaid, and before the fire at the fort.

14. "That all the conversation before related, passed between the deponent and the said Mary concerning the conspiracy before the fire at the fort, and before the proclamation issued, promising a reward to such as should make discovery of any person or persons concerned in setting fire to the houses."

15. That Mrs. Waldron who is since married to ———— Miller coming one day to the examinant's house, before the fire at the fort, Mary Burton being there, she related before her most of the particulars herein before set forth, much to the same purpose as before related: and the said Mrs. Waldron was much surprized at it.

16. "That the day the fort was fired, Mary Burton came to the deponent's house, and said to her, now you see this is the beginning of it, Mrs. Masters; they said the governor's house should be the first; you did not seem to take much notice of what I said to you; and Mary seemed to be in a very great fright and much perplexed, and said, it was a thousand pities it should not be discovered; but says she, if I was to speak what I know of it, they would not believe me, and she said, when she looked upon the houses, she thought what a city it was, that they must all come down."

17. That after the fire at the fort, the said Mary used to come frequently to the examinant's house, until the time that her master, Wilson, removed to live in the Fly, which was at May day, 1741; and she would often be talking about these matters, and of her fears and apprehensions, that she be murdered by the negroes; and she told the examinant one day, after she had been first examined by the grand jury concerning Hogg's goods, that she met one of Vaarck's negroes (Bastian) who was one of the conspirators (whose master lived near the examinant) and he asked her whether she had discovered any thing about the fires? and Mary said she answered him, no; and the negro replied, we shall soon take care that you shall not tell any more; or words to some

such purpose: and Mary said, she came immediately into the examinant's house, before she went to her master's; and she seemed to be frightened almost out of her wits, when she told the examinant this story, and said, she looked behind her all the way, expecting she should be followed and knocked on the head.

18. That after Wilson was removed into the Fly, the said Mary told the examinant, that one Sunday morning her master and mistress being gone to church, a negro who she believed did belong to old Hughson, father of John Hughson executed, came into her master Wilson's cellar-kitchen, and asked if there was a barber there? that Mary answered him no; that the said negro made a pretence that he wanted to send the boy out, the only person in the house besides herself, in order to fetch him a barber to shave him; but Mary said she was afraid he had some ill design, and would not let the boy go; and at last, when church was near out, the negro went away, and people beginning to come into the streets, the negro took to his heels and run away; and she said she thought to have got somebody to have laid hold of him, but he made too much haste out of reach: that afterwards she told her fears and apprehensions to a magistrate, and care was taken to remove her from her master Wilson's; and she was then lodged again at the under-sheriff's at the city-hall, where she was to remain, and the corporation purchased her indentures of Wilson for that purpose.

19. That this examinant was out upon the common at the execution of Quack and Cuffee, where she met the said Mary Burton, and the examinant said to her, she wondered how she had courage enough to be there; she answered, that she knew they had deserved it, and that if half the negroes in town were executed, she believed they had deserved it; that she knew a great many of them by sight, but did not know their names, nor who they belonged to.

20. That when the governor had ordered a military nightly watch to be kept in this city, that evening that Philipse's store-house was burnt, Mary, having been talking to

the examinant about the conspiracy and the several fires which had happened that day, said, that was right, and the only way to prevent farther mischief.

21. That when several fires had thus happened, the examinant was then convinced of the truth of what the said Mary had often before related to her; and the examinant's husband resolved to inform, and did inform a magistrate of what Mary had told the examinant, or of the substance of it, as the examinant's husband informed her.

22. And lastly, the examinant saith, that from the beginning of these conversations with the said Mary Burton, about these plottings and caballings between the Hughsons and the negroes, the examinant had heard the said Mary mention the names of several white persons of condition beyond the vulgar, who she said resorted some times to Hughson's, and used to go into a room with him in private, whom she suspected; and others who used to be with the negroes and the Hughson's in public, whom she said she knew, from what she had seen and heard at such meetings, were concerned in the conspiracy (whose names the examinant does not care to mention, without a promise not to insert them in her examination) but among several others, she had heard her name Corry, the dancing-master, as one particularly, who used to be with the Hughsons and the negroes when they were talking about burning the town and killing the people.

The following letter and dialogue were sent from Mr. Favieres, of the city of New-York, merchant, directed to the recorder.

Sir—Having been often interrogated concerning some discourse, I had with the negro Bastian, concerning the conspiracy, you were pleased to propose to me, that I should recollect myself as well as I could, and set down the substance of it by way of dialogue, which I have done, according to the best of my remembrance, as followeth.

Being at New-London with my sloop, the beginning of

last September, Elias Rice, commander, having sixteen negro men and one negro woman on board, who were transported for having a hand in the late plot, and have since been delivered at Hispaniola; I about that time received a letter from my wife at New-York, dated August 31, 1741, in which letter she informed me, that one John Ury had been executed the Saturday before, as one concerned in the conspiracy, and that it was the opinion of many people, that he was innocent of what had been alleged against him at court: this piece of news occasioned me to go on board, to try what I could learn from the negroes; and I was relating this account of Ury to captain Rice, in French, and Bastian, one of the transported negroes, who attended on captain Rice, being near the door of the cabin within hearing; at my saying a great many people thought him innocent, he seemed to smile and spoke as if some what surprized; he innocent! says he, he was one of the worst of them all. Upon which I said to him, Bastian, you know all that was to have been done, and you must tell me all that you know of the matter; and he answered that if I would come on board in the afternoon, he would relate to me all he knew concerning the plot, but was unwilling any of the negroes should hear him. I according to his request returned on board in the afternoon, and taking him privately into the cabin, I put the following questions to him; which, without scruple, he answered as I have penned down, or to the same effect.

Note, that most of the conversation was in French, Bastian having been bred from a boy in Mr. Fauconnier's family, where they chiefly talked that language.

Question. Bastian, seeing you are now to be transported, and that it hath pleased the governor to pardon you for a crime, wherein many of your associates have suffered death, you need not fear any dangerous consequences by giving me an impartial account of all you know concerning the negro plot, tell me all you know of that affair from the beginning to the end, without amusing me with any falsehoods; and this you may depend upon, it will in a great measure obtain a pardon likewise from God, for your many and detestable sins.

Answer. Sir you may depend upon it, that I shall declare to you nothing but what I am very certain of.

Q. Who was the first person that introduced you at Hughson's?

A. Caesar, belonging to my master.

Q. The first time you were at Hughson's, what did you do there?

A. Hughson himself filled me a bumper of liquor, and after having drank it, I found myself quite intoxicated; but I remember he brought me a book, and bid me lay my hand on it, and bid me swear, and told me if I refused it he would kill me upon the spot, finding myself in so great a stress, to save my life I took the oath.

Q. What book was it that Hughson made you swear upon, was it a bible?

A. I don't know what book it was, but by its make I thought it looked like those books you call bibles.

Q. What was it Hughson obliged you to stand to, and after what manner did you swear?

A. By lightning and thunder, and by hell flames, that I would set fire to whatever I came across, and destroy as many whites as I could.

Q. What did you propose to do, if in case you had got the upperhand of the whites; did Hughson make you any promise?

A. He promised to make us all free.

Q. Did there generally use to resort many negroes at Hughson's?

A. Yes, for I have been there many a time when I have told fifteen, often twenty, and sometimes thirty negroes.

Q. Did you use to eat and drink there, whenever you went to see Hughson?

A. We always had a good supper and never wanted for liquor.

Q. The night after the fort burnt, did you return to Hughson's?

[458]

A. No, but the night after that we were a jolly company, and had a fine supper prepared for us, and seemed all of us to be well pleased with our late good successes.

Q. Do you know any whites that were concerned with you? did you ever see any at Hughson's at your meetings?

A. I have seen Will Kane there very often, and two or three soldiers whom I knew not, and another little man who was also a stranger to me.

Q. Was that little man young or old? of what make was he? and how did he employ his time among you?

A. He was far from being a tall man, but short, very lean, and a pale visage, nor was he old, his place was at the upper end of the table; he often encouraged us to remain firm like men in our designs, he read and wrote a great deal.

Q. Do you know what he wrote?

A. I have seen him take the names of the negroes down, from time to time, by way of list.

Q. But how could Hughson, who was but a poor man, support so great an expense at his house? there were suppers every night for you all, candles and many other things, the charge of which must have been very great; this goes beyond my comprehension; for you know the person who wrote so much must have had lights to see; I say I do not know how he did to support all that charge!

A. The negroes brought what they could steal to him; the white man you speak of was short sighted, and never wrote or read without spectacles.

Q. They say he was a Romish priest; do you know any thing about that?

A. I do not know that he was a priest, but he used to exhort us like a minister, to continue stedfast in our intentions, and used to throw his hands about like a preacher; and he said to us at the meeting at Hughson's the second night after the fort was burnt, now God has prospered us in the beginning in burning the fort, and we need not fear; we must be resolute and proceed in the work, and no doubt God will prosper us in all; that the town was too much alarmed at present, but they must go on when the fine weather came, that they (the negroes) need not fear, he would forgive them their sins if they kept true to their engagements, and by-and-by the Spaniards would come, and then they should be free.

Q. Have you been baptized by that little man, they called a priest?

A. No, but I have been told by some negroes of our company, that the little man had baptized them.

Q. Is it true, you were to burn the English church?

A. Yes, we agreed to burn it last winter, but the man whom you call priest opposed it, and advised us to stay till spring, when there would be a larger congregation.

Q. Your intentions then were to destroy all the whites while they were in church; how were you to go about it? had you arms? and could you think otherwise but that many would have made their escape through the doors and windows? explain me these things as well as you can.

A. We had combustibles prepared by doctor Harry, made up into balls, which we were to set fire to and throw them upon the roof of the church, which sticking fast would set fire to the shingles; after which, guarding the doors, we were to let none pass, but destroy them all in the church with our fire arms, for we had a great number of them at Hughson's.

Q. Where did you use to keep your arms at Hughson's? for when the searchers were sent there they were not to be found.

A. I believe not, for the plot beginning to come to light, Hughson to secure himself, had them all thrown into the river; before that they were hid in a hole in the cellar.

Bastian further declared, that he had not seen the person they called a priest, since he came into jail.

James Favieres.

March 19, 1742.

James Favieres, of New-York, merchant, made oath before the recorder, that the aforegoing relation contained the substance of

[460]

the discourse that passed between him and Bastian, a negro, at the time and place above mentioned, according to the best of his remembrance.

Deposition—Elias Rice saith,

1. "That in his passage with the seventeen negroes, Burk's Sarah acknowledged that she was concerned in the plot; never was at Hughson's, but often at Comfort's amongst the negroes, a forwarding the plot, and that she had wilfully set fire to her mistress' house several times.

2. "That Ten Eyck's Dick was cooking the victuals for the ship in the passage, and the negroes suspected he had a design of poisoning them, and saw him busy with yellow stuff in shells in a bag; which upon examination the negroes looked upon to be poison, which he had from doctor Harry, the negro. Some of the negroes knew it to be poison, the same sort they saw in Guinea.

3. "H. Rutgers' Jacob and Lush's Gill denied being at Hughson's, but all the rest owned it.

4. "Bastian owned he had been a headman there, was there very often, and saw a little man there they called a priest, but never saw him after he came to jail.

5. "Tickle said he had killed fowls there: Kelly's London had carried a quarter of mutton there.

6. "Myers Cohen's Windsor had carried a turkey there: and all (except as aforesaid) owned they had many a good feast, and good liquor there.

7. "That Bastian was always during the passage, very free in owning his being engaged in the plot, and kept to the same story; and said that he had often seen Kane at Hughson's, and that he was concerned in the plot, and many more soldiers that used to come there with him, whose names he knew not.

8. "That Bastian declared, that all the negroes that were executed he had often seen at Hughson's entertainments,' and that they were concerned in the plot."

Elias Rice.

Sworn before the recorder.

[461]

Deposition.—John Thurman, of the city of New-York, baker, being duly sworn on the holy evangelists of Almighty God, deposeth,

"That after John Campbell came to live at the house where John Hughson formerly lived, by the North river, he applied to the deponent, to put his children to school to him, informing him that John Ury, who was a very good scholar, a Latinist, was to be a partner with him in keeping school; and that he the deponent would be sure to have his children well instructed, but the deponent having no good opinion of either of Campbell or the other, gave no heed to his proposal. That soon after Ury came to live in that neighbourhood, as the deponent was informed, he took upon him to preach, and was then inviting the people to come and hear him; and that some of the deponent's family, as they afterwards told him, did go to hear him: that before Ury came to live in that neighbourhood, he knew his person by sight, having seen him several times. That the day John Hughson, his wife and Peggy were executed, the deponent went upon the commons to see the execution: and as he was returning from the gallows, he saw the said Ury, near spring-garden, returning with the crowd to town, and walked along side of him till he the deponent came to the market by Bogart's the baker, when the deponent turned down towards his own house, that the deponent did at that time, and still does, think, that Ury was returning from the execution of Hughson."

John Thurman.

Sworn before the recorder.

The *information* of John Williams of the city of New-York, baker, touching the confession made to him by Will, (Ward's negro) executed for the conspiracy.

1. "That he (Williams) lived next door to Mr. Ward the clock-maker, in Duke-street, and knew his negro man Will, who was executed as a confederate in the conspiracy; that

he always had great suspicion of him, of being concerned in some mischief, having seen him at play in his master's back storehouse, with many negroes at a time, of a Sunday afternoons, playing at dice or papa; and he had heard also that this fellow had been concerned in the conspiracy at Antigua, about four or five years ago, which made him keep a very watchful eye over him.

2. "That the day Mr. Philipse's storehouse was fired, and there was an alarm that the negroes were rising, he thereupon went home to get his arms in readiness, and to secure his house and family: and as he had conceived a great jealousy of Ward's Will, he called at his house, and asked him where this negro was, in order that he might keep him in sight, and secure him; Ward answered he was back in the kitchen: and he calling him several times, Will at last answered out of the garret: he was ordered down, and Williams commanded him to keep upon his master's stoop, within his sight, and told him if he offered to stir from the door, he would shoot him: Williams having at the same time a loaded gun in his hand; and there he accordingly remained till the hurry was over.

3. "That some time afterwards, when the affairs of the plot broke out, and several persons had been executed for the same, and the proclamation was issued, promising pardon to such negroes as should come in by the time therein limited; the day before the expiration of that term, he charged Will home with being concerned, and advised, if it was so, that he would go and confess to save his life; but he stiffly denied knowing any thing of the matter, and said, think not, master, that I am such a fool; for the negroes here live as well as the white people at Antigua: I was concerned in a plot there, and had been hanged, only I turned king's evidence, and by that means got clear; I could not stay there on account of the other negroes, being apprehensive of their intending to kill me. And the next day he was impeached, and taken into custody: soon after which, Williams went to talk to Will in jail, in order to try what he could get out of him; and asked what he thought of it now?

he answered, he thought he was in the wrong, that he had not taken his advice: but he thought they were all hanged or sent off, that knew he was concerned.

4. "Then Williams asked him, what would become of him in case the plot had gone on, whether he had a greater antipathy against him than any other? he said, No; but he would have fared as the rest; he should have killed all that came in his way; for he had taken the oath of the priest; and that there was a matter of twenty or thirty of them in all, that were sworn together by the priest, a little man, with a long gown on; but he did not know him, or ever had seen him before as he know of: Williams asked him, to what they were sworn: he answered, to burn and destroy what they could: Williams asked him what would have become of his master? he answered, as he was sworn, he must have gone on to destroy what he could."

April 7, 1742.

Examination of Ann Lyng; Jemina Ross, her mother; and Jemmy; taken by the recorder and deputy town clerk.

Ann Lyng, wife of Harman Lyng of the city of New-York, mariner, declared,

"That some short time after John Ury the priest was executed, she was one Sunday morning boiling of chocolate, and Jemmy, a little boy of about six or seven years of age, who was boarded with her and her said mother, said to her, aunt Nancy, my mammy Campbell used to boil chocolate every morning, but used to give me suppan, and sometimes chocolate with it: whereupon Ann Lyng asked him, who used to eat the chocolate? he answered, his daddy Campbell (b) and Mr. Ury used to eat the chocolate; then she asked him if he knew Ury? he answered, Yes, very well: for

(b) So the child used to call him: he boarded, and went to school to him, before he came to Ann Lyng.

he used to be by, when his daddy Campbell and Hughson used to play upon a board with little pieces of wood upon it; she then asked him if he knew Hughson? he said, very well, he was a tall man, with a thin face, used to wear a red coat, and a white cap; that he often came to his daddy Campbell's, but always at night: that he knew Ury well, he used to teach him his book sometimes, and was a very little man, and lodged sometimes at his daddy Campbell's."

Mrs. Ross declared,

"That upon her said daughter's telling her what Jemmy had said, as above, she asked him questions much to the above purpose: and the child declared over again to the same effect."

Then the boy was asked some questions by the recorder and town-clerk, tending to the same purpose, concerning his knowledge of Hughson and Ury; and he described them as above, and said, they used often to be together at his daddy Campbell's, and his daddy Campbell and Hughson used to play at chequers or draughts, (as they understood, according to the child's description; for he was put in mind of it, it seems, by Ann Lyng's child having some beans given it, which it was playing with, and throwing about the floor,) and that Ury used to be by, and looking at them, and used to say, Now Campbell you will win, and now Hughson you will win.

The child also described the persons of Hughson and Ury very exactly, and said Ury used to wear spectacles, and made punch for Hughson and Campbell, whilst they were playing.

A LIST OF WHITE PERSONS,

Taken into Custody on account of the Conspiracy, in 1741.

Names of Persons.	Occupation	When committed	Arraigned	Convicted	Confessed	Executed	Discharged.
Margaret Kerry alias Salingburgh	Shoemaker and Alehouse keeper	March 4	June 2 &4 for receiving stolen goods.	June 4		June 12	
John Hughson		April 18					
Sarah Hughson wife to J Hughson		April 18					Pardoned.
Sarah Hughson, the daughter	Shoemaker and Alehouse keeper	May 6			July 8		Discharged on security for departing the province.
John Romne		May 18					
Elizabeth Romme, his wife		May 8					August 31.
Peter Connolly	Soldier	June 23	July 15 & 22	July 29		August 29	
John Ury	A Priest	June 24					
Edward Kelly	Soldier	June 25					
William Kane	Soldier	July 4					August 31.
John Coffin	Pedlar	July 6					Dec. enlisted for W. [Indies.
Edward Murphey	Soldier	July 8			July 5		
Andrew Ryan	Soldier	July 9					August 31.
David Jobnson	Hatmaker	July 9					
John Corry	Dancing master	July 13					
Thomas Hughson	Yeoman						
Nathaniel	Sons to T. Hughson						Pardoned on condition of departing the province.
Walter							
William							
Richard	Yeoman	June 12 and 13					

Corker, Fagan, and Plummer, mentioned in Kane's evidence, never found.

NEGROES.	Masters or Owners	Committed	Arraigned	Convicted	Confessed	Burnt.	Hanged.	Transported to	Discharged.
Antonio,	Peter De Lancey,	April 6,	June 13,	June 17.				Spanish W. Indies.	
Augustine, } Spaniards.	Macmullen,	April 1,	June 13,	June 17.				Madeira.	
Antonio,	Sarah Maynard,	April 1,	June 13,	June 17.					
Albany,	Mrs. Carpenter,	May 12,	June 8,	June 10.		June 12.		Madeira.	
Abraham, a free negro,		June 1,							
Adam,	J. Murray, esq.	June 26,			June 27.			Madeira.	
Brash,	Peter Jay,	May 9,	June 25,		June 25.			Madeira.	
Bastian alias Tom Peal,	Jacobus Vaarck,	May 12,	June 8,	June 10,	June 11.			Hispaniola.	
Ben,	Capt. Marshall,	June 9,	June 12,	June 13,		June 16.			
Bill alias Will,	C. Ten Eyck,	June 12,	July 3,		June 30,			Madeira.	
Bridgewater,	A. Van Horne,	June 22,	July 1,		June 27,			Hispaniola.	
Billy,	Mrs. Ellison,	June 25,	July 10,			June 16.			
Braveboy,	Mrs. Kierstede,	June 27,			June 30,			Madeira.	
Burlington,	Joseph Haines,	July 3,							July 15.
Cæsar,	Vaarck,	March 1,	April 24,	May 1,†					
Cuffee,	A. Philipse, esq.	April 6,	May 28,	May 29,		May 30,	May 11,		
Cuba, a wench,	Mrs. C. Lynch,	April 4,							5.
Curacoa Dick,	Cornelius Tiebout	May 9,	June 8,	June 10,		June 12,			
Cato,	Alderman Moore,	May 9,	July 15,						
Cæsar,	do. Pintard,	May 9,	July 3,					Madeira.	
Cuffee,	Lewis Gomez,	May 24,	June 6,	June 8,	June 22,	June 9,			
Cæsar,	Benjamin Peck,	May 25,	June 6,	June 8,	June 22,	June 9,			
Cato,	Joseph Cowley,	May 25,	June 12,	June 13,					
Cook,	Gerardus Comfort	May 26,	June 6,	June 8,		9,	June 16,		
Cambridge,	C. Codwise,	May 30,	July 10,		June 30,			Cape Francois.	
Cæsar,	Israel Horsefield,	May 30,	June 26,		June 27,			St. Thomas.	
Cato,	John Shurmur,	June 9,	June 16,	June 19,	June 27,		July 3,		

† Of a robbery, but appears to have been a principal negro conspirator:

NEGROES.	Masters or Owners	Committed	Arraigned	Convicted	Confessed	Burnt	Hanged	Transported to	Discharged.
Caesar,	Corns. Kortrecht,	June 9,	July 3,	June 13,	July 2,		June 16,	Hispaniola,	
Cato or Toby,	John Provoost,	9,	June 12,		2,				
Cuffee,	Mrs. Fortune,	22,	July 15,					Surinam.	
Cato,	Robert Benson,	23,	26,					Madeira.	July 20.
Cajoe alias Africa	Mordecai Gomez,	26,	1,		June 28,				
Caesar,	Alderman Moore,	29,							
Caesar,	Dr. Henderson,	29,	10,						15.
Cajoe,	Richard Baker,	30,							
Dundee,	Robert Todd,	May 7,	3,		24,			Cape Francois.	
Dick,	Robins,	July 8,							23.
Dublin,	Capt. Walton,	13,							23.
Deptford,	John Cruger, esq.	June 23,	June 26,		27,			Portugal.	
Dick,	C. Ten Eyck,	20,	July 15,		30,			Hispaniola.	
Dick,	Wolf,	23,	23,					Hispaniola.	23.
Diego,	Peter VanDursen,	27,							23.
Dlego,	Marschalk,								
Emanuel, a Spaniard,	Thos. Wendover,	April 6,	June 25,	June 10,	27,	June 12,		Hispaniola,	
Francis,	Jasper Bosch,	6,	8,						
Fortune,	John Wilkins,	May 22,	July 7,		May 22,		June 16,	Madeira,	
Fortune,	J. Vanderspiegle,	22,	June 12,	13,					
Fortune,	John Latham,	June 13,	July 7,		June 15,			Curacoa.	
Fortune,	David Clarkson,	25,	1,		July 2,			Madeira.	
Frank,	F. Philipse, esq.	27,							
Fortune,	Capt. Walton,	28,	1,	July 15,			July 18,		
Frank,	Henry Ryker,	30,	10,	15,			18,		
Guy,	Tim. Horsefield,	May 30.	June 26,		June 27,			St. Thomas.	20.
Galloway,	H. Rutgers,	July 2,	July 10,	15,			18,		
Gosport or Jasper,	Robert Bound,	June 29,	1,	15,				Cape Francois.	

A LIST OF NEGROES COMMITTED ON ACCOUNT OF THE CONSPIRACY.

NEGROES.	Masters or Owners.	Committed.	Arraigned.	Convicted.	Confessed.	Burnt.	Hanged.	Transported to	Discharged.
Harry,	Mrs. Kipp,	May 30	June 16	June 19	June 27		July 3		
Harry,	John Thurman,	June 9	19		22			Madeira	July 15
Hanover,	John Cruger, jun.	29							
Hercford,	Samuel M. Cohen,	29							2
Harry (Doctor)	J. Mizreal, L.I.	July 6				July 18			
Jack,	Joshua Slydall,	May 6	July 10	July 15	12			Cape Francois	
Jack,	Henry Breasted,	9	12		27			Hispaniola	
Jonneau,	Jacobus Vaarck,	13	25		July 2			Hispaniola	
Jamaica,	Thomas Ellison,	22	7	June 8				Madeira	
Jack,	Gerardus Comfort	26	6	8	June 8			Cape Francois	
Jeffery,	Capt. J. Brown,	June 15	June 6		27				
Jacob,	H. Rutgers,	23	July 1		24			Curacoa	
Jack,	J. Murray, esq.	25	June26		26			Madeira	July 20
John,	WidowVanRantz,	27	July 1						
Jack,	Jacob Abrahamse,	28	1						20
Jack,	John Roerback,	28							6
Jack,	Judah Hayes,	July 2			July 2				20
John,	Rip Van Dam, esq.	6						Madeira	
Jupiter,	Capt. Walton,	13							. 2
Kid,	C. Van Horne,	June 29							2
London,	Augustine Hicks,	May 30	June 16	June 19	June 20			Madeira	June 4
London,	Peter Marschalk,	June 9	19		July 2			Hispaniola	
London,	Edward Kelly,	12	25		June 27			Statia	
Lowe,	David Provoost,	22	26		25			Hispaniola	
London,	Ben. Wyncoop,	22			24			Madeira	
London,	Roger French,	22	July 3		July 1			Madeira	
Lewis,	AdoniahSchuyler,	27	1		3				
Mars,	Robert Benson,	12	3						

A LIST OF NEGROES COMMITTED ON ACCOUNT OF THE CONSPIRACY.

NEGROES.	Masters or Owners.	Committed.	Arraigned.	Convicted.	Confessed.	Burnt.	Hanged.	Transported to	Discharged.
Mink,	John Groesbeck,	June 12	June 16	July 10	June 18		July 18	Newfoundland	
Othello,	J. De Lancey, esq.	27	July 10	May 1*	30		May 11		
Prince,	John Auboyneau,	March 2	April 24	June 17				Newfoundland	
Pablo or Powlus a Span-[iard,	Frederick Becker,	April 6	June 13					Madeira	
Patrick,	William English,	May 9	25	26	27				
Prince,	Anthony Duane,	June 1	25						
Pompey,	Abraham Lefferts,	1	July 3		9		July 3	Madeira	
Primus,	James Debrosses,	12	3		19			St. Thomas	
Pedro,	Peter De Peyster,	13			29				
Prince,	Gabriel Crooke,	13	15		13				July 20
Pompey,	Peter De Lancey,	20	15		22			Cape Francois	
Pompey,	Jane Gilbert,	23	June 26		27			Madeira	
Pompey,	Samuel Bayard,	23	26		30			Madeira	
Phaeton,	Nicholas Bayard,	30							15
Prince,	Corns. Kortrecht,	July 1	July 23	July 10			18	Hispaniola	
Quack,	John Walters,	April 6	10	May 29	at the stake	May30			
Quack,	John Roosevelt,	May 12	May 28				18	Madeira	23
Quamino,	Eben. Pemberton,	June 12	June 19		June 22				
Quack,	Jacob Goelet,	July 4	12			June16			
Quash,	H. Rutgers,	June 9	July 23	June 13					6
Quash,	Le Roux,	July 2	June 6			9		Madeira	
Robin,	John Chambers,	April 13		8					20
Robin,	Mrs. Bickley,	July 1							11
Sarah,	De Peyster,	April 4							
Sarah,	Thomas Niblet,	May 10							
Sandy,	Thomas Niblet,	14						Hispaniola	
Sarah	Mrs. Burk,	25	July 7		1			Hispaniola	

Of a robbery, but appears to have been a principal negro conspirator.

A LIST OF NEGROES COMMITTED ON ACCOUNT OF THE CONSPIRACY.

NEGROES.	Masters or Owners.	Committed.	Arraigned.	Convicted.	Confessed.	Burnt.	Hanged.	Transported to	Discharged.
Sam,	George Rappelie,	May 30							June 4
Scipio,	Mrs. Van Borsom,	June 9	June 25		June 25				
Sterling,	Capt. Lawrence,	12	July 3		23				
Sam,	Peter Lowe,	22	June 26		July 3			Hispaniola	
Scipio,	Robert Round,	22	26		3				
Sam,	Frederick Courtlandt,	23	26		2			Cape Francois	
Scipio,	Abraham Abrahamse,	25	26		1			Madeira	
Scotland,	Nathaniel Marston,	27	July 7		June 27				
Susses,	Mrs. Beekly,	July 1			29			Curacoa	July 29
Tickle alias Will,	Mrs. Carpenter,	May 30							
Tom,	Winant Van Zandt,	30			12			Hispaniola	2
Tom,	Benjamin Moore,	June 1	June 16		18			Newfoundland	
Tom,	Capt. Rowe,	12	July 3		July 2				2
Tom,	Van Zant,	29							
Toney,	John Latham,	13	June 25	June 26					
Toney,	Mrs. Brazier,	22	26						
Tom,	Simeon Soumaien,	23	26		2		July 3	Surinam	
Toby,	Widow Brestead,	25	July 1		June 26				
Tom,	Hyer,	26	1	July 15	30			Cape Francois	
Tom,	Robert Livingston,	26						Hispaniola	
Titus,	Capt. Phœnix,	27	7					Madeira	
Tony or Tonio,	Counsellor Courtlandt,	29						Surinam	
Tom,	Peter Valette,	30							
Toby,	Hercules Wendover,	30	10	15	27				28
Toby,	Abraham Marschalk,	30			30				23
Tom,	Bradt,	Feb. 15		March 2, 1742			Mar. 13, 1742		
Venture,	Cornelius Tiebout,	June 28	1	July 15			July 18, 1741		
Wan or Juan,	Capt. Sarly,	April 6	June 13	June 17			August 15		

A LIST OF NEGROES COMMITTED ON ACCOUNT OF THE CONSPIRACY.

NEGROES.	Masters or Owners.	Committed.	Arraigned.	Convicted.	Confessed.	Burnt.	Hanged.	Transported to	Discharged.
Will, a Spaniard	Abraham Filkins,	April 6							July 20
Wan,	Dr. Nicoll,	24							June 30
Will alias Gill,	Capt. Lush,	May 24	June 25		June 27			Hispaniola	
Worcester,	Isaac Varyan,	30	19		22			Cape Francois	
Will,	Anthony Ward,	June 20	25		at the stake	July 4			
Will,	Jacobus Vaarck,	20	25						
Windsor,	Samuel Myers Cohen,	25	July 1		June 30				
Warwick,	Obadiah Hunt,	25	1		July 1			Madeira	
Will,	John Tiebout,	July 4							July 23
Wan, Indian,	Lowe,	June 12	June 19		June 19			Curacoa	
York,	Benjamin Peck,	May 30	25		27			Madeira	
York,	Peter Marschalk,	June 9	16	June 19	20		July 3*		
York,	Thomas Thomase,	20	July 6		27			Madeira	
York,	Charles Crooke,	22	June 26		27				
York,	Widow Van Rantz,	July 1	July 23					Curacoa	
York,	Gerardus Dyckink,	2							13

* In chains with John Hughson.

NEGROES INDICTED WHO WERE NOT TO BE FOUND.

Hanover;	H. Cruger's.
London,	A. Van Horne's
Ben,	Stephen Bayard's.
Pedro,	R. Stillwell's.
Ben,	Augustus Jay's.
Jack,	Governeur's.
Joe,	Holt's.

INDEX

Because of the aliases, nicknames, and variant spellings of proper names in the text of this work, the index has been prepared showing only the most commonly used name. Listed below on the left are the index entries and on the right the variants.

Allair, Alexander — Allaire
Anthony (DeLancey) — Antonio de St. Bendito; (Delancey)
Antonio (Mesnard) — Antonio de la Cruz; (Meanard)
Augustine (McMullen) — Augustine Gutierez; (M'Mullen)
Bancker, Christopher — Banker
Bastian (Vaarck) — Tom Peal
Ben (Marshall) — (Marshal)
Bohenna, Thomas — Behenna; Bohanna
Braveboy (Kierstead) — (Kiersted); (Kierstede)
Bridgwater (Van Horne) — Bridgewater
Caesar (Horsefield) — (Horsfield)
Caesar (Vaarck) — John Gwin; John Quin
Cajoe (Gomez) — Africa
Cambridge (Codweis) — (Codweise); (Codwise)
Cato (Provost) — Toby; (Provoost)
Cato (Shurmur) — (Shurmar)
Clopper, Cornelius — Cloppert
Codweis, Christopher — Codwise
Connolly, Peter — Conolly
Cook (Comfort) — Acco; Maph
Courtlandt, Stephen — Van Courtlandt? (note Stephen, Jr.)
Cuffee (Fortune) — (Vaughton)
Cuffee (Philipse) — Cuff
Danby — Denby
DeLancey, Peter — Delancey
Deriemer, Stenwick — Steenwick
Diego (Van Dursen) — (Vandursen)
Dunscomb, Samuel — Dunscombe
Emanuel (Wendover) — Manuel
Evoutzse, Peter — Evoutsee
Fortune (Vanderspeigle) — (Vanderspiegle)
Fortune (Wilkins) — (Wilkin)
Francis (Bosch) — Frank
Frank (free) — Frans
Groesbeck, John — Groesbeek
Gusie (Horsefield) — Galick; Galie; Guise; (Horsfield)
Guy (Horsefield) — (Horsfield)

Hogg, Robert	Hoggs
Horsefield, Israel	Horsfield
Horsefield, Timothy	Horsfield
Hughson, John	Hewson
Jack (Codweis)	John; (Codweise); (Codwise)
Jamaica (Ellison)	(Ellis)
Jeffery (Brown)	(Bound)
John (Van Rantz)	Wan
Juan (Sarly)	Juan de la Sylva; Wan
Kelly, Edward	Kelley
London (Kelly)	(Kelley)
Lowe, Peter	Low
Mars (Benson)	(Becker)
Mink (Groesbeck)	(Croesbeck); (Grosbeck)
Murphy, Edward	Murphey
Nicholls, Richard	(Cruger)
Neptune (Curger)	Nichols
Pablo (Becker)	Pablo Ventura Angel; Powlus; (Beecker)
Pedro (Stillwell)	Pero; (Stilwell)
Peggy	Margaret Carey; Margaret Keary; Margaret Kerry; Margaret Salinburgh; Margaret Sarinbirr; Margaret Sorubiero
Powlus	Pablo
Primus (Debrosse)	(DeBrosse)
Provost, David	Provoest
Quack (Roosevelt)	Quaco
Quack (Walter)	Quaco
Quash (Rutgers)	(Rutger)
Robin (Chambers)	(Chamber)
Romme, John	Romer
Ryan, Elizabeth	Eleanor
Sam (Courtlandt)	(Van Courtlandt)
Sam (Lowe)	(Low)
Sandy (Niblet)	Sawney
Scipio (Abrahams)	(Abraham); (Abrahamse)
Scipio (Van Borsom)	(Vanborsom); (Van Brosom)
Sterling (Lawrence)	Starling
Tickle (Carpenter)	Ticklepitcher; Tickle Pitcher; Will
Tom (Bradt)	Monkey
Tom (Rowe)	(Row); (Row'e)
Tom (Van Rant)	(Van Zant)
Tony (Courtlandt)	Jonio; Tonio
Ury, John	Jury; Doyle
Vaarck, John	Forck
Vandursen, Peter	Van Dursen
Wan (Lowe)	Indian Wan; (Low)
Webb, Joseph	Web
Wilkins, John	Wilkin
Will (Filkin)	Joseph
Will (Lush)	William

Billy (Ellison): 216, 219, 262, 375
Blanck, Mr.: 133; testifies, 134
Boelen, Abraham: grand juror, 336
Bogart, Cornelius: juror, 179
Bogart, John: juror, 190
Bogert, Henry: 31
Bohenna, Thomas: juror, 88, 155, 339
Bonett, Daniel: juror, 88
Bonnett, Mr.: 407–8
Bosch, Jasper: 150
Boswell, Mrs.: 48
Bound, Robert: 266, 337
Bradford, Andrew: 395, 396–97
Bradford, Cornelia: 395, 396-97
Bradley, Richard: xix, 43, 45, 46, 48, 51, 89, 124, 126, 129, 135, 142–43, 153, 155–56, 168–69, 340, 356–59, 376
Bradt, Divertie: 390, 394, 396–97
Brash (Jay): 54, 60–64, 118, 138, 151, 154, 164, 173, 199, 213, 219, 225, 229, 235, 257, 310, 325; confession, 217–18, 251, 258, 268; pardon, 310, 316; testifies, 311
Braveboy (Kierstead): 120, 139, 224, 232–34, 249; confession, 255–56, 260
Braveboy (Livingston): 294; pardon, 310, 316
Breasted, Henry: 265, 336
Breese, John: juror, 339
Breese, Sidney: juror, 51, 142, 339
Breton, Michael: 330
Brewer, John: juror, 167
Bridgwater (Van Horne): 201–3, 205, 270; confession, 245; pardon, 277, 291
Brinkerhoff, George: 31
Brower, Cornelius: 48; testifies, 133
Budd, Gilbert: testifies, 183
Burdet, Samuel: juror, 125
Burdett, Stephen: 330
Burger, Nicholas: 330
Burgher, Daniel: 156
Burnet, George: juror, 179
Burns, Sgt.: 27
Bursen, Jacob: 101
Burton, Mary: 17–18, 20–21, 40, 48, 64, 111, 116, 127, 129, 148,

150, 158, 170, 177, 187, 191, 287, 303, 307, 371–72, 416–17, 433–36, 438–45, 448–56; depositions, 19–20, 41–42, 44, 49, 51, 70–72, 144, 156–57, 213–16, 230, 269, 280–81, 292–93, 305–6, 308, 383; reward, 413–14; testifies, 91–93, 99, 130–32, 143–44, 156–57, 169, 179, 219, 274, 297, 310–14, 343–45, 349; threatened, 18, 42, 92, 158, 440, 451
Butchell (slave): 111, 308
Byrd, William: xvi
Byvanck, Evert: juror, 125, 179

Caesar (Henderson): 252–53, 255, 264, 294; pardon, 337
Caesar (Horsefield): 117, 221, 258, 295, 376; confession, 247; pardon, 336, 375
Caesar (Kortrecht): 148–49, 151, 153–54, 204, 239, 270; confession, 268–69; pardon, 277, 291
Caesar (Moore): 255, 326
Caesar (Murray): 227, 235, 237
Caesar (Peck): 86–88, 110–11, 113, 118, 140, 144, 151, 161–62, 201–2, 246, 254, 271–72; executed, 153; trial, 142–45, 287
Caesar (Pintard): 54, 60–64, 118, 120, 164, 173, 198–99, 203, 212, 223, 225, 228–29, 232, 235, 244, 257–58, 270, 278, 325; confession, 196, 200–202, 204, 211, 217, 242, 245–46, 259, 268, 271–72; pardon, 277, 289, 291; testifies, 220
Caesar (Vaarck): viii, xii-xv, xviii, 13–17, 19–22, 41–42, 45, 47–49, 51–52, 54–55, 57, 61–62, 67, 70–73, 76–78, 82, 86, 91–92, 94, 99, 103, 110–11, 113, 118, 120, 126, 130–132, 158–61, 172, 181, 188–91, 199–201, 204–5, 215, 223, 225–26, 228–29, 235, 242, 245, 247, 249, 254, 256–57, 259, 269, 280, 283, 285, 290, 293, 296–97, 300–302, 304, 313, 322, 328, 330, 344, 348–49, 436, 446–49, 451–52, 458; executed, 65–66; trial, 47–48

Cajoe (Baker): 258, 294
Cajoe (Faviere): 260
Cajoe (Gomez): 218, 227, 262; confession, 249–51; pardon, 310, 317
Cambridge (Codweis): 117, 294, 376; confession, 243, 247, 258
Campbell, John: 212, 215, 230, 282, 284, 290, 333–34, 353, 356, 362–63, 372–73, 462, 464–65; testifies, 359
Campbell, Mrs. John: 464; testifies, 359
Carpenter, Elizabeth: 157, 336
Cataline (Masterson): 244
Catholics: xi, 1–3, 211–12, 279, 314–16, 341–43, 364–66, 369, 376–77; involved in plot, 369–70, 377, 419, 431, 438; prior conspiracies, 421–31
Cato (Alsteyn): 120
Cato (Benson): 208, 221, 262; pardon, 276, 291
Cato (Cowley): 86–87, 118, 151, 154, 158, 161–64, 169–73, 176–77, 201–2, 230, 245–46, 258, 260, 269; executed, 178; trial, 167–71
Cato (Moore): 54, 60–64, 81, 118, 121, 173, 196–99, 201, 208, 210, 232, 238, 258, 278, 336; confession, 202–4, 211, 217, 242, 245–46, 266, 268–69, 272; pardon, 310, 317; testifies, 220
Cato (Provost): 148, 149, 151, 153–54, 161, 162, 173, 176–77, 201–2; executed, 178; trial, 167–71
Cato (Richard): 260, 305
Cato (Schurmur): 120, 139, 148–49, 151, 153–54, 161–62, 178, 197, 199, 202, 262; confession, 238–39; executed, 273; trial, 190–93
Cavillier, Eleanor: 330
Chambers, John: 43, 95, 120, 129, 142, 144, 169, 171, 179, 185, 191, 219, 240–41, 298, 311, 313, 326, 340, 343, 345, 348, 353
Charlton, James: 319; juror, 190
"Chicago 8": xx

Christian, John: 330
Clarke, George: x, xiv, xxii, 22–23, 24, 31, 34, 187, 276, 339, 350–51, 384, 387–88, 411
Clarke, John:- xxi
Clarkson, David: 218, 395–96
Clopper, Cornelius: juror, 167, 219, 310
Codweis, Christopher: 294
Coffin, John: xiii, 281–83, 286, 290, 293, 298, 309, 345–47, 383
Cohen, Abraham Meyers: 47–48, 54
Cohen, Samuel Meyers: 265, 337
Colden, Cadwallader: x; *Letters and Papers of*, xxii
Comfort, Gerardus: 81, 134, 143, 359; testifies, 135
Congo (Murray): 227, 235
Connolly, Peter: 279, 283, 383
Conspiracy: law of, ix–x, xv, xxii; suspected, viii–x, 27, 29–30, 31, 43–44, 386–91
"The Conspiracy Weapon," Herbert L. Packer: xxii
Conspirators: design, 42, 54, 59–61, 81, 91–92, 103, 126–29, 132, 143, 148–49, 158, 161, 170, 173, 180–81, 191, 195, 199–201, 203, 209–10, 217, 219–23, 228, 235, 241, 250, 254, 257, 296, 305, 309, 343–44, 408, 415, 419; Hughson's list, 160, 173, 181, 191-92, 195, 201, 216, 224, 271, 303; plan to burn church, 285, 341, 415, 460; sworn, 54, 61, 71–72, 87, 92, 112–13, 115, 119, 120, 128, 131, 149–50, 158, 160, 164, 170, 172–73, 179, 188–89, 194, 197–201, 203–6, 209, 214, 216–18, 222–24, 228–31, 239, 241, 246, 250–51, 253–54, 256–57, 263–64, 266, 268–69, 271, 282–83, 285, 287, 290, 297, 301, 311–13, 328–29, 340, 346, 348, 417, 458
Contract, Combination or Conspiracy, Milton Handler: xxii
Cook (Comfort): 81–82, 86, 110, 118, 120, 138–40, 148, 150–51, 161–62, 164, 172, 177–78, 202, 209–10, 218, 245–46, 248, 258-

[489]